Classics
in
Software
Engineering

Classics in Software Engineering

Edited by
Edward Nash Yourdon

YOURDON Press
1133 Avenue of the Americas
New York, New York 10036

Printed in the United States of America

Library of Congress Catalog Number 79-63449

ISBN: 0-917072-14-6

This book was set in Times Roman by YOURDON Press, using a PDP-11/45 running under the UNIX operating system.

CONTENTS

ACKNOWLEDGMENTS

We gratefully acknowledge the following organizations for their permission to reprint the articles in this volume:

1. "Programming Considered as a Human Activity," by E. Dijkstra, originally appeared in *Proceedings of the 1965 IFIP Congress* (Amsterdam, The Netherlands: North-Holland Publishing Co., 1965), pp. 213-17. Copyright © 1965 by North-Holland Publishing Co. Reprinted by permission.

2. "Flow Diagrams, Turing Machines and Languages with Only Two Formation Rules," by C. Böhm and G. Jacopini, is reprinted from *Communications of the ACM,* Vol. 9, No. 5 (May 1966), pp. 366-71. Copyright © 1966 by the Association for Computing Machinery, Inc. Reprinted by permission.

3. "Go To Statement Considered Harmful," by E. Dijkstra, originally appeared as a Letter to the Editor in *Communications of the ACM,* Vol. 11, No. 3 (March 1968), pp. 147-48. Copyright © 1968 by the Association for Computing Machinery, Inc. Reprinted by permission.

4. "The 'Super-Programmer Project,' " by J.D. Aron, originally appeared in a report on a conference sponsored by the NATO Science Committee, Rome, Italy, October 1969. It is reprinted from SOFTWARE ENGINEERING, CONCEPTS AND TECHNIQUES, edited by Buxton, Naur, Randell. Copyright © 1976 Litton Educational Publishing, Inc. Reprinted by permission of Van Nostrand Reinhold Company.

5. "Structured Programming," by E. Dijkstra, originally appeared in a report on a conference sponsored by the NATO Science Committee, Rome, Italy, October 1969. It is reprinted from SOFTWARE ENGINEERING, CONCEPTS AND TECHNIQUES, edited by Buxton, Naur, Randell. Copyright © 1976 Litton Educational Publishing, Inc. Reprinted by permission of Van Nostrand Reinhold Company.

6. "The Translation of 'go to' Programs to 'while' Programs," by E. Ashcroft and Z. Manna, originally appeared in *Proceedings of the 1971 IFIP Congress,* Vol. 1 (Amsterdam, The Netherlands: North-Holland Publishing Co., 1972), pp. 250-55. Copyright © 1972 by North-Holland Publishing Co. Reprinted by permission.

7. "Chief Programmer Team Management of Production Programming," by F.T. Baker, originally appeared in *IBM Systems Journal,* Vol. 11, No. 1 (1972), pp. 56-73. Reprinted by permission from *IBM Systems Journal,* Copyright © 1972 by International Business Machines Corporation.

18. "Structured Design," by W. Stevens, G. Myers, and L. Constantine, originally appeared in *IBM Systems Journal,* Vol. 13, No. 2 (May 1974), pp. 115-39. Reprinted by permission from *IBM Systems Journal,* Copyright © 1974 by International Business Machines Corporation.

19. "Programming Style: Examples and Counterexamples," by B.W. Kernighan and P.J. Plauger, originally appeared in *ACM Computing Surveys,* Vol. 6, No. 4 (December 1974), pp. 303-19. Copyright © 1974 by the Association for Computing Machinery, Inc. Reprinted by permission.

20. "Structured Programming with go to Statements," by D. Knuth, Copyright © 1974, Association for Computing Machinery, Inc., in CURRENT TRENDS IN PROGRAMMING METHODOLOGY, Vol. I, Raymond T. Yeh, ed., © 1977. Reprinted by permission of ACM and Prentice-Hall, Inc.

21. "Software Engineering," by B.W. Boehm. Copyright © 1976 by The Institute of Electrical and Electronics Engineers, Inc. Reprinted with permission, from *IEEE Transactions on Computers,* December 1976, Vol. C-25, No. 12, pp. 1226-41.

22. "Structured Analysis for Requirements Definition," by D.T. Ross and K.E. Schoman, Jr. Copyright © 1977 by The Institute of Electrical and Electronics Engineers, Inc. Reprinted with permission, from *IEEE Transactions on Software Engineering,* January 1977, Vol. SE-3, No. 1, pp. 6-15.

23. "PSL/PSA: A Computer-Aided Technique for Structured Documentation and Analysis of Information Processing Systems," by D. Teichroew and E.A. Hershey, III. Copyright © 1977 by The Institute of Electrical and Electronics Engineers, Inc. Reprinted with permission, from *IEEE Transactions on Software Engineering,* January 1977, Vol. SE-3, No. 1, pp. 41-48.

24. "Structured Analysis and System Specification," by T. DeMarco, is reprinted from the GUIDE 47 Proceedings by permission of GUIDE International Corporation. GUIDE International Corporation disclaims any responsibility for the substance of any ideas, concepts or statements contained in this article. Copyright © 1978 GUIDE International Corporation.

INTRODUCTION

When looking back on any kind of movement or revolution, one always likes to point to a beginning: "It began right *there* — it all started with so-and-so's famous speech. . . ."

If structured programming can be thought of as a revolution, then surely Dijkstra's landmark paper, "Programming Considered as a Human Activity," published in 1965, marks its beginning. Virtually the entire gospel of structured programming is contained in a few short pages: the arguments against goto statements, the notion of top-down design, the emphasis on program *correctness* and *quality* (or "elegance," as Dijkstra prefers to call it), and the strong argument against programs that modify themselves.

In addition to these fundamental concepts, there are some rather classic phrases that first appeared in this paper, and that have popped up in dozens of subsequent articles and books. For example, when discussing the "divide and conquer" approach characterizing top-down design, Dijkstra admits, "I have only a very small head, and must live with it." What seems obvious to us today was a rather novel idea in 1965: the idea that while computers were — and still are — getting faster and more powerful, human beings weren't. This theme is repeated again and again, and is essentially the entire subject matter of Dijkstra's 1972 speech, "The Humble Programmer" [included as Paper 10 in this collection].

It is in the 1965 paper, which you are about to read, that Dijkstra suggests that "the quality of . . . programmers was inversely proportional to the density of goto statements in their programs." And, it is in this early paper as well that Dijkstra recounts programming experiments identical to the ones that converted most of the rest of us to structured programming over the next several years: He rewrote unstructured programs into equivalent structured programs, and marvelled at the increase in clarity.

After reading all the pearls of wisdom that are contained in this one paper, one might well ask why the programming industry wasn't converted at once. The answer, I think, has to do with *timing* and *packaging*. In 1965, most programmers (and their managers)

1

felt that they had far more serious problems to worry about than eliminating goto statements: After all, IBM had just unleashed the 360 upon the world, and whole armies of people began trying to up-grade from Autocoder to RPG — that is, *if* they could get the hardware and the operating system to work! Programmers spent most of their time trying to figure out how to use *more* gotos, not fewer — in the hopes that doing so would help them fit some pon-derous accounting application into an 8K machine!

Another reason for slow adoption of the methods was a factor as well of the medium in which the message was presented — the IFIP Conference, which might be loosely thought of as the interna-tional version of the National Computer Conference. Prestigious and scholarly, to be sure, but its published papers attract a consider-ably smaller reading audience (at least in the United States) than, say, *Computerworld* or *Datamation*. Perhaps the only reason it at-tracted any American attention at all was that the IFIP Conference was held in New York City that year — in contrast to the 1971 Conference, which was held in Ljubljana, Yugoslavia!

An additional problem preventing widespread conversion was with the language itself! Introductory quotations came from scien-tists Ludwig Boltzmann and George Boole, names with which the average programmer is unlikely to be acquainted. Examples chosen in support of the concepts involved prime factors of a twenty-digit number — not a subject of intense interest to many programmers. Discussions in support of structured programming dealt with the features of ALGOL 60, well known to American programmers as one of their least popular languages. In short, it's a wonder anyone read the paper at all!

But once you do read it, you can see why Dijkstra has the reputation he does. His writing is succinct and yet convincing. Reading Dijkstra, someone said, has been compared to eating marzi-pan — it's best to take very small bites, chew slowly, and digest the mouthful before moving on to the next bite.

Programming Considered as a Human Activity

Introduction

By way of introduction, I should like to start this talk with a story and a quotation.

The story is about the physicist Ludwig Boltzmann, who was willing to reach his goals by lengthy computations. Once somebody complained about the ugliness of his methods, upon which complaint Boltzmann defended his way of working by stating that "elegance was the concern of tailors and shoemakers," implying that he refused to be troubled by it.

In contrast I should like to quote another famous nineteenth century scientist, George Boole. In the middle of his book, *An Investigation of the Laws of Thought*, in a chapter titled "Of the Conditions of a Perfect Method," he writes: "I do not here speak of that perfection only which consists in power, but of that also which is founded in the conception of what is fit and beautiful. It is probable that a careful analysis of this question would conduct us to some such conclusion as the following, *viz.*, that a perfect method should not only be an efficient one, as respects the accomplishment of the objects for which it is designed, but should in all its parts and processes manifest a certain unity and harmony." A difference in attitude one can hardly fail to notice.

Our unconscious association of elegance with luxury may be one of the origins of the not unusual tacit assumption that it costs to be elegant. To show that it also pays to be elegant is one of my prime purposes. It will give us a clearer understanding of the true nature of the quality of programs and the way in which they are expressed, *viz.*, the programming language. From this insight we shall try to derive some clues as to which programming language features are most desirable. Finally, we hope to convince you that the different aims are less conflicting with one another than they might appear to be at first sight.

On the quality of the results

Even under the assumption of flawlessly working machines we should ask ourselves the questions: "When an automatic computer produces results, why do we trust them, if we do so?" and after that: "What measures can we take to increase our confidence that the results produced are indeed the results intended?"

How urgent the first question is might be illustrated by a simple, be it somewhat simplified example. Suppose that a mathematician interested in number theory has at his disposal a machine with a program to factorize numbers. This process may end in one of two ways: either it gives a factorization of the number given or it answers that the number given is prime. Suppose now that our mathematician wishes to subject to this process a, say, 20 decimal number, while he has strong reasons to suppose that it is a prime number. If the machine confirms this expectation, he will be happy; if it finds a factorization, the mathematician may be disappointed because his intuition has fooled him again, but, when doubtful, he can take a desk machine and can multiply the factors produced in order to check whether the product reproduces the original number. The situation is drastically changed, however, if he expects the number given to be nonprime: if the machine now produces factors he finds his expectations confirmed and moreover he can check the result by multiplying. If, however, the machine comes back with the answer that the number given is, contrary to his expectations and warmest wishes, alas, a prime number, why on earth should he believe this?

Our example shows that even in completely discrete problems the computation of a result is not a well-defined job, well-defined in the sense that one can say: "I have done it," without paying attention to the convincing power of the result, *viz.*, to its *quality.*

The programmer's situation is closely analogous to that of the pure mathematician, who develops a theory and proves results. For a long time pure mathematicians have thought — and some of them still think — that a theorem can be proved completely, that the question whether a supposed proof for a theorem is sufficient or not, admits an absolute answer "yes" or "no." But this is an illusion, for as soon as one thinks that one has proved something, one has still the duty to prove that the first proof was flawless, and so on, ad infinitum!

One can never guarantee that a proof is correct; the best one can say "I have not discovered any mistakes." We sometimes flatter ourselves with the idea of giving watertight proofs, but in fact we do nothing but make the correctness of our conclusions plausible. So extremely plausible, that the analogy may serve as a great source of inspiration.

In spite of all its deficiencies, mathematical reasoning presents an outstanding model of how to grasp extremely complicated structures with a brain of limited capacity. And it seems worthwhile to investigate to what extent these proven methods can be transplanted to the art of computer usage. In the design of programming languages one can let oneself be guided primarily by considering "what the machine can do." Considering, however, that the programming language is the bridge between the user and the machine — that it can, in fact, be regarded as his tool — it seems just as important to take into consideration "what Man can think." It is in this vein that we shall continue our investigations.

On the structure of convincing programs

The technique of mastering complexity has been known since ancient times: *Divide et impera* (Divide and rule). The analogy between proof construction and program construction is, again, striking. In both cases the available starting points are given (axioms and existing theory versus primitives and available library programs); in both cases the goal is given (the theorem to be proved versus the desired performance); in both cases the complexity is tackled by division into parts (lemmas versus subprograms and procedures).

I assume the programmer's genius matches the difficulty of his problem and assume that he has arrived at a suitable subdivision of the task. He then proceeds in the usual manner in the following stages:

- he makes the complete specifications of the individual parts

- he satisfies himself that the total problem is solved provided he had at his disposal program parts meeting the various specifications

- he constructs the individual parts, satisfying the specifications, but independent of one another and the further context in which they will be used.

Obviously, the construction of such an individual part may again be a task of such a complexity, that inside this part of the job, a further subdivision is required.

Some people might think the dissection technique just sketched a rather indirect and tortuous way of reaching one's goals. My own feelings are perhaps best described by saying that I am perfectly aware that there is no Royal Road to Mathematics, in other words, that I have only a very small head and must live with it. I, therefore, see the dissection technique as one of the rather basic patterns of human understanding and think it worthwhile to try to create circumstances in which it can be most fruitfully applied.

The assumption that the programmer had made a suitable subdivision finds its reflection in the possibility to perform the first two stages: the specification of the parts and the verification that they together do the job. Here elegance, accuracy, clarity and a thorough understanding of the problem at hand are prerequisite. But the whole dissection technique relies on something less outspoken, *viz.*, on what I should like to call "The principle of non-interference." In the second stage above it is assumed that the correct working of the whole can be established by taking, of the parts, into account their exterior specification only, and not the particulars of their interior construction. In the third stage the principle of non-interference pops up again: here it is assumed that the individual parts can be conceived and constructed independently from one another.

This is perhaps the moment to mention that, provided I interpret the signs of current attitudes towards the problems of language definition correctly, in some more formalistic approaches the soundness of the dissection technique is made subject to doubt. Their promoters argue as follows: whenever you give of a mechanism such a two-stage definition, first, what it should do, *viz.*, its specifications, and secondly, how it works, you have, at best, said the same thing twice, but in all probability you have contradicted yourself. And statistically speaking, I am sorry to say, this last remark is a strong point. The only clean way towards language definition, they argue, is by just defining the mechanisms, because what they then will do will follow from this. My question: "How does this follow?" is wisely left unanswered and I am afraid that their neglect of the subtle, but sometimes formidable difference between the concepts *defined* and *known* will make their efforts an intellectual exercise leading into another blind alley.

After this excursion we return to programming itself. Everybody familiar with ALGOL 60 will agree that its procedure concept satisfies to a fair degree our requirements of non-interference, both in its static properties, e.g., in the freedom in the choice of local identifiers, as in its dynamic properties, e.g., the possibility to call a procedure, directly or indirectly, from within itself.

Another striking example of increase of clarity through non-interference, guaranteed by structure, is presented by all programming languages in which algebraic expressions are allowed. Evaluation of such expressions with a sequential machine having an arithmetic unit of limited complexity will imply the use of temporary store for the intermediate results. Their anonymity in the source language guarantees the impossibility that one of them will inadvertently be destroyed before it is used, as would have been possible if the computational process were described in a von Neumann type machine code.

A comparison of some alternatives

A broad comparison between a von Neumann type machine code — well known for its lack of clarity — and different types of algorithmic languages may not be out of order.

In all cases the execution of a program consists of a repeated confrontation of two information streams, the one (say *the program*) constant in time, the other (say *the data*) varying. For many years it has been thought one of the essential virtues of the von Neumann type code that a program could modify its own instructions. In the meantime we have discovered that exactly this facility is to a great extent responsible for the lack of clarity in machine code programs. Simultaneously its indispensability has been questioned: all algebraic compilers I know produce an object program that remains constant during its entire execution phase.

This observation brings us to consider the status of the variable information. Let us first confine our attention to programming languages without assignment statements and without goto statements. Provided that the spectrum of admissible function values is sufficiently broad and the concept of the conditional expression is among the available primitives, one can write the output of every program as the value of a big (recursive) function. For a sequential machine this can be translated into a constant object program, in which at run time a stack is used to keep track of the current hierarchy of calls and the values of the actual parameters supplied at these calls.

Despite its elegance a serious objection can be made against such a programming language. Here the information in the stack can be viewed as objects with nested lifetimes and with a constant value during their entire lifetime. Nowhere (except in the implicit increase of the order counter which embodies the progress of time) is the value of an already existing named object replaced by another value. As a result the only way to store a newly formed result is by putting it on top of the stack; we have no way of expressing that an earlier value now becomes obsolete and the latter's lifetime will be prolonged, although void of interest. Summing up: it is elegant but inadequate. A second objection — which is probably a direct consequence of the first one — is that such programs become after a certain, quickly attained degree of nesting, terribly hard to read.

The usual remedy is the combined introduction of the goto statement and the assignment statement. The goto statement enables us with a backward jump to repeat a piece of program, while the assignment statement can create the necessary difference in status between the successive repetitions.

But I have reasons to ask, whether the goto statement as a remedy is not worse than the defect it aimed to cure. For instance, two programming department managers from different countries and different backgrounds — the one mainly scientific, the other mainly commercial — have communicated to me, independently of each other and on their own initiative, their observation that the quality of their programmers was inversely proportional to the density of goto statements in their programs. This has been an incentive to try to do away with the goto statement.

The idea is, that what we know as *transfer of control,* i.e., replacement of the order counter value, is an operation usually implied as part of more powerful notions: I mention the transition to the next statement, the procedure call and return, the conditional clauses and the for statement; and it is the question whether the programmer is not rather led astray by giving him separate control over it.

I have done various programming experiments and compared the ALGOL text with the text I got in modified versions of ALGOL 60 in which the goto statement was abolished and the for statement — being pompous and over-elaborate — was replaced by a primitive repetition clause. The latter versions were more difficult to make: we are so familiar with the jump order that it requires some effort to forget it! In all cases tried, however, the program without the goto statements turned out to be shorter and more lucid.

The origin of the increase in clarity is quite understandable. As is well known there exists no algorithm to decide whether a given program ends or not. In other words, each programmer who wants to produce a flawless program must at least convince himself by inspection that his program will indeed terminate. In a program in which unrestricted use of the goto statement has been made, this analysis may be very hard on account of the great variety of ways in which the program may fail to stop. After the abolishment of the goto statement there are only two ways in which a program may fail to stop: either by infinite recursion, i.e., through the procedure mechanism, or by the repetition clause. This simplifies the inspection greatly.

The notion of repetition, so fundamental in programming, has a further consequence. It is not unusual that inside a sequence of statements to be repeated one or more subexpressions occur, which do not change their value during the repetition. If such a sequence is to be repeated many times, it would be a regrettable waste of time if the machine had to recompute these same values over and over again. One way out of this is to delegate to the now optimizing translator the discovery of such constant sub-expressions in order that it can take the computation of their values outside the loop. Without an optimizing translator the obvious solution is to invite the programmer to be somewhat more explicit and he can do so by introducing as many additional variables as there are constant sub-expressions within the repetition and by assigning the values to them before entering the repetition. I should like to stress that both ways of writing the program are equally misleading. In the first case the translator is faced with the unnecessary puzzle to discover the constancy; in the second case we have introduced a variable, the only function of which is to denote a constant value. This last observation shows the way out of the difficulty: besides variables the programmer would be served by *local constants,* i.e., identifiable quantities with a finite lifetime, during which they will have a constant value, that has been defined at the moment of introduction of the quantity. Such quantities are not new: the formal parameters of procedures already display this property. The above is a plea to recognize that the concept of the *local constant* has its own right of existence. If I am well informed, this has already been recognized in CPL, the programming language designed in a joint effort around the Mathematical Laboratory of the University of Cambridge, England.

The double gain of clarity

I have discussed at length that the convincing power of the results is greatly dependent on the clarity of the program, on the degree in which it reflects the structure of the process to be performed. For those who feel themselves mostly concerned with efficiency as measured in the cruder units of storage space and machine time, I should like to point out that increase of efficiency always comes down to exploitation of structure and for them I should like to stress that all structural properties mentioned can be used to increase the efficiency of an implementation. I shall review them briefly.

The lifetime relation satisfied by the local quantities of procedures allows us to allocate them in a stack, thus making very efficient use of available store; the anonymity of the intermediate results enables us to minimize storage references dynamically with the aid of an automatically controlled set of push down accumulators; the constancy of program text under execution is of great help in machines with different storage levels and reduces the complexity of advanced control considerably; the repetition clause eases the dynamic detection of endless looping and finally, the local constant is a successful candidate for a write-slow-read-fast store, when available.

Conclusion

When I became acquainted with the notion of algorithmic languages I never challenged the then prevailing opinion that the problems of language design and implementation were mostly a question of compromises: every new convenience for the user had to be paid for by the implementation, either in the form of increased trouble during translation, or during execution or during both. Well, we are most certainly not living in Heaven and I am not going to deny the possibility of a conflict between convenience and efficiency, but now I do protest when this conflict is presented as a complete summing up of the situation. I am of the opinion that it is worthwhile to investigate to what extent the needs of Man and Machine go hand in hand and to see what techniques we can devise for the benefit of all of us. I trust that this investigation will bear fruits and if this talk made some of you share this fervent hope, it has achieved its aim.

INTRODUCTION

It is likely that most programmers who have heard anything at all about structured programming also have heard the mysterious names "Böhm" and "Jacopini." "Oh, yes," they'll say, "all that structured programming stuff was proved by those guys Böhm and Jacopini somewhere in Italy." And yet it's *exceedingly* unlikely that the average programmer has read the Böhm and Jacopini paper, "Flow Diagrams, Turing Machines and Languages with Only Two Formation Rules," published in 1966.

As you begin to read the paper, it will become immediately obvious that the discussion is of an extremely abstract, theoretical nature. Serious academicians accustomed to a regular diet of such papers will no doubt wade through this one, too — but the average COBOL application programmer probably will be overwhelmed by the time he or she reaches the end of the first paragraph. I have read the paper myself several dozen times during the past twelve years, and honesty requires me to admit that I barely understand it for a period of five minutes after reading the last paragraph. It is certain that I would be at an utter loss to try to describe Böhm and Jacopini's proof to anyone else.

I say this to help prevent an inferiority complex on the part of the average reader. This *is* an important paper, and it *does* form the theoretical basis of structured programming. So you should read it. But don't feel too embarrassed if most of it is over your head. Indeed, you'll find "The Translation of 'go to' Programs to 'while' Programs," by Ashcroft and Manna [Paper 6], to be much more understandable: They, too, show that any program can be written as a structured program by simply demonstrating that any program can be *translated* into an equivalent structured program.

One last comment about the paper by Böhm and Jacopini: Note that it does not mention programming languages. It describes a set of flow diagrams as a "two-dimensional programming language," but it makes no mention of COBOL, ALGOL, PL/I, or any of the other languages that real-world programmers use. This is far more significant than you might think. What Böhm and Jacopini have proved in this paper is that any *flowchart* can be drawn from combinations of standard "structured" flowchart elements; they did *not* prove that any COBOL program can be written without goto statements. Indeed, if a programming language lacks the constructs to implement directly the Böhm and Jacopini flowcharts, goto-less programming is exceedingly difficult, if not impossible — as witnessed by such degenerate languages as FORTRAN.

This distinction between the theoretical *possibility* of structured programming, and the real-world *practicality* of structured programming is, of course, at the heart of the controversy and the squabbling that still goes on today, more than a decade after this paper was written. Examples of this controversy — the theme of which is, "Yes, we know structured programming is theoretically possible, but do we really want to do it?" — are seen in papers like Martin Hopkins' "A Case for the GOTO" [Paper 9], or Donald Knuth's "Structured Programming with go to Statements" [Paper 20].

Flow Diagrams, Turing Machines and Languages with Only Two Formation Rules

1. Introduction and summary

The set of block or flow diagrams is a two-dimensional programming language, which was used at the beginning of automatic computing and which now still enjoys a certain favor. As far as is known, a systematic theory of this language does not exist. At the most, there are some papers by Peter [1], Gorn [2], Hermes [3], Ciampa [4], Riguet [5], Ianov [6], Asser [7], where flow diagrams are introduced with different purposes and defined in connection with the descriptions of algorithms or programs.

In this paper, flow diagrams are introduced by the ostensive method; this is done to avoid definitions which certainly would not be of much use. In the first part (written by G. Jacopini), methods of normalization of diagrams are studied, which allow them to be decomposed into base diagrams of three types (first result) or of two types (second result). In the second part of the paper (by C. Böhm), some results of a previous paper are reported [8] and the results of the first part of this paper are then used to prove that every Turing machine is reducible into, or in a determined sense is equivalent to, a program written in a language which admits as formation rules only composition and iteration.

2. Normalization of flow diagrams

It is a well-known fact that a flow diagram is suitable for representing programs, computers, Turing machines, etc. Diagrams are usually composed of boxes mutually connected by oriented lines. The boxes are of functional type (see Figure 1) when they represent elementary operations to be carried out on an unspecified object x of a set X, the former of which may be imagined concretely as the set of the digits contained in the memory of a computer, the tape configuration of a Turing machine, etc. There are other boxes of predicative type (see Figure 2) which do not operate on an object but decide on the next operation to be carried out, according to whether or not a certain property of x $\in X$ occurs. Examples of diagrams are: $\Sigma(\alpha,\ \beta,\ \gamma,\ a,\ b,\ c)$ [Figure 3] and $\Omega_5(\alpha,\ \beta,\ \gamma,\ \delta,\ \epsilon,\ a,\ b,\ c,\ d,\ e)$ [see Figure 4]. It is easy to see a difference between them. Inside the diagram Σ, some parts which may be considered as a diagram can be isolated in such a way that if $\Pi(a,\ b)$, $\Omega(\alpha,\ a)$, $\Delta(\alpha,\ a,\ b)$ denote, respectively, the diagrams of Figures 5-7, it is natural to write

$$\Sigma(\alpha, \beta, \gamma, a, b, c) = \Omega(\alpha, \Delta(\beta, \Omega(\gamma, a), \Pi(b, c))).$$

Nothing of this kind can be done for what concerns Ω_5; the same happens for the entire infinite class of similar diagrams

$$\Omega_1[=\Omega],\ \Omega_2,\ \Omega_3,\ \cdots,\ \Omega_n,\ \cdots,$$

whose formation rule can be easily imagined.

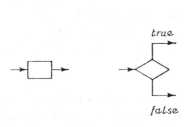

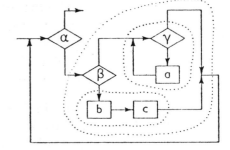

Figures 1-2. Functional and predicative boxes.   Figure 3. Diagram of Σ.

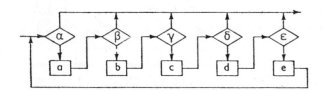

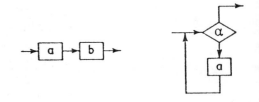

Figure 4. Diagram of Ω_5 Figures 5-6. Diagrams of Π and Ω.

Let us say that while Σ is decomposable according to subdiagrams Π, Ω and Δ, the diagrams of the type Ω_n are not decomposable. From the last consideration, which should be obvious to anyone who tries to isolate with a broken line (as was done for Σ) a part of Ω_n provided with only one input and one output, it follows that:

It is not possible to decompose all flow diagrams into a finite number of given base diagrams.

However, together with this decomposition, that could be called *strong,* another decomposition may be considered which is obtained by operating on a diagram equivalent to the one to be decomposed (that is, the diagram has to express the same transformation, whatever the meaning of the boxes contained in it may be). For instance, it may be observed that if we introduce Φ(α, *a*) [as in Figure 8] and Λ(α, *a*) [as in Figure 9] the diagrams of Φ, Λ and Ω become, respectively, equivalent to Figures 10, 11 and 12.

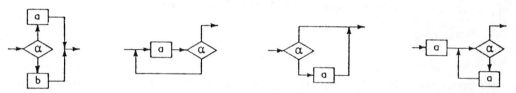

Figures 7-8. Diagrams of Δ and Φ.   Figures 9-10. Diagram of Λ and a diagram
                                                        equivalent to Φ.

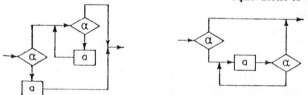

Figures 11-12. Diagrams equivalent to Λ and Ω.

Thus, the following decompositions may be accepted:

$$\Phi(\alpha, a) = \Pi(a, \Omega(\alpha, a))$$
$$\Lambda(\alpha, a) = \Delta(\alpha, \Omega(\alpha, a), a)$$
$$\Omega(\alpha, a) = \Lambda(\alpha, \Phi(\alpha, a)).$$

Nevertheless, it is to be reckoned that the above statement holds even with regard to the new wider concept of decomposability. In fact, it does not seem possible[†] for every Ω_n to find an equivalent diagram which does not contain, as a subprogram, another Ω_n or an Ω of higher order. For instance, note that

$$\Omega_3(\alpha, \beta, \gamma, a, b, c) = \Lambda(\alpha, \Pi(a, \Omega_3(\beta, \gamma, \alpha, b, c, a))$$
$$= \Omega_6(\alpha, \beta, \gamma, \alpha, \beta, \gamma, a, b, c, a, b, c)$$

and similar formulas hold for all orders of Ω.

[†]We did not, however, succeed in finding a plain and sufficiently rigorous proof of this.

The proved unfeasibility is circumvented if a new predicate is added and if, among the elementary operations, some are assumed which either add one bit of information to the object of the computation or remove one from it. The extra bits have a stack structure (formally described below as nested ordered pairs) since it is sufficient to operate and/or take decisions only on the topmost bit.

Therefore, three new functional boxes denoted by T, F, K, and a new predicative box ω are introduced. The effect of the first two boxes is to transform the object x into the ordered pair (v, x) where v can have only the values $\mathbf{t}$ (true) and $\mathbf{f}$ (false); more precisely,

$$x \xrightarrow{T} (\mathbf{t}, x), \quad x \xrightarrow{F} (\mathbf{f}, x), \quad (\mathbf{t}, x) \xrightarrow{T} (\mathbf{t}, (\mathbf{t}, x))$$

and so on. Box K takes out from an ordered pair its second component

$$(v, x) \xrightarrow{K} x, \quad (\mathbf{t}, (\mathbf{f}, (\mathbf{t}, x))) \xrightarrow{K} (\mathbf{f}, (\mathbf{t}, x)).$$

The predicate ω is defined as

$$\omega[(v, x)] = \mathbf{t} \iff v = \mathbf{t},$$

i.e., the predicate ω is verified or not according to whether the first component of the pair is T or F; ω and K are defined only on a pair; on the contrary, all the boxes α, β, γ, $\cdots$, a, b, c, $\cdots$ operating on x are not defined on a pair. The following statement holds:

If a mapping $x \rightarrow x'$ is representable by any flow diagram containing a, b, c, $\cdots$, α, β, γ, $\cdots$, it is also representable by a flow diagram decomposable into Π, Φ, and Δ and containing the same boxes which occurred in the initial diagrams, plus the boxes K, T, F and ω.

That is to say, it is describable by a formula in Π, Φ, Δ, a, b, c, $\cdots$, T, F, K, α, β, γ, $\cdots$, ω.

NOTE. A binary switch is the most natural interpretation of the added bit v. It is to be observed, however, that in certain cases if the object x can be given the property of a list, any extension of the set X becomes superfluous. For example, suppose the object of the computation is any integer x. Operations T, F, K may be defined in a purely arithmetic way:

$$x \xrightarrow{T} 2x + 1, \quad x \xrightarrow{F} 2x, \quad x \xrightarrow{K} \left[\frac{x}{2} \right]$$

and the oddity predicate may be chosen for ω. The added or canceled bit v emerges only if x is thought of as written in the binary notation system and if the actions of T, F, K, respectively, are interpreted as appending a one or a zero to the far right or to erase the rightmost digit.

To prove this statement, observe that any flow diagram may be included in one of the three types: I (Figure 13), II (Figure 14), III (Figure 15), where, inside the section lines, one must imagine a part of the diagram, in whatever way built, that is called $\mathfrak{a}$ or $\mathfrak{b}$ (not a subdiagram). The branches marked 1 and 2 may not always both be present; nevertheless, from every section line at least one branch must start.

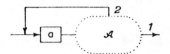

Figure 13.   Structure of a type I diagram.

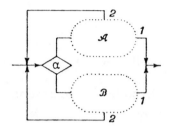

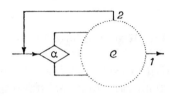

Figure 14.   Structure of a type II diagram.   **Figure 15.   Structure of a type III diagram.**

As for the diagrams of types I and II, if the diagrams in Figures 16-17, are called A and B,[†] respectively, I turns into Figure 20 and may be written

$$\Pi(\Pi(T, \Phi(\omega, \Pi(\Pi(K, a), A))), K)$$

and II turns into Figure 21, which may be written

$$\Pi(\Pi(T, \Phi(\omega, \Pi(K, \Delta(\alpha, A, B)))), K).$$

The case of the diagram of type III (Figure 15) may be dealt with as case II by substituting Figure 22, where e' indicates that subpart of e accessible from the upper entrance, and e'' that part accessible from the lower entrance.

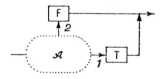

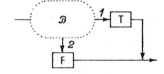

Figure 16. A-diagram.   **Figure 17. B-diagram.**

[†]If one of the branches 1 or 2 is missing, A will be simply Figure 18a or 18b, and similarly for B. If the diagram is of the type of Figure 19 where $V \{\in\}$ (T, F), it will be simply translated into $\Pi(V, A^*)$ where A^* is the whole subdiagram represented by a.

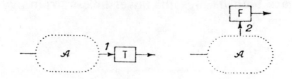

Figure 18a-b. Two special cases of the *A*-diagram.

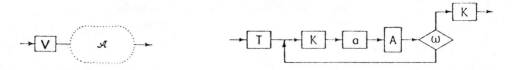

Figure 19. Diagram reducible to $\Pi(V, A^*)$.   **Figure 20. Normalization of a type I diagram.**

If it is assumed that *A* and *B* are, by inductive hypothesis,[†] representable in Π, Φ and Δ, then the statement is demonstrated.

It is thus proved possible to completely describe a program by means of a formula containing the names of diagrams Φ, Π and Δ. It can also be observed that Ω, Π and Δ could be chosen, since the reader has seen (see formula and Figure 10) that Φ can be expressed using Ω and Π. Moreover, it is observed that the predicate ω occurs only as the first argument of Φ (or, if desired, of Ω) and all the others as arguments of Δ: $\Phi(\omega, X)$ and $\Delta(\alpha, X, Y)$, etc.

Now let us define for every predicative box α, β, $\cdots$ a new functional box $\underline{\alpha}$, $\underline{\beta}$, $\cdots$ with the following meaning:

$$\underline{\alpha} \equiv \Delta(\alpha, \Pi(T, F), \Pi(F, T)) \qquad \text{(Figure 23)}$$

This simplifies the language. In fact, any $\Delta(\alpha, X, Y)$ can be replaced by (see also Figure 24):

$$\Pi(\underline{\alpha}, \Pi(\Omega(\omega, \Pi(K, \Pi(K, \Pi(X, \Pi(T, T))))),$$
$$\Pi(K, \Pi(\Omega(\omega, \Pi(K, \Pi(Y, T))), K)))).$$

Then we can simply write:

$$\Pi(X, Y) \equiv XY,$$

$$\Pi(\Pi(X, Y), Z) = \Pi(X, \Pi(Y, Z)) \equiv XYZ,$$

owing to the obvious associativity of Π. We may also write:[‡]

$$\Omega(\omega, X) \equiv (X).$$

[†]The induction really operates on the number *3N + M*, where *M* is the number of boxes *T* and *F* in the diagram and *N* is the number of all boxes of any other kind (predicates included).

[‡]The same notation is followed here as in [8].

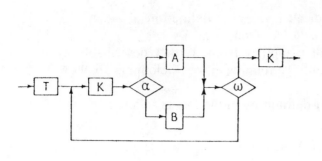

Figure 21. Normalization of a type II diagram.

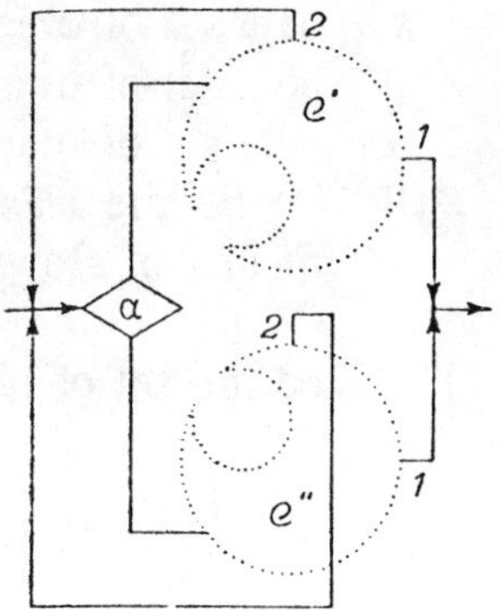

Figure 22. Normalization of a type III diagram.

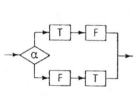

Figure 23. The diagram $\underline{\alpha}$.

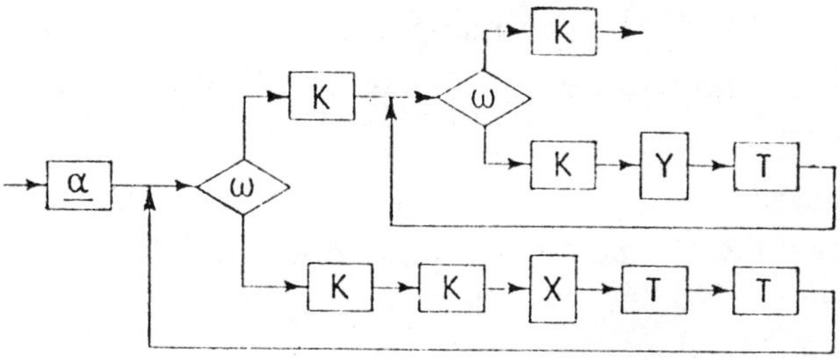

Figure 24. Transformation of $\Delta(\alpha, X, Y)$.

To sum up: every flow diagram where the operations $a, b, c, \cdots$ and the predicates $\alpha, \beta, \gamma \cdots$ occur can be written by means of a string where symbols of operations $a, b, c, \cdots, \underline{\alpha}, \underline{\beta}, \underline{\gamma}, \cdots, T, F, K$ and parentheses (,) appear. For example:

$$\Pi(a, b) = ab$$

† $\quad\Omega(\alpha, a) = \underline{\alpha}K(Ka\underline{\alpha}K)K$

† $\quad\Phi(\alpha, a) = F(Ka\underline{\alpha}K)K$

$\quad\Delta(\alpha, a, b) = \underline{\alpha}(KKaTT)K(KbT)K$

† $\quad\Lambda(\alpha, a) = \underline{\alpha}K(KaT)K$

† $\quad\Omega_2(\alpha, \beta, a, b)$

$$= F(K\underline{\alpha}(KTT)K(Ka\underline{\beta}(KTT)K(KbFT))K)K.$$

More abstractly, the main result can be summarized as follows. Let

---

†These formulas have not been obtained using the general method as described. The application of that method would make the formula even more cumbersome.

X be a set of objects x

Ψ be a set of unary predicates $\alpha, \beta, \cdots$ defined in X

O be a set of mappings $a, b, \cdots$ from X to X

$\mathcal{D}(\Psi, O)$ be the class of all mappings from X to X describable by means of flow diagrams containing boxes belonging to $\Psi \cup O$.

Y be the set of objects y defined by induction as follows:

$$\begin{cases} X \subset Y \\ y \in Y \implies (\mathbf{t}, y) \in Y, (\mathbf{f}, y) \in Y \end{cases} \tag{1}$$

ω be a predicate, defined in Y (at least on $Y - X$) by

$$\begin{cases} \omega(\mathbf{t}, x) = \mathbf{t} \\ \omega(\mathbf{f}, x) = \mathbf{f} \end{cases}$$

T, F be two mappings defined on Y by

$$T[y] = (\mathbf{t}, y)$$
$$F[y] = (\mathbf{f}, y)$$

K be a mapping defined in Y by

$$K[(\mathbf{t}, y)] = K[(\mathbf{f}, y)] = y$$

$\underline{\Psi}$ be a set of mappings $\underline{\alpha}, \underline{\beta}, \cdots$ defined on X, with values in Y as follows:

$$\underline{\alpha}[x] = \neg\alpha[x], (\alpha[x], x) \tag{2}$$

etc.

Now, given a set Z of objects z, a set Q of mappings from Z to Z, and *one* unary predicate π defined in Z, let us recursively define for every $q \in Q$ a new mapping $^\pi(q)$, written simply (q) if no misunderstanding occurs, as follows:

$$\begin{cases} \pi[z] \rightarrow (q)[z] = z \\ \sim \pi[z] \rightarrow (q)[z] = (q)[q[z]]. \end{cases}$$

For every $q_1, q_2 \in Q$, let us call $q_1 q_2$ the mapping defined by $q_1 q_2[z] = q_2[q_1[z]]$. Let us call $\mathcal{E}(\pi, Q)$ the class of mappings from Z to Z defined by induction as follows:

$$\begin{cases} Q \subset \mathcal{E}(\pi, Q) \\ q \in \mathcal{E}(\pi, Q) \Rightarrow (q) \in \mathcal{E}(\pi, Q) \\ q_1 \in \mathcal{E}(\pi, Q) \ q_2 \in \mathcal{E}(\pi, Q) \Rightarrow q_1 q_2 \in \mathcal{E}(\pi, Q). \end{cases}$$

Note the following useful properties of $\mathcal{E}$:

$$Q_1 \subset Q_2 \rightarrow \mathcal{E}(\pi, Q_1) \subset \mathcal{E}(\pi, Q_2) \tag{3}$$
$$Q_2 \subset \mathcal{E}(\pi, O_1) \rightarrow \mathcal{E}(\pi, O_1 \cup Q_2) = \mathcal{E}(\pi, Q_1). \tag{4}$$

The meaning of the last statement can easily be rewritten:

$$\mathcal{D}\,(\Psi,\,O) \subset \mathcal{E}(\omega,\,O \,\cup\, \Psi \,\cup\, \{T,\,F,\,K\}). \qquad (5)$$

3. Applications to the theory of Turing machines

In a previous paper [8], a programming language $\mathcal{P}'$ was introduced which described, in a sense specified in that paper, the family $\mathcal{B}'$ of Turing machines for a (leftward) infinite tape and any finite alphabet $\{c_1\,,\,c_2\,,\,\cdots\,,\,c_n\} \,\cup\, \{\square\}$, where $n \geqslant 1$, $\square$ is the symbol for the blank square on the tape. Using the notation of Section 2 (see Note),

$$\mathcal{B}' \equiv \mathcal{D}(\{\alpha\},\,\{\lambda,\,R\}) \qquad (6)$$

where

> α is the unary predicate true if the square actually scanned (by the Turing machine head) is blank (i.e., contains $\square$);
>
> λ is the operation of replacing the scanned symbol c_i with c_{i+1} ($c_0 \equiv c_{n+1} \equiv \square$) and shifting the head one square to the left;
>
> R is the operation of shifting the head one square, if any, to the right.

Briefly, α is a predicate, λ and R are partially defined functions[†] in the set X of tape configurations. By "tape configuration" of a Turing machine is meant the content of the tape plus the indication of the square being scanned by the machine head.

Example. If the configuration (at a certain time) is

$$x \equiv \cdots \square\,\square c_1 \underline{c_n} c_n\,,$$

then

$$\alpha[x] \equiv \mathbf{f}, \quad \lambda[x] \equiv \cdots\square\,\square\underline{c_1}\,\square c_n\,, \quad R[x] \equiv \cdots\square\,\square c_1 c_n \underline{c_n}$$

where the underscore indicates the scanned square. In [8] a language $\mathcal{P}''$ (describing a proper subfamily of Turing machines) has been shown. It was defined as follows.

> (*i*) $\lambda,\,R \in \mathcal{P}''$ (Axiom of Atomic Operations)
>
> (*ii*) $q_1,\,q_2 \in \mathcal{P}''$ implies $q_1 q_2 \in \mathcal{P}''$ (Composition Rule)
>
> (*iii*) $q \in \mathcal{P}''$ implies $(q) \in \mathcal{P}''$ (Iteration Rule)
>
> (*iv*) Only the expressions that can be derived from (*i*), (*ii*) and (*iii*) belong to $\mathcal{P}''$.

[†]For more details, see [8, 9].

Interpreting q_1, q_2 as functions from X to X, $q_1 q_2$ can be interpreted as the composition $q_2 \circ q_1$, i.e.

$$q_1 q_2 [x] \equiv q_2 [q_1 [x]] \qquad\qquad x \in X$$

and (q) can be interpreted as the composition of q with itself, n times: $q \circ \dots \circ q \equiv q^n$, i.e. $q^n [x] \equiv q[\cdots [q[x]] \cdots]$ where $q^0 [x] = x$ and $n = \mu \nu \{ \alpha [q^\nu [x]] = \mathbf{t} \}$, $\nu \geq 0$, i.e. (q) is the minimum power of q (if it exists) such that the scanned square, in the final configuration, is $\square$.

From the point of view of this paper, the set $\mathcal{B}''$ of the configuration mappings described by $\mathcal{P}''$ is

$$\mathcal{B}'' \equiv \mathcal{E}(\alpha, \{\lambda, R\}). \qquad\qquad (7)$$

The drawbacks of $\mathcal{P}''$ as opposed to $\mathcal{P}'$ are that not all Turing machines may be *directly* described by means of $\mathcal{P}''$. For instance, it was proved in [8] that the operation H^{-1} (performed by the machine, which does nothing if the scanned symbol is different from $\square$, and otherwise goes to the right until the first $\square$ is scanned) cannot be described in $\mathcal{P}''$ ($H^{-1} \notin \mathcal{B}''$).

Nevertheless, the most surprising property of $\mathcal{P}''$ is that, according to the commonest definition of "computing" a function by a Turing machine, every partial recursive function f in $m \geq 0$ variables can be evaluated by a program $P_f \in \mathcal{P}''$ (see [8]).

Although this last property enables us to build a one-one mapping (via a gödelization of the Turing machines) of $\mathcal{P}'$ in $\mathcal{P}''$, it is here preferred to find a more direct correspondence between Turing machines, without any reference to partial recursive functions. To every Turing machine M, let us associate the machine M^* whose initial (and final) tape configuration is obtained by interspersing a blank square between every two contiguous squares of the tape of M. During the computation, these auxiliary squares are used to record, from right to left, the values ν of the switch stack.

More precisely, for every configuration $x \equiv \cdots \square u_1 \cdots u_{K-1} \underline{u_K} u_{K+1} \cdots u_m$ where $u_i \in \{ \square, c_1, \cdots, c_n \}$, let us call x^* the configuration

$$x^* \equiv \cdots \square \square \square u_1 \cdots \square u_{K-1} \square u_K \square \underline{u_{K+1}} \cdots \square u_m .$$

If M designates the Turing machine which when applied[†] to configuration b gives e as the final configuration, i.e. if $M[b] = e$, then M^* is a machine such that $M^*[b^*] = e^*$.

We want to prove: $M \in \mathcal{B}', \Rightarrow M^* \in \mathcal{B}''$.

[†]For simplicity, as in (6), Turing machines and configuration mappings will be identified.

Taking advantage of the theorem (5), we may write

$$\mathscr{B}' \subset \mathscr{E}(\omega, \{\lambda, R, \underline{\alpha}, T, F, K\}). \qquad (8)$$

Following the definition (1) of Y, the mapping $x \to x^*$ is now extended to a mapping $y \to y^*$ as follows:

if $y^* \equiv \cdots \square u_{K-1} \square \underline{u}_K \cdots \Longrightarrow$

$$(\mathbf{t}, \ y)^* \equiv \cdots \square \underline{u}_{K-1} \square \ u_K \cdots, \qquad (9)$$

$$(\mathbf{f}, \ y)^* \equiv \cdots \square \ \underline{u}_{K-1} c_1 u_K \cdots.$$

Obviously,

$$M \in \mathscr{B} \Longrightarrow M \in \mathscr{E}(\omega, \{\lambda, R, \underline{\alpha}, T, F, K\})$$

and therefore

$$M^* \in \mathscr{B}'^* \Longrightarrow M^* \in \mathscr{E}(\omega^*, \{\lambda^*, R^*, \underline{\alpha}^*, T^*, F^*, K^*\}).$$

It is only necessary to prove that

$$\mathscr{E}(\omega^*, \{\lambda^*, R^*, \underline{\alpha}^*, T^*, F^*, K^*\}) \subset \mathscr{E}(\alpha, \{\lambda, R\}).$$

First, observe that for every machine $Z^* \in \mathscr{E}(\omega^*, \{\cdots\})$,

$$^{\omega^*}(Z^*) \equiv R^{\ \alpha}(LZ^*R)L,$$

where $L \equiv [\lambda R]^n \lambda$ is the operation of shifting the head one square to the left, has been proved; therefore,

$$\mathscr{E}(\omega^*, \{\cdots\}) \subset \mathscr{E}(\alpha, \{\cdots\} \cup \{\lambda, R\}).$$

Secondly, it can be easily checked that

$$\{\lambda^*, R^*, T^*, F^*, K^*\} \subset \mathscr{E}(\alpha, \{\lambda, R\}).$$

In fact,

$$\lambda^* = \lambda L, \qquad R^* = R^2, \qquad T^* = L^2,$$

$$F^* = L\lambda, \qquad K^* = R(\lambda R)R.$$

According to (4), it has been proved that

$$\mathscr{E}(\omega^*, \{\ldots\}) \subset \mathscr{E}(\alpha, \{\underline{\alpha}^*, \lambda, R\}).$$

Thirdly,

$$\underline{\alpha}^* \in \mathscr{E}(\alpha, \{\lambda, R\}).$$

From formula (2) and the convention (9) it must follow that:

$$\underline{\alpha}^*[\cdots \ \square u_2 \square u_1 \square \underline{\square} \cdots] = \cdots \square \underline{u}_2 c_1 u_1 \square \square \cdots \quad (10)$$
$$\underline{\alpha}^*[\cdots \ \square u_2 \square u_1 \square \underline{c} \cdots] = \cdots \square \underline{u}_2 \square u_1 c_1 c \cdots \quad (11)$$

where u_1, $u_2 \in \{\square, c_1, \cdots, c_n\}$ and $c \in \{c_1 \cdots, c_n\}$.

In order to implement $\underline{\alpha}^*$, the program $L^3\lambda$ [which meets conditions (10)] must be merged with $L\lambda L^2$ [which meets (11)]. A solution[†] can be written in the form

$$\underline{\alpha}^* \equiv L^3\lambda R^4(X)L^5(Y)R,$$

which obviously satisfies (10). The program (X) can be chosen mainly to copy the symbol c on the first free blank square; the program (Y), to execute the inverse operation, i.e.,

$$(X)[\cdots \square u_2 c_1 u_1 \square \underline{c} \cdots] = \cdots \underline{c} u_2 \square u_1 c_1 \square \cdots$$
$$(Y)[\cdots cu_2 \square u_1 c_1 \square \cdots] = \cdots \square \underline{u}_2 \square u_1 c_1 c \cdots$$

It is not difficult to test that the choice

$$(X) \equiv (r'L(\lambda R)\lambda L(\lambda R)L^2\lambda R^6),$$
$$(Y) \equiv (r'R^5\lambda L^4),$$

where $r' \equiv [\lambda R]^n$, gives the desired solution.

[†]The authors are indebted to the referee for this solution, which is shorter and more elegant than theirs.

References

1. R. Peter, "Graphschemata und Rekursive Funktionen," *Dialectica*, Vol. 12 (1958), pp. 373-93.

2. S. Gorn, "Specification Languages for Mechanical Languages and Their Processors," *Communications of the ACM*, Vol. 4, No. 12 (December 1961), pp. 532-42.

3. H. Hermes, *Aufzählbarkeit, Entscheidbarkeit, Berechenbarkeit* (Berlin: Springer-Verlag, 1961).

4. S. Ciampa, "Un'applicazione della Teoria dei Grafi," *Atti del Convegno Nazionale di Logica*, Vol. 5, No. 7 (Turin: April 1961), pp. 73-80.

5. J. Riguet, "Programmation et Théorie des Catégories," *Proceedings of the ICC Symposium on Symbolic Languages in Data Processing* (New York: Gordon and Breach, 1962), pp. 83-98.

6. Y.I. Ianov, "On the Equivalence and Transformation of Program Schemes," *Dokl. Akad. Nauk SSSR*, Vol. 113 (1957), pp. 39-42. (Russian)

7. G. Asser, "Functional Algorithms and Graph Schema," *Z. Math. Logik u. Grundlagen Math.*, Vol. 7 (1961), pp. 20-27.

8. C. Böhm, "On a Family of Turing Machines and the Related Programming Language," *ICC Bulletin*, Vol. 3 (July 1964), pp. 187-94.

9. _____ and G. Jacopini, "Nuove Tecniche di Programmazione Semplificanti la Sintesi di Macchine Universali di Turing," *Rend. Acc. Naz. Lincei*, Vol. 8, No. 32 (June 1962), pp. 913-22.

INTRODUCTION

To many people, Dijkstra's letter to the Editor of *Communications of the ACM,* published in March 1968, marks the true beginning of structured programming. That it influenced the industry is clear, if for no other reason than for the articles it spawned, ranging from "IF-THEN-ELSE Considered Harmful," to "The Else Must Go, Too," to "Programming Considered Harmful."

In form and content, Dijkstra's letter is similar to his 1965 paper, which appears first in this collection. Description of the inverse relationship between a programmer's ability and the density of goto statements in his program is repeated, as is the emphasis on the limited ability of the human brain. Much of the discussion is somewhat theoretical in nature, and the typical COBOL programmer will hunger for some coding examples so that he can *see* why goto statements make program logic harder to understand.

Echoing his 1965 paper, the last few paragraphs underscore once again why the subject of structured programming stayed out of the mainstream of the data processing industry for so long. As Dijkstra points out, goto statements were a subject of discussion among academicians as far back as 1959. But even today, people whom Dijkstra acknowledges — names like Wirth, Hoare, Strachey, and Landin — are not well known to business-oriented or scientific-oriented programmers, so it should be no surprise that their ideas have languished for so many years.

Go To Statement Considered Harmful

Editor:

For a number of years I have been familiar with the observation that the quality of programmers is a decreasing function of the density of **go to** statements in the programs they produce. More recently I discovered why the use of the **go to** statement has such disastrous effects, and I became convinced that the **go to** statement should be abolished from all "higher level" programming languages (i.e. everything except, perhaps, plain machine code). At that time I did not attach too much importance to this discovery; I now submit my considerations for publication because in very recent discussions in which the subject turned up, I have been urged to do so.

My first remark is that, although the programmer's activity ends when he has constructed a correct program, the process taking place under control of his program is the true subject matter of his activity, for it is this process that has to accomplish the desired effect; it is this process that in its dynamic behavior has to satisfy the desired specifications. Yet, once the program has been made, the "making" of the corresponding process is delegated to the machine.

My second remark is that our intellectual powers are rather geared to master static relations and that our powers to visualize processes evolving in time are relatively poorly developed. For that reason we should do (as wise programmers aware of our limitations) our utmost to shorten the conceptual gap between the static program and the dynamic process, to make the correspondence between the program (spread out in text space) and the process (spread out in time) as trivial as possible.

Let us now consider how we can characterize the progress of a process. (You may think about this question in a very concrete manner: suppose that a process, considered as a time succession of actions, is stopped after an arbitrary action, what data do we have to fix in order that we can redo the process until the very same point?) If the program text is a pure concatenation of, say, assignment statements (for the purpose of this discussion regarded as the descriptions of single actions) it is sufficient to point in the program text to a point between two successive action descriptions. (In the absence of **go to** statements I can permit myself the syntactic ambiguity in the last three words of the previous sentence: if we parse them as "successive (action descriptions)" we mean successive in text space; if we parse as "(successive action) descriptions" we mean successive in time.) Let us call such a pointer to a suitable place in the text a "textual index."

When we include conditional clauses (**if** B **then** A), alternative clauses (**if** B **then** $A1$ **else** $A2$), choice clauses as introduced by C.A.R. Hoare (case [i] of ($A1, A2, \ldots, An$)), or conditional expressions as introduced by J. McCarthy ($B1 \rightarrow E1, B2 \rightarrow E2, \ldots, Bn \rightarrow En$), the fact remains that the progress of the process remains characterized by a single textual index.

As soon as we include in our language procedures we must admit that a single textual index is no longer sufficient. In the case that a textual index points to the interior of a procedure body the dynamic progress is only characterized when we also give to which call of the procedure we refer. With the inclusion of procedures we can characterize the progress of the process via a sequence of textual indices, the length of this sequence being equal to the dynamic depth of procedure calling.

Let us now consider repetition clauses (like, **while** B **repeat** A or **repeat** A **until** B). Logically speaking, such clauses are now superfluous, because we can express repetition with the aid of recursive procedures. For reasons of realism I don't wish to exclude them: on the one hand, repetition clauses can be implemented quite comfortably with present day finite equipment; on the other hand, the reasoning pattern known as "induction" makes us well equipped to retain our intellectual grasp on the processes generated by repetition clauses. With the inclusion of the repetition clauses textual indices are no longer sufficient to describe the dynamic progress of the process. With each entry into a repetition clause, however, we can associate a so-called "dynamic index," inexorably counting the ordinal number of the corresponding current repetition. As repetition clauses (just as procedure calls) may be applied nestedly, we find that now the progress of the process can always be uniquely characterized by a (mixed) sequence of textual and/or dynamic indices.

The main point is that the values of these indices are outside programmer's control; they are generated (either by the write-up of his program or by the dynamic evolution of the process) whether he wishes or not. They provide independent coordinates in which to describe the progress of the process.

Why do we need such independent coordinates? The reason is — and this seems to be inherent to sequential processes — that we can interpret the value of a variable only with respect to the progress of the process. If we wish to count the number, n say, of people in an initially empty room, we can achieve this by increasing n by one whenever we see someone entering the room. In the in-between moment that we have observed someone entering the room but have not yet performed the subsequent increase of n, its value equals the number of people in the room minus one!

The unbridled use of the **go to** statement has an immediate consequence that it becomes terribly hard to find a meaningful set of coordinates in which to describe the process progress. Usually, people take into account as well the values of some well chosen variables, but this is out of the question because it is relative to the progress that the meaning of these values is to be understood! With the **go to** statement one can, of course, still describe the progress uniquely by a counter counting the number of actions performed since program start (viz. a kind of normalized clock). The difficulty is that such a coordinate, although unique, is utterly unhelpful. In such a coordinate system it becomes an extremely complicated affair to define all those points of progress where, say, n equals the number of persons in the room minus one!

The **go to** statement as it stands is just too primitive; it is too much an invitation to make a mess of one's program. One can regard and appreciate the clauses considered as bridling its use. I do not claim that the clauses mentioned are exhaustive in the sense that they will satisfy all needs, but whatever clauses are suggested (e.g. abortion clauses) they should satisfy the requirement that a programmer independent coordinate system can be maintained to describe the process in a helpful and manageable way.

It is hard to end this with a fair acknowledgment. Am I to judge by whom my thinking has been influenced? It is fairly obvious that I am not uninfluenced by Peter Landin and Christopher Strachey. Finally I should like to record (as I remember it quite distinctly) how Heinz Zemanek at the pre-ALGOL meeting in early 1959 in Copenhagen quite explicitly expressed his doubts whether the **go to** statement should be treated on equal syntactic footing with the assignment statement. To a modest extent I blame myself for not having then drawn the consequences of his remark.

The remark about the undesirability of the **go to** statement is far from new. I remember having read the explicit recommendation to restrict the use of the **go to** statement to alarm exits, but I have not been able to trace it; presumably, it has been made by C.A.R. Hoare. In [1, Sec. 3.2.1.] Wirth and

Hoare together make a remark in the same direction in motivating the case construction: "Like the conditional, it mirrors the dynamic structure of a program more clearly than **go to** statements and switches, and it eliminates the need for introducing a large number of labels in the program."

In [2] Guiseppe Jacopini seems to have proved the (logical) superfluousness of the **go to** statement. The exercise to translate an arbitrary flow diagram more or less mechanically into a jumpless one, however, is not to be recommended. Then the resulting flow diagram cannot be expected to be more transparent than the original one.

References

1. N. Wirth and C.A.R. Hoare, "A Contribution to the Development of AL-GOL," *Communications of the ACM,* Vol. 9, No. 6 (June 1966), pp. 413-32.

2. C. Böhm and G. Jacopini, "Flow Diagrams, Turing Machines and Languages with Only Two Formation Rules," *Communications of the ACM,* Vol. 9, No. 5 (May 1966), pp. 366-71.

INTRODUCTION

In many EDP organizations, structured programming is thought to mean a coding discipline *plus* a design discipline (top-down design), *plus* a discipline for reviewing programs for correctness (walkthroughs), *plus* a method of organizing the members of a programming project. Aron's paper deals with the last of these issues, completely ignoring the other disciplines of structured programming (although, interestingly, the paper was presented at the same NATO conference at which Dijkstra gave his paper, entitled "Structured Programming" [Paper 5]).

The primary reason for this paper's significance is that it shows the *beginning* of what IBM eventually called the "Chief Programmer Team." Harlan Mills, the first of IBM's chief programmers, was assigned a thirty-man-year project, to be finished in six months — by himself! For a variety of reasons, including the fact that he assembled a group of helpers for specific aspects of the project, it took six man-years to complete the job. Nevertheless, the project seemed successful enough such that IBM employed the approach again in the famous New York Times project [see Papers 7 and 11] and formalized the Chief Programmer Team concept for use throughout the entire company.

Even this first experimental project contained many of the basic concepts of the formalized Chief Programmer Team. For example, Harlan Mills had not one, but *two,* people who normally would be called "program librarians": One was a secretary, the other a trainee programmer. He also used a "language lawyer" to help deal with the intricacies of the PL/I programming language.

Perhaps the most important part of Aron's paper is the last paragraph, in which he deals with "the question of why we don't use this technique in our many other projects." Aron's explanation is crucial, because it describes precisely why most other EDP organizations have abandoned the chief programmer concept after a period of initial fascination:

> ". . . because we cannot depend upon the existence of a super-programmer in any given project and, because we must transfer our people around in order to apply the right number of resources at the right time to a contract, we have found that it is important to build our systems without dependence upon any particularly strong individual."

The "Super-Programmer Project"

I would like to describe an experiment we performed in which a single programmer, Dr. Harlan Mills, undertook to reproduce a project that had been started in a typical "army of ants" fashion and was still under way. He hoped to do in six man months what was regarded as being essentially a 30 man year project.

His approach was essentially similar to Seegmuller's scheme; his language was PL/I and he used it from the top down. He started out using PL/I as a pidgin English; he simply wrote out his abstract ideas in an English form which was closer to PL/I than it was to conversational English and, as he proceeded into more detail, he generated the remaining parts of the PL/I statement. The essentials to his procedure were (1) develop the programming system structure and (2) develop the data files and the intercommunication system within the program. He found that, having done that, it became fairly straightforward to fill in the algorithms within each program module. Now, we tried to study this project in order to determine whether it was a success or failure but we ran into difficulties; namely, that he didn't finish it in a single effort. There were interruptions, other projects along the way, so that it wasn't clear exactly what the results were. But it was clear that it didn't take six man months to do the job; it took more like six man years, which still wasn't bad since it was substantially better than the other group.

On the other hand, during the period of the experiment, the other group's objectives changed substantially because the customer changed what he wanted.

The program was called the "definitive orbit determination system" and its purpose was to build a history of orbit programs and orbit observations for space agency and air force satellites. It was to be an interactive system whereby scientists could come up to a computer, request the assembly of information from old satellite activities and study it to determine such things as the geodetic shape of the earth, distances from the earth to the moon, etc. The system itself was, I would guess, around 50,000 instructions and the file was rather large. The structure of the information in the files was diverse because it was picked up from miscellaneous jobs, none of which had been performed with the intent of storing the results in this file.

Dr. Mills had the role of chief programmer and his function was to do everything regarding generation of the program down to the final code and testing of the code. In order to assist him, however, he trained his secretary to be his interface with the computer. Naturally, he found that he had to develop a small programming support system in order to enable her to communicate with the computer, the way a secretary would, rather than the way a programmer would. And he had a little help to get that programming system built. The second thing he found was that in order to write a program in PL/I he had to spread out, like, 36 manuals on his desk. In order to get around this, first of all he requested us to assign him (part time) an expert PL/I programmer, a programmer who was expert on the internal details of OS/360 and a few other consultants. Finally he acquired what we call a programmer-technician, a trainee programmer without a degree, whose job was primarily clerical support. He found that, in order to simplify the languages that he used (PL/I, JCL and linkage editor), he had to rewrite the manuals for JCL and linkage editor. This turned out to be fairly worthwhile because it was then easy to turn the description of these procedures mechanically into a set of control cards that his secretary could conveniently use.

The estimate of the man-power required increased from his original estimate. A second point that was far more significant was that, because the job he was doing was running parallel to an existing job, we chose not to give him a direct interface with the customer. We didn't want to confuse the customer about how many different IBM groups were supporting him, so we took one of the systems analysts from the contract project and made him the simulated interface with Dr. Mills. This turned out to be a mistake, in my opinion, because it shielded Dr. Mills from all of the actual problems of customer relations.

We have a second project of this type now, dealing with an information bank for a New York City newspaper and here we do have direct contact with the customer. Progress is substantially slower, and it is obvious that Seegmuller's first point is an extremely difficult one to reach since we are dealing, at least in the case of application systems, with users who don't really know what they want; moreover, they don't realize what they want until they're into the project itself.

Now let me turn to the question of why we don't use this technique in our many other projects. First of all a chief programmer such as Dr. Mills is a very unusual individual. We started out referring to him as a super-programmer; the term may not be accurate but it is descriptive because among the other 2,000 programmers there are not more than a few of equivalent capability. The capabilities required are extremely good programming knowledge, extremely good application knowledge and a desire to work very hard on this type of problem. It was necessary in the orbit determination system to understand sufficient mathematics to develop the orbit equations and so forth, as well as understand programming. In addition it was necessary to understand a subject that is dominant in many of our application systems, namely, the problems of interface with displays and with analog input such as radars and data acquisition devices. Now, in our remaining projects, because we cannot depend upon the existence of a super-programmer in any given project and, because we must transfer our people around in order to apply the right number of resources at the right time to a contract, we have found that it is important to build our systems without dependence upon any particularly strong individual. So we set up a management and control organization that makes the best out of the resources that are normally available. If we find that, within a project, we do have a great strength then we find that the individual concerned naturally introduces more advanced ideas. But we find that it is impractical to plan our project with the confidence that we'll find such an individual in the beginning. Our current goal is to fit the best implementation approach to each new project.

INTRODUCTION

Although the structured programming movement has been with us for nearly fifteen years, it's not entirely clear where the term "structured" originated. If one had to choose a single source, the following landmark paper by Edsger Dijkstra would be it.

The theme of the paper, which was presented at a 1969 conference sponsored, strangely enough, by the North Atlantic Treaty Organization Science Committee, is intriguing. As Dijkstra points out, exhaustive testing of a computer program is virtually impossible, and testing by "sampling" also is pointless. As he says, "Program testing can be used to show the presence of bugs, but never to show their absence!" And, while rigorous mathematical proofs of program correctness are possible, they are difficult to construct, often because the programs themselves are not well suited to such analysis. So, as Dijkstra explains, rather than *first* writing a program and *then* worrying about the difficult task of constructing a proof of program correctness, it makes far better sense to ask, "For what program structures can we give correctness proofs without undue labour. . ." and then, "How do we make, for a given task, such a well-structured program?"

With this philosophy as a basis, Dijkstra concludes that program logic (or "sequencing," as he calls it) "should be controlled by alternative, conditional and repetitive clauses and procedure calls, rather than by statements transferring control to labelled points." Although he doesn't describe explicitly the IF-THEN-ELSE construct and the DO-WHILE construct, it is clear what he means. And, while he doesn't mention the implementation of these constructs in programming languages, one assumes that Dijkstra takes it for granted that any reasonable programming language would provide a direct implementation of the necessary control constructs.

Perhaps the most interesting concept in this paper comes from Dijkstra's pearl imagery. Dijkstra suggests that we visualize a program as a string of ordered pearls, in which a larger pearl describes the entire program in terms of concepts or capabilities implemented in lower-level pearls. It is clear that we are being shown, by means of a delightful, vivid analogy, the essential concepts of what is now called *top-down design*.

The only thing that detracts from this paper is the repeated emphasis that it is based on experiments with small programs. In itself, this is not surprising. Throughout the literature in the computer field, we see that small programs and small projects are the only ones that can be conducted in a "laboratory" environment. However, the concluding sentence of Dijkstra's paper may have alienated the very people who most need to understand his ideas:

> ". . . I have given but little recognition to the requirements of program development such as is needed when one wishes to employ a large crowd; I have no experience with the Chinese Army approach, nor am I convinced of its virtues."

This quote reminds me of an experience at a recent computer conference, at which one of the speakers described his own approach as a "bottom-up" strategy. What he meant, he said, was that we should begin by attacking very small problems, e.g., those requiring only twenty to thirty program statements, and learn how to solve them properly. Then we could build on that experience, and consider solving larger problems — those requiring perhaps 100-200 statements; in a few years, with our accumulated wisdom, we might consider working on problems as large as 1,000-2,000 statements. He then gave a brilliant and eloquent presentation of the solution to a twenty-statement problem.

When he finished, a member of the audience stood and announced in a loud voice that he had the misfortune of working on a project that probably would result in coding some three *million* program statements. What did the speaker suggest he do?

"Punt!" was the reply.

Do you still wonder why it took ten years for anyone to listen to the concepts of structured programming?

Structured Programming

Introduction

This working document reports on experience and insights gained in programming experiments performed by the author in the last year. The leading question was if it was conceivable to increase our programming ability by an order of magnitude and what techniques (mental, organizational or mechanical) could be applied in the process of program composition to produce this increase. The programming experiments were undertaken to shed light upon these questions.

Program size

My real concern is with intrinsically large programs. By "intrinsically large" I mean programs that are large due to the complexity of their task, in contrast to programs that have exploded (by inadequacy of the equipment, unhappy decisions, poor understanding of the problem, etc.). The fact that, for practical reasons, my experiments had thus far to be carried out with rather small programs did present a serious difficulty; I have tried to overcome this by treating problems of size explicitly and by trying to find their consequences as much as possible by analysis, inspection and reflection rather than by (as yet too expensive) experiments.

In doing so I found a number of subgoals that, apparently, we have to learn to achieve (if we don't already know how to do that).

If a large program is a composition of N "program components," the confidence level of the individual components must be exceptionally high if N is very large. If the individual components can be made with the probability "p" of being correct, the probability that the whole program functions properly will not exceed

$$P = p^N$$

for large N, p must be practically equal to one if P is to differ significantly from zero. Combining subsets into larger components from which then the whole program is composed, presents no remedy:

$$p^{N/2} * p^{N/2} \text{ still equals } p^N \ !$$

As a consequence, the problem of program correctness (confidence level) was one of my primary concerns.

The effort — be it intellectual or experimental — needed to demonstrate the correctness of a program in a sufficiently convincing manner may (measured in some loose sense) not grow more rapidly than in proportion to the program length (measured in an equally loose sense). If, for instance, the labour involved in verifying the correct composition of a whole program out of N program components (each of them individually assumed to be correct) still grows exponentially with N, we had better admit defeat.

Any large program will exist during its life-time in a multitude of different versions, so that in composing a large program we are not so much concerned with a single program, but with a whole family of related programs, containing alternative programs for the same job and/or similar programs for similar jobs. A program therefore should be conceived and understood as a member of a family; it should be so structured out of components that various members of this family, sharing components, do not only share the correctness demonstration of the shared components but also of the shared substructure.

Program correctness

An assertion of program correctness is an assertion about the net effects of the computations that may be evoked by this program. Investigating how such assertions can be justified, I came to the following conclusions:

1.   The number of different inputs, i.e. the number of different computations for which the assertions claim to hold is so fantastically high that demonstration of correctness by sampling is completely out of the question. *Program testing can be used to show the presence of bugs, but never to show their absence!*

Therefore, proof of program correctness should depend only upon the program text.

2.   A number of people have shown that program correctness can be proved. Highly formal correctness proofs have been given; also correctness proofs have been given for "normal programs," i.e. programs not written with a proof procedure in mind. As is to be expected (and nobody is to be blamed for that) the circulating examples are concerned with rather small programs and, unless measures are taken, the amount of labour involved in proving might well (will) explode with program size.

3.   Therefore, I have not focused my attention on the question "how do we prove the correctness of a given program?" but on the questions "for what program structures can we give correctness proofs without undue labour, even if the programs get large?" and, as a sequel, "how do we make, for a given task, such a well-structured program?" My willingness to confine my attention to such "well-structured programs" (as a subset of the set of all possible programs) is based on my belief that we can find such a well-structured subset satisfying our programming needs, i.e. that for each programmable task this subset contains enough realistic programs.

4.   This, what I call "constructive approach to the problem of program correctness," can be taken a step further. It is not restricted to general considerations as to what program structures are attractive from the point of view of provability; in a number of specific, very difficult programming tasks I have finally succeeded in constructing a program by analyzing how a proof could be given that a class of computations would satisfy certain requirements; from the requirements of the proof the program followed.

The relation between program and computation

Investigating how assertions about the possible computations (evolving in time) can be made on account of the static program text, I have concluded that adherence to rigid sequencing disciplines is essential, so as to allow step-wise abstraction from the possibly different routings. In particular: when programs for a sequential computer are expressed as a linear sequence of basic symbols of a programming language, sequencing should be controlled by alternative, conditional and repetitive clauses and procedure calls, rather than by statements transferring control to labelled points.

The need for step-wise abstraction from local sequencing is perhaps most convincingly shown by the following demonstration:

Let us consider a "stretched" program of the form

$$S_1; S_2; \ldots ; S_N \qquad (1)$$

and let us introduce the measuring convention that when the net effect of the execution of each individual statement S_i has been given, it takes N steps of reasoning to establish the correctness of program (1), i.e. to establish that the cumulative net effect of the N actions in succession satisfies the requirements imposed upon the computations evoked by program (1).

For a statement of the form

$$\textbf{if B then } S_1 \textbf{ else } S_2 \qquad (2)$$

where, again, the net effect of the execution of the constituent statements S_1 and S_2 has been given; we introduce the measuring convention that it takes 2 steps of reasoning to establish the net effect of program (2), viz. one for the case B and one for the case not B.

Consider now a program of the form

$$\textbf{if } B_1 \textbf{ then } S_{11} \textbf{ else } S_{12};$$
$$\textbf{if } B_2 \textbf{ then } S_{21} \textbf{ else } S_{22};$$
$$.$$
$$.$$
$$.$$
$$\textbf{if } B_N \textbf{ then } S_{N1} \textbf{ else } S_{N2} \qquad (3)$$

According to the measuring convention it takes 2 steps per alternative statement to understand it, i.e. to establish that the net effect of

$$\textbf{if } B_i \textbf{ then } S_{i1} \textbf{ else } S_{i2}$$

is equivalent to that of the execution of an abstract statement S_i. Having N such alternative statements, it takes us 2N steps to reduce program (3) to one of the form of program (1); to understand the latter form of the program takes us another N steps, giving 3N steps in toto.

If we had refused to introduce the abstract statements S_i but had tried to understand program (3) directly in terms of executions of the statements S_{ij}, each such computation would be the cumulative effect of N such statement executions and would as such require N steps to understand it. Trying to understand the algorithm in terms of the S_{ij} implies that we have to distinguish between 2^N different routings through the program and this would lead to $N*2^N$ steps of reasoning!

I trust that the above calculation convincingly demonstrates the need for the introduction of the abstract statements S_i. An aspect of my constructive approach is not to reduce a given program (3) to an abstract program (1), but to start with the latter.

Abstract data structures

Understanding a program composed from a modest number of abstract statements again becomes an exploding task if the definition of the net effect of the constituent statements is sufficiently unwieldy. This can be overcome by the introduction of suitable abstract data structures. The situation is greatly analogous to the way in which we can understand an ALGOL program operating on integers without having to bother about the number representation of the implementation used. The only difference is that now the programmer must invent his own concepts (analogous to the "ready-made" integer) and his own operations upon them (analogous to the "ready-made" arithmetic operations).

In the refinement of an abstract program (i.e. composed from abstract statements operating on abstract data structures) we observe the phenomenon of "joint refinement." For abstract data structures of a given type a certain representation is chosen in terms of new (perhaps still rather abstract) data structures. The immediate consequence of this design decision is that the abstract statements operating upon the original abstract data structure have to be redefined in terms of algorithmic refinements operating upon the new data structures in terms of which it was decided to represent the original abstract data structure. Such a joint refinement of data structure and associated statements should be an isolated unit of the program text: it embodies the immediate consequences of an (independent) design decision and is as such the natural unit of interchange for program modification. It is an example of what I have grown into calling "a pearl."

Programs as necklaces strung from pearls

I have grown to regard a program as an ordered set of pearls, a "necklace." The top pearl describes the program in its most abstract form, in all lower pearls one or more concepts used above are explained (refined) in terms of concepts to be explained (refined) in pearls below it, while the bottom pearl eventually explains what still has to be explained in terms of a standard interface (=machine). The pearl seems to be a natural program module.

As each pearl embodies a specific design decision (or, as the case may be, a specific aspect of the original problem statement) it is the natural unit of interchange in program modification (or, as the case may be, program adaptation to a change in problem statement).

Pearls and necklace give a clear status to an "incomplete program," consisting of the top half of a necklace; it can be regarded as a complete program to be executed by a suitable machine (of which the bottom half of the necklace gives a feasible implementation). As such, the correctness of the upper half of the necklace can be established regardless of the choice of the bottom half.

Between two successive pearls we can make a "cut," which is a manual for a machine provided by the part of the necklace below the cut and used by the program represented by the part of the necklace above the cut. This manual serves as an interface between the two parts of the necklace. We feel this form of interface more helpful than regarding data representation as an interface between operations, in particular more helpful towards ensuring the combinatorial freedom required for program adaptation.

The combinatorial freedom just mentioned seems to be the only way in which we can make a program as part of a family or "in many (potential) versions" without the labour involved increasing proportional to the number of members of the family. The family becomes the set of those selections from a given collection of pearls that can be strung into a fitting necklace.

Concluding remarks

Pearls in a necklace have a strict logical order, say "from top to bottom." I would like to stress that this order may be radically different from the order (in time) in which they are designed.

Pearls have emerged as program modules when I tried to map upon each other as completely as possible, the numerous members of a class of related programs. The abstraction process involved in this mapping turns out (not, amazingly, as an afterthought!) to be the same as the one that can be used to reduce the amount of intellectual labour involved in correctness proofs. This is very encouraging.

As I said before, the programming experiments have been carried out with relatively small programs. Although, personally, I firmly believe that they show the way towards more reliable composition of really large programs, I should like to stress that as yet I have *no* experimental evidence for this. The experimental evidence gained so far shows an increasing ability to compose programs of the size I tried. Although I tried to do it, I feel that I have given but little recognition to the requirements of program development such as is needed when one wishes to employ a large crowd; I have no experience with the Chinese Army approach, nor am I convinced of its virtues.

INTRODUCTION

Some of the papers presented in this book already have been widely circulated; others were published in well-known journals, like *IBM Systems Journal,* but largely were ignored when they first appeared; and then there are the obscure papers like this one by Ashcroft and Manna, which was presented at the 1971 IFIP Conference in Ljubljana, Yugoslavia. It's not that the *ideas* in the paper are obscure — it's just that very few people in the mainstream EDP community attended the Conference, and precious few copies of the conference proceedings ever found their way into American libraries. It is, however, a paper that many people over the years have wanted to read, particularly since it deals with a subject also mentioned by Knuth ("Structured Programming with go to Statements" [see Paper 20]), Wulf ("A Case Against the GOTO" [Paper 8]), and Böhm and Jacopini ("Flow Diagrams, Turing Machines and Languages with Only Two Formation Rules" [Paper 2]).

The subject of the Ashcroft and Manna paper is the translation of unstructured programs into equivalent structured programs. Although Wulf's paper sets forth a more practical, step-by-step mechanism for such translations, Ashcroft and Manna give an extremely detailed, extremely theoretical presentation, providing an important addition to the work of Böhm and Jacopini — but it's definitely for the more serious students of computer science.

The larger issue of "restructuring" is ignored by Ashcroft and Manna, and, to a large extent, by everyone else. The issue began as a theoretical question: Could *any* program be written as a structured program? Böhm and Jacopini answered the question in the affirmative by demonstrating that any *arbitrary* program could be translated into an equivalent structured program. Wulf, Knuth, and Ashcroft and Manna shifted the emphasis of the question slightly: Could one translate an existing program into a structured program that still would have the same topology as the original program? To most people, the mere question suggested heresy, perverting the very idea of writing structured programs! Rather than writing bad code and then cleaning it up, they argued, we should begin by writing good code in the first place.

But the larger issue of restructuring does exist. The vast mountains of unstructured code, which already were written before structured programming came along, clearly can't be thrown away. Members of the average EDP organization have to live with their code, for better or worse, for a period of ten years or more before they can afford to discard it. Do Ashcroft and Manna have the solution for these people? Can we take existing unstructured code and translate it into more maintainable, structured code? And, more important, can we do it *mechanically?*

In principle, we can. Indeed, the Ashcroft-Manna algorithm has been built into so-called structuring engines such as the one described by Guy de Balbine in "Better Manpower Utilization Using Automatic Restructuring."* But there are questions that still have not been completely answered: For example, can one really trust such an automatic translation process? What if the original unstructured program worked *because of* its use of syntactically illegal COBOL statements — not in spite of, but because of illegal statements that the compiler ignored, or for which it produced mysterious object code that accidentally produced the right result!

Another somewhat ironic situation could occur that would hamper the success of an automatic translation process: After living with a program for ten years, a veteran maintenance programmer may have become intimately familiar with the rat's-nest unstructured logic, and a mechanical translation of the program into a structured form actually might be *less* understandable! Of course, it is unlikely that a structuring engine could improve anything but the control structures (and perhaps the formatting, if a PRETTYPRINT function is included); the data-names still might be so cryptic that nobody would be able to understand the program. Moreover, the program might be part of a larger system suffering from all the problems of, say, pathological connections or global data areas.

So, it is not entirely clear that the world really wants mechanical structuring algorithms. However, since situations do exist in which the capability *might* be useful, it is a very good idea to be familiar with the kind of translation mechanisms that Ashcroft and Manna present.

---

*Balbine's paper appears as part of the *AFIPS Proceedings of the 1975 National Computer Conference,* Vol. 44, (Montvale, N.J.: AFIPS Press, 1975), pp. 319-34.

The Translation
of 'go to' Programs
to 'while' Programs

1. GENERAL DISCUSSION

1.1. Introduction

The first class of programs we consider are simple *flowchart programs* constructed from assignment statements (that assign terms to variables) and test statements (that test quantifier-free formulas) operating on a "state vector" $\bar{x}$. The flowchart program begins with a unique start statement of the form

where $\bar{x}_{\text{input}}$ is a subvector of $\bar{x}$, indicating the variables that have to be given values at the beginning of the computation. It ends with a unique halt statement of the form

where $\bar{x}_{\text{output}}$ is a subvector of $\bar{x}$, indicating the variables whose values will be the desired result of the computation.

We make no assumptions about the domain of individuals, or about the operations and predicates used in the statements. Thus our flowchart programs are really flowchart schemas (see, for example, Luckham, Park and Paterson [1]) and all the results can be stated in terms of such schemas.

51

Let P_1 be any flowchart program of the form shown in Figure 1. Note that, for example, the statement $\bar{x} \leftarrow e(\bar{x})$ stands for any sequence of assignment statements whose net effect is the replacement of vector $\bar{x}$ by a new vector $e(\bar{x})$. Similarly, the test $p(\bar{x})$, for example, stands for any quantifier-free formula with variables from x. The flowchart program P_1 will be used as an example throughout the paper.

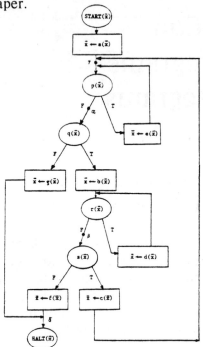

Figure 1. The flowchart program P_1.

In order to write such flowchart programs in a conventional programming language, *goto* statements are required. There has recently been much discussion (see, for example, Dijkstra [2]) about whether the use of *goto* statements makes programs difficult to understand, and whether the use of *while* or *for* statements is preferable. In addition, it is quite possible that simpler proof methods of the validity and equivalence of programs may be found for programs without *goto* statements (see, for example, Stark [3]). It is clearly relevant to this discussion to consider whether the abolition of *goto* statements is really possible.

Therefore the second class of programs we consider are *while programs*, i.e., Algol-like programs consisting only of *while* statements of the form *while* ⟨quantifier-free formula⟩ *do* ⟨statement⟩, in addition to conditional, assignment and block* statements. As before, each program starts with a unique start statement, START($\bar{x}_{\text{input}}$), and ends with a unique halt statement, HALT($\bar{x}_{\text{output}}$).

---

*A block statement is denoted by any sequence of statements enclosed by square brackets.

Since both classes of programs use the same kind of start and halt statements, we can define the equivalence of two programs independently of the classes to which they belong. Two programs (with the same input subvectors $\bar{x}_{input}$ and the same output subvectors $\bar{x}_{output}$) are said to be *equivalent* if for each assignment of values to x_{input} either both programs do not terminate or both terminate with the same values in $\bar{x}_{output}$.

1.2. Translation to while programs by adding variables

1.2.1. Extending the state vector $\bar{x}$

We can show that by allowing extra variables which keep crucial past values of some of the variables in $\bar{x}$, one can effectively translate every flowchart program into an equivalent while program (ALGORITHM I). The importance of this result is that original "topology" of the program is preserved, and the new program is of the same order of efficiency as the original program. However, we shall not enter into any discussion as to whether the new program is superior to the original one or not.

This result, considered in terms of schemas, can be contrasted with those of Paterson and Hewitt [4] (see also Strong [5]). They showed that although it is not possible to translate all recursive schemas into flowchart schemas, it is possible to do this for "linear" recursive schemas, by adding extra variables. However, as they point out, the flowchart schemas produced are less efficient than the original recursive schemas.

As an example, ALGORITHM I will give the following while program which is equivalent to the flowchart program P_1 (Figure 1):

```
 START(x̄);
 x̄ ← a(x̄);
┌ ─ ─ ─ ─ ─ ─ ─ ─ ─ ─ ─ ─ ─ ─ ─ ─ ┐
│ while p (x̄) do x̄ ← e(x̄);          │
│ ȳ ← x̄;                             │
│ if q(x̄) then [x̄ ← b(x̄); while r(x̄) do x̄ ← d(x̄)]; │
└ ─ ─ ─ ─ ─ ─ ─ ─ ─ ─ ─ ─ ─ ─ ─ ─ ┘
 while q(ȳ) ∧ s(x̄) do
     [x̄ ← c(x̄);
 ┌ ─ ─ ─ ─ ─ ─ ─ ─ ─ ─ ─ ─ ─ ─ ─ ┐
 │ while p(x̄) do x̄ ← e(x̄);        │
 │ ȳ ← x̄;                          │
 │ if q(x̄) then                    │
 └ _ _ [x̄ ← b(x̄); while r(x̄) do x̄ ← d(x̄)] ┘ ];
 if q(ȳ) then x̄ ← f(x̄) else x̄ ← g(x̄);
 HALT(x̄).
```

If the test $q(\bar{x})$ uses only a subvector of $\bar{x}$, then the algorithm will indicate that the vector of extra variables y need only be of the same length as this subvector.

Note that on each cycle of the main while statement, the state vector $\bar{x}$ is at point β, while $\bar{y}$ holds the preceding values of $\bar{x}$ at point α.

Note also that the two subprograms enclosed in broken lines are identical. This is typical of the programs produced by the algorithm. One might use this fact to make the programs more readable by using "subroutines" for the repeated subprograms.

Because of space limitations we cannot present ALGORITHM I in this paper. The detailed algorithm can be found in the preliminary report of this paper (CS 188, Computer Science Dept., Stanford University).

1.2.2. Adding boolean variables

The translation of flowchart programs into while programs by the addition of boolean variables is not a new idea. Böhm and Jacopini [6] and Cooper [7] (see also Bruno and Steiglitz [8]) have shown that every flowchart program can be effectively translated into an equivalent while program (with one while statement) by introducing new boolean variables into the program, new predicates to test these variables, together with assignments to set them *true* or *false*. The boolean variables essentially simulate a program counter, and the while program simply interprets the original program. On each repetition of the while statement, the next operation of the original program is performed, and the "program counter" is updated. As noted by Cooper and Bruno and Steiglitz themselves, this transformation is undesirable since it changes the "topology" (loop-structure) of the program, giving a program that is less easy to understand. For example, if a while program is written as a flowchart program and then transformed back to an equivalent while program by their method, the resulting while program will not resemble the original.

We give an algorithm (ALGORITHM II) for transforming flowchart programs to equivalent while programs by adding extra boolean variables, which is an improvement on the above method. It preserves the "topology" of the original program and in particular it does not alter while-like structure that may already exist in the original program.

For the flowchart program P_1 (Figure 1), for example ALGORITHM II will produce the following while program.

```
START(x̄);
x̄ ← a(x̄);
t ← true;
while t do
     [while p(x̄) do x ← e(x̄);
     if q(x̄) then [x̄ ← b(x̄);
          while r(x̄) do x̄ ← d(x̄);
          if s(x̄) then x̄ ← c(x̄)
               else [x̄ ← f(x); t ← false]]
          else [x̄ ← g(x̄); t ← false]];
HALT(x̄).
```

Note that each repetition of the main while statement starts from point γ and proceeds either back to γ or to δ. In the latter case, t is made *false* and we subsequently exit from the while statement.

1.3. Translation to while programs without adding variables

It is natural at this point to consider whether every flowchart program can be translated into an equivalent while program without adding extra variables (i.e., using only the original state vector $\bar{x}$). We show that this cannot be done in general, and in fact there is a flowchart program of the form of Figure 1 which is an appropriate counter-example.

A similar negative result has been demonstrated by Knuth and Floyd [9] and Scott [private communication]. However, the notion of equivalence considered by those authors is more restrictive in that it requires equivalence of computation sequences (i.e., the sequence of assignment and test statements in order of execution) and not just the equivalence of final results of computation as we do. Thus, since our notion of equivalence is weaker, our negative result is stronger.

2. ALGORITHM II: TRANSLATION BY ADDING BOOLEAN VARIABLES

The second algorithm, ALGORITHM II, translates flowchart programs to equivalent while programs by adding boolean variables. It makes use of the fact that every flowchart program (without the start and halt statements) can be decomposed into blocks where a block is any piece of flowchart program with only one exit (but possibly many entrances). This is obvious since in particular the whole body of the given flowchart program can be considered as such a block. The aim, whenever possible, is to get blocks containing at most one top-level test statement (i.e., test statement not contained in inner blocks) since such blocks can be represented as a piece of while program without adding boolean variables. In particular, if a while program is expressed as a flowchart program, this latter program can always be decomposed into such simple blocks, and the algorithm will give us back the original while program.

For any given flowchart program we construct the equivalent while program by induction on the structure of the blocks.

For each entrance b_i to block B we consider that part B_i of the block reachable from b_i. We then recursively construct an equivalent piece of while program $\widetilde{B_i}(\bar{x}, \bar{t})$* as follows. There are two cases to consider:

Case 1:   (a) B_i contains at most one top-level test statement.

    or   (b) B_i contains no top-level loops.

---

*t is a (possibly empty) vector of additional boolean variables introduced by the translation.

In both cases $\widetilde{B_i}(x,\ t)$ is the obvious piece of while program requiring at most one top-level while statement (and no extra boolean variables).

Case 2: B_i contains two or more top-level test statements and at least one top-level loop.

In this case we choose a set of points on top-level arcs of B_i (called "cut-set" points) such that each top-level loop contains at least one such point. One point on the exit arc of the block is also included in this set. We shall translate B_i into a piece of while program $\widetilde{B_i}(\bar{x},\ \bar{t})$ with one top-level while statement in such a way that each iteration of the while statement follows the execution of B_i from one cut-set point to the next. In this case, $\widetilde{B_i}(\bar{x},\ \bar{t})$ includes boolean variables introduced to keep track of the current cut-set point. Note that n boolean variables $t_1,\ t_2,\ \ldots,\ t_n$ are sufficient to distinguish between k cut-set points, $2^{n-1} < k \leq 2^n$.

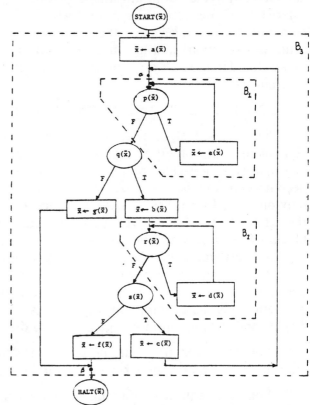

Example: We shall illustrate the method using again the flowchart program P_1 (Figure 1). We decompose P_1 into blocks as shown in Figure 2. Blocks B_1 and B_2 are of type 1 and can each be written as a single while statement. Block B_3 is of type 2 with a single top-level loop. Thus it is sufficient to choose points α and β as the cut-set points. To distinguish between α and β we need one boolean variable, t say. We can therefore generate the while program given on the preceding page which is equivalent to the flowchart program P_1.

Figure 2. The flowchart program P_1 (for ALGORITHM II).

3. THE NEGATIVE RESULT

We consider the flowchart program P_2 (Figure 3) which has the structure of Figure 1. The domain D is the set of all pairs of strings such that the first string, called "head," is any *finite* string over letters {g, h}, and the second string, called "tail," is any *infinite** string over letters {α, β, γ}, with at most one occurrence of γ.

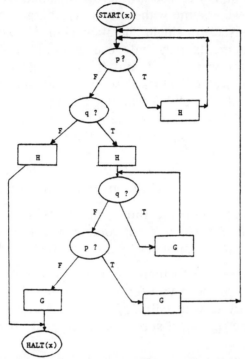

Where test *p* means "is 'α' the leftmost letter in tail"; test *q* means "is 'β' the leftmost letter in tail"; operation *G* means "erase the leftmost letter in tail and add 'g' on the right of head"; and operation *H* means "erase the leftmost letter in tail and add 'h' on the right of head."

Figure 3. The flowchart program P_2.

During a computation of P_2, the only changes in the value of the program variable are deletion of leftmost letters from the tail and adding letters *g* or *h* to the right of the head. The tests in the program simply look at the tail, and therefore the computation is determined by the tail of the initial value. Thus, since the program terminates if and only if both tests *p* and *q* are false, it implies that P_2 terminates if and only if the tail of the initial value contains γ. Another important feature of any computation of P_2 is that whenever the leftmost letter of the tail is α, the next but one operation must be operation *H*. Similarly, whenever the leftmost letter is β, the next but one operation must be *G*.

---

*Note that the domain is non-enumerable. However, we can in fact restrict the tails to the enumerable domain of ultimately periodic strings, i.e., infinite strings which eventually repeat some finite substring indefinitely.

Let us assume that we have a while program P_2^* equivalent to P_2 which also has one variable and the same domain D. Although we could allow the assignment statements of P_2^* to use any terms obtained by compositions of the operations G and H, we assume without loss of generality that each assignment statement in P_2^* consists of a single operation G or H. The tests in the conditional and while statements may only use quantifier-free formulas obtained from tests p and q, and operations G and H. Since we use only one variable, it follows that the sequences of values describing corresponding computations of P_2^* and P_2 are identical. Note also that since there is a bound on the depth of terms in the quantifier-free formulas, there is a bound, M say, on the number of leftmost letters in the tail that can affect the decision of any test in P_2^*. Finally, without loss of generality we shall make the restriction that there is no redundant while statement in P_2^*; i.e., there is no while statement with a uniform bound on the number of its iterations in terminating computations.

Since P_2^* must contain some (non-redundant) while statement, let W be any while statement in P_2^* which is not contained or followed by another while statement. The point in P_2^* immediately after W we shall denote by A.

Lemma: For all n $(n \geqslant 0)$ there exist strings a, $c \in \{\alpha, \beta\}^*$ and $d \in \{\alpha, \beta\}^\infty$ $(\,|c| = n)^\dagger$ such that for all strings $b \in \{\alpha, \beta\}^*$ the computation of P_2^* starting with tail $abc\gamma d$ passes A with some tail $\underline{ab}c\gamma d$, where $\underline{ab}$ is some rightmost substring of ab (possibly empty).

From this lemma we immediately obtain the following corollary.

Corollary. For every n, $n \geqslant 0$, there exists a finite computation of P_2^* which passes through A with more than n operations still to be performed.

But this contradicts the fact that since there is no while statement following A, the number of operations that P_2^* can perform after A is bounded.

Proof of Lemma: By induction on n.

Base step. Choose any computation starting with tail $a' a'' b' \gamma d'$ $(a', a'', b' \in \{\alpha, \beta\}^*$, $d' \in \{\alpha, \beta\}^\infty$ and $|a''| = M)$ that enters W with tail $a'' b' \gamma d'$. (Such computation exists by non-redundancy of W.)

Since at most M leftmost letters of the tail can effect the decision of any test, on entering W the main test can only look at a''. Therefore the test will be true for any tail starting with a''.

---

†i.e., a and c are finite strings (possibly empty) over $\{\alpha, \beta\}$, d is an infinite string over $\{\alpha, \beta\}$ and the length of c is n.

In particular, the computation starting with tail $a'a''b\gamma a''d'$, *for any b* $\{\alpha,$ $\beta\}^*$, also enters W at the same point, i.e., with tail $a''b\gamma a''d'$. Since the computation is finite, it must subsequently pass point A, but (noting that the test in W must be false when passing A) it cannot pass A with tail $a''d'$.

Hence, with $a = a'a''$, $d = a''d'$, for all strings b in $\{\alpha, \beta\}^*$, the computation starting with $ab\gamma d$ must pass A with some tail $\underline{ab}\gamma d$ where $\underline{ab}$ is some rightmost substring of ab.

Induction step. Assume we have strings a, $c \in \{\alpha, \beta\}^*$ and $d \in \{\alpha, \beta\}^\infty$, $|c| = n$, such that for all strings b in $\{\alpha, \beta\}^*$ the computation starting with tail $abc\gamma d$ passes A with some tail $\underline{abc}\gamma d$ where $\underline{ab}$ is some rightmost substring of ab.

We find a string $c' \in \{\alpha, \beta\}^*$, $|c'| = n+1$, such that for all strings b' in $\{\alpha, \beta\}^*$ the computation starting with tail $ab'c'\gamma d$ passes A with some tail $\underline{ab'}c'\gamma d$ where $\underline{ab'}$ is some rightmost substring of ab'.

There are three cases to consider:

(i)   For all nonempty strings b, the corresponding substring $\underline{ab}$ is nonempty. In this case *we take c' to be αc.*[†]

For any string b' in $\{\alpha, \beta\}^*$ the computation starting with tail $ab'\alpha c\gamma d$, passes A with tail $\underline{ab'}\alpha c\gamma d$, where $\underline{ab'}$ is a rightmost substring of ab'.

(ii)   For some nonempty string $b = b''\alpha$ ($b'' \in \{\alpha, \beta\}^*$), the substring $\underline{ab}$ is empty, i.e., there exists computation S starting with $ab''\alpha c\gamma d$ that passes A with $c\gamma d$. In this case *we take c' to be βc.*

By earlier remarks about P_2 and P_2^*, it follows that the next operation in S after passing A must be H.

Now, for *any string b' in* $\{\alpha, \beta\}^*$ the computation starting with tail $ab'\beta c\gamma d$ must pass A with some tail $\underline{ab'}\beta c\gamma d$ where $\underline{ab'}\beta$ is some rightmost substring of $ab'\beta$.

$\underline{ab'}\beta$ cannot be empty because this would mean that this computation passes A with the same tail $c\gamma d$ as for S but in this case the next operation to be performed is G. This is impossible, since the course of computation from A must be determined by the tail at this point.

[†]We could equally well take c' to be βc and consider computations starting with tail $ab'\beta c\gamma d$.

Hence, the computation must pass A with some tail $\underline{ab}' \beta c \gamma d$ (i.e., $\underline{ab}' c' \gamma d$) where ab' is a rightmost substring of ab'.

(iii) For some nonempty string $b = b'' \beta$ ($b'' \in \{\alpha, \beta\}^*$), the substring $\underline{ab}$ is empty. In this *case we take c' to be αc.*

We proceed as in case (ii) with α and β interchanged and G and H interchanged.

Acknowledgement

We are indebted to David Cooper for stimulating discussions and mainly for his idea of using cut-set points which we have adopted in ALGORITHM II. We are also grateful to Donald Knuth for his critical reading of the manuscript and subsequent helpful suggestions.

The research reported here was supported in part by the Advanced Research Projects Agency of the Office of the Secretary of Defense (SD-183).

References

1. D.C. Luckham, D.M.R. Park, and M.S. Paterson, "On Formalized Computer Programs," *Journal of Computer and System Sciences,* Vol. 4, No. 3 (June 1970), pp. 220-49.

2. E.W. Dijkstra, "Go To Statement Considered Harmful," *Communications of the ACM,* Vol. 11, No. 3 (March 1968), pp. 147-48.

3. R. Stark, "A Language for Algorithms," *Computer Journal,* Vol. 14, No. 1 (February 1971), pp. 40-44.

4. M.S. Paterson and C.E. Hewitt, "Comparative Schematology," unpublished memo.

5. H.R. Strong, "Translating Recursion Equations into Flowcharts," *Journal of Computer and System Sciences,* Vol. 5, No. 3 (June 1971), pp. 254-85.

6. C. Böhm and G. Jacopini, "Flow Diagrams, Turing Machines and Languages with Only Two Formation Rules," *Communications of the ACM,* Vol. 9, No. 5 (May 1966), pp. 366-71.

7. D.C. Cooper, "Böhm and Jacopini's Reduction of Flowcharts," *Communications of the ACM,* Vol. 10, No. 8 (August 1967), pp. 463-73.

8. J. Bruno and K. Steiglitz, "The Expression of Algorithms by Charts," *Journal of the ACM,* Vol. 19, No. 3 (July 1972), pp. 517-25.

9. D.E. Knuth and R.W. Floyd, "Notes on Avoiding 'go to' Statements," *Information Processing Letters,* Vol. 1, No. 1 (February 1971), pp. 23-31; see also Stanford University Computer Science Technical Report, Vol. CS148 (Stanford, Calif.: January 1970).

INTRODUCTION

As is evident from some of the other material reprinted in this book, much of the early discussion about structured programming and the related techniques was conducted by academic people and was published in scholarly journals, thus escaping the attention of the average software professional. In the rare instances in which structured programming *was* brought to the attention of the real-world programmer, the subject usually was greeted with loud hoots: "Bah! Humbug! What do those academic types know about *real* programming? By God, *they* should have to write a payroll system under a tight deadline with XYZ's version of COBOL. Then they'd stop yapping!"

It's precisely because of this traditionally academic association that Terry Baker's article in the January 1972 *IBM Systems Journal* was so important. IBM's name, for the first time, was associated with top-down design, structured programming, and the related disciplines. Granted, *IBM Systems Journal* is not as widely read as *Datamation* or *Computerworld,* but it attracts more readers than the proceedings of the IFIP Conferences. The article served to call popular attention to the new techniques, and, as happened with virtual memory and several other technological developments, caused a substantial number of people in the field to believe that IBM *invented* structured programming! Who invented structured programming clearly is debatable, but IBM's role in popularizing it is indisputable.

Many of Baker's topics deserve mention, either because of their initial impact, or because of their long-term implications. The first noteworthy concept is the major topic of the paper: the Chief Programmer Team. Baker's description of the team is a good one, and is illustrated with a real case study. The fact that the concept has been expanded and refined in later works, such as Fred Brooks's *The Mythical Man-Month* (Reading, Mass.: Addison-Wesley, 1975), should not detract from its worth. Nor should the realization, some seven years after the article's publication, that the Chief Programmer Team concept probably will never work in an ordinary EDP organization, for the following reasons: There are precious few chief programmers. Those that do exist are very expensive, and are not interested in working on small computers and mundane applications. In short, the Chief Programmer Team concept probably will work only in companies that are in the EDP business to make a profit. In most other companies, data processing is regarded as a necessary evil, and programmers (chief and indians alike) are tolerated with the greatest reluctance.

Similarly, the concept of the program librarian, discussed at length by Baker, is less popular today than when it was first introduced. The concept of a program *library* is an important one, and its use has indeed been accepted, but the idea of hiring a human being to create, maintain, and control the library is becoming increasingly less popular.

Most of the other structured concepts discussed by Baker still are used widely. Interestingly, Baker mentions top-down testing, but seems to attach relatively little importance to it, whereas I think it is one of *the* most important structured techniques. Baker also mentions structured programming, of course, and refers to Böhm and Jacopini as the source of the idea; what's interesting is his emphasis on the formatting of structured code, and his effort to show how structured programming works with real languages such as PL/I and assembler.

The other major significance of Baker's paper relates to the so-called New York Times project. For several years following publication of the paper, programmers quoted Baker's figures as proof that structured programming increases productivity by a factor of two or five, depending on your viewpoint. Statistics from a companion paper, "System Quality Through Structured Programming" [Paper 11], have been used by many EDP professionals to prove that structured programming leads to more reliable software. Indeed, the productivity and reliability figures of the New York Times project *are* impressive, but one has to wonder whether the Hawthorne Effect was a factor: Were the programmers more productive because they knew they were working on a special project? Or were they more productive simply because they were extraordinarily gifted programmers? Was the success of the New York Times project the result of the people or was it because of the particular *organization* of the people?

Questions like these still are being debated, and they will continue to be debated for several years to come. Significantly, Baker's paper first brought the questions to everyone's attention.

Chief Programmer
Team Management of
Production Programming

Production programming projects today are often staffed by relatively junior programmers with at most a few years of experience. This condition is primarily the result of the rapid development of the computer and the burgeoning of its applications. Although understandable, such staffing has at least two negative effects on the costs of projects. First, the low average level of experience and knowledge frequently results in less-than-optimum efficiency in programming design, coding, and testing. Concurrently, the more experienced programmers, who have both the insight and knowledge needed to improve this situation, are frequently in second- or third-level management positions where they cannot effectively or economically do the required detailed work of programming.

Another kind of ineffectiveness appears on many projects, which derives from the typical project structure wherein each programmer has complete responsibility for all aspects of one or a small set of modules. This means that, in addition to normal programming activities such as design, coding, and unit testing, the programmer maintains his own decks and listings, punches his own corrections, sets up his own runs, and writes reports on the status of all aspects of his subsystem. Furthermore, since there are few if any guidelines (let alone standards) for doing any of these essentially clerical tasks, the results are highly individualized. This frequently leads to serious problems in subsystem integration, system testing, documentation, and inevitably to a lack of concentration and a general loss of effectiveness throughout the project. Because such clerical work is added to that of programming, more programmers are required for a given size system than would be necessary if the programming and clerical work were separated. There are also many more opportunities for misunderstanding when there is a larger number of interpersonal interfaces. This approach to multiprogrammer projects appears to have evolved naturally, beginning in the days when one-programmer projects were the rule rather than the exception. With the intervening advances in methods and technology, this is not a necessary, desirable, or efficient way to do programming today.

Chief programmer teams

H.D. Mills has studied the present large, undifferentiated, and relatively inexperienced team approach to programming projects and suggests that it could be supplemented — perhaps eventually replaced — by a smaller, functionally specialized, and skilled team [1]. The proposed organization is compared with a surgical team in which chief programmers are analogous to chief surgeons, and the chief programmer is supported by a team of specialists (as in a surgical team) whose members assist the chief, rather than write parts of the program independently.

A chief programmer is a senior-level programmer who is responsible for the detailed development of a programming system. The chief programmer produces a critical nucleus of the programming system in full, and he specifies and integrates all other programming for the system as well. If the system is sufficiently monolithic in function or small enough, he may produce it entirely.

Permanent members of a team consist of the chief programmer, his backup programmer, and a programming librarian. The backup programmer is also a senior-level programmer. The librarian may be either a programmer technician or a secretary with additional technical training. Depending on the size and character of the system under development, other programmers, analysts, and technicians may be required.

The chief programmer, backup programmer, and librarian produce the central processing capabilities of the system. This programming nucleus includes job control, linkage editing, and some fraction of source-language programming for the system — including the executive and, usually, the data management subsystems.

Specific functional capabilities of the system may be provided by other programmers and integrated into the system by the chief programmer. Functional capabilities might involve very complex mathematical or logical considerations and require a variety of programmers and other specialists to produce them.

Thus the team organization directly attacks the problems previously described. By organizing the team around a skilled and experienced programmer who performs critical parts of the programming work, better performance can be expected. Also, because of the separation of the clerical and the programming activities, fewer programmers are needed, and the number of interfaces is reduced. The results are more efficient implementation and a more reliable product.

A team experiment

Programming for *The New York Times* information bank was selected as a project suitable for testing the validity of the chief programmer team principles. Since the programming had to interface with non-IBM programs and non-IBM hardware, this experiment involved most of the types of problems generally encountered in large system development. Besides serving as a proving ground for chief programmer team operational techniques, the project sheds light on three key questions bearing on the utility of the approach: (1) Is the team a feasible organization for production programming? (2) What are the implications of the wide deployment of teams? and (3) How can a realistic evolution be made? The main theme of this paper is a discussion of these questions. Before beginning, however, we present a technical description of the project, which was performed under a contract between The New York Times Company and the IBM Federal Systems Division.

Information bank system

The heart of the information bank system is a conversational subsystem that uses a data base consisting of indexing data, abstracts, and full articles from *The New York Times* and other periodicals. Although a primary object of the system is to bring the clipping file (morgue) to the editorial staff through terminals, the system may also be made available to remote users. This is a dedicated, time-sharing system that provides document retrieval services to 64 local terminals (IBM 4279/4506 digital TV display subsystems) and up to one hundred twenty remote lines with display or typewriter terminals.

Figure 1 is a diagram of the data flow in the conversational subsystem, which occupies a 200 to 240K byte partition of a System/360 (depending on the remote line configuration) under the System/360 Disk Operating System (DOS/360). Most of the indexing data and all of the system control data are stored on an IBM 2314 disk storage facility. Abstracts of all articles are stored on an IBM 2321. The full text of all articles is photographed and placed on microfiche, and is accessible to the system through four TV cameras contained in a microfiche retrieval device called the RISAR that was developed by Foto-Mem. A video switch allows the digital TV display consoles to receive either computer-generated character data from the control unit or article images from the RISAR. Users have manual scan and zoom controls to assist in studying articles and can alternate between abstract and article viewing through interaction with the CPU.

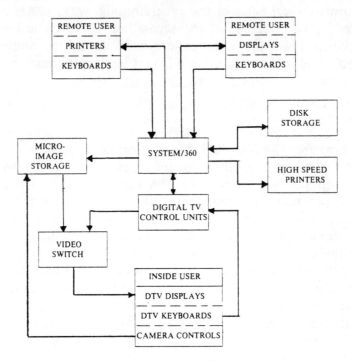

Figure 1. Conversational subsystem data flow.

Users scan the data base via a thesaurus of all descriptors (index terms) that have been used in indexing the articles. This thesaurus contains complete information about each descriptor, often including scope notes and suggested cross references. Descriptors of interest may be selected and saved for later use in composing an inquiry. Experienced users, who are familiar with the thesaurus, may key in precise descriptors directly. When the descriptor specification is complete, inquirers supply any of the following known bibliographic data that further limits the range of each article in which they are interested:

- Date or date range
- Publication in which the articles appeared
- Sources other than staff reporters from which an article has been prepared
- Types of article (e.g., editorial or obituary)
- Articles with specific types of illustrations (e.g., maps and graphs)
- Section number where an article was published

- Pages (e.g., front-page articles)
- Columns
- Relative importance of the article desired (on an eight-point scale)

Users may further specify their retrieval by combining descriptors that must appear in eligible articles by relating them in AND, OR, and NOT Boolean logic expressions.

The article search is performed in two phases. An inverted index derives an initial list of articles that satisfy the Boolean inquiry statement. Articles on this list are then looked up in a file of bibliographic data and further culled on the basis of any other specified data. When the search is complete, the inquirer may elect to sort the article references into ascending or descending chronological order before he begins viewing.

Because there are only four cameras available in the RISAR, the system limits article viewing to reduce contention. Thus the inquirer views abstracts of the retrieval articles and selects the most relevant ones for full viewing when a camera becomes available. Inquirers may also request hard copies of specified abstracts and articles. Remote users cannot view the full articles directly. The references in displayed abstracts, however, identify the corresponding articles for off-line retrieval from other sources or through the mail.

A few other significant features of the conversational subsystem may be of interest. It incorporates several authorization features that inhibit unauthorized access to the system and fulfill the conditions of copyright law and other legal agreements. Inquirers who need assistance may key a special code and be placed in keyboard communication with an expert on system files and operations. This expert may also broadcast messages of general interest to all users. Several priority categories exist to allocate resources to inquirers and to control response time. In addition to inquirer facilities, the conversational subsystem allows indexers using the digital TV terminals to compose and edit indexing data for articles being entered into the system data base.

Figure 2 shows the relationship of the conversational subsystem to the supporting subsystems. The indexing data previously mentioned is processed by the data entry edit subsystem and produces transactions for entering data into or modifying the system files. Also produced is a separate set of transactions for preparing a published index. The file maintenance subsystem modifies the six interrelated files that constitute the system data base, and also prepares file backups. Security data used by the conversational subsystem to identify users and determine their authority is prepared by the authorization file subsystem. The conversational subsystem interacts with users by presenting messages on one of three levels ranging from concise to tutorial, and the message file subsystem prepares and maintains the message file. During operation of the conversational subsystem, users may request hard copy of abstracts and/or articles. The abstracts and the microfiche addresses of the designated articles are printed by the deferred print subsystem. The conversational subsystem also transmits a variety of data on its operation to the log/statistics file, and the corresponding subsystem. A log containing a summary of operations is printed. Billing data for subscribers are passed to billing programs written by *The Times*. Usage data are passed back to be added to the data base. Usage statistics are passed to the statistics reporting subsystem, which produces detailed reports on overall system usage, descriptor (index term) usage, abstract usage, and full article usage.

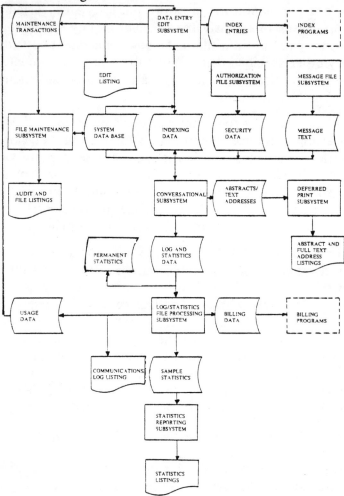

Figure 2. Information bank system.

Team organization and methodology

The methods discussed in this paper have been individually tried in other projects. What we have done is to integrate, consistently apply, and evaluate the following four programming management techniques that constitute the methodology of chief programmer teams:

- Functional organization
- Program production library
- Top-down programming
- Structured programming

Functional organization

Since our contracts have more legal, financial, administrative, and reporting requirements associated with them than internal projects of corresponding size, a project manager coordinates these activities in all except the smallest contracts. Administrative and technical problems are jointly handled by the chief programmer and the project manager, thereby permitting the team and especially the chief programmer to concentrate on the technical aspects of the project.

A functional organization also segregates the creative from the clerical work of programming. Because the clerical work is similar in all programming projects, standard procedures can be easily created so that a secretary performs the duties of program maintenance and computer scheduling.

Program production library

We have developed a program library system to isolate clerical work from programming and thereby enhance programmer productivity. The system currently in use is the Programming Production Library (PPL). The PPL, shown in Figure 3, includes both machine and office procedures for defining the clerical duties of a programming project. The PPL procedures promote efficiency and visibility during the program development stages.

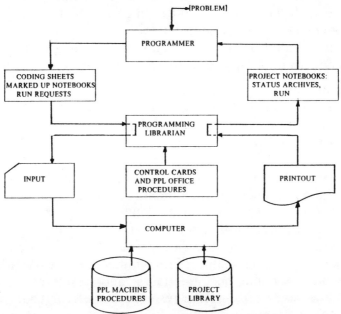

Figure 3. Programming Production Library.

The PPL comprises four parts. The machine-readable *internal library* is a group of sublibraries, each of which is a data set containing all current project programming data. These data may be source code, relocatable modules, linkage-editing statements, object modules, job control statements, or test information. The status of the internal library is reflected in the human-readable *external library* binders that contain current listings of all library members and archives consisting of recently superseded listings. The *machine procedures* consist of standard computer steps for such procedures as the following:

- Updating libraries
- Retrieving modules for compilations and storing results
- Linkage editing of jobs and test runs
- Backing up and restoring libraries
- Producing library status listings

Office procedures are clerical rules used by librarians to perform the following duties:

- Accepting directions marked in the external library
- Using machine procedures
- Filing updated status listings in the external library
- Filing and replacing pages in the archives

A programmer using the PPL works only with the external library. Using standard conventions, he enters directly into the external library binders the changes to be made or work to be done. He then gives these changes to the librarian. Later he receives the updated external library binders, which reflect the new status of the internal library. The external library is always current and is organized to facilitate use by programmers. A chronological history of recent runs contained in the archive binders is retained to assist in disaster recovery. The programmers are thus freed from handling decks, filing listings, keypunching, and spending unnecessary time in the machine area.

The PPL procedures are similar to other library maintenance systems and consist solely of Job Control Language (JCL) statements and standard utility control statements. By combining standard machine procedures, standard office procedures, and project libraries, the trained librarians provide a versatile programming service that allows a team to make more effective use of its time. The PPL also assists in improving productivity and quality by providing visibility of the work, thereby allowing team members to be aware of the status of modules that they are integrating. Such visibility also permits members to be certain of interface requirements. The internal working languages of a team are the code and statements in the libraries, rather than a separate set of documents that lag behind actual status. Programmers read each other's code in order to communicate definitions, interfaces, and details of operation. Only when a question arises that cannot be resolved by reading code is it necessary to consult another programmer directly.

Top-down programming

The third technique implemented and tested is that of top-down programming. Although most programming system design is done from the top down, most implementations are done from the bottom up. That is, units are typically written and integrated into subsystems that are in turn integrated at higher and higher levels into the final system. The top-down approach inverts the order of the development process. Figure 4 depicts the essence of the top-down approach. Following system design, all JCL and link-edit statements are written together with a base system. The second-level modules are then written while the base system is being checked out with dummy second-level modules and dummy files where necessary. Third-level modules are then written while the second-level modules are being integrated with the base system. This development cycle is repeated for as many levels as necessary. Even within a module, the top-down approach is used by writing and running a nucleus of control code first. Then functional code is added to the control code in an incremental fashion.

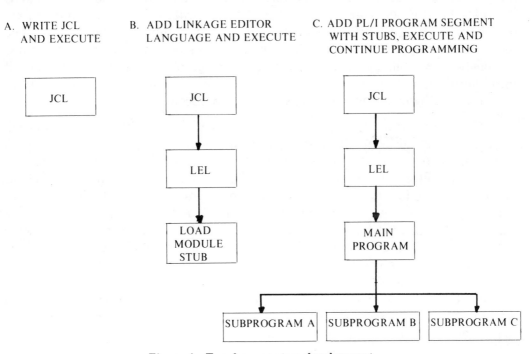

A. WRITE JCL AND EXECUTE

B. ADD LINKAGE EDITOR LANGUAGE AND EXECUTE

C. ADD PL/I PROGRAM SEGMENT WITH STUBS, EXECUTE AND CONTINUE PROGRAMMING

Figure 4. Top-down system development.

Structured programming

Structured programming, also used in the information bank project, is a method of programming according to a set of rules that enhance a program's readability and maintainability. The rules are a consequence of a structure theorem in computer science described by Böhm and Jacopini [2]. The rules state that any proper program — a program with one entry and one exit — can be written using only the following programming progressions that are also illustrated in Figure 5.

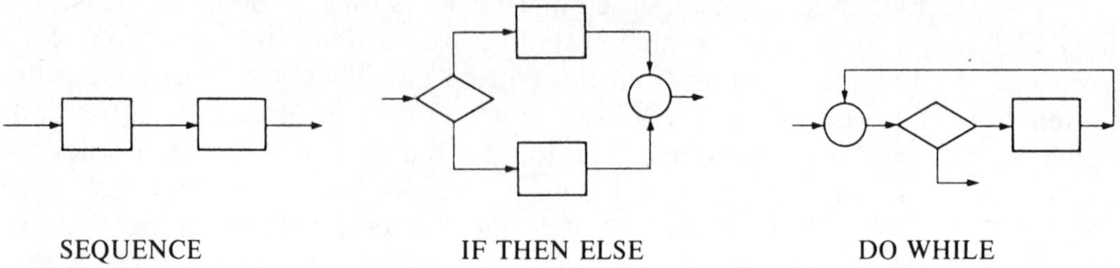

| SEQUENCE | IF THEN ELSE | DO WHILE |

Figure 5. Structured programming.

Although these rules may seem restrictive and may require a programmer to exercise more thought when first using them, several advantages ensue. With the elimination of GO TOs, one can read a program from top to bottom with no jumps and one can see at a glance the conditions required for modifying a block of code. For the same reason, tests are easier to specify. Further, the rules assist in allowing a program unit to be written using the top-down approach by writing control statements first and then function statements. The use of CALLs to dummy subroutines or INCLUDEs of empty members permits compilation and debugging at a much earlier stage of programming. Finally, if meaningful identifiers are used, a program becomes self-documenting and the need for lengthy comments and flow charts is reduced.

Conventions to support the use of structured programming are required. A set of rules has been developed to format source code so that indentation corresponds to logical depth. If extensive change is necessary, a program is available to reformat the source code [3]. To make minor changes such as moving some code a few columns, a utility program may be written or an existing one modified. Also, the lengths of individual blocks of source code are small to enhance readability and encourage a top-down approach. The objective is to have no block exceed a single listed page, or about fifty lines. Finally, by extending the range of structured programming progressions, efficiency of object code can be significantly improved, and source code readability is not impaired. Thus, iterative DOs with or without a WHILE clause and a simulated ALGOL-like CASE statement based on a subscripted GO TO statement and a LABEL array were permitted in our project.

Structured programming has been described in terms of languages with block structures such as PL/I, ALGOL, or JOVIAL. It is possible to introduce a simulated block structure into other types of languages and then to develop structuring rules for them also. This has been done for System/360 Assembler Language, a low-level language, through a set of macros that introduce and delimit blocks and provide DO WHILE, IF THEN ELSE and CASE-type figures. Further, if the long identifiers permitted by Assembler H are used, the source code is even more readable.

System development

This section discusses how the previously described techniques have been used in developing the information bank. The project was originally staffed with a chief programmer, a backup programmer, a system analyst (who was also a programmer), and a project manager. Since a project requirement was that the information bank operate under the System/360 Disk Operating System (DOS/360), the backup programmer began developing a version of the programming production library (PPL) that would operate under DOS/360. In parallel, the chief programmer and the system analyst began developing a detailed set of functional specifications. The first product of the team was a book of specifications that served as a detailed statement of the project objectives.

The team, at this point, reoriented itself from an analysis group into a development group, and a programmer technician was added to serve as a librarian. The system analyst began detailed design of system externals, such as the messages, communication log, and statistics reports. The chief programmer and backup programmer worked together on designing the various subsystems and their interfaces.

File maintenance subsystem

Since the system is heavily file oriented, efficient retrieval and the capability of adding large volumes of new material daily were requirements. Therefore, the chief and backup programmers initially emphasized the development of an interrelated set of six files that provide the necessary file attributes. Declarations of structures for these files were the first members placed in the library. Detailed file maintenance and retrieval algorithms were developed before any further design was done.

A substantial amount of data already existed on magnetic tape. Therefore, to begin building files for debugging and testing the system, it was desirable that the file maintenance subsystem be developed. This subsystem was designed to consist of two major programs and several minor ones. The chief programmer and backup programmer each began work on one of the major programs. Working in top-down fashion, control nuclei for each major program were developed. Functional code was gradually added to these nuclei to handle different types of file maintenance transactions until the programs were complete. The minor programs were then produced similarly.

Because of the early need for the file maintenance programs, an independent acceptance test was held for this subsystem. One of the functions performed by the backup programmer was the development of a test plan that specified all functions of the subsystem requiring testing and an orderly sequence for performing the test using actual data and transactions. An indication of the quality achievable by the chief programmer team is afforded by the fact that no errors were detected during the subsystem test. In fact, no errors have been detected during fifteen months of operation subsequent to the test.

Data entry subsystem

While the file maintenance subsystem was being developed, the chief programmer and system analyst designed an on-line system for keying and correcting indexing data destined for information bank files and for *The New York Times Index.* This indexing system became the data entry subsystem and additions to the conversational subsystem. The *Index* had previously been prepared by a programming system from data obtained by keying a complex free-form indexing language onto paper tape. The existing language was, therefore, extended to include the fields needed by the conversational subsystem and formalized by expressing it in Backus-Naur form. Because it was likely that the language would be modified as the project evolved, we decided to perform the editing of indexing data using syntax-direct techniques. (Another programmer was added to the team to develop the data entry subsystem around the syntax-directed editor.)

After the file maintenance subsystem had been delivered and the externals of the system specified, the system analyst programmed the authorization file subsystem, the message file subsystem, the log/statistics file processing subsystem, and the deferred print subsystem. (Another programmer was added, who wrote the statistics reporting subsystem.)

The chief programmer and backup programmer developed the conversational subsystem. Again, operating in top-down fashion, first programmed was the nucleus consisting of a time-sharing supervisor and the part of the terminal-handling package required to support the digital TV terminals. This nucleus was debugged with a simple function module that echoed back to a display material that was typed on the keyboard. After the nucleus was operational, development of the functions of the retrieval system itself commenced. System functions were programmed in retrieval order, so that new functions could be debugged and tested using existing operational functions, and an inquiry could proceed as far as programming existed to support it. All debugging was done in the framework of the conversational subsystem itself, and because of the time-sharing aspects of the system, several programmers could debug their programs simultaneously. The ability to modify tests as results were displayed at a terminal was helpful in checking out new code. Two programmers were added to the team to write functional code. A third programmer was added to extend the terminal-handling package for the 2260 and 2265 display terminals, and for the 2740 communication terminal. These programmers rapidly acquired sufficient knowledge of the interface with the time-sharing supervisor to write functional code despite their short participation on the team.

System testing

During this development process, the backup programmer prepared a test plan for the rest of the system to be used with realistic inquiries for the test. Although some errors were found during a five-week period of functional and performance testing, all were relatively small, and did not involve the basic logic of the system. Most errors were found in the functional code that had been most recently added to the system and had been the least exercised. The performance parts of the testing measured both sustained load handling and peak load handling. In spite of the fact that the performance tests were run on a System/360 Model 40 with three 2314 disk storage facilities as files, instead of on the System/360 Model 50 with seven disk storage facilities for which the performance objectives had been developed, performance objectives were successfully met.

Productivity

A key objective of the chief programmer team approach was to demonstrate increased productivity of the team over an equal number of conventionally organized programmers. This section discusses data on the productivity of the team and their strategy for using their time. Typical productivity measures are computed to facilitate comparison with other projects. Table 1 breaks down the staff months applied on the project, and Table 2 displays measures of amounts of source code produced.

Table 1. Analysis of Project Staffing by Time and Type of Work

Work type	Staff time (man months)											
				Programmer								
	Chief	Backup	Analyst	1	2	3	4	5	Technician	Manager	Sec'y	Total
Requirements Analysis	2.5	1.0	8.0	0.5	–	–	–	–	–	–	–	12.0
System design	4.0	4.0	4.5	1.0	–	–	–	–	–	–	–	13.5
Unit design, programming, debugging, and testing	12.0	14.0	10.0	13.0	4.5	2.8	3.7	4.5	–	–	–	64.5
Documentation	2.0	2.0	4.5	1.5	0.2	0.2	0.3	0.3	–	–	–	11.0
Secretarial	–	–	–	–	–	–	–	–	–	–	7.0	7.0
Librarian	–	–	–	–	–	–	–	–	5.5	–	2.0	7.5
Manager	3.5	2.0	–	–	–	–	–	–	–	11.0	–	16.5
Total	24.0	23.0	27.0	16.0	4.7	3.0	4.0	4.8	5.5	11.0	9.0	132.0

Table 2. Lines of Source Coding by Difficulty and Level

| | Level | | |
Difficulty	High	Low	Total
Hard	5034	–	5034
Standard	44247	4513	48760
Easy	27897	1633	29530
Total	77178	6146	83324

Standardized definitions have been used in preparing these tables and achieving comparable measures of productivity. *Source lines* are eighty-character records in the library that have been incorporated into the information bank and consist of the following kinds of statements:

- Programming language

- Linkage-editor control

- Job control

Source coding has been broken into the following three levels of difficulty, which are summarized in Table 2:

- *Easy coding* has few interactions with other system elements. (Most of the support programs are in this category.)

- *Standard coding* has some interactions with other system elements. (Examples are the functional parts of the conversational subsystem and the data entry edit subsystem.)

- *Difficult coding* has many interactions with other system elements. (This category is limited to the control elements of the conversational subsystem.)

Source coding types have been categorized as one of the following:

- *High-level* coding in a language such as PL/I, COBOL, or JCL

- *Low-level* coding such as assembler language and linkage-editor control statements

Table 3 presents some simple measures of programmer productivity based on the same coding used for producing Tables 1 and 2. The first row includes work done on unit design, coding, debugging, and acceptance testing. The second row summarizes professional work, which includes system design and documentation, but not librarian support. The third row includes all programming and librarian support. The last row presents the productivity of the entire team on the completed system (excluding requirements analysis).

Table 3. Programmer Productivity

Organization	Source lines per programmer day
Unit design, programming, debugging, and testing	65
All professional	47
With librarian support	43
Entire team	35

Team experience and conclusions

The chief programmer team approach appears to be desirable for the type of project discussed in this paper because programmer efficiency was substantially improved. The quality of the programming was demonstrated by nearly error-free acceptance testing with real data, by successful operation after delivery, and by its acceptance by system users.

The information bank system was specified, developed, and tested during a 132 man-month project. The team, in this experiment, was a relatively experienced one, and it performed at an above-average level. Comparing results of this experiment with results for comparable projects that were organized more conventionally, we believe that chief programmer teams applying the methods described in this paper should probably be able to double normal productivity. In addition, the quality of the completed programs should be superior to conventionally produced programs in terms of lower levels of errors remaining, self-documentation, and ease of maintenance.

Another valuable experience of the chief programmer team approach was its manageability. The team had a lower than usual ratio of professional-to-support personnel. Because the number of people actually doing professional work was small, communications problems were significantly reduced. The chief programmer was more knowledgeable about the progress of the work than programming managers generally are because of his direct involvement in it and because the techniques used (particularly the Programming Production Library, top-down programming, and structured programming) made the status of the work highly visible and understandable. This knowledge allowed both him and his management to react to problems sooner and more effectively than might have been the case had they been more detached from the work.

The relatively small size of the team made it highly responsive to change. The original functional specification went through six revisions, yet it was possible to adapt readily to major changes, even those occurring after programming was well along. Improved communication achieved through the consistent application of top-down programming, structured programming, and the PPL all contributed to team adaptability.

A functional organization was applied both within the team and to the project organization as a whole. Within the team, the functional distribution of work allowed team members to concentrate on those aspects of the job for which they were best equipped and most productive. At the project level, the functional organization allowed the chief programmer to concentrate on technical progress of the programming, both internally and in his relations with the system users. A very effective relationship was established between the chief programmer and the project manager, and no problems arose from the dual interface with the users — who fully understood the responsibilities of each of the managers. During a period when the chief programmer was off of the project, the backup programmer successfully ran the project.

The functional organization effectively broadened the range of career opportunities in the programming field by allowing senior programmers to continue to be productive in a technical capacity. Downward, the team approach offers programming-related clerical opportunities to nonprogramming personnel. The team, as originally constituted, included a programmer technician for the clerical function, but two problems arose with this approach. The work did not require a programmer technician because the PPL procedures were well enough defined that no programming knowledge was required to operate it. Also, neither librarian support nor secretarial support became full-time jobs on the project. We, therefore, combined the two functions and trained a secretary to perform them. With two weeks of on-the-job training, the secretary was capable of acting as librarian by using the PPL. Combining the two jobs also worked well from a work-load standpoint because when programming work was heavy, then documentation was light, and vice versa.

The programming techniques and standards used by the team to enhance productivity and visibility also worked as planned. Top-down programming was similarly successful. System logic for one of the major programs ran correctly the first time and never required a change as the program was expanded to its full size. This was helpful in debugging, since programs usually ran to completion, and the rare failures were readily traceable to newly added functions. Top-down programming also alleviated the interface problems normally associated with multiprogrammer projects, because interfaces were always defined and coded before any coding functions that made use of the interfaces.

The Programming Production Library run by the librarian-secretary achieved its objectives of removing many of the clerical aspects of programming from the programmer and of making the project more visible and, hence, more manageable. It also encouraged modularity of the programs and made top-down programming practical and effective.

Whereas the experiment was successful, there are still some unanswered questions and unsolved problems. Most obvious, perhaps, is whether the approach can be extended to larger projects. The best estimate at this time is that it probably can, but it needs to be tried. The general approach would be to begin a project with a single high-level team to do overall system design and nucleus development. After the nucleus is functioning, programmers on the original team could become chief programmers on teams developing major subsystems. The original team would assume control, review, validation, and testing duties and perform integration of the subsystems into the overall system. The process could be repeated at lower levels if necessary. It might appear that such a top-down evolution of the development process would increase the project time vis-à-vis the bottom-up approach. This is not necessarily true because of parallel development and integration, and it may take even less time. In any case, the risk should be substantially reduced because of the better visibility and management control in the team methodology.

A second major question concerns team composition and training. Because the team is a close-knit unit producing a large system at a faster-than-usual pace, close cooperation and good communication are essential. It is, therefore, desirable that team members be experienced professionals trained in the techniques described. Although a team may include one or possibly two less experienced programmers, larger teams would force the chief programmer to spend too high a percentage of his time in detailed training and supervision thereby reducing his own productivity. One solution may be to place newly trained programmers in program maintenance or in projects that are extending existing systems before placing them on teams that are developing new systems.

The selection of the chief programmer from among several candidates may be more difficult than was at first anticipated. The chief programmer is responsible for team management and for technical representation of the project to a customer and to his own management. Therefore, management ability and experience are necessary qualifications. A chief programmer must also possess the creativity and drive to make significant technical contributions of his own and to assist other team members in making their contributions. This essential combination of skills rarely appears in the same individual. Thus the use of aptitude testing should probably be considered as part of the selection process. Potential chief programmers should of course first serve as backup programmers to obtain first-hand experience before taking on their own projects.

One final question that has frequently been asked is whether chief programmers are willing to accept the technical and managerial challenges of large projects with few people. Experienced chief programmers have responded to the challenges and have found that it leads to a degree of satisfaction that is hard to match.

To summarize, there is little in the chief programmer team organization and methodology that has not been previously tried. Laid bare, it is basically a functional organization of programming projects coupled with the use of tried and true tools to improve productivity and quality. It works well when it all fits snugly together and is applied in a consistent fashion over an entire project. Continuing evolution shows promise of making the programming production process more economical and more manageable.

References

1. H.D. Mills, *Chief Programmer Teams: Principles and Procedures,* IBM Corporation, Report No. FSC 71-5108 (Gaithersburg, Md.: IBM Federal Systems Division, 1971).

2. C. Böhm and G. Jacopini, "Flow Diagrams, Turing Machines and Languages with Only Two Formation Rules," *Communications of the ACM,* Vol. 9, No. 5 (May 1966), pp. 366-71.

3. K. Conrow and R.G. Smith, "NEATER2: A PL/I Source Statement Reformatter," *Communications of the ACM,* Vol. 13, No. 11 (November 1970), pp. 669-75.

INTRODUCTION

This is one of two companion papers presented at the 25th ACM National Conference in October 1972, a time when the debate about goto statements was reaching its peak. Indeed, so intense was the argument that the issue was considered to be almost separate and distinct from the concept of structured programming.

Wulf's viewpoint, reflected in the title of the paper, is that goto statements are dangerous, and should be avoided. Wulf admits that not all gotos are bad; as he says, ". . . this argument addresses the *use* of the goto rather than the goto itself." There are legitimate uses of the goto, but they are rare and can be eliminated altogether with proper high-level language constructs.

One of Wulf's main themes is borrowed from Dijkstra, namely, that program *correctness* is becoming more and more important, and that it cannot be achieved by conventional testing. If proofs of correctness (either formal or informal) are the way of the future, then — as Wulf illustrates with a small programming example — it is essential that the code be written in a well-structured fashion. Regrettably, this still is an issue that most real-world programmers ignore: They argue that their programs are so complex that they can't develop correctness proofs *regardless* of whether their code is structured or unstructured; so they usually opt for the easiest coding approach, which (in languages like COBOL) may not be well-structured at all.

Wulf also demonstrates in this paper a mechanism for converting unstructured code into equivalent structured code.* The method is taken directly from Böhm and Jacopini, but is considerably easier to understand when Wulf explains it.

Finally, Wulf addresses the practical possibility of eliminating the goto statement; he considers the two most common practical objections to be *convenience* and *efficiency*. Whether or not structured

---

*The subject of converting unstructured logic to structured logic is discussed in greater detail by Ashcroft and Manna in "The Translation of 'go to' Programs to 'while' Programs" [Paper 6].

programming is convenient, he argues, is largely a function of the programming language. With suitable constructs to express the various forms of loops and decisions, together with some escape constructs to exit prematurely from the middle of a block structure, the goto is hardly ever missed. Here Wulf speaks from experience that few could claim in 1972: He and his colleagues already had been programming for three years in a systems implementation language called BLISS, a language that has no goto statement!

Wulf's comment regarding efficiency has become a classic: "More computing sins are committed in the name of efficiency (without necessarily achieving it) than for any other single reason — including blind stupidity." He recognizes that there are applications or, more commonly, *portions* of applications in which efficiency is a valid issue, but maintains that the problem of efficiency is best left to optimizing compilers, a point with which most people agree today. Wulf's final, and perhaps most effective, argument against the goto and in favor of well-structured code follows: In the long run, optimizing compilers will be able to generate considerably better object code for structured programs than for rat's-nest programs.

The 1972 ACM Conference at which Wulf presented his paper was considerably more accessible than, say, the 1971 IFIP Conference in Yugoslavia. Certainly, a reasonable number of practicing industry-oriented programmers attended, and Wulf's paper must have had some impact on them, but his message reached only a very small percentage of the potential audience. Indeed, there are many programming shops *today* in which Wulf's paper is just as relevant as it was in 1972, shops in which debates about the goto statement still are being waged.

A Case Against the GOTO

Introduction

It has been suggested that the use of the **goto** construct is undesirable, is bad programming practice, and that at least one measure of the "quality" of a program is inversely related to the number of **goto** statements contained in it. The rationale behind this suggestion is that it is possible to use the **goto** in ways which obscure the logical structure of a program, thus making it difficult to understand, modify, debug, and/or prove its correctness. It is quite clear that not all uses of the **goto** are obscure, but the hypothesis is that these situations fall into one of a small number of cases and therefore explicit and inherently well-structured language constructs may be introduced to handle them. Although the suggestion to ban the **goto** appears to have been a part of the computing folklore for several years, to this author's knowledge the suggestion was first made in print by Professor E.W. Dijkstra in a letter to the editor of the *Communications of the ACM* in 1968 [1].

In this paper we shall examine the rationale for the elimination of the **goto** in programming languages, and some of the theoretical and practical implications of its (total) elimination.

Rationale

At one level, the rationale for eliminating the **goto** has already been given in the introduction. Namely, it is possible to use the **goto** in a manner which obscures the logical structure of a program to a point where it becomes virtually impossible to understand [1, 3, 4]. It is *not* claimed that *every* use of the **goto** obscures the logical structure of a program; it is only claimed that it is *possible* to use the **goto** to fabricate a "rat's nest" of control flow which has the undesirable properties mentioned above. Hence this argument addresses the *use* of the **goto** rather than the **goto** itself.

As the basis for a proposal to totally eliminate the **goto** this argument is somewhat weak. It might reasonably be argued that the undesirable consequences of unrestricted branching may be eliminated by enforcing restrictions on the *use* of the **goto** rather than eliminating the construct. However, it will be seen that any rational set of restrictions is equivalent to eliminating the construct if an adequate set of other control primitives is provided. The strong reasons for eliminating the **goto** arise in the context of more positive proposals for a programming methodology which makes the **goto** unnecessary. It is not the purpose of this paper to explicate these methodologies (variously called "structured programming," "constructive programming," "stepwise refinement," etc.); however, since the major justification for eliminating the **goto** lies in this work, a few words are in order.

It is, perhaps, pedantic to observe that the present practice of building large programming systems is a mess. Most, if not all, of the major operating systems, compilers, information systems, etc. developed in the last decade have been delivered late, have performed below expectation (at least initially), and have been filled with "bugs." This situation is intolerable, and has prompted several researchers [2, 3, 4, 5, 6, 7, 8, 9] to consider whether a programming methodology might be developed to correct this situation. This work has proceeded from two premises:

1. Dijkstra speaks of our "human inability to do much" (at one time) to point up the necessity of decomposing large systems into smaller, more "human size" chunks. This observation is hardly startling, and in fact, most programming languages include features (modules, subroutines, and macros, for example) to aid in the mechanical aspects of this decomposition. However, the further observation that the particular decomposition chosen makes a significant difference to the understandability, modifiability, etc., of a program and that there is an *a priori* methodology for choosing a "good" decomposition is less expected.

2. Dijkstra has also said that debugging can show the presence of errors, but never their absence. Thus ultimately we will have to be able to prove the correctness of the programs we construct (rather than "debug" them) since their sheer size prohibits exhaustive testing. Although some progress has been made on the automatic proof of the correctness of programs (c.f., [10, 11, 12, 23, 24]), this approach appears to be far from a practical reality. The methodology proposed by Dijkstra (and others) proceeds so that the construction of a program guides a (comparatively) simple and intuitive proof of its correctness.

The methodology of "constructive programming" is quite simple and, in this context, best described by an (partial) example. Let us consider the problem of producing a KWIC* index. Construction of the program proceeds in a series of steps in which each step is a refinement of some portion of a previous step. We start with a single statement of the function to be performed:

       Step 1: PRINTKWIC

We may think of this as being an instruction in a language (or machine) in which the notion of generating a KWIC index is primitive. Since this operation is not primitive in most practical languages, we proceed to define it:

       Step 2: PRINTKWIC: generate and save all interesting circular shifts
                         alphabetize the saved lines
                         print alphabetized lines

Again, we may think of each of these lines as being an instruction in an appropriate language; and again, since they are not primitive in most existing languages, we must define them; for example:

       Step 3a: generate and save all interesting circular shifts:

              for each line in the input **do**
                begin
                generate and save all interesting
                    shifts of "this line"
                end
     etc.

---

*For those who may not be familiar with a KWIC (key word in context) index, the following description is adequate for this paper.

A KWIC system accepts a set of *lines*. Each *line* is an ordered set of *words* and each *word* is an ordered set of *characters*. A *word* may be one of a set of *uninteresting* words ("a," "the," "of," etc.), otherwise it is a *key* word. Any line may be circularly shifted by removing its first word and placing it at the end of the line. The KWIC index system generates an ordered (alphabetically by the first word) listing of all circular shifts of the input lines such that no line in the output begins with an uninteresting word.

The construction of the program proceeds by small steps* in this way until ultimately each operation is expressed in the available primitive operations of the target language. We shall not carry out the details since the objective of this paper is not to be a tutorial on this methodology. However, note that the methodology achieves the goals set out for it. Since the context is small at each step it is relatively easy to understand what is going on; indeed, it is easy to prove that the program will work correctly if the primitives from which it is constructed are correct. Moreover, proving the correctness of the primitives used at step ι is a small set of proofs (of the same kind) at step $\iota+1$. (In the terminology of this methodology, step ι is an *abstraction* from its implementation in step $\iota+1$.)

Now, the constructive programming methodology relates to eliminating the **goto** in the following way. It is crucial to the constructive philosophy that it should be possible to define the behavior of each primitive action at the ιth step independent of the context in which it occurs. If this were not so, it would not be possible to prove the correctness of these primtives at the $\iota+1$st step without reference to their context in the ιth step. In particular, this suggests (using flow chart terminology) that it should be possible to represent each primitive at the ιth step by a (sub) flow chart with a single entry and a single exit path. Since this must be true at each step of the construction, the final flow chart of a program constructed in this way must consist of a set of totally nested (sub) flow charts. Such a flow chart can be constructed without an explicit **goto** if conditional and looping constructs are available.

Consider, now, programs which can be built from only simple conditional and loop constructs. To do this we will use a flow chart representation because of the explicit way in which it manifests control. We assume two basic flow chart elements, a "process" box and a "binary decision" box:

These boxes are connected by directed line segments in the usual way. We are interested in two special "**goto**-less" constructions fabricated from these primitives: a simple loop and an n-way conditional, or "case," construct. We consider these forms "**goto**-less" since they contain single entry and exit points and hence might reasonably be provided in a language by explicit syntactic constructs. (The loop considered here obviously does not correspond to all vari-

---

*A more complete explication of the methodology would concern itself with the nature and order of the decisions made at each step as well as the fact that they are small. See [22] for an analysis of two alternative decompositions of a KWIC system similar to the one defined here.

ants of initialization, test before or after the loop body, etc. These variants would not change the arguments to follow and have been omitted.)

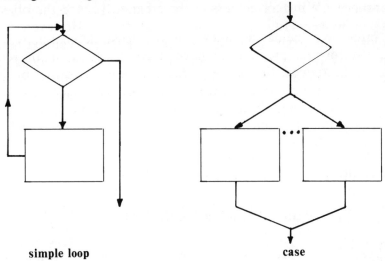

simple loop   case

Consider the following three transformations (T1, T2, T3) defined on arbitrary flow charts:

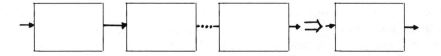

T1. Any linear sequence of process boxes may be mapped into a single process box.

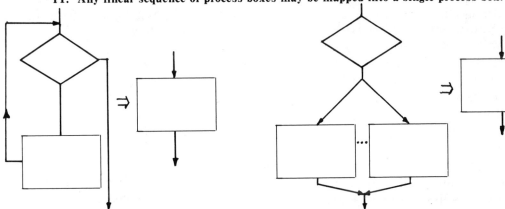

T2. Any simple loop may be mapped into a process box.

T3. Any n-way "case" construct may be mapped into a process box.

Any graph (flow chart) which may be derived by a sequence of these transformations we shall call a "reduced" form of the original. We shall say that a graph which may be reduced to a single node by some sequence of transformations is "**goto**-less" (independent of whether actual **goto** statements are used in its encoding) and that the sequence of transformations defines a set of nested "control environments." The sequence of transformations applied in order to reduce a graph to a single node may be used as a guide to both understanding and proving the correctness of the program [2, 4, 6, 7, 19].

The property of being "**goto**-less" in the sense defined above is a necessary condition for the program to have been designed by the constructive methodology. Moreover, the property depends only upon the topology of the program and not on the primitives from which it is synthesized; in particular, a **goto** statement might have been used. However, not only can such programs be constructed without a **goto** if conditionals and loops are available, but *any* use of a **goto** which is not equivalent to one of these will destroy the requisite topology. Hence any set of restrictions (on the *use* of the **goto**) which is intended to achieve this topology is equivalent to eliminating the **goto**.

The theoretical possibility of eliminating the GOTO

It is possible to express the evaluation of an arbitrary computable function in a notation which does not have an explicit **goto**. This is not particularly surprising since: (1) several formal systems of computability theory, e.g., recursive functions, do not use the concept; (2) (pure) LISP does not use it; and (3) van Wijngaarden [13], in defining the semantics of Algol, eliminated labels and **goto**'s by systematic substitution of procedures. However, this does not say that an algorithm for the evaluation of these functions is especially convenient or transparent in **goto**-less form. Alan Perlis has referred to similar situations as the "Turing Tarpit" in which everything is possible, but nothing is easy.

Knuth and Floyd [14] and Ashcroft and Manna [15] have shown that given an arbitrary flow chart it is *not* possible to construct another flow chart (using the same primitives and no additional variables) which performs the same algorithm and uses only simple conditional and loop constructs; of course other algorithms exist that compute the same function and which can be expressed with only simple conditionals and loops. The example given in Ashcroft and Manna of an algorithm which cannot be written in **goto**-less form without adding additional variables is:

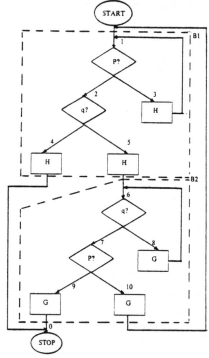

By enclosing some of the regions of the flow chart in dotted lines and labeling them (B1 and B2) as shown on the previous page, and further abstracting from the details of the process and decision structure, the abstract structure of this example is:

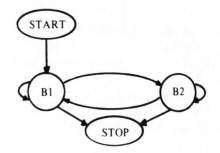

The reader is referred to [15] for a proof that such programs cannot be constructed from simple looping and conditional constructs unless an additional variable is added. Intuitively, however, it should be clear from the abstraction of the example that neither B1 nor B2 is inherently nested within the other. Moreover, the existence of multiple exit paths from B1 and B2 make it impossible to impose a superior (simple) loop (which inherently has a single exit path) to control the iteration between them unless some mechanism for path selection (e.g., an additional variable) is introduced.

In [21] Böhm and Jacopini show that an arbitrary flow chart program may be translated into an equivalent one with a single "while statement" by introducing new boolean variables, predicates to test them, and assignment statements to set them. A variant of this scheme involving the addition of a single integer variable, call it "α," which serves as a "program counter," is given below.

Suppose some flow chart program contains a set of process boxes assigned arbitrary integer labels $i_1, i_2, \ldots, i_n$, and decision boxes assigned arbitrary integer labels $i_{n+1}, i_{n+2}, \ldots, i_m$. (By convention assume the $\boxed{STOP}$ box is assigned the label zero, and the entry box is assigned the label one.) For each process box, i_j, create a new box, i_j', identical to the former except for the addition of the assignment "$\alpha \leftarrow i_k$" where i_k is the label of the successor of i_j in the original program. For each decision box, i_l, create the macro box, i_l',

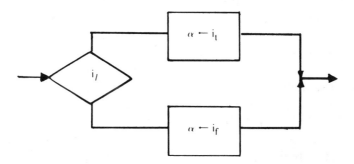

where i_t and i_f are the labels of the successors of the **true** and **false** branches of the decision box, i_l, in the original program. Now create the following flow chart:

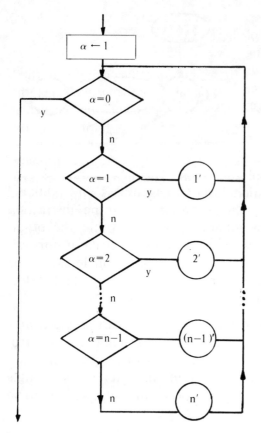

Thus, for example, the Ashcroft and Manna example given earlier (the labels are given on the earlier diagram) becomes (see right):

Constructions such as the one given at right are undesirable not only because of their inefficiency, but because they destroy the topology (loop structure) and locality of the original program and thus make it extremely difficult to understand. Nevertheless, the construction serves to illustrate the point that adding (at least one) control variable is an effective device for eliminating the **goto**. Ashcroft and Manna have given algorithms for translating arbitrary programs into **goto**-less form (with additional variables) which preserve the efficiency and topology of the original program.

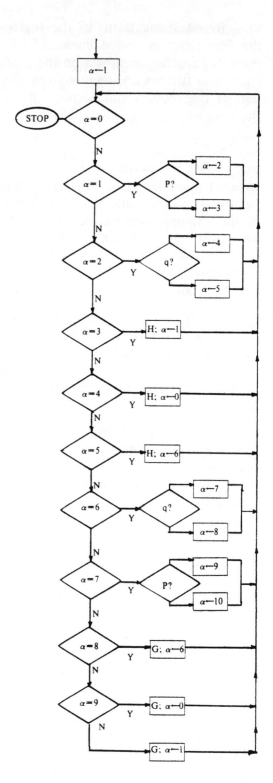

The practical possibility of eliminating the GOTO

As discussed in the previous section, it is theoretically possible to eliminate the **goto**. Moreover, there can be little quarrel with the *objectives* of the constructive programming methodology. A consequence of the particular methodology presented above is that it produces **goto**-less programs, thus the **goto** is unnecessary in programs produced according to this methodology. A key, perhaps the key, issue, then, is whether it is *practical* to remove the **goto**. In particular there is an appropriate suspicion among practicing programmers* that coding without the **goto** is both inconvenient and inefficient. In this section we shall investigate these two issues, for, if it is inconvenient or grossly inefficient to program without the **goto** then the practicality of the methodology is in question.

Convenience:

Programming without the **goto** is *not* (necessarily) inconvenient. The author is one of the designers, implementors, and users of a "systems implementation language," Bliss [16, 17, 18]; Bliss does not have **goto**. The language has been in active use for three years; we have thus gained considerable practical experience programming without the **goto**. This experience spans many people and includes several compilers, a conversational programming system (APL), an operating system, as well as numerous applications programs.

The inescapable conclusion from the Bliss experience is that the purported inconvenience of programming without a **goto** is a myth! Programmers familiar with languages in which the **goto** is present go through a rather brief and painless adaptation period. Once past this adaptation period they find that the lack of a **goto** is not a handicap; on the contrary, the invariant reaction is that the enforced discipline of programming without a **goto** structures and simplifies the task.

Bliss is not, however, a simple **goto**-less language; that is, it contains more than simple **while-do** and **if-then-else** (or **case**) constructs. There are natural forms of control flow that occur in real programs which, if not explicitly provided for in the language, either require a **goto** so that the programmer may synthesize them, or else will cause the programmer to contort himself to mold them into a **goto**-less form (e.g., in terms of the construction in the previous section). Contortion obscures and is therefore antipathetic with the constructive philosophy; hence the approach in Bliss has been to provide explicit forms of these natural constructs which are also inherently well-structured. In [19] the author analyzes the forms of control flow which are not easily realized in a simple **goto**-less language and uses this analysis to motivate the facilities in

*Including this author when he first read Dijkstra's letter in 1968.

Bliss. Here we shall merely list some of the results of that analysis as they manifest themselves in Bliss (and might manifest themselves in any **goto**-less language):

1. A collection of "conventional" control structures: Many of the inconveniences of a simple **goto**-less language are eliminated by simply providing a fairly large collection of more-or-less "conventional" control structures. In particular, for example, Bliss includes: control "scopes" (blocks and compounds), conditionals (both **if-then-else** and **case** forms), several looping constructs (including **while-do, do-while**, and stepping forms), potentially recursive procedures, and co-routines.

2. Expression Language: As noted in an earlier section, one mechanism for expressing algorithms in **goto**-less form is through the introduction of at least one additional variable. The value of this variable serves to encode the state of the computation and direct subsequent flow. This is a common programming practice used even in languages in which the **goto** is present (e.g., the FORTRAN "computed **goto**"). Bliss is an "expression language" in the sense that every construct, including those which manifest control, is an expression and computes a value. The value of an expression (e.g., a block or loop) forms a natural and convenient implicit state variable.

3. Escape Mechanism: Analysis of real programs strongly suggests that one of the most common "good" uses of a **goto** is to prematurely terminate execution of a control environment — for example, to exit from the middle of a loop before the usual termination condition is satisfied. To accommodate this form of control Bliss* allows any expression (control environment) to be labeled; an expression of the form "**leave** <label> **with** <expression>" may be executed within the scope of this labeled environment. When a **leave** expression is executed two things happen: (1) control immediately passes to the end of the control environment (expression) named in the **leave**, and (2) the value of the named environment is set to that of the <expression> following the **with**. Note that the **leave** expression is a restricted form of forward branch just as the various forms of loop constructs are restricted backward jumps. In both cases the constructs are less general, and less dangerous, than the general **goto**.

---

*A somewhat different form of the Bliss escape is described in [19]; the form described in [19] has been replaced by that described above.

In summary, then, our experience with Bliss supports the notion that programming without the **goto** is no less convenient than with it. This conclusion rests heavily on the assumption that the **goto** was not merely removed from some existing language, but that a coherent selection of well-structured constructs were assembled as the basis of the control component of the new language. It would be unreasonable to expect that merely removing the **goto** from an existing language, say FORTRAN or PL/I, would result in a convenient notation. On the other hand, it is *not* unreasonable to expect that a relatively small set of additions to an existing language, especially the better structured ones such as Algol or PL/I, could reintroduce the requisite convenience. While not a unique set of solutions, the control mechanisms in Bliss are one model on which such a set of additions might be based.

Efficiency:

More computing sins are committed in the name of efficiency (without necessarily achieving it) than for any other single reason — including blind stupidity. One of these sins is the construction of a "rat's nest" of control flow which exploits a few common instruction sequences. This is precisely the form of programming which must be eliminated if we are ever to build correct, understandable, and modifiable systems.

There *are* applications (e.g., "real time" processing) and there *are* (a few) portions of every program where efficiency is crucial. This is a real issue. However, the appropriate mechanism for achieving this efficiency is a highly optimizing compiler, not incomprehensible source code. In this context it is worth noting another benefit of removing the **goto** — a benefit which the author did not fully appreciate until the Bliss compiler was designed — namely, that of global optimization. The presence of **goto** in a block-structured language with dynamic storage allocation forces runtime overhead for jumping out of blocks and procedures and may imply a distributed overhead to support the possibility of such jumps. Eliminating the **goto** removes both of these forms of overhead. More important, however, is that: (1) the scope of a control environment is statically defined, and (2) all control appears as one of small set of explicit control constructs. A consequence of (1) is that the Fortran-H compiler [20], for example, expends a considerable amount of effort in order to achieve roughly the same picture of overall control as that implicit in the text of a Bliss program. The consequence of (2) is that the compiler need only deal with a small number of well-defined control forms; thus failure to optimize a peculiarly constructed variant of a common control structure is impossible. Since flow analysis is pre-requisite to global optimization, this benefit of eliminating the **goto** must not be underestimated.

Summary

One goal of our profession must be to produce large programs of predictable reliability. To do this requires a methodology of program construction. Whatever the precise shape of this methodology, whether the one sketched earlier or not, one property of that methodology must be to isolate (sub) components of a program in such a way that the proof of the correctness of an abstraction from these components can be made independent of both their implementation and the context in which they occur. In particular this implies that unrestricted branching between components cannot be allowed.

Whether or not a language contains a **goto** and whether or not a programmer uses a **goto** in some context is related, in part, to the variety and extent of the other control features of the language. If the language fails to provide important control constructs, then the **goto** is a crutch from which the programmer may synthesize them. The danger in the **goto** is that the programmer may do this in obscure ways. The advantage in eliminating the **goto** is that these same control structures will appear in regular and well-defined ways. In the latter case, both the human and the compiler will do a better job of interpreting them.

References

1. E.W. Dijkstra, "Go To Statement Considered Harmful," *Communications of the ACM,* Vol. 11, No. 3 (March 1968), pp. 147-48.

2. _____, "A Constructive Approach to the Problem of Program Correctness," *BIT,* Vol. 8, No. 3 (1968), pp. 174-86.

3. _____, "Structured Programming," *Software Engineering, Concepts and Techniques, Proceedings of the NATO Conferences,* eds. P. Naur, B. Randell, and J.N. Buxton (New York: Petrocelli/Charter, 1976), pp. 222-26.

4. _____, *Notes on Structured Programming,* 2nd ed., Technische Hogeschool Eindhoven, Report No. EWD-248, 70-WSK-0349 (Eindhoven, The Netherlands: April 1970); see also *Structured Programming,* O.-J. Dahl, E.W. Dijkstra, and C.A.R. Hoare (New York: Academic Press, 1972).

5. P. Naur, "Proof of Algorithms by General Snapshots," *BIT,* Vol. 6, No. 4 (1966), pp. 310-16.

6. _____, "Programming by Action Clusters," *BIT,* Vol. 9, No. 3 (1969), pp. 250-58.

7. C.A.R. Hoare, "Proof of a Program: FIND," *Communications of the ACM,* Vol. 14, No. 1 (January 1971), pp. 39-45.

8. N. Wirth, "Program Development by Stepwise Refinement," *Communications of the ACM,* Vol. 14, No. 4 (April 1971), 221-27.

9. D.L. Parnas, "Information Distribution Aspects of Design Methodology," *Proceedings of the 1971 IFIP Congress* (Amsterdam, The Netherlands: North-Holland Publishing Co., 1971), pp. 339-44; see also Carnegie-Mellon University, Computer Science Technical Report (Pittsburgh: 1971).

10. J. King, "A Program Verifier," Ph.D. Thesis, Carnegie-Mellon University, 1969.

11. Z. Manna, "Termination of Algorithms," Ph.D. Thesis, Carnegie-Mellon University, 1968.

12. _____, "The Correctness of Programs," *Journal of Computer & System Sciences,* Vol. 3 (May 1969), pp. 119-27.

13. A. van Wijngaarden, "Recursive Definition of Syntax and Semantics," *Formal Language Description Languages,* ed. T.B. Steel (Amsterdam, The Netherlands: North-Holland Publishing Co., 1966).

14. D. Knuth and R.W. Floyd, "Notes on Avoiding 'go to' Statements," *Information Processing Letters,* Vol. 1, No. 1 (February 1971), pp. 23-31, 177; see also Stanford University, Computer Science Technical Report, Vol. CS148 (Stanford, Calif.: January 1970).

15. E. Ashcroft and Z. Manna, "The Translation of 'go to' Programs to 'while' Programs," *Proceedings of the 1971 IFIP Congress,* Vol. I (Amsterdam, The Netherlands: North-Holland Publishing Co., 1972), pp. 250-55; see also Stanford University, AI Memo AIM-138, STAN CS-71-88 (Stanford, Calif.: January 1971).

16. W.A. Wulf, et al., *BLISS/11 Reference Manual,* Carnegie-Mellon University, Computer Science Department Report No. AD-739964 (Pittsburgh: March 1972).

17. W.A. Wulf, D.B. Russell, and A.N. Habermann, "BLISS: A Language for Systems Programming," *Communications of the ACM,* Vol. 14, No. 12 (December 1971), pp. 780-90.

18. W.A. Wulf, et al., "Reflections on a Systems Programming Language," *Proceedings of the SIGPLAN Symposium on Systems Implementation Languages* (October 1971).

19. W.A. Wulf, "Programming without the GOTO," *Proceedings of the 1971 IFIP Congress,* Vol. 1 (Amsterdam, The Netherlands: North-Holland Publishing Co., 1972), pp. 408-13.

20. E.S. Lowry and C.W. Medlock, "Object Code Optimization," *Communications of the ACM,* Vol. 12, No. 1 (January 1969), pp. 13-22.

21. C. Böhm and G. Jacopini, "Flow Diagrams, Turing Machines and Languages with Only Two Formation Rules," *Communications of the ACM,* Vol. 9, No. 5 (May 1966), pp. 366-71.

22. D. Parnas, "On the Criteria to Be Used in Decomposing Systems into Modules," *Communications of the ACM,* Vol. 15, No. 12 (December 1971), pp. 1053-58.

23. Z. Manna, S. Ness, and J. Vuillemin, "Inductive Methods for Proving Properties of Programs," *Communications of the ACM,* Vol. 16, No. 8 (August 1973), pp. 491-502.

24. R. Burstall, "An Algebraic Description of Programs with Assertions, Verification and Simulation," *Proceedings of the ACM Conference on Proving Assertions About Programs, SIGPLAN Notices,* Vol. 7, No. 1 (January 1972), pp. 7-14.

INTRODUCTION

A second paper presented at the 1972 ACM National Conference provides an important counterpart to Wulf's "A Case Against the GOTO" [Paper 8]. It is Martin Hopkins' plea for sensible use of the goto statement, and should be read immediately after the Wulf paper. It is not, as its title, "A Case for the GOTO," would lead one to believe, in support of indiscriminate use of the goto.

Hopkins sets forth several good arguments in favor of retaining the goto statement in our programming languages, and warns against "extremists" who advocate abolishing the goto entirely. He argues that elimination of the goto is viewed as a kind of magic that will solve all programming problems, an observation that many veteran structured programmers finally are coming to understand after seeing first-hand that structured code is not necessarily equivalent to good code. Indeed, as Hopkins points out, the goto statement is only one issue of programming style; overemphasizing its importance tends to make people forget about a variety of other style issues: proper naming conventions, proper formatting, proper use of recursion and iteration, and so on.

Several valid arguments are made by Hopkins, but my greatest concern is that the average reader won't read those arguments carefully. Indeed, many will get no further than the title. "See," they'll exclaim, "at least there's one guy with some sense! He says that he's in favor of the goto!" It is important to stress that Hopkins does not favor the use of goto statements; nor does he argue against structured programming or any other disciplined form of program construction. He simply argues that there are times when use of the goto statement is justified. Thus, his main argument is simply to keep the goto statement in our programming *languages,* so that it can be used if necessary. Certainly, it must be kept in the current versions of FORTRAN and COBOL; indeed, even in the more powerful languages, like PL/I, the goto may be useful as a means of simulating certain structured constructs.

Like Wulf, Hopkins concludes his paper with a review of some practical issues concerning the goto statement, pointing out those "ugly" programming situations in which the goto is the easiest way to construct the logic (for example, a one-time program that has to be patched at 3 A.M.). Unfortunately, most people — myself included — tend to be skeptical about such a scenario. There are precious few one-time programs. Moreover, quick-and-dirty patches done in the middle of the night have a way of becoming permanent, much to the dismay of the next generation of maintenance programmers.

On the subject of efficiency, Hopkins makes a cautious plea for retaining the goto statement. Obviously, optimization ought to be considered *after* the program is working, and *after* it has become evident that optimization is necessary; wherever possible, the programmer should seek to optimize his program by developing better algorithms and better data structures. But, when all else fails, Hopkins says, we need the freedom to use goto statements to speed up our logic. In rebuttal to Wulf, Hopkins says that we eventually may be able to depend on optimizing compilers to do this for us, but that such global optimization is a goal of the future rather than an available option. Unfortunately, that comment still is true today!

A Case for the GOTO

Introduction

It is with some trepidation that I undertake to defend the **goto** statement, a construct, which while ancient and much used has been shown to be theoretically unnecessary [1] and in recent years has come under so much attack [2]. In my opinion, there have been far too many **goto** statements in most programs, but to say this is not to say that **goto** should be eliminated from our programming languages. This paper contains a plea for the retention of **goto** in both current and future languages. Let us first examine the context in which the controversy occurs.

A wise philosopher once pointed out to a lazy king that there is no royal road to geometry. After discovering, in the late fifties, that programming was *the* computer problem, a search was made during the sixties for the royal road to programming. Various paths were tried including comprehensive operating systems, higher level languages, project management techniques, time sharing, virtual memory, programmer education, and applications packages. While each of these is useful, they have not solved the programming problem. Confronted with this unresolved problem and with few good ideas on the horizon, some people are now hoping that the royal road will be found through style, and that banishment of the **goto** statement will solve all. The existence of this controversy and the seriousness assigned to it by otherwise very sensible people are symptoms of a malaise in the computing community. We have few promising new ideas at hand. I also suspect that the controversy reflects something rather deep in human nature, the notion that language is magic and the mere utterance of certain words is dangerous or defiling. Is it an accident that "goto" has four letters?

Having indicated my belief that this controversy is not quite as momentous as some have made out, it is appropriate to point out some beneficial aspects. First, interest has been focused on programming style and while style is not everything it does have a great deal of importance. Second, the popularity of the no **goto** rule is, in large part, due to the fact that it is a simple rule which does improve the code produced by most programmers. As we shall see, this is not sufficient grounds for banishing the construct from our languages, although it may well justify teaching alternative methods of programming to beginners or restricting its use on a project. Perhaps the most beneficial aspect of the controversy will be to encourage the use of block structure languages and to discourage use of our most popular languages, COBOL and FORTRAN as they are not well suited to programming without the **goto**.

The principal motivation behind eliminating the **goto** statement is the hope that the resulting programs will not look like a bowl of spaghetti. Instead they will be simple, elegant and easy to read, both for the programmer who is engaged in composition and checkout as well as the poor soul attempting future modification. By avoiding **goto** one guarantees that a program will consist entirely of one-in-one-out control structures. It is easy to read a properly indented program without **goto** statements, which is written in a block structure language. The possible predecessors of every statement are obvious and, with the exception of loops, all predecessors are higher on the page. (I assume nobody writes inner procedures longer than a page anymore?) Why then should we retain the **goto** statement in our current and future programming languages?

Theoretical considerations

It has been demonstrated that there are flow charts which cannot be converted to a procedural notation without **goto** statements [3, 4]. It turns out though that this result is not really an argument for the retention of **goto** as there are means by which a procedure can be *rewritten* in a systematic manner to eliminate all instances of **goto**. An almost trivial method is to introduce a new variable which can be thought of as the instruction counter along with tests and sets of this counter. The method is fully described by Böhm and Jacopini [1]. The results of this procedure when applied to a large program with many instances of **goto** would usually be a program which is less readable than the original program with **goto** statements. However, nobody seems to be advocating using such unconsidered methods.

The real issue is that theoretical work has suggested a number of techniques that can be used to rewrite programs, eliminating the instances of **goto**. These include replication of code (node splitting), the introduction of new variables and tests as well as the introduction of procedures. Any of these techniques, when used with discretion, can increase the readability of code. The question is whether there are any instances when the application of such methods decreases clarity or produces some other undesirable effect. Whether or not to retain the **goto** does not seem to be a theoretical issue. It is rather a matter of taste, style and the practical considerations of day to day computer use.

Alternatives to GOTO

With respect to current languages which are in wide use such as COBOL and FORTRAN, there is the practical consideration that the **goto** statement is necessary. Even where a language is reasonably well-suited to programming without the **goto**, the elimination of this construct may be at once too loose and too restrictive. PL/I provides some interesting examples here. One exits from an Algol procedure when the flow of control reaches the end bracket. PL/I provides an additional mechanism, an explicit RETURN statement. Consider the table look up in Fig. 1 which is similar to an example of Floyd and Knuth [4]. The problem is to find an instance of X in the vector A and if there is no instance of X in A, then make a new entry in A of the argument X. In either case the index of the entry is returned. A count of the number of matches associated with each entry in A is also maintained in an associated vector, B. In this example there are no **goto** statements but the two RETURN statements cause an exit from both the procedure and the iterative DO. Thus the procedure has control structures which have more than one exit and one-in-one-out control structures were a principal reason for avoiding **goto**. Should the PL/I programmer add a rule forbidding RETURN? The procedure could then be rewritten as in Fig. 2. This involves the introduction of a new variable, SWITCH, and a new test. If one assumes that the introduction of gratuitous identifiers and tests is undesirable perhaps RETURN is a desirable construct even though it can result in multiple exit control structures. It is my feeling that procedures with several RETURN statements are easy to read and modify because they follow the top to bottom pattern and maintain the obvious predecessor characteristic, while avoiding the introduction of new variables. RETURN is therefore preferable to the alternative of introducing new variables and tests.

However, RETURN is a very specialized statement. It only permits an exit from one level of one type of control, the procedure. One could generalize the construct to apply to multiple levels of control and to DO groups or BEGIN blocks as well as procedures. This is exactly the flavor of the BLISS **leave** [6] construct. Lacking such language, the PL/I user must content himself with **goto**. But is this a bad thing? The good programmer, who understands the potential complexity which results from excessive use of **goto**, will attempt to recast such an algorithm. Failing to find an elegant restatement, he will insert the label and its associated **goto** out of the desired control structure. The label stands there as a warning to the reader of the routine that this is a procedure with more than the usual complexity. Note also that the label point catches the eye. It is immediately apparent when looking at this statement that it has an unusual predecessor. The careful reader will want to consult a cross reference listing to determine the potential flow of control. Note that the BLISS **leave** construct is somewhat less than ideal here. In BLISS when one examines the code which follows a bracket terminating a level of control, its potential predecessors are not immediately apparent. One must look upward on the page for its associated label, which indicates a potential unusual predecessor and then find the **leave**. It is my feeling that unusual exits from levels of control should be avoided. The multiple level case is especially ugly. Where such constructs are necessary, it should be made completely obvious to all. Statements such as the BLISS **leave** encourage unusual exits from multiple levels of control. One should not cover up the fact that there is an awkward bit of logic by the introduction of a new control construct.

```
LOOK_UP:
    PROC (X);
        DO I = 1 TO A_TOP;
            IF A(I) = X   THEN
                DO:
                    B(I) = B(I) + 1;
                    RETURN (I);
                END;
        END;
        A(I) = X;
        B(I) = 1;
        A_TOP = A_TOP +1;
        RETURN (I);
    END;
```

Figure 1

```
LOOK_UP2:
    PROC (X);
        SWITCH = 1;
        DO I = 1 TO A_TOP WHILE (SWITCH = 1);
            IF A(I) = X THEN
                SWITCH = 0;
        END;
    IF SWITCH = 0  THEN
            B(I) = B(I) + 1;
        ELSE
            DO;
                A(I) = X;
                B(I) = 1;
                A_TOP = A_TOP + 1;
            END;
        RETURN(I);
    END;
```

Figure 2

Another interesting PL/I control construct is the ON unit. This is a named block which is automatically invoked on certain events such as overflow, but it can also be invoked explicitly by a statement of the form:

SIGNAL   CONDITION (name);

The name is established dynamically and need not be declared in the scope of the SIGNAL. This facility often eliminates the need to pass special error return parameters or test a return code which indicates abnormal termination of a lower level procedure. After completion of an ON unit activated by SIGNAL, control is passed back to the statement following the SIGNAL. This is usually not useful. One wants to terminate the signaling block and the only way to do this in PL/I is with a **goto** out of the ON unit. Is SIGNAL permissible under the no **goto** criteria? Elimination of **goto** seems too restrictive here as SIGNAL is a useful facility which can eliminate much messy programming detail. However, the natural consequence of using the SIGNAL statement is to terminate an ON unit with a **goto**. Perhaps it is best to admit that there is no very good alternative to a **goto** statement in this situation.

GOTO **as a basic building block**

The lack of a **case** statement in PL/I is a clear deficiency. The resourceful programmer will construct one out of a **goto**. This does not make up for the lack of a **case** statement, but it does point up an interesting and highly legitimate use of **goto**. One can use it as a primitive to construct more advanced and elegant control structures. Imaginative programmers will, from time to time, develop new control constructs as Hoare invented the **case** statement [5]. Those that are worthwhile will be informally defined and implemented with a macro preprocessor. The better ones will appear in experimental compilers and eventually the best will find their way into the standard languages. Such inventions are often very hard to implement with macro preprocessors for existing languages without use of the **goto** construct. There is still room for the incorporation of unusual control mechanisms into existing block structure languages. Decision tables are a prime example. One way of handling decision tables is to have a preprocessor convert them to source language statements. If a convenient translation process introduces **goto** statements, this is not important as the basic documentation is at the decision table level. The source language is treated as an internal language. The ease of translation is more important than the introduction of **goto** statements.

Another related reason for retaining **goto** even in our newest languages is that it is often possible to use a language as the target to which one translates a secondary source language. If the secondary language has **goto** or even a different set of control constructs, then translation could be very difficult without a **goto** in the target language. In other words source languages and their associated compilers are useful building blocks for the development of special constructs or languages and elimination of **goto** decreases the range of usefulness of a language.

GOTO as an escape

Part of the reason for retaining **goto** is that the world is not always a very elegant place and sometimes a **goto** is a useful, if ugly, tool to handle an awkward situation. Algorithms are often messy. Sometimes this may be due to inherent complexity. I suspect, however, that most of the time it is because not enough time or intelligence has been applied. Where time or intelligence are lacking, a **goto** may do the job. Every program will not be published. Many may be used only once. I tend to sympathize with the programmer who fixes up a one time program at 3:00 a.m. with a **goto**. Of course, there is always the danger that the programmer will lapse into bad habits but I am willing to take that chance. Perhaps it is an opportunity, for when the intelligent supervisor reads the code of those under him, he can focus on any **goto** statements. A programmer should be able to justify each use of **goto**.

I have avoided discussing performance, which like death and taxes, none of us can avoid forever. Suppose a procedure runs too slowly or takes up too much space. A rewrite of the procedure or restructuring of the data may be in order. But if that fails one may be driven to a rewrite in assembly language. There is an intermediate alternative which may solve the problem without resort to an assembler. The programmer who writes structured programs uses certain techniques such as the introduction of procedures and the repetition of code which can result in the loss of time and space. Given the idiosyncracies of many compilers, a little reorganization of code and a few **goto** statements inserted by a clever programmer can often improve performance. This is not a practice which I recommend for those starting a project, even where it is known to have stringent performance requirements. One should give up a structured program in a higher level language only after performance bottlenecks have been clearly identified and then only give up what is absolutely necessary. My guess is that very few such situations will exist but when they do, a slightly contorted procedure in a higher level language may be an attractive alternative to one written in assembly language. The villain here is the compiler which produces bad code in some situations. Would elimination (as opposed to avoidance) of **goto** significantly ease the task of compiler writers and thus help us to get better object code? It is difficult to do justice to this problem as there are so many different compiling techniques and some would be helped and some would not. My feeling is that elimination of the **goto** would not dramatically ease the problems of compiler writers. Even in compilers which do extensive control flow analysis, a small percentage of implementation effort is devoted to that task. A more interesting subject for compiler writers is the identification of those optimizations which improve the performance of programs written with none or very few **goto** statements. Viewed in this light the existence of well-structured programs imposes an additional obligation and more work on compiler writers. This is work which they should eagerly accept so that programmers will not have to make the trade-off between a well-structured program and one that performs well. More work is required in this area.

Varieties of programming style

The **goto** issue is part of the larger topic of overall programming style. One of my worries is that we will become the prisoners of one currently fashionable "classical" style. Perhaps other rules of style are better. For example we might say that only a **goto** which was directed forward was elegant. Perhaps it is useful to restrict ourselves to standard type labels such as "PROC_EXIT." Vagaries of style or fashion need not disturb students who should be taught in a rather constrained way which is established by the teacher. Also, those working on large projects will have to conform to standards. However, experienced programmers and language designers of taste and imagination will want to experiment and they should be encouraged to do so. APL provides an interesting example of a diverse style. A computed **goto**, in the form of a right pointing arrow exists in APL, but other than function invocation there are no control constructs such as IF THEN ELSE or an iteration statement. Surprisingly one does not get a maze of **goto** statements in a well-written APL function, for the powerful array operators can be used in situations where loops occur in other languages. Sequential execution of statements thus becomes the general rule and few right pointing arrows are required. Whether an algorithm written in APL is clearer than the same algorithm written in a block structure language seems to be a matter on which intelligent people of taste will disagree.

Elegance in programming involves more than avoiding **goto**, and beyond the **goto** controversy there are a great many other important issues of style. There is the question about the clarity of array operations in APL and PL/I, as well as structure operations in COBOL and PL/I. To what extent are implicit conversions a subsumption of extraneous detail and in what instances do they produce surprising results? There are many questions about optimal size and complexity with respect to expressions, nesting of IF and iteration statements as well as the size and complexity of procedures. To what extent do declarations properly subsume detail and to what extent do they leave the meaning of a statement unclear unless one is simultaneously examining the declaration? Under what circumstances, if any, should functions have side effects or should iteration replace recursion? To what extent can we eliminate assignment? These and other questions are subtle but important stylistic problems which we are likely to pass over if we concentrate too heavily on the relatively simple and unimportant issue of **goto**.

Conclusion

goto should be retained in both current and future languages because it is useful in a limited number of situations. Programmers should work hard to produce well-structured programs with one-in-one-out control structures which have no **goto** statements. Where this is not possible, we should not think that elegance is achieved with a magic language formula. It is far better to admit the awkwardness and use the **goto**. Furthermore, **goto** is a useful means to synthesize more complex control structures and increases the usefulness of a language as a target to which other languages can be translated. Viewed in the light of practical programming as an ultimate escape, **goto** can also be justified if not encouraged. Finally our wisdom has not yet reached the point where future languages should eliminate the **goto**. If future work indicates that by avoiding **goto** we can gain some important advantage such as routine proofs that programs are correct, then the decision to retain the **goto** construct should be reconsidered. But until then, it is wise to retain it.

References

1. C. Böhm and G. Jacopini, "Flow Diagrams, Turing Machines and Languages with Only Two Formation Rules," *Communications of the ACM,* Vol. 9, No. 5 (May 1966), pp. 366-71.

2. E.W. Dijkstra, "Go To Statement Considered Harmful," *Communications of the ACM,* Vol. 11, No. 3 (March 1968), pp. 147-48.

3. E. Ashcroft and Z. Manna, "The Translation of 'go to' Programs to 'while' Programs," *Proceedings of the 1971 IFIP Congress,* Vol. I (Amsterdam, The Netherlands: North-Holland Publishing Co., 1972), pp. 250-55; see also Stanford University, AI Memo, AIM-138, STAN CS-71-88 (Stanford, Calif.: January 1971).

4. D.E. Knuth and R.W. Floyd, "Notes on Avoiding 'go to' Statements," *Information Processing Letters,* Vol. 1, No. 1 (February 1971), pp. 23-31; see also Stanford University, Computer Science Technical Report, Vol. CS148, (Stanford, Calif.: January 1970).

5. N. Wirth and C.A.R. Hoare, "A Contribution to the Development of ALGOL," *Communications of the ACM,* Vol. 9, No. 6 (June 1966), pp. 413-32.

6. W.A. Wulf, D.B. Russell, and A.N. Habermann, "BLISS: A Language for Systems Programming," *Communications of the ACM,* Vol. 14, No. 12 (December 1971), pp. 780-90.

INTRODUCTION

In my opinion, Dijkstra's "Humble Programmer" ought to be required reading for everyone who claims that programming is his or her profession. To me, it ranks as one of the great classics in the field, providing an educational experience for the junior programmer, and truly delightful reading for the veteran. It serves as a wonderful reminder of the good old days of the computer field, and offers an excellent summary of the philosophies and guiding principles by which we try to do our jobs. The concepts expressed are eloquent and profound, sometimes controversial, and generally thought-provoking.

I worry that some of the most eloquent remarks cannot be appreciated by today's programmers: For example, Dijkstra says, ". . . when we had a few weak computers, programming became a mild problem, and now that we have gigantic computers, programming has become an equally gigantic problem." Most of us who began our careers on 1K or 4K machines will smile in appreciation, but will the remarks mean anything to the programmer of the 1980s who will begin his or her career on a 16-megabyte computer? When Dijkstra states, ". . . one of the most important aspects of any computing tool is its influence on the thinking habits of those who try to use it," I wonder whether today's hobbyist programmer, with his build-it-at-home computer and subset of BASIC, has any idea of what Dijkstra is talking about.

There are the controversial comments, too: For instance, Dijkstra refers to FORTRAN as an infantile disorder, and PL/I as a fatal disease. Curiously enough, even though he praises such obscure languages as LISP, he does not seem to acknowledge the existence of the two languages that account for probably 75 percent of all the computer programs written today: COBOL and RPG.

It is in this paper as well that Dijkstra suggests that the primary resistance to the so-called structured revolution will come from educational institutions, and from the political backlash of an EDP organization that would prefer to maintain the status quo. I personally agree with this, having experienced such resistance first-hand in

111

my own work as a consultant and educator. You may or may not agree, but you certainly will find Dijkstra's comments worth reading.

The Humble Programmer

Editor's note: The following article was presented as the 1972 ACM Turing Award Lecture at the ACM Annual Conference, Boston, on August 14, 1972.

As a result of a long sequence of coincidences I entered the programming profession officially on the first spring morning of 1952, and as far as I have been able to trace, I was the first Dutchman to do so in my country. In retrospect the most amazing thing is the slowness with which, at least in my part of the world, the programming profession emerged, a slowness which is now hard to believe. But I am grateful for two vivid recollections from that period that establish that slowness beyond any doubt.

After having programmed for some three years, I had a discussion with van Wijngaarden, who was then my boss at the Mathematical Centre in Amsterdam — a discussion for which I shall remain grateful to him as long as I live. The point was that I was supposed to study theoretical physics at the University of Leiden simultaneously, and as I found the two activities harder and harder to combine, I had to make up my mind, either to stop programming and become a real, respectable theoretical physicist, or to carry my study of physics to a formal completion only, with a minimum of effort, and to become . . . , yes what? A programmer? But was that a respectable profession? After all, what was programming? Where was the sound body of knowledge that could support it as an intellectually respectable discipline? I remember quite vividly how I envied my hardware colleagues, who, when asked about their professional competence, could at least point out that they knew everything about vacuum tubes, amplifiers and the rest, whereas I felt that, when faced with that question, I would stand empty-handed. Full of misgivings I knocked on van Wijngaarden's office door, asking him whether I could speak to him for a moment; when I left his office a number of hours later, I was another person. For after having listened to my problems patiently, he agreed that up till that moment there was not much of a programming discipline, but then he went on to explain quietly that automatic computers were here to stay, that we were just at the beginning and could not I be one of the persons called to make programming a respectable discipline in the years to come? This was a turning point in my life and I completed my study of physics formally as quickly as I could. One moral of the above story is, of course, that we must be very careful when we give advice to younger people: sometimes they follow it!

Two years later, in 1957, I married, and Dutch marriage rites require you to state your profession and I stated that I was a programmer. But the municipal authorities of the town of Amsterdam did not accept it on the grounds that there was no such profession. And, believe it or not, but under the heading "profession" my marriage record shows the ridiculous entry "theoretical physicist"!

So much for the slowness with which I saw the programming profession emerge in my own country. Since then I have seen more of the world, and it is my general impression that in other countries, apart from a possible shift of dates, the growth pattern has been very much the same.

Let me try to capture the situation in those old days in a little bit more detail, in the hope of getting a better understanding of the situation today. While we pursue our analysis, we shall see how many common misunderstandings about the true nature of the programming task can be traced back to that now distant past.

The first automatic electronic computers were all unique, single-copy machines and they were all to be found in an environment with the exciting flavor of an experimental laboratory. Once the vision of the automatic computer was there, its realization was a tremendous challenge to the electronic technology then available, and one thing is certain: we cannot deny the courage of the groups that decided to try to build such a fantastic piece of equipment. For fantastic pieces of equipment they were: in retrospect one can only wonder that those first machines worked at all, at least sometimes. The overwhelming problem was to get and keep the machine in working order. The preoccupation with the physical aspects of automatic computing is still reflected in the names of the older scientific societies in the field, such as the Association for Computing Machinery or the British Computer Society, names in which explicit reference is made to the physical equipment.

What about the poor programmer? Well, to tell the honest truth, he was hardly noticed. For one thing, the first machines were so bulky that you could hardly move them and besides that, they required such extensive maintenance that it was quite natural that the place where people tried to use the machine was the same laboratory where the machine had been developed. Secondly, the programmer's somewhat invisible work was without any glamour: you could show the machine to visitors and that was several orders of magnitude more spectacular than some sheets of coding. But most important of all, the programmer himself had a very modest view of his own work: his work derived all its significance from the existence of that wonderful machine. Because that was a unique machine, he knew only too well that his programs had only local significance, and also because it was patently obvious that this machine would have a limited lifetime, he knew that very little of his work would have a lasting value. Finally, there is yet another circumstance that had a profound influence on the programmer's attitude toward his work: on the one hand, besides being unreliable, his machine was usually too slow and its memory was usually too small, i.e. he was faced with a pinching shoe, while on the other hand its usually somewhat queer order code would cater for the most unexpected constructions. And in those days many a clever programmer derived an immense intellectual satisfaction from the cunning tricks by means of which he contrived to squeeze the impossible into the constraints of his equipment.

Two opinions about programming date from those days. I mention them now; I shall return to them later. The one opinion was that a really competent programmer should be puzzle-minded and very fond of clever tricks; the other opinion was that programming was nothing more than optimizing the efficiency of the computational process, in one direction or the other.

The latter opinion was the result of the frequent circumstance that, indeed, the available equipment was a painfully pinching shoe, and in those days one often encountered the naive expectation that, once more powerful machines were available, programming would no longer be a problem, for then the struggle to push the machine to its limits would no longer be necessary and that was all that programming was about, wasn't it? But in the next decades something completely different happened: more powerful machines became available, not just an order of magnitude more powerful, even several orders of magnitude more powerful. But instead of finding ourselves in a state of eternal bliss with all programming problems solved, we found ourselves up to our necks in the software crisis! How come?

There is a minor cause: in one or two respects modern machinery is basically more difficult to handle than the old machinery. Firstly, we have got the I/O interrupts, occurring at unpredictable and irreproducible moments; compared with the old sequential machine that pretended to be a fully deterministic automaton, this has been a dramatic change, and many a systems programmer's grey hair bears witness to the fact that we should not talk lightly about the logical problems created by that feature. Secondly, we have got machines equipped with multilevel stores, presenting us problems of management strategy that, in spite of the extensive literature on the subject, still remain rather elusive. So much for the added complication due to structural changes of the actual machines.

But I called this a minor cause; the major cause is . . . that the machines have become several orders of magnitude more powerful! To put it quite bluntly: as long as there were no machines, programming was no problem at all; when we had a few weak computers, programming became a mild problem, and now we have gigantic computers, programming has become an equally gigantic problem. In this sense the electronic industry has not solved a single problem, it has only created them — it has created the problem of using its products. To put it in another way: as the power of available machines grew by a factor of more than a thousand, society's ambition to apply these machines grew in proportion, and it was the poor programmer who found his job in this exploded field of tension between ends and means. The increased power of the hardware, together with the perhaps even more dramatic increase in its reliability, made solutions feasible that the programmer had not dared to dream about a few years before. And now, a few years later, he *had* to dream about them and, even worse, he had to transform such dreams into reality! Is it a wonder that we found ourselves in a software crisis? No, certainly not, and as you may guess, it was even predicted well in advance; but the trouble with minor prophets, of course, is that it is only five years later that you really know that they had been right.

Then, in the mid sixties something terrible happened: the computers of the so-called third generation made their appearance. The official literature tells us that their price/performance ratio has been one of the major design objectives. But if you take as "performance" the duty cycle of the machine's various components, little will prevent you from ending up with a design in which the major part of your performance goal is reached by internal housekeeping activities of doubtful necessity. And if your definition of price is the price to be paid for the hardware, little will prevent you from ending up with a design that is terribly hard to program for: for instance the order code might be such as to enforce, either upon the programmer or upon the system, early binding decisions presenting conflicts that really cannot be resolved. And to a large extent these unpleasant possibilities seem to have become reality.

When these machines were announced and their functional specifications became known, many among us must have become quite miserable; at least I was. It was only reasonable to expect that such machines would flood the computing community, and it was therefore all the more important that their design should be as sound as possible. But the design embodied such serious flaws that I felt that with a single stroke the progress of computing science had been retarded by at least ten years; it was then that I had the blackest week in the whole of my professional life. Perhaps the most saddening thing now is that, even after all those years of frustrating experience, still so many people honestly believe that some law of nature tells us that machines have to be that way. They silence their doubts by observing how many of these machines have been sold, and derive from that observation the false sense of security that, after all, the design cannot have been that bad. But upon closer inspection, that line of defense has the same convincing strength as the argument that cigarette smoking must be healthy because so many people do it.

It is in this connection that I regret that it is not customary for scientific journals in the computing area to publish reviews of newly announced computers in much the same way as we review scientific publications: to review machines would be at least as important. And here I have a confession to make: in the early sixties I wrote such a review with the intention of submitting it to Communications, but in spite of the fact that the few colleagues to whom the text was sent for their advice urged me to do so, I did not dare to do it, fearing that the difficulties either for myself or for the Editorial Board would prove to be too great. This suppression was an act of cowardice on my side for which I blame myself more and more. The difficulties I foresaw were a consequence of the absence of generally accepted criteria, and although I was convinced of the validity of the criteria I had chosen to apply, I feared that my review would be refused or discarded as "a matter of personal taste." I still think that such reviews would be extremely useful and I am longing to see them appear, for their accepted appearance would be a sure sign of maturity of the computing community.

The reason that I have paid the above attention to the hardware scene is because I have the feeling that one of the most important aspects of any computing tool is its influence on the thinking habits of those who try to use it, and because I have reasons to believe that that influence is many times stronger than is commonly assumed. Let us now switch our attention to the software scene.

Here the diversity has been so large that I must confine myself to a few stepping stones. I am painfully aware of the arbitrariness of my choice, and I beg you not to draw any conclusions with regard to my appreciation of the many efforts that will have to remain unmentioned.

In the beginning there was the EDSAC in Cambridge, England, and I think it quite impressive that right from the start the notion of a subroutine library played a central role in the design of that machine and of the way in which it should be used. It is now nearly 25 years later and the computing scene has changed dramatically, but the notion of basic software is still with us, and the notion of the closed subroutine is still one of the key concepts in programming. We should recognize the closed subroutine as one of the greatest software inventions; it has survived three generations of computers and it will survive a few more, because it caters for the implementation of one of our basic patterns of abstraction. Regrettably enough, its importance has been underestimated in the design of the third generation computers, in which the great number of explicitly named registers of the arithmetic unit implies a large overhead on the subroutine mechanism. But even that did not kill the concept of the subroutine, and we can only pray that the mutation won't prove to be hereditary.

The second major development on the software scene that I would like to mention is the birth of FORTRAN. At that time this was a project of great temerity, and the people responsible for it deserve our great admiration. It would be absolutely unfair to blame them for short-comings that only became apparent after a decade or so of extensive usage: groups with a successful look-ahead of ten years are quite rare! In retrospect we must rate FORTRAN as a successful coding technique, but with very few effective aids to conception, aids which are now so urgently needed that time has come to consider it out of date. The sooner we can forget that FORTRAN ever existed, the better, for as a vehicle of thought it is no longer adequate: it wastes our brainpower, and it is too risky and therefore too expensive to use. FORTRAN's tragic fate has been its wide acceptance, mentally chaining thousands and thousands of programmers to our past mistakes. I pray daily that more of my fellow-programmers may find the means of freeing themselves from the curse of compatibility.

The third project I would not like to leave unmentioned is LISP, a fascinating enterprise of a completely different nature. With a few very basic principles at its foundation, it has shown a remarkable stability. Besides that, LISP has been the carrier for a considerable number of, in a sense, our most sophisticated computer applications. LISP has jokingly been described as "the most intelligent way to misuse a computer." I think that description a great compliment because it transmits the full flavor of liberation: it has assisted a number of our most gifted fellow humans in thinking previously impossible thoughts.

The fourth project to be mentioned is ALGOL 60. While up to the present day FORTRAN programmers still tend to understand their programming language in terms of the specific implementation they are working with — hence the prevalence of octal or hexadecimal dumps — while the definition of LISP is still a curious mixture of what the language means and how the mechanism works, the famous Report on the Algorithmic Language ALGOL 60 is the fruit of a genuine effort to carry abstraction a vital step further and to define a programming language in an implementation-independent way. One could argue that in this respect its authors have been so successful that they have created serious doubts as to whether it could be implemented at all! The report gloriously demonstrated the power of the formal method BNF, now fairly known as Backus-Naur-Form, and the power of carefully phrased English, at least when used by someone as brilliant as Peter Naur. I think that it is fair to say that only very few documents as short as this have had an equally profound influence on the computing community. The ease with which in later years the names ALGOL and ALGOL-like have been used, as an unprotected trademark, to lend glory to a number of sometimes hardly related younger projects is a somewhat shocking compliment to ALGOL's standing. The strength of

BNF as a defining device is responsible for what I regard as one of the weaknesses of the language: an over-elaborate and not too systematic syntax could now be crammed into the confines of very few pages. With a device as powerful as BNF, the Report on the Algorithmic Language ALGOL 60 should have been much shorter. Besides that, I am getting very doubtful about AL-GOL 60's parameter mechanism: it allows the programmer so much combinatorial freedom that its confident use requires a strong discipline from the programmer. Besides being expensive to implement, it seems dangerous to use.

Finally, although the subject is not a pleasant one, I must mention PL/I, a programming language for which the defining documentation is of a frightening size and complexity. Using PL/I must be like flying a plane with 7,000 buttons, switches, and handles to manipulate in the cockpit. I absolutely fail to see how we can keep our growing programs firmly within our intellectual grip when by its sheer baroqueness the programming language — our basic tool, mind you! — already escapes our intellectual control. And if I have to describe the influence PL/I can have on its users, the closest metaphor that comes to my mind is that of a drug. I remember from a symposium on higher level programming languages a lecture given in defense of PL/I by a man who described himself as one of its devoted users. But within a one-hour lecture in praise of PL/I, he managed to ask for the addition of about 50 new "features," little supposing that the main source of his problems could very well be that it contained already far too many "features." The speaker displayed all the depressing symptoms of addiction, reduced as he was to the state of mental stagnation in which he could only ask for more, more, more. . . . When FORTRAN has been called an infantile disorder, full PL/I, with its growth characteristics of a dangerous tumor, could turn out to be a fatal disease.

So much for the past. But there is no point in making mistakes unless thereafter we are able to learn from them. As a matter of fact, I think that we have learned so much that within a few years programming can be an activity vastly different from what it has been up till now, so different that we had better prepare ourselves for the shock. Let me sketch for you one of the possible futures. At first sight, this vision of programming in perhaps already the near future may strike you as utterly fantastic. Let me therefore also add the considerations that might lead one to the conclusion that this vision could be a very real possibility.

The vision is that, well before the seventies have run to completion, we shall be able to design and implement the kind of systems that are now straining our programming ability at the expense of only a few percent in man-years of what they cost us now, and that besides that, these systems will be virtually free of bugs. These two improvements go hand in hand. In the latter respect software seems to be different from many other products, where as a rule a higher quality implies a higher price. Those who want really reliable software will discover that they must find means of avoiding the majority of bugs to start with, and as a result the programming process will become cheaper. If you want more effective programmers, you will discover that they should not waste their time debugging — they should not introduce the bugs to start with. In other words, both goals point to the same change.

Such a drastic change in such a short period of time would be a revolution, and to all persons that base their expectations for the future on smooth extrapolation of the recent past — appealing to some unwritten laws of social and cultural inertia — the chance that this drastic change will take place must seem negligible. But we all know that sometimes revolutions do take place! And what are the chances for this one?

There seem to be three major conditions that must be fulfilled. The world at large must recognize the need for the change; secondly, the economic need for it must be sufficiently strong; and, thirdly, the change must be technically feasible. Let me discuss these three conditions in the above order.

With respect to the recognition of the need for greater reliability of software, I expect no disagreement anymore. Only a few years ago this was different: to talk about a software crisis was blasphemy. The turning point was the Conference on Software Engineering in Garmisch, October 1968, a conference that created a sensation as there occurred the first open admission of the software crisis. And by now it is generally recognized that the design of any large sophisticated system is going to be a very difficult job, and whenever one meets people responsible for such undertakings, one finds them very much concerned about the reliability issue, and rightly so. In short, our first condition seems to be satisfied.

Now for the economic need. Nowadays one often encounters the opinion that in the sixties programming has been an overpaid profession, and that in the coming years programmer salaries may be expected to go down. Usually this opinion is expressed in connection with the recession, but it could be a symptom of something different and quite healthy, *viz.* that perhaps the programmers of the past decade have not done so good a job as they should have done. Society is getting dissatisfied with the performance of programmers and of their products. But there is another factor of much greater weight. In the present situation it is quite usual that for a specific system, the price to be paid for the development of the software is of the same order of magnitude as the price of the hardware needed, and society more or less accepts that. But hardware manufacturers tell us that in the next decade hardware prices can be expected to drop with a factor of ten. If software development were to continue to be the same clumsy and expensive process as it is now, things would get completely out of balance. You cannot expect society to accept this, and therefore we *must* learn to program an order of magnitude more effectively. To put it in another way: as long as machines were the largest item on the budget, the programming profession could get away with its clumsy techniques; but that umbrella will fold very rapidly. In short, also our second condition seems to be satisfied.

And now the third condition: is it technically feasible? I think it might be, and I shall give you six arguments in support of that opinion.

A study of program structure has revealed that programs — even alternative programs for the same task and with the same mathematical content — can differ tremendously in their intellectual manageability. A number of rules have been discovered, violation of which will either seriously impair or totally destroy the intellectual manageability of the program. These rules are of two kinds. Those of the first kind are easily imposed mechanically, *viz.* by a suitably chosen programming language. Examples are the exclusion of goto-statements and of procedures with more than one output parameter. For those of the second kind, I at least — but that may be due to lack of competence on my side — see no way of imposing them mechanically, as it seems to need some sort of automatic theorem prover for which I have no existence proof. Therefore, for the time being and perhaps forever, the rules of the second kind present themselves as elements of discipline required from the programmer. Some of the rules I have in mind are so clear that they can be taught and that there never needs to be an argument as to whether a given program violates them or not. Examples are the requirements that no loop should be written down without providing a proof for termination or without stating the relation whose invariance will not be destroyed by the execution of the repeatable statement.

I now suggest that we confine ourselves to the design and implementation of intellectually manageable programs. If someone fears that this restriction is so severe that we cannot live with it, I can reassure him: the class of intellectually manageable programs is still sufficiently rich to contain many very realistic programs for any problem capable of algorithmic solution. We must not forget that it is *not* our business to make programs; it is our business to design classes of computations that will display a desired behavior. The suggestion of confining ourselves to intellectually manageable programs is the basis for the first two of my announced six arguments.

Argument one is that, as the programmer only needs to consider intellectually manageable programs, the alternatives he is choosing from are much, much easier to cope with.

Argument two is that, as soon as we have decided to restrict ourselves to the subset of the intellectually manageable programs, we have achieved, once and for all, a drastic reduction of the solution space to be considered. And this argument is distinct from argument one.

Argument three is based on the constructive approach to the problem of program correctness. Today a usual technique is to make a program and then to test it. But: program testing can be a very effective way to show the presence of bugs, but it is hopelessly inadequate for showing their absence. The only effective way to raise the confidence level of a program significantly is to give a convincing proof of its correctness. But one should not first make the program and then prove its correctness, because then the requirement of providing the proof would only increase the poor programmer's burden. On the contrary: the programmer should let correctness proof and program grow hand in hand. Argument three is essentially based on the following observation. If one first asks oneself what the structure of a convincing proof would be and, having found this, then constructs a program satisfying this proof's requirements, then these correctness concerns turn out to be a very effective heuristic guidance. By definition this approach is only applicable when we restrict ourselves to intellectually manageable programs, but it provides us with effective means for finding a satisfactory one among these.

Argument four has to do with the way in which the amount of intellectual effort needed to design a program depends on the program length. It has been suggested that there is some law of nature telling us that the amount of intellectual effort needed grows with the square of program length. But, thank goodness, no one has been able to prove this law. And this is because it need not be true. We all know that the only mental tool by means of which a very finite piece of reasoning can cover a myriad of cases is called "abstraction"; as a result the effective exploitation of his powers of abstraction must be regarded as one of the most vital activities of a competent programmer. In this connection it might be worthwhile to point out that the purpose of abstracting is *not* to be vague, but to create a new semantic level in which one can be absolutely precise. Of course I have tried to find a fundamental cause that would prevent our abstraction mechanisms from being sufficiently effective. But no matter how hard I tried, I did not find such a cause. As a result I tend to the assumption — up till now not disproved by experience — that by suitable application of our powers of abstraction, the intellectual effort required to conceive or to understand a program need not grow more than proportional to program length. A by-product of these investigations may be of much greater practical significance, and is, in fact, the basis of my fourth argument. The by-product was the identification of a number of patterns of abstraction that play a vital role in the whole process of composing programs. Enough is known about these patterns of abstraction that you could devote a lecture to each of them. What the familiarity and conscious knowledge of these patterns of abstraction imply dawned upon me when I realized that, had they been common knowledge 15 years ago, the step from BNF to syntax-directed compilers, for instance, could have taken a few minutes instead of a few years. Therefore I present our recent knowledge of vital abstraction patterns as the fourth argument.

Now for the fifth argument. It has to do with the influence of the tool we are trying to use upon our own thinking habits. I observe a cultural tradition, which in all probability has its roots in the Renaissance, to ignore this influence, to regard the human mind as the supreme and autonomous master of its artifacts. But if I start to analyze the thinking habits of myself and of my fellow human beings, I come, whether I like it or not, to a completely different conclusion, *viz.* that the tools we are trying to use and the language or notation we are using to express or record our thoughts are the major factors determining what we can think or express at all! The analysis of the influence that programming languages have on the thinking habits of their users, and the recognition that, by now, brainpower is by far our scarcest resource, these together give us a new collection of yardsticks for comparing the relative merits of various programming languages. The competent programmer is fully aware of the strictly limited size of his own skull; therefore he approaches the programming task in full humility, and among other things he avoids clever tricks like the plague. In the case of a well-known conversational programming language I have been told from various sides that as soon as a programming community is equipped with a terminal for it, a specific phenomenon occurs that even has a well-established name: it is called "the one-liners." It takes one of two different forms: one programmer places a one-line program on the desk of another and either he proudly tells what it does and adds the question, "Can you code this in less symbols?" — as if this were of any conceptual relevance! — or he just says, "Guess what it does!" From this observation we must conclude that this language as a tool is an open invitation for clever tricks; and while exactly this may be the explanation for some of its appeal, *viz.* to those who like to show how clever they are, I am sorry, but I must regard this as one of the most damning things that can be said about a programming language. Another lesson we should have learned from the recent past is that the development of "richer" or "more powerful" programming languages was a mistake in the sense that these baroque monstrosities, these conglomerations of idiosyncrasies, are really unmanageable, both mechanically and mentally. I see a great future for very systematic and very modest programming languages. When I say "modest," I mean that, for instance, not only ALGOL 60's "for clause," but even FORTRAN's "DO loop" may find themselves thrown out as being too baroque. I have run a little programming experiment with really experienced volunteers, but something quite unintended and quite unexpected turned up. None of my volunteers found the obvious and most elegant solution. Upon closer analysis this turned out to have a common source: their notion of repetition was so tightly connected to the idea of an associated controlled variable to be stepped up, that they were mentally blocked from seeing the obvious. Their solutions were less efficient, needlessly hard to understand, and it took them a very long time to find them. It was a revealing, but also shocking experience for me. Finally, in one respect one hopes that tomorrow's programming languages will differ greatly from what we are used to now: to a much greater extent than hitherto they should invite us to reflect in the structure of what we write down all abstractions needed to cope conceptually with the complexity of what we are designing. So much for the greater adequacy of our future tools, which was the basis of the fifth argument.

As an aside I would like to insert a warning to those who identify the difficulty of the programming task with the struggle against the inadequacies of our current tools, because they might conclude that, once our tools will be much more adequate, programming will no longer be a problem. Programming will remain very difficult, because once we have freed ourselves from the circumstantial cumbersomeness, we will find ourselves free to tackle the problems that are now well beyond our programming capacity.

You can quarrel with my sixth argument, for it is not so easy to collect experimental evidence for its support, a fact that will not prevent me from believing in its validity. Up till now I have not mentioned the word "hierarchy," but I think that it is fair to say that this is a key concept for all systems embodying a nicely factored solution. I could even go one step further and make an article of faith out of it, *viz.* that the only problems we can really solve in a satisfactory manner are those that finally admit a nicely factored solution. At first sight this view of human limitations may strike you as a rather depressing view of our predicament, but I don't feel it that way. On the contrary, the best way to learn to live with our limitations is to know them. By the time that we are sufficiently modest to try factored solutions only, because the other efforts escape our intellectual grip, we shall do our utmost to avoid all those interfaces impairing our ability to factor the system in a helpful way. And I can not but expect that this will repeatedly lead to the discovery that an initially untractable problem can be factored after all. Anyone who has seen how the majority of the troubles of the compiling phase called "code generation" can be tracked down to funny properties of the order code will know a simple example of the kind of things I have in mind. The wider applicability of nicely factored solutions is my sixth and last argument for the technical feasibility of the revolution that might take place in the current decade.

In principle I leave it to you to decide for yourself how much weight you are going to give to my considerations, knowing only too well that I can force no one else to share my beliefs. As in each serious revolution, it will provoke violent opposition and one can ask oneself where to expect the conservative forces trying to counteract such a development. I don't expect them primarily in big business, not even in the computer business; I expect them rather in the educational institutions that provide today's training and in those conservative groups of computer users that think their old programs so important that they don't think it worthwhile to rewrite and improve them. In this connection it is sad to observe that on many a university campus the choice of the central computing facility has too often been determined by the demands of a few established but expensive applications with a disregard of the question, how many thousands of "small users" who are willing to write their own programs are going to suffer from this choice. Too often, for instance, high-energy physics seems to have blackmailed the scientific community with the price of its remaining experimental equipment. The easiest answer, of course, is a flat denial of the technical feasibility, but I am afraid that you need pretty strong arguments for that. No reassurance, alas, can be obtained from the remark that the intellectual ceiling of today's average programmer will prevent the revolution from taking place: with others programming so much more effectively, he is liable to be edged out of the picture anyway.

There may also be political impediments. Even if we know how to educate tomorrow's professional programmer, it is not certain that the society we are living in will allow us to do so. The first effect of teaching a methodology — rather than disseminating knowledge — is that of enhancing the capacities of the already capable, thus magnifying the difference in intelligence. In a society in which the educational system is used as an instrument for the establishment of a homogenized culture, in which the cream is prevented from rising to the top, the education of competent programmers could be politically unpalatable.

Let me conclude. Automatic computers have now been with us for a quarter of a century. They have had a great impact on our society in their capacity of tools, but in that capacity their influence will be but a ripple on the surface of our culture compared with the much more profound influence they will have in their capacity of intellectual challenge which will be without precedent in the cultural history of mankind. Hierarchical systems seem to have the property that something considered as an undivided entity on one level is considered as a composite object on the next lower level of greater detail; as a result the natural grain of space or time that is applicable at each level decreases by an order of magnitude when we shift our attention from one level to the next lower one. We understand walls in terms of bricks, bricks in terms of crystals, crystals in terms of molecules, etc. As a result the number of levels that can be distinguished meaningfully in a hierarchical system is kind of proportional to the logarithm of the ratio between the largest and the smallest grain, and therefore, unless this ratio is very large, we cannot expect many levels. In computer programming our basic building block has an associated time grain of less than a microsecond, but our program may take hours of computation time. I do not know of any other technology covering a ratio of 10^{10} or more: the computer, by virtue of its fantastic speed, seems to be the first to provide us with an environment where highly hierarchical artifacts are both possible and necessary. This challenge, *viz.* the confrontation with the programming task, is so unique that this novel experience can teach us a lot about ourselves. It should deepen our understanding of the processes of design and creation; it should give us better control over the task of organizing our thoughts. If it did not do so, to my taste we should not deserve the computer at all!

It has already taught us a few lessons, and the one I have chosen to stress in this talk is the following. We shall do a much better programming job, provided that we approach the task with a full appreciation of its tremendous difficulty, provided that we stick to modest and elegant programming languages, provided that we respect the intrinsic limitations of the human mind and approach the task as Very Humble Programmers.

INTRODUCTION

Baker published two papers in 1972 that, taken as companion pieces, contributed significantly to the credibility of structured programming. The earlier paper, "Chief Programmer Team Management of Production Programming" [Paper 7], discusses the theory of the Chief Programmer Team and describes the New York Times system in considerable detail. The following paper, "System Quality Through Structured Programming," concentrates on the actual working product.

Indeed, the primary reason for reading this second paper is that it presents *real* data about *real* bugs in a non-trivial system produced with structured programming, top-down testing, and related techniques. Because it is a real system — the New York Times presumably paid real money for it! — it has been used for years to help convince skeptics and cynics that structured programming actually works. Of course, people are no longer quite as impressed by a project that took place during 1969 and 1970, and there *are* other examples and case studies that can be used. But for quite a long time, this was *the* case study on structured programming.

Notice, as you read, that Baker makes an important distinction between the different types of bugs found in the New York Times system. He refers to "incorrect functions," "omitted functions," and "misinterpreted functions." An incorrect function is defined by Baker as one that is implemented but that does not operate correctly: a coding error (or possibly a design error). An omitted function also could be interpreted as a design or coding error, but a misinterpreted function implies something rather different: It implies a communication problem between the user, the systems analyst, and/or the programmer.

This last type of bug, the misinterpreted function, is of particular interest to me. It can occur as a result of poor specifications (for which more recent techniques like structured analysis can provide a remedy); but it also can happen even with the best specifications, simply because building a software system involves imperfect communication between human beings. Since this is the case, *top-down testing,* a technique that certainly was used in the Times project, is particularly important: It helps expose these misunderstandings and faulty communications as early as possible. Baker doesn't emphasize this, but it is widely recognized now.

You should keep one last point in mind when you read this paper: It was written after approximately two years of operational experience with the system; consequently, it does not represent the last word on the quality or reliability of the New York Times system. During the summer of 1975, several papers appeared in popular computer journals and numerous discussions were presented at computer conferences, all debating the success of the Times project. Some claimed (based on informal discussions with a few of the Times maintenance programmers) that the quality of the software was considerably lower than that suggested by Baker; others stoutly maintained that the software was continuing to run at the same high level of reliability reported by Baker in 1971.

The issue never was completely resolved, and by now no one really cares. What is important to recognize is that to get a *true* feeling for the impact of the structured techniques on system quality, one should count the number of bugs and measure (if there is a meaningful way to do it) the ease of maintenance *ten* years after a system is put into operation, as well as during the first year. So, whether or not the results of the Times project were what Baker believed them to be, his early reporting gave structured programming a much-needed boost.

System Quality Through Structured Programming

Introduction

Experience in development and maintenance of large computer-based systems for government and industry has led the IBM Federal Systems Division to the formulation of a new approach to production programming. This approach, which couples a new kind of programming organization (a Chief Programmer Team) with formal tools for using structured programming in system development [1], was recently applied on a contract with The New York Times for an online information system. Compared to experience on similar contracts in the past, the approach resulted in increased programmer productivity coupled with improved quality. An earlier paper [2] describes the approach in detail and gives productivity measures in a form which should allow comparability to other systems. Following a brief description of the system and a review of the approach, this paper discusses the quality of the system as observed during a thorough acceptance test and in the initial period of operation following its delivery.

The Information Bank system and its development

The New York Times Information Bank is an online system which will eventually replace the clipping file (morgue) now used by the Times to provide background information for articles being written. An inquirer may interact with the on-line system to select index terms, specify document parameters (e.g., date of publication, section of the paper), and view article abstracts until he has identified those articles relevant to his immediate needs. Reporters and editors at the Times do this by means of an IBM 4506 Digital TV display unit which can display either text transmitted from the IBM System/360 Model 40 Central Processing Unit or images from standard TV cameras, and transmit text to the System/360 from a standard keyboard. They may also view the full original articles, which are stored in a microfiche retrieval device containing TV cameras capable of being switched to the IBM 4506's under System/360 control.

While editorial support is the main purpose of the system, a number of other features are provided. In addition to the 40 terminals mentioned above, another 24 IBM 4506 units without article viewing capability are interfaced to the on-line system for use by indexers keying index terms, abstracts and document parameters for eventual entry into the system files. The Times is marketing the retrieval service, and up to 500 remote terminals may be added to the system. (While remote users cannot view the articles on their terminals, they can view the abstracts, which provide information sufficient to permit retrieval of the articles from back issue files or from microfilm.) The on-line system (the "Conversational Subsystem") is supported by other subsystems which provide the security data and interactive message texts used by it, edit the keyed indexing data, maintain the system files, print abstracts and clipping references so that users may receive hard copy, log all major interactions with the system and maintain and print statistics on its use. All programs operate on the 360/40 under control of the Disk Operating System.

The system was developed by a Chief Programmer Team, a functional programming organization similar in concept to a surgical team. Members of the team are specialists who assist the Chief Programmer in developing a program system, much as nurses, anesthesiologists and laboratory personnel assist a surgeon in performing an operation. A team is organized around a nucleus of a Chief Programmer, a Backup Programmer and a Programming Librarian. The Chief Programmer is both the prime architect and the key coder of the system. The Backup Programmer works closely with the Chief to design and produce the system's key elements, as well as providing essential insurance that development can continue should the Chief leave the project. The Programming Librarian is responsible for maintenance and operation of a program library system used to keep all system programs and data both internally in machineable form and externally in well-organized, highly readable form. This Team nucleus, usually assisted by a systems analyst, designs and begins development of the system. The Team is then augmented by additional programmers who produce the remainder of the code under the close supervision of the Chief and Backup Programmers. "Egoless programming," [3] featuring careful code review by team members other than the original programmer, is practiced throughout.

In addition to the functional organization and the enhanced cooperation fostered by the program library system, the Team operates in a highly disciplined fashion using principles of structured programming described by Dijkstra [4] and formalized by Mills [5, 6]. These couple a top-down, evolutionary approach to systems development with the application of formal rules governing control flow within modules. In the top-down approach a nucleus of control code is written and debugged first. Function code is then written incrementally and added to the already operational system. This approach eliminates the need for throwaway drivers and reduces integration problems typically encountered at the end of a project. It also improves reliability because code is debugged within the actual system and because major portions of the system, including critical control code, are operational during almost the entire development period. The rules governing control flow are a consequence of a program structure theorem proved by Böhm and Jacopini [7]. This states that any proper program — a program with one entry and one exit — can be written using only the programming progressions illustrated in Figure 1.

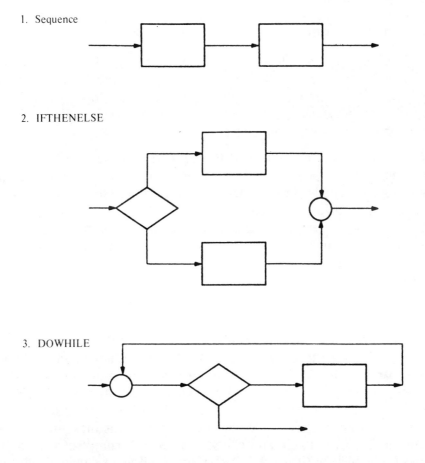

Figure 1. Progressions allowed in structured programming.

Application of these rules permits a program to be read from beginning to end with no control jumps. It therefore simplifies testing and greatly enhances the visibility and understandability of programs. Finally, it supports the writing of program modules in top-down fashion by enhancing the ability to write and debug control code before adding function code.

Debugging experience

Throughout the development of the system, progress was noticeably enhanced due to the use of structured programming and the library. Although no statistics on number of errors or number of runs per module were kept, it was apparent from a qualitative standpoint that both were significantly reduced when compared to similar systems on which team members had previously worked. In a number of cases, program nuclei consisting of two to four hundred source statements ran correctly the first time. In all cases, debugging was clearly faster. Identification of paths to be tested was greatly facilitated by the use of only those formalized control structures permitted by our structured programming conventions.

Acceptance test experience

The system was developed in two major steps. To allow the Times to prepare data for the system files and for debugging and testing of the on-line system, the File Maintenance Subsystem was developed first. Following delivery of that subsystem, the Conversational Subsystem and the rest of the supporting subsystems were developed.

Rigorous and extensive formal testing was performed prior to acceptance by the Times of each of these major phases of the system. For each phase, a test plan was developed jointly by IBM and the Times. Each plan was designed specifically to test all functions included in that phase and was derived principally from the detailed functional specifications agreed upon by the two parties. Data to test these functions were then prepared exclusively by the Times, and these acceptance tests were conducted by the Times with IBM personnel in attendance. All the functional tests were rerun after all problems identified had been corrected, so that corrections could not have undetected effects on parts of the system already tested.

The File Maintenance Subsystem contained 12,029 lines of source code (about 14 percent of the overall system). The test plan for it contained tests for 171 separate functions required in creating and maintaining system files. Acceptance testing lasted a week and also covered all operational aspects of the subsystem, including the elaborate backup and recovery procedures incorporated to ensure preservation of the valuable data. Listings and hexadecimal dumps of all files were made and checked to ensure compliance with predicted file content and specified formats. No errors at all were detected during any of the testing of the File Maintenance Subsystem.

Acceptance testing of the Conversational Subsystem, which contained 38,990 lines of source code (about 47 percent of the overall system), was carried out during a five-week period. The first two weeks were devoted to single-thread (one user signed on from an IBM 4506) testing of the 286 separate functions itemized in the Test Plan. Seventeen errors were detected during this testing, all in the interaction processing modules and none in the time-sharing control program.

Following the single-thread testing, multiple-thread testing was conducted. All the previous tests were repeated with multiple users executing them asynchronously from IBM 4506's. No additional errors were discovered during this testing. Finally, the tests were repeated a third time from IBM 2740 and IBM 2265 terminals, serving to test the remote terminal handling features of the system. While all function was verified to be identical to that observed using the IBM 4506's, three errors were detected in the control program. These all had to do with handling of unusual types of transmission errors on remote lines.

Finally, "free-form" testing allowed for several periods of retrievals by typical users under conditions when any errors or anomalies detected could be carefully recorded and analyzed. No errors were detected during this type of testing. In addition to the formal acceptance testing, system performance was measured to compare normal and peak load performance to a set of performance goals specified by the Times. Even though the system was operating on an IBM 360/40 with three disk drives, instead of the IBM 360/50 with seven drives which had been proposed and accepted on the basis of the performance goals, the goals were still met.

In all, twenty errors were discovered in the Conversational Subsystem during the five weeks of testing. Only two of those caused abnormal termination of the system; in other words, most of the coding errors were of such a nature that the system continued to function even though output was incorrect. Also, only nine represented bugs in the usual sense; the remaining eleven errors represented functions which had not been incorporated into the coding, or coding which performed as we expected but not as the Times desired. It is also of interest to note that twelve of the errors were in code written during the last two months of the nine-month coding period, and all were in code written during the last four months.

Acceptance testing of the Data Entry Edit Subsystem, which contained 13,421 lines of source code (about 16 percent of the overall system) was carried out during the third week. Pre-defined entries were keyed to test all identified features of this subsystem. However, due to pressure of other duties on the part of the indexers, little free-form testing was conducted. One error (misinterpreted function) was detected in this subsystem as a result of the formal tests.

The five other supporting subsystems, containing 18,884 lines of source code (about 23 percent of the overall system), primarily prepare files and tables for use by the Conversational Subsystem and produce listings, logs and statistical reports on the basis of outputs from it. Because of the variety of conditions required for and ensuing from these tests, it was agreed that the smaller subsystems would be sufficiently tested without the need for additional data. These subsystems were run on a regular basis during the five weeks of acceptance testing, and no errors were detected in any of them.

The complete system contained 83,324 lines of source code. Table I summarizes the total of twenty-one errors found during formal and free-form acceptance testing of the system. In the tables, "incorrect function" refers to code which operated improperly; "omitted function" refers to specifications not implemented; and "misinterpreted function" refers to code which did not perform precisely the functions specified.

Table I — Errors Identified During Acceptance Testing

Subsystem	Source Lines	Error Type			
		Incorrect Function	Omitted Function	Misinter-preted Function	Total
File Maintenance	12,029	0	0	0	0
Conversational	38,990	9	8	3	20
Data Entry Edit	13,421	0	0	1	1
Other	18,884	0	0	0	0
Total	83,324	9	8	4	21

Operational Experience

The File Maintenance Subsystem was delivered in June, 1970. It was used during 1970 and early 1971 to build files for the acceptance testing described above. Beginning in November, 1971, it has been in use on a daily basis to add to the files new data keyed by the indexers and several years of past data converted from tapes used to publish The New York Times Index. Only two errors have been discovered in this subsystem, neither of which affected the data base. One of these involved incorrect function and the other misinterpreted function.

The Conversational Subsystem was delivered in June, 1971. It was used for experimental and demonstration purposes until November, 1971. Since that time it has been operational eight hours a day for online indexing and for inquiries designed to ensure the consistency of the operational files now being constructed. A total of seven errors have been discovered since delivery. Only one of these resulted in abnormal termination of the system, and this was due to lack of any capability in the System/360 Disk Operating System to handle the particular file error condition which caused it. (Additional application coding was added to circumvent the possibility of this error occurring again.)

The Data Entry Edit Subsystem was also delivered in June, 1971, and became operational on a daily basis in November, 1971. It had the least formal testing of any of the subsystems and has had a number of extensions made to it since delivery. Sixteen errors have been identified in this subsystem.

The five other supporting subsystems have been used on an intermittent basis since their delivery in June, 1971. No errors have been detected in any of these during that period.

Table II summarizes the operating experience to date which has resulted in a total of 25 errors being identified, only thirteen of which involved incorrect function. This represents about three errors per 10,000 lines of code, a result which informal comparisons suggest is substantially better than average. From another standpoint, there was about one error for each five man-months of effort on the project. In fact, the programs written by the Chief and Backup Programmers had about one error per year of effort on their parts.

Table II — Errors Identified During Operation

		Error Type			
Subsystem	Source Lines	Incorrect Function	Omitted Function	Misinterpreted Function	Total
File Maintenance	12,029	1	0	1	2
Conversational	38,990	4	3	0	7
Data Entry Edit	13,421	8	5	3	16
Other	18,884	0	0	0	0
Total	83,324	13	8	4	25

Consequently, initial operation has been very smooth. The important Conversational Subsystem has only suffered one abnormal termination due to an error in thirteen months of experimentation and operation; the other five errors prevented a single user from completing an inquiry or entering indexing data but permitted continued operation. To the best of our knowledge, no errors have been created in the files during two years of operation of the File Maintenance Subsystem. The experience with the Data Entry Edit Subsystem has not been as good, and it has suggested some changes in procedure discussed below.

Conclusions

Structured programming, and the organization and tools used to achieve it, were key factors in developing this kind of system. The fact that most of the errors encountered during acceptance testing were in code written during the last two months tended to confirm our expectations that the longer period of operation permitted by the top-down approach would lead to a more reliable system. The application of the program structure rules made it thoroughly practical for programmers to read, check and criticize each other's code and nearly eliminated the need for flowcharts as a means of communication. The Chief Programmer and Backup Programmer together reviewed much of the code on the project, particularly that of the more junior members of the team. This ensured that specifications and standards were being adhered to and that code would function as intended. Numerous problems were identified by code reviews which would otherwise have led to problems later.

The program library system used was also a major factor in improving quality. Ensuring that up-to-date versions of programs and data were always available reduced problems frequently encountered due to use of obsolete versions. For instance, when programmers were ready to use an interface, they could directly include the appropriate declarations into their code instead of writing their own version. When the interface changed, it was only necessary to recompile to incorporate a new version into all affected programs. In addition to reducing interface problems, the library system facilitated study of code to allow one programmer to adapt an approach used by another instead of re-creating it. Most importantly, it permitted the ready review and criticism of code by others as described above. As a side benefit, the availability of all this information in usable form reduced the need to get it verbally and thus further reduced errors due to distraction or interruption.

While it was not essential to structured programming, the use of the functional Chief Programmer Team organization had three major benefits in the area of program quality. First, the use of senior people directly in the design and programming process led to a cleaner, more rapidly implemented design. Second, use of a programming librarian to do many of the clerical tasks associated with creating, updating and maintaining programs reduced interruptions and diversions which tend to cause programming errors. Finally, the higher degree of specialization and smaller number of programmers led to a reduction in the number of misunderstandings and inconsistencies.

This project has suggested two areas in which further work needs to be done. First, it may not always be possible to follow a strictly top-down approach in development of a large programming system. If a system organization, viewed as a tree structure, is narrow and tall, then a pure top-down approach may take too much elapsed time to be practical. Second, a more rigorous approach to code review needs to be developed. In retrospect, a number of the problems encountered in the Data Entry Edit Subsystem after delivery were of such a nature that they would probably have been caught earlier if all the code had been read. The Chief and Backup Programmers did much functional coding themselves on the project, but it would probably have been more effective for them to have reviewed more code and written less. This would have reduced productivity slightly but would have eliminated a number of the remaining problems.

While the initial objective of the approach was improvement in production programming productivity, it became apparent that the same methods also resulted in increased quality. Experience gained on this project is leading IBM to more experimentation with structured programming and Chief Programmer Teams, and limited results to date confirm the conclusions reached here.

References

1. H.D. Mills, *Chief Programmer Teams: Principles and Procedures,* IBM Corporation, Report No. FSC 71-5108 (Gaithersburg, Md.: IBM Federal Systems Division, 1971).

2. F.T. Baker, "Chief Programmer Team Management of Production Programming," *IBM Systems Journal,* Vol. 11, No. 1 (January 1972), pp. 56-73.

3. G.M. Weinberg, *The Psychology of Computer Programming* (New York: Van Nostrand Reinhold, 1971), p. 72.

4. E.W. Dijkstra, *Notes on Structured Programming,* 2nd ed., Technische Hogeschool Eindhoven, Report No. EWD-248, 70-WSK-03 (Eindhoven, The Netherlands: April 1970); also in *Structured Programming,* O.-J. Dahl, E.W. Dijkstra, and C.A.R. Hoare (New York: Academic Press, 1972).

5. H.D. Mills, *Mathematical Foundations for Structured Programming,* IBM Corporation, Report No. FSC 72-6012 (Gaithersburg, Md.: IBM Federal Systems Division, 1972).

6. _____, "Top-Down Programming in Large Systems," *Debugging Techniques in Large Systems,* ed. R. Rustin (Englewood Cliffs, N.J.: Prentice-Hall, 1971), pp. 41-55.

7. C. Böhm and G. Jacopini, "Flow Diagrams, Turing Machines and Languages with Only Two Formation Rules," *Communications of the ACM,* Vol. 9, No. 5 (May 1966), pp. 366-71.

INTRODUCTION

D.L. Parnas has had an enormous impact on program design — or "structured design," as most people now call it — but his published work has been read by a surprisingly small number of EDP professionals. The following paper, which appeared in the December 1972 issue of *Communications of the ACM,* is included in this collection of structured programming classics because it is the source of many now-familiar concepts and phrases. It is the source for the phrase "information hiding," and is probably Parnas' best-known, if little-read, work.

In this paper, Parnas attacked the whole mystique of modularization, asking questions that, for the most part, had been entirely ignored by the EDP profession: What is a module? What distinguishes a good module from a bad one? How do we go about modularizing a program? And he posed his argument at a time when "modular programming" still was very much a buzzword.

Most of his argument is based on one example: the KWIC index system. Two different modularizations are presented in this paper, and it becomes apparent that one of them is substantially superior to the other — superior, that is, if one defines superiority in terms of ease of maintenance.

If you're like me, you probably will become puzzled halfway through the presentation of his example. "Where did these two modularizations come from?" you'll find yourself asking. "What would make the average programmer stupid enough to come up with the first kind of modularization, and how would he be clever enough to invent the second, demonstrably superior, one?" If these questions occur to you, be patient: Parnas does provide the answers later on in the paper. As he points out, the first modularization probably was derived from flowcharting the problem — an approach still used by many people today. And the second modularization came from a careful consideration of the design decisions that were *likely to change.*

One of the most useful contributions made by Parnas in this paper is the list of *practical* suggestions — specifically, a list of the typical kinds of design decisions that should be hidden within a single module. For those who find information hiding a vague topic, the examples help considerably.

For a long time, Parnas' work seemed to be unrelated to many of the other developments in the structured field, despite the effort Parnas makes in this paper to relate his ideas to the hierarchical design concepts that Dijkstra was publishing at about the same time. More recently, though, it has become evident that his ideas fit neatly into the realm of structured design, and that they are quite compatible with, say, the ideas presented by Stevens, Myers, and Constantine in "Structured Design" [Paper 18]. The typical consequence of *not* hiding information is excessive coupling between modules, to use the term first introduced by Constantine; and one also could argue that information hiding is a *design heuristic,* much like the "span of control" heuristic presented by Stevens, Myers, and Constantine.

On the Criteria to Be Used in Decomposing Systems Into Modules

Introduction

A lucid statement of the philosophy of modular programming can be found in a 1970 textbook on the design of system programs by Gauthier and Ponto [1, ¶ 10.23], which we quote below:*

> A well-defined segmentation of the project effort ensures system modularity. Each task forms a separate, distinct program module. At implementation time each module and its inputs and outputs are well-defined, there is no confusion in the intended interface with other system modules. At checkout time the integrity of the module is tested independently; there are few scheduling problems in synchronizing the completion of several tasks before checkout can begin. Finally, the system is maintained in modular fashion; system errors and deficiencies can be traced to specific system modules, thus limiting the scope of detailed error searching.

Usually nothing is said about the criteria to be used in dividing the system into modules. This paper will discuss that issue and, by means of examples, suggest some criteria which can be used in decomposing a system into modules.

---

*Reprinted by permission of Prentice-Hall, Englewood Cliffs, N.J.

A brief status report

The major advancement in the area of modular programming has been the development of coding techniques and assemblers which (1) allow one module to be written with little knowledge of the code in another module, and (2) allow modules to be reassembled and replaced without reassembly of the whole system. This facility is extremely valuable for the production of large pieces of code, but the systems most often used as examples of problem systems are highly-modularized programs and make use of the techniques mentioned above.

Expected benefits of modular programming

The benefits expected of modular programming are: (1) managerial — development time should be shortened because separate groups would work on each module with little need for communication; (2) product flexibility — it should be possible to make drastic changes to one module without a need to change others; (3) comprehensibility — it should be possible to study the system one module at a time. The whole system can therefore be better designed because it is better understood.

What is modularization?

Below are several partial system descriptions called *modularizations*. In this context "module" is considered to be a responsibility assignment rather than a subprogram. The *modularizations* include the design decisions which must be made *before* the work on independent modules can begin. Quite different decisions are included for each alternative, but in all cases the intention is to describe all "system level" decisions (i.e. decisions which affect more than one module).

Example system 1: A KWIC index production system

The following description of a KWIC index will suffice for this paper. The KWIC index system accepts an ordered set of lines, each line is an ordered set of words, and each word is an ordered set of characters. Any line may be "circularly shifted" by repeatedly removing the first word and appending it at the end of the line. The KWIC index system outputs a listing of all circular shifts of all lines in alphabetical order.

This is a small system. Except under extreme circumstances (huge data base, no supporting software), such a system could be produced by a good programmer within a week or two. Consequently, none of the difficulties motivating modular programming are important for this system. Because it is impractical to treat a large system thoroughly, we must go through the exercise of treating this problem as if it were a large project. We give one modularization which typifies current approaches, and another which has been used successfully in undergraduate class projects.

Modularization 1 — We see the following modules:

Module 1: Input. This module reads the data lines from the input medium and stores them in core for processing by the remaining modules. The characters are packed four to a word, and an otherwise unused character is used to indicate the end of a word. An index is kept to show the starting address of each line.

Module 2: Circular Shift. This module is called after the input module has completed its work. It prepares an index which gives the address of the first character of each circular shift, and the original index of the line in the array made up by module 1. It leaves its output in core with words in pairs (original line number, starting address).

Module 3: Alphabetizing. This module takes as input the arrays produced by modules 1 and 2. It produces an array in the same format as that produced by module 2. In this case, however, the circular shifts are listed in another order (alphabetically).

Module 4: Output. Using the arrays produced by module 3 and module 1, this module produces a nicely formatted output listing all of the circular shifts. In a sophisticated system the actual start of each line will be marked, pointers to further information may be inserted, and the start of the circular shift may actually not be the first word in the line, etc.

Module 5: Master Control. This module does little more than control the sequencing among the other four modules. It may also handle error messages, space allocation, etc.

It should be clear that the above does not constitute a definitive document. Much more information would have to be supplied before work could start. The defining documents would include a number of pictures showing core formats, pointer conventions, calling conventions, etc. All of the interfaces between the four modules must be specified before work could begin.

This is a modularization in the sense meant by all proponents of modular programming. The system is divided into a number of modules with well-defined interfaces; each one is small enough and simple enough to be thoroughly understood and well programmed. Experiments on a small scale indicate that this is approximately the decomposition which would be proposed by most programmers for the task specified.

Modularization 2 — We see the following modules:

Module 1: Line Storage. This module consists of a number of functions or subroutines which provide the means by which the user of the module may call on it. The function call $CHAR(r,w,c)$ will have as value an integer representing the c th character in the r th line, w th word. A call such as $SETCHAR(r,w,c,d)$ will cause the c th character in the w th word of the r th line to be the character represented by d (i.e. $CHAR(r,w,c) = d$). $WORDS(r)$ returns as value the number of words in line r. There are certain restrictions in the way that these routines may be called; if these restrictions are violated, the routines "trap" to an error-handling subroutine which is to be provided by the users of the routine. Additional routines are available which reveal to the caller the number of words in any line, the number of lines currently stored, and the number of characters in any word. Functions *DELINE* and *DELWRD* are provided to delete portions of lines which have already been stored. A precise specification of a similar module has been given in [3] and [8] and we will not repeat it here.

Module 2: INPUT. This module reads the original lines from the input media and calls the line storage module to have them stored internally.

Module 3: Circular Shifter. The principal functions provided by this module are analogs of functions provided in module 1. The module creates the impression that we have created a line holder containing not all of the lines but all of the circular shifts of the lines. Thus the function call *CSCHAR*(l,w,c) provides the value representing the c th character in the w th word of the l th circular shift. It is specified that (1) if $i < j$ then the shifts of line i precede the shifts of line j, and (2) for each line the first shift is the original line, the second shift is obtained by making a one-word rotation to the first shift, etc. A function *CSSETUP* is provided which must be called before the other functions have their specified values. For a more precise specification of such a module, see [8].

Module 4: Alphabetizer. This module consists principally of two functions. One, *ALPH*, must be called before the other will have a defined value. The second, *ITH*, will serve as an index. *ITH*(i) will give the index of the circular shift which comes i th in the alphabetical ordering. Formal definitions of these functions are given [8].

Module 5: Output. This module will give the desired printing of set of lines or circular shifts.

Module 6: Master Control. Similar in function to the modularization above.

Comparison of the two modularizations

General. Both schemes will work. The first is quite conventional; the second has been used successfully in a class project [7]. Both will reduce the programming to the relatively independent programming of a number of small, manageable, programs.

Note first that the two decompositions may share all data representations and access methods. Our discussion is about two different ways of cutting up what *may* be the same object. A system built according to decomposition 1 could conceivably be identical *after assembly* to one built according to decomposition 2. The differences between the two alternatives are in the way that they are divided into the work assignments, and the interfaces between modules. The algorithms used in both cases *might* be identical. The systems are substantially different even if identical in the runnable representation. This is possible because the runnable representation need only be used for running; other representations are used for changing, documenting, understanding, etc. The two systems will not be identical in those other representations.

Changeability. There are a number of design decisions which are questionable and likely to change under many circumstances. This is a partial list.

1. Input format.

2. The decision to have all lines stored in core. For large jobs it may prove inconvenient or impractical to keep all of the lines in core at any one time.

3. The decision to pack the characters four to a word. In cases where we are working with small amounts of data it may prove undesirable to pack the characters; time will be saved by a character per word layout. In other cases we may pack, but in different formats.

4. The decision to make an index for the circular shifts rather than actually store them as such. Again, for a small index or a large core, writing them out may be the preferable approach. Alternatively, we may choose to prepare nothing during *CSSETUP*. All computation could be done during the calls on the other functions such as *CSCHAR*.

5. The decision to alphabetize the list once, rather than either (a) search for each item when needed, or (b) partially alphabetize as is done in Hoare's FIND [2]. In a number of circumstances it would be advantageous to distribute the computation involved in alphabetization over the time required to produce the index.

By looking at these changes we can see the differences between the two modularizations. The first change is confined to one module in both decompositions. For the first decomposition the second change would result in changes in every module! The same is true of the third change. In the first decomposition the format of the line storage in core must be used by all of the programs. In the second decomposition the story is entirely different. Knowledge of the exact way that the lines are stored is entirely hidden from all but module 1. Any change in the manner of storage can be confined to that module!

In some versions of this system there was an additional module in the decomposition. A symbol table module (as specified in [3]) was used within the line storage module. This fact was completely invisible to the rest of the system.

The fourth change is confined to the circular shift module in the second decomposition, but in the first decomposition the alphabetizer and the output routines will also know of the change.

The fifth change will also prove difficult in the first decomposition. The output module will expect the index to have been completed before it began. The alphabetizer module in the second decomposition was designed so that a user could not detect when the alphabetization was actually done. No other module need be changed.

Independent Development. In the first modularization the interfaces between the modules are the fairly complex formats and table organizations described above. These represent design decisions which cannot be taken lightly. The table structure and organization are essential to the efficiency of the various modules and must be designed carefully. The development of those formats will be a major part of the module development and that part must be a joint effort among the several development groups. In the second modularization the interfaces are more abstract; they consist primarily in the function names and the numbers and types of the parameters. These are relatively simple decisions and the independent development of modules should begin much earlier.

Comprehensibility. To understand the output module in the first modularization, it will be necessary to understand something of the alphabetizer, the circular shifter, and the input module. There will be aspects of the tables used by output which will only make sense because of the way that the other modules work. There will be constraints on the structure of the tables due to the algorithms used in the other modules. The system will only be comprehensible as a whole. It is my subjective judgment that this is not true in the second modularization.

The criteria

Many readers will now see what criteria were used in each decomposition. In the first decomposition the criterion used was to make each major step in the processing a module. One might say that to get the first decomposition one makes a flowchart. This is the most common approach to decomposition or modularization. It is an outgrowth of all programmer training which teaches us that we should begin with a rough flowchart and move from there to a detailed implementation. The flowchart was a useful abstraction for systems with on the order of 5,000–10,000 instructions, but as we move beyond that it does not appear to be sufficient; something additional is needed.

The second decomposition was made using "information hiding" [4] as a criterion. The modules no longer correspond to steps in the processing. The line storage module, for example, is used in almost every action by the system. Alphabetization may or may not correspond to a phase in the processing according to the method used. Similarly, circular shift might, in some circumstances, not make any table at all but calculate each character as demanded. Every module in the second decomposition is characterized by its knowledge of a design decision which it hides from all others. Its interface or definition was chosen to reveal as little as possible about its inner workings.

Improvement in circular shift module

To illustrate the impact of such a criterion let us take a closer look at the design of the circular shift module from the second decomposition. Hindsight now suggests that this definition reveals more information than necessary. While we carefully hid the method of storing or calculating the list of circular shifts, we specified an order to that list. Programs could be effectively written if we specified only (1) that the lines indicated in circular shift's current definition will all exist in the table, (2) that no one of them would be included twice, and (3) that an additional function existed which would allow us to identify the original line given the shift. By prescribing the order for the shifts we have given more information than necessary and so unnecessarily restricted the class of systems that we can build without changing the definitions. For example, we have not allowed for a system in which the circular shifts were produced in alphabetical order, *ALPH* is empty, and *ITH* simply returns its argument as a value. Our failure to do this in constructing the systems with the second decomposition must clearly be classified as a design error.

In addition to the general criteria that each module hides some design decision from the rest of the system, we can mention some specific examples of decompositions which seem advisable.

1. A *data structure*, its internal linkings, *accessing procedures and modifying procedures* are part of a single module. They are not shared by many modules as is conventionally done. This notion is perhaps just an elaboration of the assumptions behind the papers of Balzer [9] and Mealy [10]. Design with this in mind is clearly behind the design of BLISS [11].

2. *The sequence of instructions necessary to call a given routine and the routine itself are part of the same module.* This rule was not relevant in the Fortran systems used for experimentation but it becomes essential for systems constructed in an assembly language. There are no perfect general calling sequences for real machines and consequently they tend to vary as we continue our search for the ideal sequence. By assigning responsibility for generating the call to the person responsible for the routine we make such improvements easier and also make it more feasible to have several distinct sequences in the same software structure.

3. The *formats of control blocks* used in queues in operating systems and similar programs *must be hidden* within a "control block module." It is conventional to make such formats the interfaces between various modules. Because design evolution forces frequent changes on control block formats, such a decision often proves extremely costly.

4. *Character codes, alphabetic orderings, and similar data should be hidden* in a module for greatest flexibility.

5. The sequence in which certain items will be processed should (as far as practical) be hidden within a single module. Various changes ranging from equipment additions to unavailability of certain resources in an operating system make sequencing extremely variable.

Efficiency and implementation

If we are not careful the second decomposition will prove to be much less efficient than the first. If each of the functions is actually implemented as a procedure with an elaborate calling sequence there will be a great deal of such calling due to the repeated switching between modules. The first decomposition will not suffer from this problem because there is relatively infrequent transfer of control between modules.

To save the procedure call overhead, yet gain the advantages that we have seen above, we must implement these modules in an unusual way. In many cases the routines will be best inserted into the code by an assembler; in other cases, highly specialized and efficient transfers would be inserted. To successfully and efficiently make use of the second type of decomposition will require a tool by means of which programs may be written as if the functions were subroutines, but assembled by whatever implementation is appropriate. If such a technique is used, the separation between modules may not be clear in the final code. For that reason additional program modification features would also be useful. In other words, the several representations of the program (which were mentioned earlier) must be maintained in the machine together with a program performing mapping between them.

A decomposition common to a compiler and interpretor for the same language

In an earlier attempt to apply these decomposition rules to a design project we constructed a translator for a Markov algorithm expressed in the notation described in [6]. Although it was not our intention to investigate the relation between compiling and interpretive translators of a language, we discovered that our decomposition was valid for a pure compiler and several varieties of interpretors for the language. Although there would be deep and substantial differences in the final running representations of each type of compiler, we found that the decisions implicit in the early decomposition held for all.

This would not have been true if we had divided responsibilities along the classical lines for either a compiler or interpretor (e.g. syntax recognizer, code generator, run time routines for a compiler). Instead the decomposition was based upon the hiding of various decisions as in the example above. Thus register representation, search algorithm, rule interpretation etc. were modules and these problems existed in both compiling and interpretive translators. Not only was the decomposition valid in all cases, but many of the routines could be used with only slight changes in any sort of translator.

This example provides additional support for the statement that the order in time in which processing is expected to take place should not be used in making the decomposition into modules. It further provides evidence that a careful job of decomposition can result in considerable carryover of work from one project to another.

A more detailed discussion of this example was contained in [8].

Hierarchical structure

We can find a program hierarchy in the sense illustrated by Dijkstra [5] in the system defined according to decomposition 2. If a symbol table exists, it functions without any of the other modules, hence it is on level 1. Line storage is on level 1 if no symbol table is used or it is on level 2 otherwise. Input and Circular Shifter require line storage for their functioning. Output and Alphabetizer will require Circular Shifter, but since Circular Shifter and line holder are in some sense compatible, it would be easy to build a parameterized version of those routines which could be used to alphabetize or print out either the original lines or the circular shifts. In the first usage they would not require Circular Shifter; in the second they would. In other words, our design has allowed us to have a single representation for programs which may run at either of two levels in the hierarchy.

In discussions of system structure it is easy to confuse the benefits of a good decomposition with those of a hierarchical structure. We have a hierarchical structure if a certain relation may be defined between the modules or programs and that relation is a partial ordering. The relation we are concerned with is "uses" or "depends upon." It is better to use a relation between programs since in many cases one module depends upon only part of another module (e.g. Circular Shifter depends only on the output parts of the line holder and not on the correct working of *SETWORD*). It is conceivable that we could obtain the benefits that we have been discussing without such a partial ordering, e.g. if all the modules were on the same level. The partial ordering gives us two additional benefits. First, parts of the system are benefited (simplified) because they use the services of lower* levels. Second, we are able to cut off the upper levels and still have a usable and useful product. For example, the symbol table can be used in other applications; the line holder could be the basis of a question answering system. The existence of the hierarchical structure assures us that we can "prune" off the upper levels of the tree and start a new tree on the old trunk. If we had designed a system in which the "low level" modules made some use of the "high level" modules, we would not have the hierarchy, we would find it much harder to remove portions of the system, and "level" would not have much meaning in the system.

Since it is conceivable that we could have a system with the type of decomposition shown in version 1 (important design decisions in the interfaces) but retaining a hierarchical structure, we must conclude that hierarchical structure and "clean" decomposition are two desirable but *independent* properties of a system structure.

Conclusion

We have tried to demonstrate by these examples that it is almost always incorrect to begin the decomposition of a system into modules on the basis of a flowchart. We propose instead that one begins with a list of difficult design decisions or design decisions which are likely to change. Each module is then designed to hide such a decision from the others. Since, in most cases, design decisions transcend time of execution, modules will not correspond to steps in the processing. To achieve an efficient implementation we must abandon the assumption that a module is one or more subroutines, and instead allow subroutines and programs to be assembled collections of code from various modules.

---

*Here "lower" means "lower numbered."

References

1. R.L. Gauthier and S.D. Ponto, *Designing Systems Programs* (Englewood Cliffs, N.J.: Prentice-Hall, 1970).

2. C.A.R. Hoare, "Proof of a Program: FIND," *Communications of the ACM,* Vol. 14, No. 1 (January 1971), pp. 39-45.

3. D.L. Parnas, "A Technique for Software Module Specification with Examples," *Communications of the ACM,* Vol. 15, No. 5 (May 1972), pp. 330-36.

4. _____, "Information Distribution Aspects of Design Methodology," *Proceedings of the 1971 IFIP Congress* (Amsterdam, The Netherlands: North-Holland Publishing Co., 1971); also Carnegie-Mellon University, Computer Science Technical Report (Pittsburgh, Pa.: 1971).

5. E.W. Dijkstra, "The Structure of the 'THE'-Multiprogramming System," *Communications of the ACM,* Vol. 11, No. 5 (May 1968), 341-46.

6. B. Galler and A.J. Perlis, *A View of Programming Languages* (Reading, Mass.: Addison-Wesley, 1970).

7. D.L. Parnas, "A Course on Software Engineering," *Proceedings of the ACM SIGCSE Technical Symposium* (March 1972).

8. _____, "On the Criteria to be Used in Decomposing Systems into Modules," *Communications of the ACM,* Vol. 15, No. 12 (December 1972), pp. 1053-58.

9. R.M. Balzer, "Dataless Programming," *AFIPS Proceedings of the 1967 Fall Joint Computer Conference,* Vol. 31 (Montvale, N.J.: AFIPS Press, 1967), pp. 535-44.

10. G.H. Mealy, "Another Look at Data," *AFIPS Proceedings of the 1967 Fall Joint Computer Conference,* Vol. 31 (Montvale, N.J.: AFIPS Press, 1967), pp. 525-34.

11. W.A. Wulf, D.B. Russell, and A.N. Habermann, "BLISS: A Language for Systems Programming," *Communications of the ACM,* Vol. 14, No. 12 (December 1971), pp. 780-90.

INTRODUCTION

Wirth's "On the Composition of Well-Structured Programs" is one of three papers selected from the December 1974 issue of *ACM Computing Surveys.* Together with Knuth's "Structured Programming with go to Statements" [Paper 20] and Kernighan and Plauger's "Programming Style: Examples and Counterexamples" [Paper 19], it provides an excellent overview of the whole subject of structured programming and top-down decomposition of programs.

While the paper may be a little too theoretical for the average reader, the examples given by Wirth are extremely instructive. For example, after four pages of a delightful philosophical review of the dismal state of the art of programming, Wirth launches into examining a total of five sample programs — all involving an ALGOL-like pseudocode that will be somewhat unfamiliar to the average COBOL programmer, and all involving applications that he wouldn't care about. If you're a COBOL programmer, all I can say is, be patient! Spend the time to read through the examples and to study the code that Wirth presents; it really is worth the effort.

For example, one point comes through very clearly after reading Wirth's third, fourth, and fifth examples: "mechanical" translations of an unstructured program into a goto-less program usually will result in clumsy code. Another lesson we learn from reading Wirth's examples — and one that appears in the other two papers selected from the same issue of *ACM Computing Surveys* — is that a piece of program logic often needs to be rewritten three or four times before it can be considered an elegant, professional piece of code. Most programmers violently object to this concept, even though they are quite happy to revise and rewrite a narrative English document three or four times before they are satisfied with its style. The objection to revising program logic in order to improve the style usually is related to the amount of time it takes. In fact, revising program logic usually takes relatively little time, and the vastly improved program can be maintained at a considerably lower cost.

If you manage to stick with Wirth through his examples, you'll find his concluding remarks about structured programming a true delight. As he says, ". . . the method of stepwise decomposition and refinement of the programming task automatically leads to **goto**-free programs; the absence of jumps is not the initial aim, but the final outcome of the exercise." And that says it all!

On the Composition of Well-Structured Programs

Introduction

In the first decade of computers, say up to the early sixties, computers were quite limited in their power. The task of the programmer was to formulate algorithms in the specific order codes of these machines so that they were utilized as effectively as possible. Primarily because of their limitations, this task was achieved by collecting sets of clever techniques and startling tricks, and by finding applications for them as frequently as possible. Examples of such techniques were the programmed self-modification of parts of the program, such as, for instance, the conversion of conditional jumps into dummy instructions and vice versa, or the sharing of store for functionally independent, but never simultaneously used auxiliary variables.

Tricks were necessary at this time, simply because machines were built with limitations imposed by a technology in its early development stage, and because even problems that would be termed "simple" nowadays could not be handled in a straightforward way. It was the programmers' very task to push computers to their limits by whatever means available. We should recall that the absence of index registers (and indirect addressing), for example, made automatic code modification a mere necessity (see also [1, 2]).

The essence of programming was understood to be the *optimization of the efficiency* of particular machines executing particular algorithms. As computers grew more powerful, the problems posed to the programmers grew proportionally, and as a result, the growing power of hardware did not ease, but rather increased the burden. The elimination of deficiencies, errors and blunders — called debugging — became the overwhelming problem.

Understandably, the remedy was sought in the development and use of better tools in the form of programming languages. The amount of resistance and prejudices which the farsighted originators of FORTRAN had to overcome to gain acceptance of their product is a memorable indication of the degree to which programmers were preoccupied with efficiency, and to which trickology had already become an addiction. However, once these adversities and fears had been overcome, FORTRAN had a tremendous impact — an impact that is still felt today. ALGOL 60 followed several years later; it went beyond FORTRAN in several significant respects, but essentially shared the same purpose and intention. In particular, it extended to the level of statements what FORTRAN had introduced on the level of (arithmetic) expressions: *structure.* But ALGOL 60 was not very successful when measured by its frequency of use in technical and commercial applications. There are many reasons for this, one being that it appeared on the scene when the relevance of structure had not yet been widely recognized, and its restrictiveness against the use of clever tricks was considered to be a handicap and a deficiency. The law of the "Wild West of Programming" was still held in too high esteem! The same inertia that kept many assembly code programmers from advancing to use FORTRAN is now the principal obstacle against moving from a "FORTRAN style" to a structured style.

As the power of computers on the one side, and the complexity and size of the programmer's task on the other continued to grow with a speed unmatched by any other technological venture, it was gradually recognized that the true challenge does not consist in pushing computers to their limits by saving bits and microseconds, but in being capable of organizing large and complex programs, and assuring that they specify a process that for all admitted inputs produces the desired results. In short, it became clear that any amount of efficiency is worthless if we cannot provide *reliability* [4]. But how can this reliability be provided? Here structure enters the scene as the one essential tool for mastering complexity, the effective means of converting a seemingly senseless mass of bits or characters into meaningful and intelligible information. We must recognize the strong and undeniable influence that our language exerts on our ways of thinking, and in fact defines and delimits the abstract space in which we can formulate — give form to — our thoughts.

But now the term *structured programming* has been coined, and it seems finally to be achieving what the term "structured language" was unable to suggest. It was first used by E.W. Dijkstra [3], and has spread with various interpretations and connotations since then. It is the expression of a conviction that the programmers' knowledge must not consist of a bag of tricks and trade secrets, but of a general intellectual ability to tackle problems systematically, and that particular techniques should be replaced (or augmented) by a method. At its heart lies an *attitude* rather than a recipe: the admission of the limitations of our minds. The recognition of these limitations can be used to our advantage, if we carefully restrict ourselves to writing programs which we can manage intellectually, where we fully understand the totality of their implications.

1. Intellectual manageability of programs

Our most important mental tool for coping with complexity is *abstraction*. Therefore, a complex problem should not be regarded immediately in terms of computer instructions, bits, and "logical words," but rather in terms and entities natural to the problem itself, abstracted in some suitable sense. In this process, an abstract program emerges, performing specific operations on abstract data, and formulated in some suitable notation — quite possibly natural language. The operations are then considered as the constituents of the program which are further subjected to decomposition to the next "lower" level of abstraction. This process of *refinement* continues until a level is reached that can be understood by a computer, be it a high-level programming language, FORTRAN, or some machine code [5, 6].

For the intellectual manageability, it is crucial that the constituent operations at each level of abstraction are connected according to sufficiently simple, well understood *program schemas*, and that each operation is described as a piece of program with *one starting point* and a *single terminating point*. This allows defining states of the computation (P, Q), i.e., relations among the involved variables, and attaching them to the starting and terminating points of each operation (S). It is immaterial, at this point, whether these states are defined by rigorous mathematical formulas (i.e., by predicates of logical calculus) or by sufficiently clear and informative sentences, or by a combination of both. The important point is that the programmer has the means to gain clarity about the interface conditions between the individual building blocks out of which he composes his program [7].

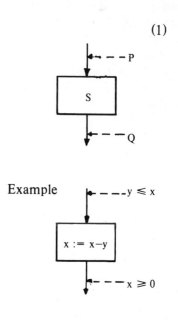

An example may clarify the issues at this point. The reader should be aware that any example that is sufficiently short to fit onto a single page cannot be much more than a metaphor, probably unconvincing to habitual skeptics. The important thing is to abstract from the example and to imagine the same method being applied to large programming problems.

Example 1: Sequential merging

Given a set of $n = 2^N$ integer variables $a_1 \cdots a_n$, find a recipe to permute their values such that $a_1 \le a_2 \le \cdots \le a_n$ using the principle of sequential merging. Thus, we are to sort under the assumption of strictly sequential access. Briefly told, we shall use the following algorithm:

1) Pick individual components $a_i^{(1)}$ and merge them into ordered pairs, depositing them in a variable $a^{(2)}$.

2) Pick the ordered pairs from $a^{(2)}$ and merge them pairwise into ordered quadruples, depositing them in a variable $a^{(3)}$.

3) Continue this game, each time doubling the size of the merged subsequences, until a single sequence of length $n = 2^N$ is generated.

At the outset, we notice that two variables $a^{(1)}$ and $a^{(2)}$ suffice, if the items are alternately shuttled between them. We shall introduce a single array variable A with $2n$ components, such that $a^{(1)}$ is represented by $A[1] \cdots A[n]$ and $a^{(2)}$ is represented by $A[n+1] \cdots A[2n]$. Each of these two conceptually independent parts has two points of sequential access, or read/write heads. These are to be denoted by pairs of index variables i, j and k, l respectively. We may now visualize the sort process as a repeated transfer under merging of tuples *up* and *down* the array A.

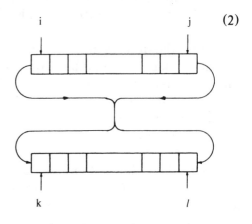

(2)

The first version of our program is evidently a repetition of the merge shuttle of p-tuples, where each time around p is doubled and the direction of the shuttle is changed. As a consequence, we need two variables, one to denote the tuple size, one to denote the direction. We will call them p and *up*. Note that each repetitive operation must contain a change of its (control) variables within the loop, an initialization in front of the loop, and a termination condition. We easily convince ourselves of the correctness of the following program:

$up: = true; p: = 1;$ (3)
repeat 1: "initialize indices *i, j, k,* and *l*";
      2: "merge *p*-tuples from *i*- and
          j-sequences into *k*- and
          l-sequences";
          $up: = \neg up; p: = 2*p$
until $p = n$

Statement-1 is easily expressed in terms of simple assignments depending on the direction of the merge pass:

1: **if** *up* **then** (4)
    begin $i: = 1; j: = n;$
        $k: = n+1; l: = 2*n$
    end
  else
    begin $k: = 1; l: = n;$
        $i: = n+1; j: = 2*n$
    end

Statement-2 describes the repeated merging of *p*-tuples; we shall control the repetition by counting the number *m* of items merged. The sources are designated by the indices *i* and *j;* the destination alternates between indices *k* and *l*. Instead of introducing a new variable standing alternately for *k* and *l*, we use the simple solution of interchanging *k* and *l* after each *p*-tuple merge, and letting *k* denote the destination index at all times. Clearly, the increment of *k* has then to alternate between the values +1 and −1; to denote the increment, we introduce the auxiliary variable *h*. We can easily convince ourselves that the following refinement is correct:

2: **begin** $m: = n; h: = 1;$ (5)
    repeat $m: = m-2*p;$
      3: "merge one *p*-tuple from
         each of *i* and *j* to *k*, in-
         crement *k* after each
         move by *h*"; $h: = -h;$
      4: "exchange *k* and *l*"
    until $m = 0$
  end

Whereas statement-4 is easily expressed as a sequence of simple assignments, statement-3 involves more careful planning. It describes the actual merge operation, i.e., the repeated comparison of the two incoming items, the selection of the lesser one, and the stepping up of the corresponding index. In order to keep track of the number of items taken from the two sources, we introduce the two counter variables *q* and *r*. It must be noted that the merge always exhausts only one of the two sources, and leaves the other one nonempty. Therefore, the leftover tail must subsequently be copied onto the output sequence. These deliberations quickly lead to the following description of statement-3:

$$3: \quad \textbf{begin } q := p; r := p; \qquad\qquad\qquad (6)$$
$$\textbf{repeat } \{\text{select the smaller item}\}$$
$$\textbf{if } A[i] < A[j] \textbf{ then}$$
$$\textbf{begin } A[k] := A[i];$$
$$k := k+h; i := i+1;$$
$$q := q-1$$
$$\textbf{end}$$
$$\textbf{else}$$
$$\textbf{begin } A[k] := A[j];$$
$$k := k+h; j := j-1;$$
$$r := r-1$$
$$\textbf{end}$$
$$\textbf{until } (q = 0) \lor (r = 0);$$
$$5: \text{ "copy tail of } i\text{-sequence"};$$
$$6: \text{ "copy tail of } j\text{-sequence"}$$
$$\textbf{end}$$

The manner in which the tail copying operations are stated demands that they be designed to have no effect, if initially their counter is zero. Use of a repetitive construct testing for termination *before* the first execution of the controlled statement is therefore mandatory.

$$5: \quad \textbf{while } q \neq 0 \textbf{ do} \qquad\qquad\qquad (7)$$
$$\textbf{begin } A[k] := A[i];$$
$$k := k+h;$$
$$i := i+1; q := q-1$$
$$\textbf{end}$$

$$6: \quad \textbf{while } r \neq 0 \textbf{ do}$$
$$\textbf{begin } A[k] := A[j];$$
$$k := k+h;$$
$$j := j-1; r := r-1$$
$$\textbf{end}$$

This concludes the development and presentation of this program, if a computer is available to accept statements of this form, i.e., if a suitable compiler is available.

In passing, I should like to stress that we should not be led to infer that actual program conception proceeds in such a well organized, straightforward, "top-down" manner. Later refinement steps may often show that earlier decisions are inappropriate and must be reconsidered. But this neat, *nested factorization* of a program serves admirably well to keep the individual building blocks intellectually manageable, to explain the program to an audience and to oneself, to raise the level of confidence in the program, and to conduct informal, and even formal proofs of correctness. The emerging modularity is particularly welcome if programs have to be adjusted to changed or extended specifications. This is a most essential advantage, since in practice few programs remain constant for a long time. The reader is urged to rediscover this advantage by generalizing this merge-sort program by allowing n to be any integer greater than 1.

Example 2: Squares and palindromes

List all integers between 1 and N whose squares have a decimal representation which is a palindrome. (A palindrome is a sequence of characters that reads the same from both ends.)

The problem consists in finding sequences of digits that satisfy two conditions: they must be palindromes, and they must represent squares. Consequently, there are two ways to proceed: either generate all palindromes (with log N^2 digits) and select those which represent squares, or generate all squares and then select those whose representations are palindromes. We shall pursue the second method, because squares are simpler to generate (with conventional programming facilities), and because for a given N there are fewer squares than palindromes. The first program draft then consists of essentially a single repetitive statement.

$$n := 0; \tag{8}$$
repeat $n := n+1$; generate square;
   if decimal representation of square
      is a palindrome
     then write n
until $n = N$

The next step is the decomposition of the complicated, verbally described statements into simpler parts. Obviously, before testing for the palindrome property, the decimal representation of the square must have been computed. As an interface between the individual parts we introduce auxiliary variables. They represent the result of one step and function as the argument of the successive step.

$d[1] \cdots d[L]$ an array of decimal digits
L the number of digits computed
p a Boolean variable

(note that $L = entier(2\ log\ N) + 1$)

The refined version of (8) becomes

$$n := 0; \tag{9}$$
repeat $n := n+1$; $s := n*n$;
   $d :=$ decimal representation of s;
   $p := d$ is a palindrome;
   if p **then** *write* (n)
until $n = N$

and we can proceed to specify the three component statements in even greater detail. The computation of a decimal representation is naturally formulated as the repeated computation of individual digits starting "at the right."

$$L : = 0; \tag{10}$$
```
repeat L : = L+1;
    separate the rightmost digit of s,
        call it d[L]
until s = 0
```

The separation of the least significant digit is now easily expressed in terms of elementary arithmetic operations as shown in (12). Hence, the next task is the decomposition of the computation of the palindrome property p of d. It is plain that it also consists of the repeated, sequential comparison of corresponding digits. We start by picking the first and the last digits, and then proceed inwards. Let i and j be the indices of the compared digits.

$$i : = 1; j : = L; \tag{11}$$
```
repeat compare the digits;
    i : = i+1; j : = j−1
until (i ≥ j) or digits are unequal
```

A last refinement leads to a complete solution entirely expressed in terms of a conventional programming language with adequate structuring facilities.

$$n : = 0; \tag{12}$$
```
repeat n : = n+1; s : = n*n; L : = 0;
    repeat L : = L+1;
        r : = s div 10; d[L] : = s − 10*r;
        s : = r
    until s = 0;
    i : = 1; j : = L;
    repeat p : = d[i] = d[j];
        i : = i+1; j : = j−1
    until (i ≥ j) or ¬p;
    if p then write (n)
until n = N
```

This ends the presentation of Example 2.

2. Simplicity of composition schemes

In order to achieve intellectual manageability, the elementary composition schemes must be simple. We have encountered most of the truly fundamental ones in this second example. They encompass *sequencing*, *conditioning*, and *repetition* of constituent statements. I should like to elaborate on what is meant by simplicity of composition scheme. To this end, let us select as example the repetitive scheme expressed as

while B **do** S $\tag{13}$

It specifies the repeated execution of the constituent statement S, while — at the outset of each repetition — condition B is satisfied. The simplicity consists in the ease with which we can infer properties about the **while** statement from known properties of the constituent statement. In particular, assume that we know that S leaves a property P on its variables unchanged or *invariant* whenever B is true initially; this may be expressed formally as

$$P \wedge B \; \{S\} \; P \tag{14a}$$

according to the notation introduced by Hoare [8]. Then we may infer that the **while** statement also leaves P invariant, regardless of the number of times S was repeated. Since the repetition process terminates only after condition B has become false, we may infer that in addition to P, also $\neg B$ holds after the execution of the **while** statement. This inference may be expressed formally as

$$P \; \{\textbf{while } B \textbf{ do } S\} \; P \wedge \neg B \tag{14b}$$

This formula contains the essence of the entire **while**-construct. It teaches us to look for an invariant property P, and to consider the result of the repetition to be the logical combination of P and the negation of the continuation condition B. A similar pattern of inference governs the **repeat**-construct used in the preceding examples. Assuming that we can prove

$$Q \vee (P \wedge \neg B) \; \{S\} \; P \tag{15a}$$

about S, then we may conclude that

$$Q \; \{\textbf{repeat } S \textbf{ until } B\} \; P \wedge B \tag{15b}$$

holds for the **repeat**-construct.

There remains the question, whether all programs can be expressed in terms of hierarchical nestings of the few elementary composition schemes mentioned. Although in principle this is possible, the question is rather, whether they can be expressed conveniently, and whether they *should* be expressed in such a manner. The answer must necessarily be subjective, a matter of taste, but I tend to answer affirmatively. At least an attempt should be made to stick to elementary schemes before using more elaborate ones. Yet, the temptation to rescind this rule is real, and the chance to succumb is particularly great in languages offering a facility like the **goto** statement, which allows the instantaneous invention of any form of composition, and which is the key to any kind of structural irregularity.

The following short example illustrates a typical situation, and the issues involved.

Example 3: Selecting distinct numbers

Given is a sequence of (not necessarily different) numbers r_0, r_1, r_2, $\cdots$. Select the first n distinct numbers and assign them sequentially to an array variable a with n elements, skipping any number r_i that had already occurred. (The sequence r may, for instance, be obtained from a pseudo-random number generator, and we can rest assured that the sequence r contains at least n different numbers.)

An obvious formulation of a program performing this task is the following:

```
for i : = 1 to n do                           (16)
begin L : get(r);
    for j : = 1 to i−1 do
      if a[j ] = r then goto L;
    a[i ] : = r
end
```

It cannot be denied that this "obvious" solution has been suggested by the tradition of expressing a repeated action by a **for** statement (or a DO loop). The task of computing a value for a is decomposed into n identical steps of computing a single number $a[i]$ for $i = 1 \cdots n$. Another influence leading to this formulation is the tacit assumption that the probability of two elements of the sequence being equal is reasonably small. Hence, the case of a candidate r being equal to some $a[j]$ is considered as the exception: it leads to a break in the orderly course of operations and is expressed by a jump. The elimination of this break is the subject of our further deliberations.

Of course, the **goto** statement may be easily — almost mechanically — replaced in a transcription process leading to the following **goto**-less version.

```
for i : = 1 to n do                           (17)
begin
  repeat get(r); ok : = true;
      j : = 1;
    while (j<i )∧ok do
      begin ok : = a[j ]≠ r; j : = j+1
      end
  until ok;
  a[i ] : = r
end
```

The transcription consists of the replacement of the **for** statement with a fixed termination condition depending on the running index j by a more flexible **while** statement allowing for more complicated, composite termination (or rather continuation) conditions. But this solution appears quite unattractive. It is admittedly less transparent than the program using a jump, in spite of the fact that the most frequently heard objection to the use of jumps is that they

obscure the program. The other objection is that the **goto**-less version (17) requires more comparisons and tests, and hence is less efficient.

The crux of the matter is that well-structured programs should not be obtained merely through the formalistic process of eliminating **goto** statements
from programs that were conceived with that facility in mind, but that they
must emerge from a proper design process. Two alternative solutions are
presented here as illustrations.

In the first case, we abandon the notion that the program must necessarily
be based on the statement

$$\textbf{for } i := 1 \textbf{ to } n \textbf{ do} \qquad\qquad (18)$$
$$a[i] := \text{the next suitable number}$$

and consider the basic iteration step to consist of the generation of the next element of the sequence r, followed by the test for its acceptability.

```
i : = 1;                                           (19)
while i ≤ n do
begin generate next r;
   assign it to a[i];
   check whether all a[j] are different from a[i];
   if so, proceed by incrementing i
end
```

This form makes it obvious that we are in trouble, if the sequence r should be
such that i cannot be incremented any longer. Written in terms of our programming language, (19) becomes

```
i : = 1;                                           (20)
while i ≤ n do
begin get(r);
   a[i] : = r; j : = 1;
   while a[j] ≠ r do j : = j+1;
   if i = j then i : = i+1
end
```

The second approach to this problem retains the basic concept of the solution as shown in (18). From there, its development is characterized by the following two snapshots:

```
for i : = 1 to n do                                (21)
   repeat generate the next r;
      check its acceptability
   until acceptable
```

```
for i : = 1 to n do                                (22)
   repeat get(r);
      a[i] : = r; j : = 1;
      while a[j] ≠ r do j : = j+1;
   until i = j
```

In contrast to (20), this solution consists of *three* nested repetitions instead of only two, and therefore seems inferior at first sight. In fact, however, solution (22) turns out to be even more economical. The reason is that in (20) the test for continuation $i \leq n$ is actually unnecessary whenever $i \neq j$, since $i \neq j$ in this case implies $i < j$, and because i has not been altered since the last evaluation of $i \leq n$. Of course, program (22) is considerably more efficient than the original form with a jump (16).

This terminates our consideration of Example 3.

The question remains open, of course, whether jumps can *always* be avoided without disadvantage. I shall not venture to answer this question, particularly because the term "disadvantage" is sufficiently vague to admit many interpretations. But there is evidence of the existence of some characteristic and reasonably frequent situations which are expressed only with difficulty in terms of the language construct introduced above. A particular case is the *loop with exit(s) in the middle.* Lately it has led language designers to introduce specific constructs mirroring this case [12]. It turns out, however, that it is most difficult to find a satisfactory and linguistically suggestive formulation, and that sometimes solutions are invented that seem to merely replace the symbol **goto** by another word, such as **exit** or **jump**. For example, the construct

$$\begin{aligned}&\textbf{loop } S1; \qquad\qquad\qquad\qquad\qquad\qquad\qquad (23)\\&\quad\textbf{exit if } P;\\&\qquad S2\\&\textbf{end}\end{aligned}$$

with the parametric statements $S1$, $S2$, and the termination condition P might be adopted to express the program

$$\begin{aligned}&\text{L1: } \textbf{begin } S1; \qquad\qquad\qquad\qquad\qquad\qquad (24)\\&\quad\textbf{if } P \textbf{ then goto } \text{L2};\\&\quad S2; \textbf{ goto } \text{L1}\\&\text{L2: } \textbf{end}\end{aligned}$$

in a more concise and **goto**-free form.

Expressing (24) in terms of the basic repetitive statement forms does, indeed, often lead to undesirable complications, such as unnecessary reevaluation of conditions, or duplication of parts of the program, as is shown by the two proposals (25) and (26).

$$\begin{aligned}&\textbf{repeat } S1; \qquad\qquad\qquad\qquad\qquad\qquad\qquad (25)\\&\quad\textbf{if } \neg P \textbf{ then } S2\\&\textbf{until } P\end{aligned}$$

$$\begin{aligned}&S1; \qquad\qquad\qquad\qquad\qquad\qquad\qquad\qquad\quad (26)\\&\textbf{while } \neg P \textbf{ do}\\&\quad\textbf{begin } S2; S1 \textbf{ end}\end{aligned}$$

Loop structures

The following, and last two, examples of problems are added to show that often the need for an *exit in the middle* construct is based on a preconceived notion rather than on a real necessity, and that sometimes an even better solution is found when sticking to the fundamental constructs.

Example 4: A scanner

The task is to construct a piece of program which, each time it is activated, scans an input sequence of characters, delivering as a result the next character, but skipping over blanks and over so-called comments. A comment is defined as any sequence of characters starting with a left bracket and ending with a right bracket.

This scanner could typically occur as part of a compiler. A common solution is indicated by the following flowchart (*next* denotes the operation of reading the next character and assigning it to the result variable *x)*.

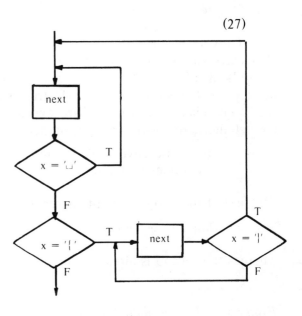

(27)

This program clearly exhibits the loop structure with exit in the middle, satisfying the one-entry-one-exit prerequisite. Instead of proposing a suggestive form for this construct in sequential language, however, let me tackle the posed problem in a different manner. Recognizing the main purpose of the program as being the reading of the next character, with the additional request for skipping over blanks and comments, I propose a first version as follows:

>*next;* (28)
>**while** *x* **in** {'⎵', '{'} **do**
>   "skip blanks and comments"

The correctness of this program is easily established, assuming that the statement in quotes performs what it says, and nothing more. The definition of the **while** statement guarantees that the resulting value of *x* is neither a blank nor a comment, no matter in what way blanks and comments are skipped.

The refinement of the statement in quotes is guided by the fact that upon its initiation x is either a blank or an opening bracket.

       if $x = $ '␣' **then** *next* **else**   (29)
           "skip comment"

where the last statement is expressed, with obvious reasoning, as

       begin repeat *next* **until** $x = $ '}';   (30)
        next
       end

Only knowledge about the expected *frequencies of occurrence* of individual characters can be a reason to choose another form of this program on the grounds of efficiency. For the sake of argument, let us assume that short sequences of blanks are particularly frequent and that, on the other hand, immediately adjacent comments are extremely rare. This leads us to an equally correct alternative form of (29), namely

       "skip consecutive blanks, if any";   (31)
       "skip comment, if any"

The first of the two statements is readily expressed as

       while $x = $ '␣' **do** *next*   (32)

whereas the second is already elaborated in (30).

(33)

Example 5: Integer multiplication

Assume that we are to design a program to multiply two non-negative integers a and b with the use of addition, doubling, and halving only. Let the result be represented by a variable z. A well-known and efficient method is shown by the flowchart at right:

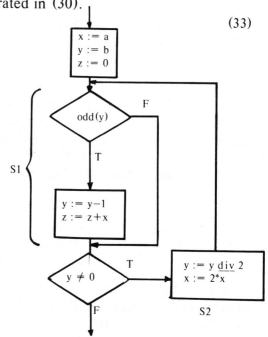

This program, once again, clearly exhibits the loop structure with exit in the middle, and therefore cannot be expressed as a single **while** statement. It is usually squeezed into the simple loop form by displacing the loop termination test, positioning it in front of statement $S1$. The program then obtains the well-known form

$$x : = a; y : = b; z : = 0; \qquad\qquad (34)$$
$$\textbf{while } y \neq 0 \textbf{ do}$$
$$\quad \textbf{begin if } odd(y) \textbf{ then}$$
$$\qquad \textbf{begin } y : = y{-}1; z : = z{+}x$$
$$\qquad \textbf{end};$$
$$\quad\quad y : = y \textbf{ div } 2; x : = 2{*}x$$
$$\quad \textbf{end}$$

This clearly does not change the effect of the program, because if $y = 0$ at entry to $S1$, then $S1$ has no effect and, in particular, leaves y unchanged; and if $y \neq 0$, then the only additional effect incurred by the modified version is on the auxiliary variables x and y in the case of $y = 1$. But this additional effect is quite undesirable, not so much because of the additional, superfluous, and useless computation, but because this operation may be harmful by causing overflow of the arithmetic unit. Should we therefore resort to the exit-in-the-middle version?

A different solution was shown to me by E.W. Dijkstra. He proposed to tackle the problem at its roots, instead of trying to remedy a preconceived proposal. The most obvious multiplication algorithm under the stated constraints is the following:

$$x : = a; y : = b; z : = 0; \qquad\qquad (35)$$
$$\textbf{while } y \neq 0 \textbf{ do}$$
$$\quad \textbf{begin } \{y > 0 \text{ and } x{*}y{+}z = a{*}b\}$$
$$\qquad y : = y{-}1; z : = z{+}x$$
$$\quad \textbf{end}$$

Before we start out trying to improve this version, we observe that at the outset of each repetition two conditions are satisfied.

1. $y > 0$ follows from the fact that y is a non-negative integer and not equal to zero.

2. $x{*}y{+}z = a{*}b$ is invariant under the two repeated assignments. (To verify this claim, substitute $y{-}1$ for y and $z{+}x$ for $z;$ this yields $x{*}(y{-}1){+}(z{+}x) = x{*}y{+}z = a{*}b$, i.e., the original equation.) At entry the equation is satisfied, since $z = 0$, $x = a$, $y = b$.

Note that the invariant equation combined with the negation of the continuation condition yields $(y = 0)$ and $(x*y+z = a*b)$, i.e., the desired result $z = a*b$.

If we now insert any statement at the place of the invariant which leaves the product $x*y$ unchanged, the result of the program will evidently remain the same. Such a statement is, e.g., the pair of assignments

$$y : = y \text{ div } 2; \, x : = 2*x \tag{36}$$

under the condition that y is even. But if a relation is invariant over a statement, it remains so regardless of how often the statement is executed. This suggests the following, quite evidently correct, efficient, and elegant solution. It contains no exit-in-the-middle loop.

$$
\begin{aligned}
&x : = a; y : = b; z : = 0; \tag{37}\\
&\textbf{while } y \neq 0 \textbf{ do}\\
&\textbf{begin } \{y > 0 \text{ and } x*y+z = a*b\}\\
&\quad \textbf{while } even(y) \textbf{ do}\\
&\qquad \textbf{begin } y : = y \text{ div } 2; \, x : = 2*x\\
&\qquad \textbf{end};\\
&\quad y : = y{-}1; \, z : = z+x\\
&\textbf{end}
\end{aligned}
$$

So much for examples, whose purpose was to sketch and elucidate the basic ideas behind the methods of structured programming and stepwise refinement.

Conclusions

Skeptics will, of course, doubt that these methods represent any progress over the techniques of the old days — in fact, that they are *methods* at all. I can merely say that in my own experience, the new approach has improved my attitudes and abilities towards programming very considerably, and the experiences of others confirm this impression [10, 11]. A systematic, orderly, and transparent approach is mandatory in any sizable project nowadays, not only to make it work properly, but also to keep the programming cost within reasonable bounds. It is the very fact that computation has become very cheap in contrast with salaries of programmers, that squeezing the machines to yield their utmost in speed has become much less important than reliability, correctness, and organizational clarity. It is not only more urgent, but also much more costly to correct an efficient, but erroneous program, than to speed up a relatively slow, but correct program. In the past, the debugging phase has taken a ridiculously large percentage of the development cost in most large projects. The aim now is to eliminate the necessity of debugging by creating bug-free products in the first place. Doesn't this bring to mind the medical slogan "prevention is better than healing"!

The criticism has been voiced that the method of structured programming is in essence nothing more than programming by painstakingly avoiding the use of jumps (**goto** statements). One may, indeed, come to this conclusion by looking at the entire issue in the reverse direction. But in fact, the method of stepwise decomposition and refinement of the programming task automatically leads to **goto**-free programs; the absence of jumps is not the initial aim, but the final outcome of the exercise. The claim that structured programming was invented by proving that all programs can be formulated without **goto** statements is therefore based on a fundamental misunderstanding.

The question of whether jumps enter the picture or not is basically a matter of the level of decomposition or refinement to which the programming process is carried. Ultimately — that is in machine code — there can be no doubt about the presence of jump instructions. The moral of the story is that jumps must not be used in the initial conception of a general algorithmic strategy, and in fact should be delayed as long as possible. With today's state of technology, the introduction of jump instructions can be left to compilers of languages that offer adequate, judiciously chosen, disciplined structuring facilities.

One of the essential facilities for this purpose, besides conditional and repetitive statements, is the *recursive procedure.* In many cases it emerges as the natural formulation of a solution, such as, for instance, in most cases of backtracking algorithms. Hardly anywhere else can a natural, concise, and often self-explanatory solution be made more obscure and mystifying than by replacing its recursive formulation by one in terms of repetition and — well — jumps. This process should definitely be left to a compiler, as it concerns what is called *coding* rather than programming (code = system of symbols used in ciphers, secret messages, etc. [Webster]). Modern programming systems, however, offer efficient implementations of recursion, and thereby make "programming around recursion" a largely unnecessary exercise.

Whereas a teacher should not and must not pay attention to "percent issues" as to efficiency while explaining and exemplifying methods of composing well-structured programs, a professional programmer may well be forced to do so. He may sometimes find a dogma of sticking exclusively to a restricted set of program structuring schemas too much of a straight-jacket, and the temptation to break out too powerful. This will be the case as long as compilers are insufficiently sophisticated to take full advantage of disciplined structuring. Naturally, there will always be situations where a compiler is either denied the full information needed for successful code optimization, or where it would be unable to infer the necessary conditions. It is therefore entirely possible that in the future a more interactive mode of operation between compiler and programmer will emerge, at least for the very sophisticated professional. The purpose of this interaction would not, however, be the development of an algorithm or the debugging of a program, but rather its *improvement under invariance of correctness.*

The foregoing discussion also implies an answer to the question of whether structured programming in an unstructured language (such as FORTRAN) is possible. It is not. What is possible, however, is structured programming in a "higher level" language and subsequent hand-translation into the unstructured language. The corollary is that whereas this approach may be practicable with the almost superhuman discipline of a compiler, it is highly unsuited for *teaching* programming. Recognizing that there may be valid economic reasons for learning *coding* in, say, FORTRAN, the use of an unstructured language to teach *programming* — as the art of systematically developing algorithms — can no longer be defended in the context of computer science education. The lack of an adequate modern tool on the available computing facility is the only remaining excuse.

The last remark concerns an aspect of "structured programming" that has not been illuminated by the foregoing examples: structuring considerations of program and data are often closely related. Hence, it is only natural to subject also the specification of data to a process of stepwise refinement. Moreover, this process is naturally carried out simultaneously with the refinement of the program. A language must, therefore, not only offer program structuring facilities, but an adequate set of systematic data structuring facilities as well. An example of this direction of language development is the programming language PASCAL [12, 13]. The importance of this aspect of programming is particularly evident, as we recognize the data as the ultimate object of our interest: they represent the arguments and results of all computing processes. Only structure enables the programmer to recognize meaning in the computed information.

Acknowledgment

The author is grateful to P.J. Denning for kindly posing the problem treated in Example 3.

References

1. E.W. Dijkstra, "Some Meditations on Advanced Programming," *Proceedings of the 1962 IFIP Congress* (Amsterdam, The Netherlands: North-Holland Publishing Co., 1963), pp. 535-38.

2. _____, "The Humble Programmer," *Communications of the ACM,* Vol. 15, No. 10 (October 1972), pp. 859-66.

3. _____, "Notes on Structured Programming," *Structured Programming,* O.-J. Dahl, E.W. Dijkstra, and C.A.R. Hoare (New York: Academic Press, 1972).

4. P. Naur, B. Randell, and J.N. Buxton, eds., *Software Engineering, Concepts and Techniques, Proceedings of the NATO Conferences* (New York: Petrocelli/Charter, 1976).

5. N. Wirth, "Program Development by Stepwise Refinement," *Communications of the ACM,* Vol. 14, No. 4 (April 1971), pp. 221-27.

6. _____, *Systematic Programming* (Englewood Cliffs, N.J.: Prentice-Hall, 1973).

7. P. Naur, "Proof of Algorithms by General Snapshots," *BIT,* Vol. 6, No. 4 (1966), pp. 310-16.

8. C.A.R. Hoare, "An Axiomatic Approach to Computer Programming," *Communications of the ACM,* Vol. 12, No. 10 (October 1969), pp. 576-80, 583.

9. W.A. Wulf, "Programming Without the GOTO," *Proceedings of the 1971 IFIP Congress,* Vol. 1 (Amsterdam, The Netherlands: North-Holland Publishing Co., 1972), pp. 408-13.

10. F.T. Baker, "Chief Programmer Team Management of Production Programming," *IBM Systems Journal,* Vol. 11, No. 1 (January 1972), pp. 56-73.

11. U. Ammann, "The Method of Structured Programming Applied to the Development of a Compiler," *Proceedings of the 1973 International Computing Symposium* (Amsterdam, The Netherlands: North-Holland Publishing Co., 1974), pp. 93-100.

12. N. Wirth, "The Programming Language Pascal," *Acta Informatica,* Vol. 1, No. 1 (1971), pp. 35-63.

13. K. Jensen and N. Wirth, "PASCAL — User Manual and Report," *Lecture Notes in Computer Science,* Vol. 18 (New York: Springer-Verlag, 1974).

References

INTRODUCTION

In December 1973, *Datamation* devoted its entire issue to the subject of structured programming. The issue included five interrelated papers covering top-down design, Chief Programmer Teams, structured programming, and related subjects. I have selected four of those papers for inclusion in this collection, and will discuss each of them in this single introduction.

McCracken's article, "Revolution in Programming: An Overview," probably attracted more attention than the others, largely because of its dramatic title. More important, however, than the content of the article was the emphasis given to a relatively unfamiliar subject by a man known throughout the industry for his FORTRAN and COBOL textbooks. After structured programming had been discussed for years at computer conferences and in scholarly journals, *the* well-known Daniel McCracken announced in *the* most popular computer magazine that:

> "Structured programming is a major intellectual invention, one that will come to be ranked with the subroutine concept or even the stored program concept."

Aside from such attention-getting comments, there's not a great deal of technical detail in McCracken's paper, which clearly was intended primarily to be an overview introduction to the other papers in that issue.

Donaldson's article, entitled "Structured Programming," presents the subject in somewhat more detail than McCracken, although considerably *less* detail than most of the other papers presented in this book. This is understandable, of course. *Datamation* caters to an audience of managers and senior technical people who are interested in concepts and trends, but who usually have neither the time nor the interest to wade through highly technical details. Although the paper is significant for its inclusion in a popular magazine, there are two crucial weaknesses: First, the paper gives the impression that structured programming is a simple, straightforward matter in FORTRAN and COBOL — an impression that probably led to a great deal of disillusionment on the part of innocent programmers who took Donaldson at his word. Second, the example chosen by Donaldson to compare the virtues of structured code with the ugliness of unstructured code is not at all convincing, because the example is not one of a real program.

This second weakness is remedied in the third *Datamation* paper, entitled "Structured Programming: A Top-Down Approach," by Miller and Lindamood. This paper presents an excellent example of the disadvantages of writing unstructured code in FORTRAN, as well as a distinctly improved structured version in IFTRAN. The authors give most of the credit to Dijkstra for popularizing the concept of structured programming, a tribute that is well-deserved and that continues to this day. However, as Knuth points out in his "Structured Programming with go to Statements" [Paper 20], a number of others in addition to Dijkstra actually contributed to the popularization of the subject within the academic community.

Baker and Mills collaborated on the final of the *Datamation* papers selected for this collection. In many ways, "Chief Programmer Teams" summarizes the discussion in Baker's "Chief Programmer Team Management of Production Programming" and "System Quality Through Structured Programming" presented as the seventh and eleventh papers in this book, respectively. Baker and Mills's paper is interesting in that it provides historical perspective on IBM's evolving interest in the subject of structured programming. Baker's earlier papers were published in January and September of 1972. The *Datamation* paper, as we have seen, appeared in December 1973. By late 1973, as is apparent from the *Datamation* paper, IBM had begun considering the application of Chief Programmer Teams to larger projects — that is, to "teams of teams," and had used the chief programmer approach on additional projects: The Skylab support system is mentioned briefly by Baker and Mills as an example of a 400,000-statement system developed with the same approach as that used on the original New York Times system.

Revolution in Programming:
An Overview

Structured programming is a major intellectual invention, one that will come to be ranked with the subroutine concept or even the stored program concept.

What *is* structured programming? Extravagant claims have been heard for several years, but few people would venture a definition. In fact, it is not clear that there exists a simple definition as yet, but several threads seem to run through the discussions.

The theoretical framework is usually traced to a paper by Böhm and Jacopini. They showed that it is possible to write any program using only three structures:

1. Simple sequence; in the absence of instructions to the contrary, statements are executed in the order written.

2. IF-THEN-ELSE; combine with statement brackets (begin and end) so that groups of statements can be included in the THEN and ELSE clauses. In fact, the THEN and ELSE clauses may contain any of the three structures, recursively.

3. A loop control mechanism such as DO-WHILE or DO-UNTIL.

Using only these constructions, assuming that they are available in the language being used or can somehow be simulated, it is possible to write programs that can be read from top to bottom without ever branching back to something earlier. The GOTO statement is not needed at all, although most people would admit that there are occasional situations where efficiency dictates its use. Programs are accordingly *much* easier to read and understand.

Sometimes the elimination or minimization of GOTO's is presented as the whole point of structured programming, but that is getting the matter backwards. The real situation is that when the three basic structures are used correctly, there simply isn't much occasion to consider using the GOTO.

Harlan Mills extended this result by adding the requirement that a program module have only one entry point and one exit point; with this restriction it becomes possible to prove whether a program is correct. Program proving isn't yet a practical matter for programs of realistic size, but the theory influences the daily practice of programming anyway.

A set of conventions, the details of which depend on the language being used, dictate how to indent program statements so as to make the structure more obvious to the reader of the program. A simple example from FORTRAN is to indent all the statements in the range of a DO by some consistent amount; DO's within DO's are further indented, and so forth.

It seems to be a matter of disbelief in some quarters that such a simple idea as consistent indentation could make much difference, but the practical experience of lots of programmers is that it does. It may in fact make the program harder to write, but the reading is greatly simplified. And when a program has to be maintained it is the reading that is crucial. Following such a practice also makes it much easier for another programmer to check a program for correctness.

Large projects in the past have had reported coding rates in the range of two or three statements per man-day. Since it would be difficult to spend more than ten minutes writing three statements, it is clear that a lot of time was being wasted, presumably in debugging and recoding modules that didn't interface properly with other modules. Structured programming, together with the idea of top-down programming, greatly reduces this waste. The net effect is that although the initial coding is harder, overall programmer efficiency goes up dramatically.

It has been said that skilled programmers have pretty much been using structured programming for years, anyway. This isn't really true. The discipline imposed by using only the three basic program structures and following indentation rules rigidly, improves the performance of even the best programmers. Perhaps more important, it can greatly enhance the effectiveness of the rest of us, who are not geniuses and who sometimes program in rather sloppy ways if left to our own devices.

Historically, recognition of the idea of structured programming seems to date from a famous letter in the *Communications of the ACM* by Professor E.W. Dijkstra of the Netherlands. The title attached to the letter, published in

March of 1968, was "Go To Statement Considered Harmful." The letter attracted considerable attention and puzzlement at the time. I well remember asking people, "Do you understand what Dijkstra is talking about?" The representative answer was: "I'm sure it's important, but I don't really quite understand it." This perplexity was caused in part by the fact that some of the few published articles were rather difficult to obtain, and circulated in a sort of underground library.

So long as the matter seemed to be a theoretical issue that most people could not quite get a good grasp of, nothing much happened. Then came the IBM work for the *New York Times*, with reports of greatly increased programmer productivity and very greatly reduced coding error rates (one detected error per 10,000 lines of coding, or one per man-year)! Absolutely incredible, but these were the facts. The IBM project involved more than just structured programming, to be sure, notably the concept of F.T. Baker of the chief programmer team. But the participants assure me that structured programming was most definitely part of the reason for the amazing results.

What was for a few years an underground ivory tower — to mix metaphors a bit — has now come out in the open as a very important thing indeed. The practicality of the theory has been demonstrated in a fashion that simply cannot be ignored, and one hears of lots of demonstration projects underway, elsewhere within IBM and in many other organizations.

This is a development that could revolutionize programming in several ways. The most obvious benefits are increased productivity and reduced error rates. Programming is perhaps on the verge of becoming a science instead of a craft. The analogy has been made that the hardware people have known for years that any logic circuit can be made up from a few basic primitives, such as the "and" and "or" operations. Programming is now approaching something of the same maturity.

There will also be a strong effect on the use of procedure-oriented languages. Of those in wide use today, only ALGOL and PL/I are anywhere close to suitable for easy use in structured programming. Applying these ideas even in FORTRAN will make for better FORTRAN programs, but it is clear that FORTRAN is not an ideal language for structured programming. And since ALGOL, sad to say, has not caught on in a big way in the U.S., that leaves PL/I. I predict that within the three-to-five-year future, there will be, at long last, a swing to PL/I, precisely because it is well-suited for structured programming.

Structured Programming

Recent shifts in emphasis have occurred in the field of software development. The primary requirement to be met in software development has always been to perform the function specified for the software. But, where at one time secondary emphasis was placed only on software efficiency, that is, core and time required, today three other factors are recognized as requiring special emphasis. These factors are reliability, maintainability, and extensibility. The emphasis on these factors has increased because their economic importance has been recognized. Software maintenance and modification account for a substantial portion of total software expenditures and, as the volume of existing software grows, so does the expense of maintenance and modification. This trend can be counteracted by designing and implementing software in a way that minimizes errors and maximizes the ease with which errors are corrected and modifications are made; hence, reliability, maintainability, and extensibility. While much work is needed to determine how best to design and implement software with these characteristics, there are already some techniques known that contribute materially to these aims.

The development of these new techniques has been motivated by a desire to reduce the cost of developing and maintaining software. The technique discussed in this article does so by reducing a program's complexity and increasing its clarity. The high cost of programming today is due in large measure to the complexity of the programs. As a result of this complexity, the program development process is characterized by a large number of mistakes and a great deal of waste and rework. To the practicing programmer this may not seem like an accurate description; certainly it is a pessimistic one. But when you step back and look at the programming process from the proper perspective and compare it with other scientific disciplines, you will find that the picture *is* bleak.

Program complexity causes problems not only during development but also during maintenance of a program. When a program must be modified to correct a bug or provide a new feature, the complexity of the program makes its operation hard to decipher — even if the person doing the maintenance developed the program originally. Furthermore, once the program is deciphered, inserting the change and insuring that it works correctly is made difficult by program complexity. The expense of program maintenance is becoming more and more important as the volume of programs in existence increases. Use of the technique described in this article can reduce the cost of maintenance dramatically — say, by 50%.

Improvement in program clarity also benefits program development and maintenance. Program clarity is its "understandability"; that is, the ease with which a person unfamiliar with the program (it may even be the original developer) reads code to determine what it does and how it operates. Improved program clarity will decrease the cost of program development and maintenance.

Reduced program complexity can be thought of as a process of removing things from the program: obscure structures, complicated control paths, redundant and obsolete code, meaningless notes, etc. Improving program clarity can be thought of as a process of adding things to the program: self-explanatory labels, good notes, code layout and indentation that has information content for the reader, more levels of modularity, etc.

A technique known as structured programming has been developed which offers improvements in both program complexity and program clarity. Structured programming is a manner of organizing and coding programs that makes the programs easily understood and modified. Easy modification in turn permits easy maintenance of the product and easy building of a new product using this product as a base. Much has been written about structured programming in the last couple of years and its definition varies from writer to writer. However, the fundamental message is "simplify your control paths."

Much of a program's complexity arises from the fact that the program contains many jumps to other parts of the program — jumps both forward and backward in the code. These jumps make it difficult to follow the logic of the program and difficult to be sure at any given point of the program what present conditions are (such as what the state of variables is, what other paths of the program have already been executed or are yet to be executed, etc.). Furthermore, as a program undergoes change during its development period, as it gets further debugged during its maintenance period, and as it gets modified in subsequent new projects, the complexity of the program grows alarmingly. New jumps are inserted, increasing the complexity. In some cases, new code is added because the programmer cannot find existing code that performs the desired function, or isn't sure how the existing code works, or is afraid to disturb the existing code for fear of undoing another desirable function, and the result, after many modifications, is a program that is nearly unintelligible. This is the software equivalent of being shop-worn; the time when it is better to throw the whole thing out and start over.

In a structured program, any program function can be performed using one of three control structures (see Fig. 1): 1. simple sequence, 2. selection, 3. repetition. Any kind of processing, any combination of decisions, any sort of logic, can be accommodated with one of these control structures or a combination of these structures. Each structure is characterized by a simple and single point of transfer of control into the structure, and a single point of transfer of control out of the structure. These structures can be combined to form a program that is very simple in the sense that control flows from top to bottom or from beginning to end. There is no back-tracking. The control structures can be nested, as shown in Fig. 2, but they retain their characteristic of single-entry/single-exit.*

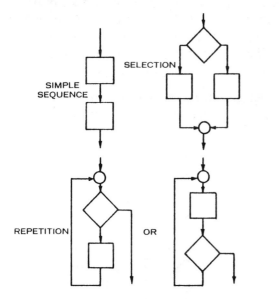

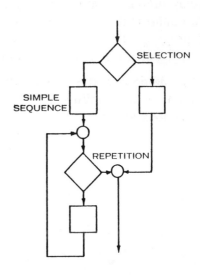

Figure 1. Control structures.   **Figure 2. Nesting of control structures.**

*A proof of the ability of these structures to accommodate any program requirement can be found in Böhm, C., and G. Jacopini, "Flow Diagrams, Turing Machines and Languages with Only Two Formation Rules," *Communications of the ACM*, May 1966, pp. 366-371.

The three control structures can be constructed in any programming language. Thus, structured programming can be practiced by anyone, although the difficulty of it varies with the language you are using. Some high-level languages have language features or constructs that correspond directly to these control structures. PL/I, for example, has IF-THEN-ELSE and DO constructs which perform selection and repetition functions, respectively. COBOL has IF-THEN-ELSE, and a PERFORM construct that performs the repetition function. FORTRAN has a simple IF construct, and a DO construct. Most other high-level languages have equivalent or closely equivalent capabilities. Structured programming can be approximated in assembly language particularly if a powerful macro facility is available, but if assembly language is used many of the benefits sought with structured programming are lost, as discussed below. In a high-level language with suitable capabilities, structured programming produces code that is very clear and intelligible.

Use of the three classical control structures of structured programming in their pure form results in inefficiency in two situations. This inefficiency is avoided through the use of a variant of the selection structure and a slight relaxation of the single-exit rule. The first situation is that handled in conventional programming by computed-GOTO's or switches; the case where only one of a series of functions is to be performed depending on the value of a variable. This is really a generalization of the selection function (IF-THEN-ELSE) from a two-valued to a multi-valued operation as shown in Fig. 3. The second situation arises when the programmer wishes to terminate a repetition block abnormally, as in Fig. 4, and the languages do not explicitly allow this. Although such an abnormal termination violates the single-entry/single-exit rule of structured programming, it may produce significant savings in space and time. If properly flagged, this practice maintains the spirit of structured programming.

In addition to the use of the restricted control structures, many other refinements and attributes have been attached to structured programming. We shall now look at these.

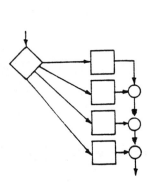

Figure 3. From a two-valued to a multi-valued operation.

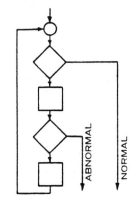

Figure 4. An abnormal termination of a repetition block.

Routine lengths should be limited to a manageable size. The size is usually expressed as a number of lines, say 50, or as a displayable unit such as one crt screenful or one printer page.

This size restriction helps limit programs to a comprehensible unit; one that can be "held in the mind." In addition, since the unit has a single entry and a single exit and no arbitrary jumps to other parts of the program, there is little need for page-turning or for holding several places in a listing to which you must constantly refer.

Careful indenting of coding to show nesting levels also gives increased clarity to the code.

Structured programming, combined with some traditional coding practices such as good annotation, descriptive labels, and judicious spacing in the source code, greatly clarifies source coding. This increased clarity, and the reduced complexity of structured programs are responsible for another advantage of a structured program: its correctness is more easily proven than that of an unstructured program. There are two senses in which this is true. First, since the flow of control is simpler in a structured program, the development and execution of test cases to adequately debug the program is simpler. Second, since the program is more understandable, its correctness is more easily proved by reading, that is, by desk checking. Compared to unstructured programs, structured programs are very easy to read and verify for correctness. The use of structured programming and of more desk checking, therefore, will improve the quality of programs and reduce the cost of their development. In the future, structured programming may make correctness-proving easier in another way.

There is a study of program proof-of-correctness in which the correctness of a program is proved analytically, similar to the proving of a mathematical theorem. However, this work has not yet produced any practical results. No methodology has been developed that is better than the proving system used today by practicing programmers, that is, debugging on the hardware. The proof-of-correctness methods that have been developed are very cumbersome and require more work to prove the program than it takes to debug the program in the conventional way. It is likely that the representation of algorithms for computers will have to be simplified in order that analytical proving can become practical. Structured programming is one step toward that simplification.

Fig. 5 outlines the same function coded in an unstructured program and in a structured program. The dashed lines indicate various program statements. GOTO's (conditional and unconditional) and RETURN's are shown in order to indicate the flow of control, shown by the arrows in the diagram. The program on the left is not structured. Notice the complexity of the flow of control. Note too that this program has no backward GOTO's, which would further add to its complexity. This form of programming, the traditional form, is very bug-prone, difficult to understand (even for the program's author), and hard to modify.

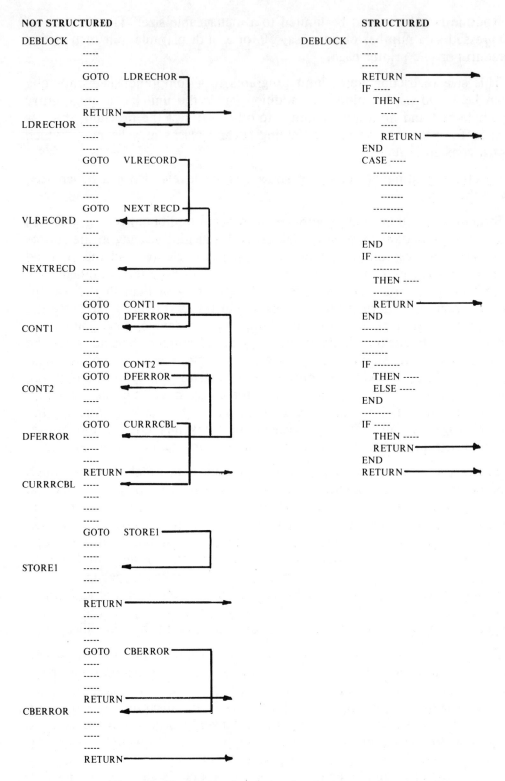

Figure 5. Unstructured and structured programming example.

The program on the right is fully structured. There are no GOTO's, although multiple RETURN's are used for efficiency as described earlier. Control flows uniformly from top to bottom. Each block of code is clearly shown by indentation. The only exception to the simple flow of control is that the program can exit at any one of five points. Necessary program functions are accomplished with various constructs such as IF and CASE (which performs a computed-GOTO function). The structured program is simpler to write, easier to read and understand, and easier to modify. Furthermore, it will usually have fewer bugs when written.

Structured Programming: Top-Down Approach

Structured programming, if the current level of interest and controversy within the computing community is any measure, is an idea whose time has come. You hear about it at conferences, there is increasing mention of the concept in the literature, and, very likely, there are numerous hallway discussion groups trying to unravel the difference between what is and isn't structured programming.

Some of the early successes reported to have been achieved with structured programming techniques include spectacular increases in programmer productivity and correspondingly spectacular decreases in overall software system error rates. One spokesman is reported to have announced that with structured programming " . . . we have observed programmer error rates on the order of one per programmer man-year, or one per 10,000 lines of code." This statement, when viewed against the current increasing concern for the unreliability of software — and what to do about it — suggests that something more than a simple technique is involved. If that kind of productivity and reliability is involved, further study of the techniques which produced it is certainly warranted.

In a very general way, structured programming is a reflection of the concern with form and the interrelationships which exist between the attributes of a "good" program and what the program is supposed to do. Thus, the intense interest in structured programming may be a manifestation of a coming maturation of computing, which is intrinsically a human activity.

What's it all about?

No one "invented" structured programming. A few people, however, have contributed to its development by providing enthusiasm for the idea. Certainly, E.W. Dijkstra can be considered the common-law father of some of the underlying concepts. The now-famous "GOTO letter," which warned that GOTO statements were potentially hazardous to the state of mind of programmers charged with debugging complex and intertwined codes, was the starting point for much of the current interest. Subsequently, Dijkstra's "Notes on Structured Programming" has been widely circulated in the underground press, and has converted many a soul to Dijkstra's version of "right thinking." Along the way, a slightly different thrust — one which dealt with the necessity for certain degrees of clarity of thought during the design (and possibly during the implementation) phases of software system design — surfaced in Dijkstra's description of the "THE" operating system. These two concepts will be discussed in detail later on.

A slightly different approach, which falls into the category of structured programming, was that described by F.T. Baker. That technique, called the "chief programmer team" approach to system design and system implementation, was used with startling success in an IBM programming effort on behalf of the *New York Times;* IBM implemented a complex information retrieval system using only a handful of highly skilled programmers, all under the direction of a chief programmer, in a rather short time. More importantly, it is claimed that the resulting software system had virtually no errors and has run satisfactorily from the day it was implemented. The approach used combined good management with the use of special structured programming techniques.

Some basic notions about what constitutes structured programming have evolved from these sources. The main ideas seem to be:

1.   The construction of programs without the use of GOTO statements (and, consequently, without the necessity for statement labels). This may require certain extensions to the more common procedure languages, as will be made clear below.

2.   The use of strict rules for the top-down design and implementation of a system of programs, and the requirement that the components adhere to a hierarchical form as much as possible.

3.   The generalization of the notion of "abstract resource," so that a hierarchically organized software system obeys some additional rules about the way it performs operations on the "objects" it manipulates.

At the current time it is not possible to say which of these is the basis of structured programming. Indeed, the concept may be an amalgam of these and other ideas, but each is rich enough to require some additional explanation.

GOTO-less programming

In Dijkstra's GOTO letter, he argued that the blatant use of GOTO statements — unconditional transfers of control — resulted in unnecessarily complex flow patterns leading to difficult debugging efforts on the part of programmers. His suggestion was to avoid the GOTO statement as much as possible. The result would be program code which more accurately reflected the relationship between the static and the dynamic behavior of the program. The result of that would be a better correspondence between what the programmer uses (the source code listing) and what the program is supposed to do (the source code translated, linked, loaded, and executed).

The fundamental difficulty with the GOTO statement is that it distracts the reader of the program by forcing him to examine the program in an unnatural way. For example, consider the FORTRAN program fragment below:

```
Line 1:    IF (A.GT.20) GOTO 2
Line 2:    IF (A.GT.10) GOTO 1
Line 3:    X = 5.0
Line 4:    GOTO 3
Line 5:  1 X = 6.0
Line 6:    GOTO 3
Line 7:  2 X = 4.0
Line 8:  3 CONTINUE
```

To understand what is going on in this program, the programmer would consider the conditional statements in the sequence presented. First, if "A.GT.20" is true, the program continues execution at Line 7. Next, if "A.GT.20" is false but "A.GT.10" is true, the program continues execution at Line 5. Only if both conditionals fail does the program perform Line 3, and then control passes to Line 8. To a FORTRAN-experienced eye this may not seem to be very difficult code structure, but if the eventual target, the label "3," were several pages away (and if the labels "1" and "2" were not so conveniently located) there would be a considerable amount of page flipping in order to discern the intended meaning of the program.

This problem would be eliminated, or at least greatly simplified, if the program were organized so that there was greater "locality." In a sense, achieving this kind of correspondence between static placement of statements and dynamic flow depends on the vague concept of "program style." It is also clear that there would have to be some additional features in the FORTRAN language. (There is no intention here to generate another programming language; the widespread use of FORTRAN makes the question of an appropriate set of extensions to FORTRAN for support of structured programming an important one.) To illustrate how this program segment would look in GOTO-free form, we can rewrite it in IFTRAN as follows:

```
Line 1:  IF (A.GT.20)
Line 2:     X = 4.0
Line 3:  ORIF (A.GT.10)
Line 4:     X = 6.0
Line 5:  ELSE
Line 6:     X = 5.0
Line 7:  END IF
```

In this example, the IF, ORIF, and ELSE statements behave very much like similar statements in such languages as ALGOL, PL/I and JOVIAL. The resulting value of X, after the set of checks on the value of A, is evident by the organization of the statements. Because there are no GOTO statements there are no labels and there is a direct correspondence between the static form of the program and the dynamic flow during execution.

Many languages, including those just mentioned, have the facilities to support GOTO-free programming without modification. PL/I and ALGOL have been used extensively as structured programming languages.

Besides the apparent advantages of logical "locality" with better IF statement forms than commonly available (in FORTRAN, at least) there is the related problem of dealing with iterations of one form or another. FORTRAN requires a label as the target of a DO statement and that is esthetically unsatisfying. The syntax of the DO WHILE iteration form ordinarily has been found sufficient.

The question arises naturally: can all programs be written without the use of statement labels? Yes, according to Böhm and Jacopini. The program structures which result from a label-free conditional statement and a DO WHILE statement are sufficient to express any algorithm. Not every program which currently has labels can be converted into a label-free program, however; Manna has shown that it may be necessary to introduce certain "flag" variables in order to eliminate GOTO's and labels completely.

Other enrichments of common programming languages are under consideration as additional means to bring the textual form of the source language the programmer reads into closer correlation with the dynamics during execution. Sullivan outlines a number of such additions for PL/I, for example.

Top-down design

Merely removing all of the GOTO statements will not "structure" the programs; in fact, even though GOTO-free programs are intrinsically easier to read and debug than their labelled counterparts, the form and style of the expression of the algorithms is not explicitly changed by avoidance of the GOTO. Structured programming is also concerned with ways of developing complicated program structures in an orderly manner.

This point is the major feature of the "chief programmer team" approach. This approach to software development (which is now being practiced by a small but growing minority of IBM programmers) involves the following additional ideas:

1. Design of the software system should proceed from the top to the bottom. This is called "top-down" design.

2. Implementation of the software system should also proceed in a top-down fashion, and program "stubs" (which simulate the presence of yet-to-be-implemented modules) should be used as early as possible.

3. Individual program modules should be as short as possible, preferably no longer than one page of machine output, to facilitate partitioning of logic into individual chunks which are easy to debug.

4. Overall control of the software development should be in the hands of a highly competent and experienced chief programmer, upon whose shoulders fall all questions of module-to-module interfacing and testing.

Thus, embedded within techniques which are purely management related are strict rules of hierarchical design. There are two major advantages of a strictly hierarchical form for a software system. First, adhering to the hierarchical constraints forces the organization of the software system along "natural" algorithmic boundaries; individual program modules tend to organize themselves so that each performs some specific function. The result is that each module is easier to debug and so the entire system is easier to debug.

During implementation, just after the design stage is complete, the hierarchical organization is filled out with program stubs which simulate the operation of the modules and provide the means to operate the entire system from the beginning of the implementation phase.

Second, performing the complete system design from the topmost levels ensures that the software will adequately meet its design goals, and that any failures exhibited when implementation begins will become apparent as early as possible. This translates into a smaller number of implementation iterations; if the initial top-down design is good enough, the number of implementation iterations may be reduced to one. There would be no more multiple releases if a strictly hierarchical implementation scheme were followed.

The early results of this type of software design/implementation environment are heartening. The *New York Times* system was apparently completed in record time, with an unprecedented absence of major errors. Several other projects are yielding similar results.

The chief IBM proponent of hierarchical design and implementation is Harlan Mills, who has reported some initial experiences.

Abstract resources

The ideas underlying hierarchical structuring of software systems are a partial outgrowth of the work of Dijkstra. In a landmark paper on Dijkstra's experience with the development of the "THE" multiprogramming system Dijkstra discussed his views on the use of abstract resources in the structure of software systems. In his opinion, each level of the hierarchy of software modules which comprise a system generates an abstract resource which is supported by the lower levels of the hierarchy, and which is available to the higher levels of the hierarchy. Thus, at one level the programming amounts to manipulation of the abstract resources supported by the next lower level of the hierarchy. The programs at that level manipulate abstractions — the abstractions of the resource, whatever it may be — and at the same time participate in generating a higher level of abstraction for the next layer of the hierarchy to manipulate.

An example may help to clarify these concepts. Suppose that a software package is to be built to retrieve information from a file. A file can be considered a collection of "vectors," and each vector may lie on some sector of a disc, for example. In turn, each vector is composed of words, each word is composed of bytes, and each byte composed of bits. The hierarchy of resources needed in order to retrieve single bits from a file is the following:

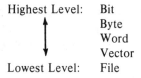

Highest Level:	Bit
	Byte
	Word
	Vector
Lowest Level:	File

A set of programs would be written to manipulate files — in this case, to locate and extract particular vectors. The next level of programs would operate solely on vectors, extracting words from vectors retrieved by the file manipulating programs. In turn, the next level of abstraction would be represented by a set of programs which extract bytes from words; at the top would be the capability to extract bits from bytes.

In implementing the software system for this hierarchy of resources, Dijkstra advises that special care be taken to assure that each level is "complete," at least in the sense that it will always be true that the desired operations at one level are actually supportable by the abstract resource provided by the underlying level. He doesn't say just how to do this; there appears to be no mathematical theory which could apply to this problem, either.

It is important to note that this concept of abstraction bears only a slight resemblance to the concept of "modularity." A highly modular implementation is one in which specific functions are performed by specific modules (and nowhere else); on the other hand, a system which preserves a hierarchy of abstract resources would appear to require modularity as a minimum, and perhaps a great deal more "structure."

The relationship between Dijkstra's ideas and those of Mills is yet to be completely revealed. Mills' work on the theory of structured programming is more concerned with clarity of exposition and ease of debugging than with preservation of levels of abstraction. Dijkstra's work on the subject is ambivalent on issues of clarity. The discussion is likely to go on for some time.

We have seen that "structured programming" is an aggregation of three main ideas: 1. the inherent properties of GOTO-free programming, 2. the application of management techniques to the process of top-down design and implementation of software systems, and 3. the idea of having levels within a hierarchy of software modules lie in specific relations with one another. Collectively, these techniques seem to produce surprisingly reliable systems with relative ease and seem to have inherent qualities of reliability not possible with other implementation techniques.

While structured programming represents a concern with the specific forms programs take, it also represents some first steps toward a deeper understanding of the intrinsic nature of programming, and of the factors which distinguish "good" from "not-so-good" programming. At this point, it appears that structured programming is a viable alternative worth early-on use in a variety of circumstances.

Bibliography

1. Ashcroft, E. and Z. Manna. "The Translation of 'go to' Programs to 'while' Programs." *Proceedings of the 1971 IFIP Congress,* Vol. I. Amsterdam, The Netherlands: North-Holland Publishing Co., 1972, pp. 250-55. See also Stanford University AI Memo AIM-138, STAN CS-71-88. Stanford, Calif.: 1971.

2. Baker, F.T. "Chief Programmer Team Management of Production Programming." *IBM Systems Journal,* Vol. 11, No. 1 (January 1972), pp. 56-73.

3. Böhm, C. and G. Jacopini. "Flow Diagrams, Turing Machines and Languages with Only Two Formation Rules." *Communications of the ACM,* Vol. 9, No. 5 (May 1966), pp. 366-71.

4. Dijkstra, E.W. "Go To Statement Considered Harmful." *Communications of the ACM,* Vol. 11, No. 3 (March 1968), pp. 147-48.

5. _____. "The Structure of the 'THE'-Multiprogramming System." *Communications of the ACM,* Vol. 11, No. 5 (May 1968), pp. 341-46.

6. _____. *Notes on Structured Programming,* 2nd ed. Technische Hogeschool Eindhoven, Report No. EWD-248, 70-WSK-03. Eindhoven, The Netherlands: April 1970. See also O.-J. Dahl, E.W. Dijkstra, and C.A.R. Hoare. *Structured Programming.* New York: Academic Press, 1972.

7. _____. "The Humble Programmer." *Communications of the ACM,* Vol. 15, No. 10 (October 1972), pp. 859-66.

8. Miller, E.F., Jr. *Extensions to FORTRAN and Structured Programming — An Experiment.* General Research Corporation, Report No. RM-1608. Santa Barbara, Calif.: March 1972.

9. Mills, H.D. *Mathematical Foundations for Structured Programming.* IBM Corporation, Report No. FSC 72-6012. Gaithersburg, Md.: IBM Federal Systems Division, 1972.

10. _____. "Top-Down Programming in Large Systems," *Debugging Techniques in Large Systems,* ed. R. Rustin. Englewood Cliffs, N.J.: Prentice-Hall, 1971, pp. 41-55.

11. Sullivan, J.E. *Extending PL/I for Structured Programming.* Mitre Corporation, Report No. MTR-2353 (Bedford, Mass.: March 1972).

Chief Programmer Teams

There is a myth these days that programming consists of a little strategic thinking at the top (program design), and a lot of coding at the bottom. But one small statistic is sufficient to explode that myth.

Including all overhead, five to ten debugged instructions are coded per man-day on a large production programming project. The coding time for these instructions cannot exceed more than a few minutes of an eight-hour day. What do programmers do with their remaining time? They debug.

Programmers usually spend more time debugging code than they do writing it. They are also apt to spend even more time reworking code (and then debugging that code) due to faulty logic or faulty communication with other programmers. In short, it is the thinking errors, more than the coding errors, which limit programming productivity.

The problem is as much one of organization as of technology. To address this, IBM has developed a programming organization called a chief programmer team.

A chief programmer team represents a new managerial approach to production programming. While the approach is made possible by recent technical advances in programming, it also incorporates a fundamental change in managerial framework which includes restructuring the work of programming into specialized jobs, defining relationships among specialists, developing new tools to permit these specialists to interface effectively with a developing, visible project; and providing for training and career development of personnel within these specialties.

This approach contrasts sharply with that of conventional programming groups which frequently suffer from lack of functional separation, discipline, and teamwork. By moving the programming production process from private art to public practice, chief programmer team operations substantially improve the manageability, quality, and productivity of programming.

In addition to the organizational approach, chief programmer team operations are based on two major innovative disciplines. The first is provided by a development support library (DSL) in which all programs under development are maintained by a programming secretary in a visible, standardized form. The second discipline, introduced in a practical way by IBM, is structured programming (SP), which defines a top-down sequence for program unit creation and testing and a technical standard for the coding of each unit.*

Chief programmer team operations provide increased productivity by sharply reducing the debugging and reworking required in a project. The initial coding requires the same amount of time, but the design level thinking is transmitted deeper into the coding by technical and organizational means. SP displays program organization and interactions more effectively for the coding process. More competent, but fewer, people do the coding with carefully orchestrated teamwork. The result is increased productivity, and even more significant, improvements in the reliability and maintainability of the code produced.

This is accomplished by dividing the work of a programming project among special skills addressed to each type of work, rather than simply parceling out a project among programmer generalists, with all the attendant problems of communication and integration. Recognizing that program design capability is a scarce commodity, the work is organized around a senior architect/programmer. This key programmer operates in a disciplined team environment rather than as an individual. There are checks and balances in the restructuring to ensure the integrity of the team effort.

The nucleus of a chief programmer team consists of a chief programmer, a backup programmer, and a programming secretary. This nucleus is standardized to provide management continuity, not only for programming expertise but also for project recording and documentation. Requirements for additional personnel are defined by the chief programmer; a typical team will involve three to five programmers, a secretary, and other specialists. In addition, a project officer may be part of a team to help the chief programmer with administrative,

---

*See articles by Donaldson, and Miller and Lindamood in this book.

financial, legal, and personnel matters, thus allowing him to concentrate on technical management.

The chief programmer team allows for professional growth and technical excellence in programming. Since delegated clerical procedures are used to maintain programming system development in a structured form, more time and energy can be allocated to developing key technical skills and building the deliverable system. This creative environment provides good training for other programmers associated with a team and prepares them for future team leadership.

Team member responsibilities

The chief programmer is a technical manager to whom all team members report directly, but whose principal job is to design and code programs. The chief programmer codes central, critical segments of a programming system and specifies programs for other team members to complete using SP techniques. The programs done by others are reviewed and incorporated into the developing system under the immediate supervision of the chief programmer.

The chief programmer is a professional programming manager who maintains organization discipline and bears project responsibility. His managerial duties are simplified by the structure and the continuous project interaction of the team.

Project management exposure is reduced by the use of a backup programmer, so that a second person is totally familiar with the developing project and its rationale. The backup programmer, a peer of the chief programmer in program design and development, is involved in every aspect of the work and participates in making all important decisions. He can assume the leadership role at any time, if required.

He also participates in the system design and in the coding of the key parts of the system under the direction of the chief programmer. In addition, the backup programmer serves as a research assistant for the chief programmer in programming strategy and tactics, allowing the chief programmer to concentrate on the central problems of system development. Finally, he can provide test planning for the system independent of the chief programmer.

The job of programming secretary is standard in every chief programmer team, and is independent of the subject matter of the project. A programming secretary maintains the records of a project in the development support library in both an internal (machine-readable) and an external (human-readable) form.

The external project records of a chief programmer team are maintained in a set of filed listings that define the current status and previous history of the project. Current status is maintained in loose-leaf notebooks, each headed by a directory and followed by an alphabetized list of member modules. When members and directories are updated and replaced in the status notebooks, the replaced copies are logged in chronological journals. All results of test runs are also maintained in journals.

The main function of a programming secretary is to maintain this current status of program and test data so that programmers can work more effectively and with fewer errors. A by-product of this function is a significant saving in clerical work on the part of the programmers.

In addition to maintaining the DSL, a programming secretary performs secretarial duties in maintaining all other project records. The workload balances well for one secretary on a team. In the middle of a project, DSL maintenance predominates; at the beginning and end, design and documentation create a great deal of paperwork.

It is significant in chief programmer team operations that the programming secretary is a full-fledged, professional team member, not simply a pooled assistant to the programmers on the team.

The reintroduction of senior people such as the chief and backup programmers into detailed program coding recognizes a new set of circumstances in comprehensive modern operating systems. The job control language (JCL), data management and utility facilities, and high-level source languages are so complex that there is both a need and an opportunity for using senior personnel at the detailed coding level.

The need is to make the best possible use of a very extensive and complicated set of facilities. The functions of such systems are impressive, but they are called into play by language forms that require much study, experience, and sustained mental effort to use effectively.

The opportunity also exists for a good deal of work reduction and simplification in the application being written, both in original programming and later in maintenance. For example, the intelligent use of a high-level data management capability may eliminate the need to develop a private file processing system. Finding such an intelligent use is not an easy job, but it can bring about substantial reduction in code required and easier system maintenance.

Development support library

The DSL is a system of office and machine procedures that permits the isolation and delegation of secretarial, clerical, keypunching, and machine operations in programming systems development. The office procedures create input for the machine procedures from programmer-generated material, and file output in project notebooks and archives of the external library. The machine procedures maintain and process library data on a disc file in the internal library, including procedures for performing all runs from initial source code entry through final system testing.

Programmers create or alter the project status by writing programs or data on coding sheets, by marking corrections in the status notebooks, and by requesting runs. The programming secretary is responsible for the preparation and execution of all runs and the filing of output. Fig. 1 illustrates the relationship between the people, the DSL, and the procedures. Because of this functional breakup of work, each programmer can work on more coding in parallel than is normally expected.

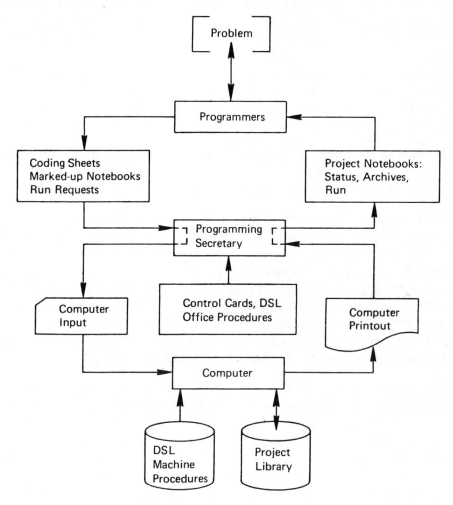

Figure 1. Development support library.

The DSL represents a concept in which people work on a common product rather than on separate, isolated products. Chief programmer team members communicate through this visible product. While the programming secretary is responsible for maintaining the notebooks and archives of the DSL, the chief programmer is responsible for its contents. This structure of responsibility permits a new level of management standardization in project record keeping.

The DSL permits a chief programmer to exercise a wider span of detailed control over the programming, resulting in fewer programmers doing the same job. This reduces communication requirements and allows still more control in the programming. With structured programming, this span of detailed control over code can be greatly expanded beyond present practice; the DSL plays a crucial role in this expansion.

As noted, the chief programmer team concept is primarily an organizational method of increasing programmer productivity. Several components of the method have been tried before. While the chief programmer team bears a superficial similarity to a close-knit programming team working under a lead programmer, two innovations distinguish it from such situations. First is the functional organization and disciplined approach used in the DSL operations. Second is the introduction of structured programming, which results in a new order of quality, productivity and understandability.

In chief programmer team operations, the traditional ad hoc mystique of a developing program is reduced. The visibility of the DSL motivates each team member to think more accurately and consistently about his specific job.

IBM has introduced a set of standards which enables structured programming techniques to be applied to production programming. These standards permit the chief programmer to read, understand, and validate all program data developed by other programmers on the team; this motivates better programming. The other programmers, in turn, read and understand programs written by the chief programmer that define the program stubs with which they must interface. While this organization results in the benefits of "egoless programming," as described by Weinberg, it goes further in ensuring that at least two programmers fully understand every line of the developing program.

The separation of skills forces a high degree of public practice. For example, the programming secretary is responsible for picking up all computer output, good or bad, and filing it in the notebooks and archives of the DSL where they become part of the public record. By contrast, in traditional programming operations, the bad runs go into the wastebasket, often destroying information of latent value, and certainly destroying information about errors of carelessness or ignorance. The identification of all computer runs and program data as public assets, not private property, is a key principle in chief programmer team operations.

Group of teams

About 100,000 lines of source code appears to be a practical maximum for a single team. Larger systems will require the extension of the organization to a group of teams.

In an approach now being tried, overall system design and development of key control code are being carried out by a single team of skilled programmer/analyst/managers under overall chief and backup programmers. When the core system is operational, some members of the original team will become chief programmers of subordinate teams developing major functional subsystems. The nucleus of the original team will complete the control coding and then become the technical monitor of the developing functional coding. That team will control all specification and design changes, and integrate the subsystems into the overall system as they evolve in a top-down fashion. As the system nears completion, programmers on the lower level teams may proceed to other assignments. Because of the original team's detailed familiarity with the entire system and the use of the tools described above, it will supervise testing and turnover of the system.

Although the techniques have been described above in the context of a chief programmer team, they need not all be applied to realize substantial benefits. Fig. 2 illustrates the relationship of the individual ideas described.

DSL's are the foundation for the entire method. They provide visibility of the developing programs and the basis for a more functional breakup of the programming process. Structured programming at the individual module level may be applied at any point in the development of a system, even during its operation as modules are rewritten to add new functions. SP requires a DSL to provide effective support for the hierarchical organization and inclusion of code as a module evolves.

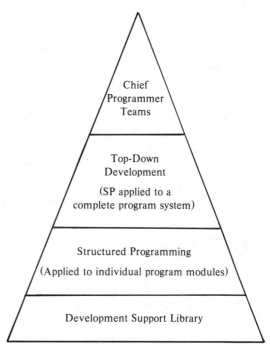

Figure 2. Techniques and their relationship.

When a complete new program system is begun, SP can be applied in a more extensive form ("top-down development") to the development sequence of the entire system. It, too, requires a DSL and presupposes SP at the module level.

A chief programmer team is designed to make the most effective use of the three programming techniques. If one applies the techniques rigorously to development of a moderately sized system, it is hard to avoid creating an organization similar if not identical to that of a team.

To institute the techniques in an existing organization, it is most practical to develop and install a DSL and to begin applying SP to new modules being written. As SP experience is gained and the support tools become familiar, an entire new program system can be developed. At this time, a chief programmer team nucleus can be established using two experienced programmers and a programming secretary familiar with SP. As the system evolves, additional programmers can be added to complete its development.

The information bank of *The New York Times* was produced under contract by a chief programmer team which specified and designed the system and developed over 83,000 lines of original high-level language source code. The task took 22 months. By today's productivity standards for systems of comparable complexity, such a task would require several times the 11 man-years of effort actually used by the team.

The information bank was developed using SP so that no integration period was required between the completion of detailed coding and delivery for acceptance testing. In other words, the integration work was completed parallel with, rather than after, unit coding. As a result of the high-precision coding techniques, the acceptance testing and subsequent system operation have been nearly error-free. For example, the file processing system (delivered one week after unit coding was completed) passed a week of acceptance tests without error, and ran 20 months until the first error was detected. In the first 13 months of operation of the on-line retrieval system, only one program error was detected that resulted in system failure. The chief and backup programmers produced code that had one detected error per man-year of effort.

Future implications

The New York Times' information bank project was a forerunner of many other internal and customer projects. These results show the possibility of a new level of manageability in programming projects through a combination of technical and organization standards. The results also show a significant decrease in error incidence and a corresponding increase in productivity, all with greater job satisfaction and less trauma in project completion.

There is a third property resulting from chief programmer team operations — harder to measure than manageability and quality, but even more important: the integrity and comprehensibility of the product for maintenance and growth. This occurs because an entirely new technical standard for design quality is enforced in structured programming systems.

At a more specific personal level, achievable targets for applications programming (as opposed to system programming — i.e., for system control programs) are 10,000 lines of source code and one error per man-year. This target includes system and program design, documentation and testing time as well as actual coding time. These targets were achieved by the principal programmers on the chief programmer team performing on the information bank project.

While *The Times* project was still under way, it became apparent that the techniques and organization were effective. Within the IBM Federal Systems Division, programmers and programming managers were trained in structured programming. Similar courses have been given in other IBM divisions, and management techniques have been developed for SP projects.

A number of projects have since begun using SP techniques, and chief programmer teams are active in many of them. Several have already been successfully completed. One of the largest was the mission simulation system used in preparation and training for Skylab operations. The software for this totalled about 400,000 lines of source code produced over a two-year period using SP techniques. Productivity was again significantly higher than that previously experienced in comparable efforts.

More remarkably, the software was delivered on the original schedule in spite of 1,200 formal changes in the requirements, coupled with cuts in manpower and computer budgets. One of the striking facts about this development was that the rate at which computer time was used remained nearly constant from the 9th to the 24th month, a consequence of the continuous integration performed as part of the top-down development process. There was no overtime peak at the end of the project. Similar results are being achieved in other projects at IBM, both for products and for internal systems.

". . . As long as there were no machines, programming was no problem at all; when we had a few weak computers, programming became a mild problem; now that we have gigantic computers, programming has become an equally gigantic problem." E.W. Dijkstra, in the 1972 Turing Award Lecture, has articulated the problem. The problem is as much one of organization as of technology, and the chief programmer team is primarily an organizational solution.

Further application and extension of the concepts could move the programming process a long way toward a true professional discipline with a recognized, standard methodology.

Bibliography

1.   Baker, F.T. "Chief Programmer Team Management of Production Programming." *IBM Systems Journal,* Vol. 11, No. 1 (January 1972), pp. 56-73.

2.   _____. "System Quality Through Structured Programming." *AFIPS Proceedings of the 1972 Fall Joint Computer Conference,* Vol. 41, Part I. Montvale, N.J.: AFIPS Press, 1972, pp. 339-44.

3.   Böhm, C., and G. Jacopini. "Flow Diagrams, Turing Machines and Languages with Only Two Formation Rules." *Communications of the ACM,* Vol. 9, No. 5 (May 1966), pp. 366-71.

4.   Dijkstra, E.W. *Notes on Structured Programming,* 2nd ed. Technische Hogeschool Eindhoven, Report No. EWD-248, 70-WSK-03. Eindhoven, The Netherlands: April 1970. See also Dahl, O.-J., E.W. Dijkstra, and C.A.R Hoare, *Structured Programming,* New York: Academic Press, 1972.

5.   _____. "The Humble Programmer" (1972 ACM Turing Award Lecture). *Communications of the ACM,* Vol. 15, No. 10 (October 1972), pp. 859-66.

6.   McHenry, R.C. *Management Concepts for Top-Down Structured Programming.* IBM Corporation, Report No. FSC 73-0001, Gaithersburg, Md.: IBM Federal Systems Division, 1973.

7.   Mills, H.D. *Mathematical Foundations for Structured Programming.* IBM Corporation, Report No. FSC 72-6012, Gaithersburg, Md.: IBM Federal Systems Division, 1972.

8.   _____. "Top-Down Programming in Large Systems." *Debugging Techniques in Large Systems,* ed. R. Rustin. Englewood Cliffs, N.J.: Prentice-Hall, 1971, pp. 41-55.

9.   Weinberg, G.M. *The Psychology of Computer Programming.* New York: Van Nostrand Reinhold, 1971.

INTRODUCTION

A number of papers were published throughout the 1960s and early 1970s on program design, most commonly with titles incorporating the phrase "modular design," or "modular programming." But Stevens, Myers, and Constantine were the first to use the term "structured design." Their paper, published in 1974, became the precursor of a number of books on the subject.*

The "Structured Design" paper does a good job of introducing the concepts of coupling, cohesion, design heuristics (span of control, scope of effect/scope of control, among others), and the graphic notations of structure charts. At the basic conceptual level, the ideas first presented in this paper have not changed in the ensuing publication of textbooks. Indeed, the primary justification for massive textbooks on structured design seems to be the need for examples and case studies. Even though the following paper is twenty-five pages long, it has few examples to illustrate concepts that, when first presented, are often completely alien to the average data processing professional.

The basic concepts and terms set forth in the paper remain valid although some changes or refinements have evolved since the paper's publication in *IBM Systems Journal.*† Myers adds such terms as "classical" cohesiveness, and "informational" cohesiveness; and Yourdon/Constantine add "procedural" cohesiveness to the original list of six that are presented in the paper.

On a practical level, it has become evident that the test for functional cohesiveness proposed in this paper (and later repeated in the various textbooks) is fraught with danger: It is altogether too easy for a designer to describe one of his modules in such a way that a bad module sounds good, or a good module sounds bad. By using

---

*See also Myers' *Reliable Software Through Composite Design* (New York: Petrocelli/Charter, 1975); his more recent *Composite/Structured Design* (New York: Van Nostrand Reinhold, 1978); and Yourdon and Constantine's *Structured Design: Fundamentals of a Discipline of Computer Program and System Design* (New York: YOURDON Press, 1975; Englewood Cliffs, N.J.: Prentice-Hall, 1979).

†For example, in both of Myers' books and in the Yourdon/Constantine text, the "levels of cohesiveness" are slightly different from those presented in this early paper.

the concepts of cohesiveness and coupling *together,* this difficulty usually can be overcome. The designer uses cohesiveness as a guiding principle when creating modules in the first place, and he uses the guidelines proposed in this paper to evaluate the cohesiveness of his modules — up to the point where the issue becomes clouded by semantics. Then he switches to an evaluation of his design based on coupling: If the design shows evidence of strong coupling, then the cohesiveness of the modules was probably low, regardless of the eloquent module description the designer may have used to convince himself (and others) that it was functionally cohesive. Unfortunately, that important relationship between cohesion and coupling is virtually ignored in this paper.

The other major weakness in the paper is its overly sketchy description of a design methodology variously referred to as "transform analysis," "source-transform-sink analysis," and "dataflow analysis." The paper introduces the concept of dataflow diagrams, but does not elaborate upon them, or give the designer any guidelines for drawing good ones. And the example used to show the transformation of a dataflow diagram into a hierarchy of modules (expressed as a HIPO diagram or a structure chart) is so trivial as to be meaningless to the average reader.

It was not until a year after this paper was published that textbooks began providing sufficient detail to fill in some of these gaps; and it was not until two years later that the emerging technology of structured analysis added a crucial element to the dataflow analysis concept — namely, that the dataflow diagram could be developed by the user and the systems analyst as part of the requirements definition phase of a project.

Yet even with these shortcomings, "Structured Design" remains an important paper — given further credibility by its publication in *IBM Systems Journal.* If you've never been exposed to structured design, hopefully the paper will whet your appetite; or if you've read some of the more recent texts, you should find it interesting to see the kind of progress that has been made since 1974.

Structured Design

Structured design is a set of proposed general program design considerations and techniques for making coding, debugging, and modification easier, faster, and less expensive by reducing complexity [1]. The major ideas are the result of nearly ten years of research by Mr. Constantine [2]. His results are presented here, but the authors do not intend to present the theory and derivation of the results in this paper. These ideas have been called *composite design* by Mr. Myers [3, 4, 5]. The authors believe these program *design* techniques are compatible with, and enhance, the *documentation* techniques of HIPO [6] and the *coding* techniques of structured programming [7].

These cost-saving techniques always need to be balanced with other constraints on the system. But the ability to produce simple, changeable programs will become increasingly important as the cost of the programmer's time continues to rise.

General considerations of structured design

Simplicity is the primary measurement recommended for evaluating alternative designs relative to reduced debugging and modification time. Simplicity can be enhanced by dividing the system into separate pieces in such a way that pieces can be considered, implemented, fixed, and changed with minimal consideration or effect on the other pieces of the system. Observability (the

ability to easily perceive how and why actions occur) is another useful consideration that can help in designing programs that can be changed easily. Consideration of the effect of reasonable changes is also valuable for evaluating alternative designs.

Mr. Constantine has observed that programs that were the easiest to implement and change were those composed of simple, independent modules.
The reason for this is that problem solving is faster and easier when the problem can be subdivided into pieces which can be considered separately. Problem
solving is hardest when all aspects of the problem must be considered simultaneously.

The term *module* is used to refer to a set of one or more contiguous program statements having a name by which other parts of the system can invoke
it and preferably having its own distinct set of variable names. Examples of
modules are PL/I procedures, FORTRAN mainlines and subprograms, and, in
general, subroutines of all types. Considerations are always with relation to the
program statements *as coded*, since it is the programmer's ability to understand
and change the *source* program that is under consideration.

While conceptually it is useful to discuss dividing whole programs into
smaller pieces, the techniques presented here are for designing simple, independent modules originally. It turns out to be difficult to divide an existing
program into separate pieces without increasing the complexity because of the
amount of overlapped code and other interrelationships that usually exist.

Graphical notation is a useful tool for structured design. Figure 1 illustrates a notation called a *structure chart* [8], in which:

1.   There are two modules, A and B.

2.   Module A *invokes* module B. B is
     subordinate to A.

3.   B receives an input parameter *X* (its
     name in module A) and returns a
     parameter *Y* (its name in module A).
     (It is useful to distinguish which cal-
     ling parameters represent data passed
     to the called program and which are
     for data to be *returned* to the caller.)

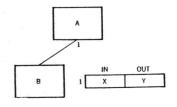

Figure 1. A structure chart.

Coupling and communication

To evaluate alternatives for dividing programs into modules, it becomes
useful to examine and evaluate types of "connections" between modules. A
connection is a reference to some label or address defined (or also defined)
elsewhere.

The fewer and simpler the connections between modules, the easier it is to understand each module without reference to other modules. Minimizing connections between modules also minimizes the paths along which changes and errors can propagate into other parts of the system, thus eliminating disastrous "ripple" effects, where changes in one part cause errors in another, necessitating additional changes elsewhere, giving rise to new errors, etc. The widely used technique of using common data areas (or global variables or modules without their own distinct set of variable names) can result in an enormous number of connections between the modules of a program. The complexity of a system is affected not only by the number of connections but by the degree to which each connection couples (associates) two modules, making them interdependent rather than independent. Coupling is the measure of the strength of association established by a connection from one module to another. Strong coupling complicates a system since a module is harder to understand, change, or correct by itself if it is highly interrelated with other modules. Complexity can be reduced by designing systems with the weakest possible coupling between modules.

The degree of coupling established by a particular connection is a function of several factors, and thus it is difficult to establish a simple index of coupling. Coupling depends (1) on how complicated the connection is, (2) on whether the connection refers to the module itself or something inside it, and (3) on what is being sent or received.

Coupling increases with increasing complexity or obscurity of the interface. Coupling is lower when the connection is to the normal module interface than when the connection is to an internal component. Coupling is lower with data connections than with control connections, which are in turn lower than hybrid connections (modification of one module's code by another module). The contribution of all these factors is summarized in Table 1.

Table 1. Contributing factors

	Interface complexity	Type of connection	Type of communication
low	simple, obvious	to module by name	data
COUPLING			control
high	complicated, obscure	to internal elements	hybrid

Interface complexity

When two or more modules interface with the same area of storage, data region, or device, they share a common environment. Examples of common environments are:

- A set of data elements with the EXTERNAL attribute that is copied into PL/I modules via an INCLUDE statement or that is found listed in each of a number of modules.

- Data elements defined in COMMON statements in FORTRAN modules.

- A centrally located "control block" or set of control blocks.

- A common overlay region of memory.

- Global variable names defined over an entire program or section.

The most important structural characteristic of a common environment is that it couples every module sharing it to every other such module without regard to their functional relationship or its absence. For example, only the two modules XVECTOR and VELOC might actually make use of data element X in an "included" common environment of PL/I, yet changing the length of X impacts *every* module making any use of the common environment, and thus necessitates recompilation.

Every element in the common environment, whether used by particular modules or not, constitutes a separate path along which errors and changes can propagate. Each element in the common environment adds to the complexity of the total system to be comprehended by an amount representing all possible pairs of modules sharing that environment. Changes to, and new uses of, the common area potentially impact all modules in unpredictable ways. Data references may become unplanned, uncontrolled, and even unknown.

A module interfacing with a common environment for some of its input or output data is, on the average, more difficult to use in varying contexts or from a variety of places or in different programs than is a module with communication restricted to parameters in calling sequences. It is somewhat clumsier to establish a new and unique data context on each call of a module when data passage is via a common environment. Without analysis of the entire set of sharing modules or careful saving and restoration of values, a new use is likely to interfere with other uses of the common environment and propagate errors into other modules. As to future growth of a given system, once the commitment is made to communication via a common environment, any new module will have to be plugged into the common environment, compounding the total complexity even more. On this point, Belady and Lehman [9], observe that "a well-structured system, one in which communication is via passed parameters through defined interfaces, is likely to be more growable and require less effort to maintain than one making extensive use of global or shared variables."

The impact of common environments on system complexity may be quantified. Among M objects there are $M(M-1)$ ordered pairs of objects. (Ordered pairs are of interest because A and B sharing a common environment complicates both, A being coupled to B and B being coupled to A.) Thus a common environment of N elements shared by M modules results in $NM(M-1)$ first order (one level) relationships or paths along which changes and errors can propagate. This means 150 such paths in a FORTRAN program of only three modules sharing the COMMON area with just 25 variables in it.

It is possible to minimize these disadvantages of common environments by limiting access to the smallest possible subset of modules. If the total set of potentially shared elements is subdivided into groups, all of which are *required* by some subset of modules, then both the size of each common environment and the scope of modules among which it is shared is reduced. Using "named" rather than "blank" COMMON in FORTRAN is one means of accomplishing this end.

The complexity of an interface is a matter of how much information is needed to state or to understand the connection. Thus, obvious relationships result in lower coupling than obscure or inferred ones. The more syntactic units (such as parameters) in the statement of a connection, the higher the coupling. Thus, extraneous elements irrelevant to the programmer's and the modules' immediate task increase coupling unnecessarily.

Type of connection

Connections that address or refer to a module as a whole by its name (leaving its contents unknown and irrelevant) yield lower coupling than connections referring to the internal elements of another module. In the latter case, as for example the use of a variable by direct reference from within some other module, the entire content of that module may have to be taken into account to correct an error or make a change so that it does not make an impact in some unexpected way. Modules that can be used easily without knowing anything about their insides make for simpler systems.

Consider the case depicted in Figure 2. GETCOMM is a module whose function is getting the next command from a terminal. In performing this function, GETCOMM calls the module READT, whose function is to read a line from the terminal. READT requires the address of the terminal. It gets this via an externally declared data element in GETCOMM, called TERMADDR. READT passes the line back to GETCOMM as an argument called LINE. Note the arrow extending from *inside* GETCOMM to *inside* READT. An arrow of this type is the notation for references to internal data elements of another module.

Now, suppose we wish to add a module called GETDATA, whose function is to get the next data line (i.e., not a command) from a (possibly) different terminal. It would be desirable to use module READT as a subroutine of GET-DATA. But if GETDATA modifies TERMADDR in GETCOMM before calling READT, it will cause GETCOMM to fail since it will "get" from the wrong terminal. Even if GETDATA restores TERMADDR after use, the error can still occur if GETDATA and GETCOMM can ever be invoked "simultaneously" in a multiprogramming environment. READT would have been more usable if TERMADDR had been made an input argument to READT instead of an externally declared data item as shown in Figure 3. This simple example shows how references to internal elements of other modules can have an adverse effect on program modification, both in terms of cost and potential bugs.

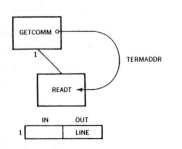

Figure 2. Module connections.

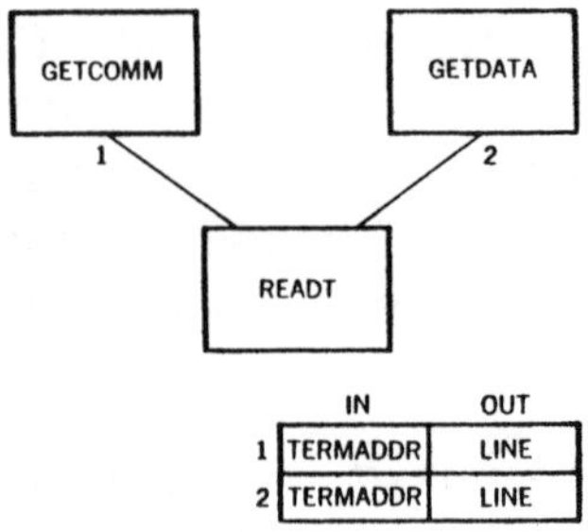

Figure 3. Improved module connections.

Type of communication

Modules must at least pass data or they cannot functionally be a part of a single system. Thus connections that pass data are a necessary minimum. (Not so the communication of control. In principle, the presence or absence of requisite input data is sufficient to define the circumstances under which a module should be activated, that is, receive control. Thus the explicit passing of control by one module to another constitutes an additional, theoretically inessential form of coupling. In practice, systems that are *purely* data-coupled require special language and operating system support but have numerous attractions, not the least of which is they can be fundamentally simpler than any equivalent system with control coupling [10].)

Beyond the practical, innocuous, minimum control coupling of normal subroutine calls is the practice of passing an "element of control" such as a switch, flag, or signal from one module to another. Such a connection affects the execution of another module and not merely the data it performs its task upon by involving one module in the internal processing of some other module. Control arguments are an additional complication to the essential data arguments required for performance of some task, and an alternative structure that eliminates the complication always exists.

Consider the modules in Figure 4 that are control-coupled by the switch PARSE through which EXECNCOMM instructs GETCOMM whether to return a parsed or unparsed command.   Separating the two distinct functions of GETCOMM results in a structure that is simpler as shown in Figure 5.

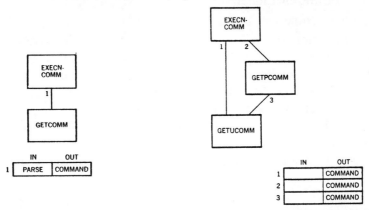

Figure 4. **Control-coupled modules.**   Figure 5. **Simplified coupling.**

The new EXECNCOMM is no more complicated; where once it set a switch and called, now it has two alternate calls.   The sum of GETPCOMM and GETUCOMM is (functionally) less complicated than GETCOMM was (by the amount of the switch testing).   And the two small modules are likely to be easier to comprehend than the one large one.   Admittedly, the immediate gains here may appear marginal, but they rise with time and the number of alternatives in the switch and the number of levels over which it is passed.   Control coupling, where a called module "tells" its caller what to do, is a more severe form of coupling.

Modification of one module's code by another module may be thought of as a hybrid of data and control elements since the code is dealt with as data by the modifying module, while it acts as control to the modified module.   The target module is very dependent in its behavior on the modifying module, and the latter is intimately involved in the other's internal functioning.

Cohesiveness

Coupling is reduced when the relationships among elements *not* in the same module are minimized.   There are two ways of achieving this — minimizing the relationships among modules and maximizing relationships among elements in the same module.   In practice, both ways are used.

The second method is the subject of this section.   "Element" in this sense means any form of a "piece" of the module, such as a statement, a segment, or a "subfunction."   Binding is the measure of the cohesiveness of a module.   The objective here is to reduce coupling by striving for high binding. The scale of cohesiveness, from lowest to highest, follows:

1. Coincidental.
2. Logical.
3. Temporal.
4. Communicational.
5. Sequential.
6. Functional.

The scale is not linear. Functional binding is much stronger than all the rest, and the first two are much weaker than all the rest. Also, higher-level binding classifications often include all the characteristics of one or more classifications below it *plus* additional relationships. The binding between two elements is the highest classification that applies. We will define each type of binding, give an example, and try to indicate why it is found at its particular position on the scale.

Coincidental binding

When there is no meaningful relationship among the elements in a module, we have coincidental binding. Coincidental binding might result from either of the following situations: (1) An existing program is "modularized" by splitting it apart into modules. (2) Modules are created to consolidate "duplicate coding" in other modules.

As an example of the difficulty that can result from coincidental binding, suppose the following sequence of instructions appeared several times in a module or in several modules and was put into a separate module called X:

```
A = B + C
GET CARD
PUT OUTPUT
IF B = 4, THEN E = 0
```

Module X would probably be coincidentally bound since these four instructions have no apparent relationships among one another. Suppose in the future we have a need in one of the modules originally containing these instructions to say GET TAPERECORD instead of GET CARD. We now have a problem. If we modify the instruction in module X, it is unusable to all of the other callers of X. It may even be difficult to *find* all of the other callers of X in order to make any other compatible change.

It is only fair to admit that, independent of a module's cohesiveness, there are instances when any module can be modified in such a fashion to make it unusable to all its callers. However, the *probability* of this happening is very high if the module is coincidentally bound.

Logical binding

Logical binding, next on the scale, implies some logical relationship between the elements of a module. Examples are a module that performs all input and output operations for the program or a module that edits all data.

The logically bound, EDIT ALL DATA module is often implemented as follows. Assume the data elements to be edited are master file records, updates, deletions, and additions. Parameters passed to the module would include the data and a special parameter indicating the type of data. The first instruction in the module is probably a four-way branch, going to four sections of code — edit master record, edit update record, edit addition record, and edit deletion record.

Often, these four functions are also intertwined in some way in the module. If the deletion record changes and requires a change to the edit deletion record function, we will have a problem if this function is intertwined with the other three. If the edits are truly independent, then the system could be simplified by putting each edit in a separate module and eliminating the need to decide which edit to do for each execution. In short, logical binding usually results in tricky or shared code, which is difficult to modify, and in the passing of unnecessary parameters.

Temporal binding

Temporal binding is the same as logical binding, except the elements are also related in time. That is, the temporally bound elements are executed in the same time period.

The best examples of modules in this class are the traditional "initialization," "termination," "housekeeping," and "clean-up" modules. Elements in an initialization module are logically bound because initialization represents a logical class of functions. In addition, these elements are related in time (i.e., at initialization time).

Modules with temporal binding tend to exhibit the disadvantages of logically bound modules. However, temporally bound modules are higher on the scale since they tend to be simpler for the reason that *all* of the elements are executable at one time (i.e., no parameters and logic to determine which element to execute).

Communicational binding

A module with communicational binding has elements that are related by a reference to the same set of input and/or output data. For example, "print and punch the output file" is communicationally bound. Communicational binding is higher on the scale than temporal binding since the elements in a module with communicational binding have the stronger "bond" of referring to the same data.

Sequential binding

When the output data from an element is the input for the next element, the module is sequentially bound. Sequential binding can result from flow-charting the problem to be solved and then defining modules to represent one or more blocks in the flowchart. For example, "read next transaction and up-date master file" is sequentially bound.

Sequential binding, although high on the scale because of a close relationship to the problem structure, is still far from the maximum — functional binding. The reason is that the procedural processes in a program are usually distinct from the *functions* in a program. Hence, a sequentially bound module can contain several functions or just part of a function. This usually results in higher coupling and modules that are less likely to be usable from other parts of the system.

Functional binding

Functional binding is the strongest type of binding. In a functionally bound module, all of the elements are related to the performance of a single function.

A question that often arises at this point is what is a function? In mathematics, $Y = F(X)$ is read "Y is a function F of X." The function F defines a transformation or mapping of the independent (or input) variable X into the dependent (or return) variable Y. Hence, a function describes a transformation from some input data to some return data. In terms of programming, we broaden this definition to allow functions with no input data and functions with no return data.

In practice, the above definition does not clearly describe a functionally bound module. One hint is that if the elements of the module all contribute to accomplishing a single goal, then it is probably functionally bound. Examples of functionally bound modules are "Compute Square Root" (input and return parameters), "Obtain Random Number" (no input parameter), and "Write Record to Output File" (no return parameter).

A useful technique in determining whether a module is functionally bound is writing a sentence describing the function (purpose) of the module, and then examining the sentence. The following tests can be made:

1. If the sentence *has* to be a compound sentence, contain a comma, or contain more than one verb, the module is probably performing more than one function; therefore, it probably has sequential or communicational binding.

2. If the sentence contains words relating to time, such as "first," "next," "then," "after," "when," "start," etc., then the module probably has sequential or temporal binding.

3. If the predicate of the sentence doesn't contain a single specific object following the verb, the module is probably logically bound. For example, Edit All Data has logical binding; Edit Source Statement may have functional binding.

4. Words such as "initialize," "clean-up," etc., imply temporal binding.

Functionally bound modules *can* always be described by way of their elements using a compound sentence. But if the above language is unavoidable while still completely describing the module's function, then the module is probably not functionally bound.

One unresolved problem is deciding how far to divide functionally bound subfunctions. The division has probably gone far enough if each module contains no subset of elements that could be useful alone, and if each module is small enough that its entire implementation can be grasped all at once, i.e., seldom longer than one or two pages of source code.

Observe that a module can include more than one type of binding. The binding between two elements is the highest that can be applied. The binding of a module is lowered by every element pair that does not exhibit functional binding.

Predictable modules

A predictable, or well-behaved, module is one that, when given the identical inputs, operates identically each time it is called. Also, a well-behaved module operates independently of its environment.

To show that dependable (free from errors) modules can still be unpredictable, consider an oscillator module that returns zero and one alternately and dependably when it is called. It might be used to facilitate double buffering. Should it have multiple users, each would be required to call it an even number of times before relinquishing control. Should any of the users have an error that prevented an even number of calls, all other users will fail. The operation of the module given the same inputs is not constant, resulting in the module not being predictable even though error-free. Modules that keep track of their own state are usually not predictable, even when error-free.

This characteristic of predictability that can be designed into modules is what we might loosely call "black-boxness." That is, the user can understand what the module does and use it without knowing what is inside it. Module "black-boxness" can even be enhanced by merely adding comments that make the module's function and use clear. Also, a descriptive name and a well-defined and visible interface enhance a module's usability and thus make it more of a black box.

Tradeoffs to structured design

The overhead involved in writing many simple modules is in the execution time and memory space used by a particular language to effect the call. The designer should realize the adverse effect on maintenance and debugging that may result from striving just for minimum execution time and/or memory. He should also remember that programmer cost, is, or is rapidly becoming, the major cost of a programming system and that much of the maintenance will be in the future when the trend will be even more prominent. However, depending on the actual overhead of the language being used, it is very possible that a structured design can result in less execution and/or memory overhead rather than more due to the following considerations:

For memory overhead

1. Optional (error) modules may never be called into memory.

2. Structured design reduces duplicate code and the coding necessary for implementing control switches, thus reducing the amount of programmer-generated code.

3. Overlay structuring can be based on actual operating characteristics obtained by running and observing the program.

4. Having many single-function modules allows more flexible, and precise, grouping, possibly resulting in less memory needed at any one time under overlay or virtual storage constraints.

For execution overhead

1. Some modules may only execute a few times.

2. Optional (error) functions may never be called, resulting in zero overhead.

3. Code for control switches is reduced or eliminated, reducing the total amount of code to be executed.

4. Heavily used linkage can be recompiled and calls replaced by branches.

5. "Includes" or "performs" can be used in place of calls. (However, the complexity of the system will increase by at least the extra consideration necessary to prevent duplicating data names and by the difficulty of creating the equivalent of call parameters for a well-defined interface.)

6. One way to get fast execution is to determine which parts of the system will be most used so all optimizing time can be spent on those parts. Implementing an initially structured design allows the testing of a working program for those critical

modules (and yields a working program prior to any time spent optimizing). Those modules can then be optimized separately and reintegrated without introducing multitudes of errors into the rest of the program.

Structured design techniques

It is possible to divide the design process into general program design and detailed design as follows. General program design is deciding *what* functions are needed for the program (or programming system). Detailed design is *how* to implement the functions. The considerations above and techniques that follow result in an identification of the functions, calling parameters, and the call relationships for a structure of functionally bound, simply connected modules. The information thus generated makes it easier for each module to then be separately designed, implemented, and tested.

Structure charts

The objective of general program design is to determine what functions, calling parameters, and call relationships are needed. Since flowcharts depict *when* (in what order and under what conditions) blocks are executed, flowcharts unnecessarily complicate the general program design phase. A more useful notation is the structure chart, as described earlier and as shown in Figure 6.

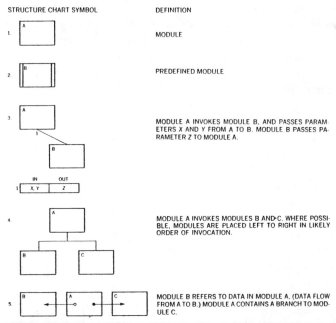

STRUCTURE CHART SYMBOL   DEFINITION

1. MODULE

2. PREDEFINED MODULE

3. MODULE A INVOKES MODULE B, AND PASSES PARAMETERS X AND Y FROM A TO B. MODULE B PASSES PARAMETER Z TO MODULE A.

4. MODULE A INVOKES MODULES B AND C. WHERE POSSIBLE, MODULES ARE PLACED LEFT TO RIGHT IN LIKELY ORDER OF INVOCATION.

5. MODULE B REFERS TO DATA IN MODULE A. (DATA FLOW FROM A TO B.) MODULE A CONTAINS A BRANCH TO MODULE C.

THE MORE COMPREHENSIVE "PROPOSED STANDARD GRAPHICS FOR PROGRAM STRUCTURE," PREFERRED BY MR. CONSTANTINE AND WIDELY USED OVER THE PAST SIX YEARS BY HIS CLASSES AND CLIENTS, USES SEPARATE ARROWS FOR EACH CONNECTION, SUCH AS FOR THE CALLS FROM A TO B AND FROM A TO C, TO REFLECT STRUCTURAL PROPERTIES OF THE PROGRAM. THE CHARTING SHOWN HERE WAS ADOPTED FOR COMPATIBILITY WITH THE HIERARCHY CHART OF HIPO.

Figure 6. Definitions of symbols used in structure charts.

To contrast a structure chart and a flowchart, consider the following for the same three modules in Figure 7 — A which calls B which calls C (coding has been added to the structure chart to enable the proper flowchart to be determined; B's code will be executed first, then C's, then A's). To design A's interfaces properly, it is necessary to know that A is responsible for invoking B, but this is hard to determine from the flowchart. In addition, the structure chart can show the module connections and calling parameters that are central to the consideration and techniques being presented here.

The other major difference that drastically simplifies the notation and analysis during general program design is the absence in structure charts of the decision block. Conditional calls can be so noted, but "decision designing" can be deferred until detailed module design. This is an example of where the *design* process is made simpler by having to consider only part of the design problem. Structure charts are also small enough to be worked on all at once by the designers, helping to prevent suboptimizing parts of the program at the expense of the entire problem.

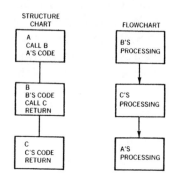

Figure 7. Structure chart compared to flowchart.

Common structures

A shortcut for arriving at simple structures is to know the general form of the result. Mr. Constantine observed that programs of the general structure in Figure 8 resulted in the lowest-cost implementations. It implements the input-process-output type of program, which applies to most programs, even if the "input" or "output" is to secondary storage or to memory.

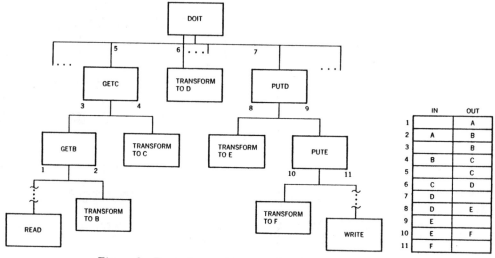

Figure 8. Basic form of low-cost implementation.

In practice, the sink leg is often shorter than the source one. Also, source modules may produce output (e.g., error messages) and sink modules may request input (e.g., execution-time format commands).

Another structure useful for implementing parts of a design is the transaction structure depicted in Figure 9. A "transaction" here is any event, record, or input, etc., for which various actions should result. For example, a command processor has this structure. The structure may occur alone or as one or more of the source (or even sink) modules of an input-process-output structure. Analysis of the transaction modules follows that of a transform module, which is explained later.

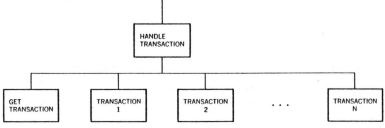

Figure 9. Transaction structure.

Designing the structure

The following procedure can be used to arrive at the input-process-output general structure shown previously.

Step One. The first step is to sketch (or mentally consider) a functional picture of the problem. As an example, consider a simulation system. The rough structure of this problem is shown in Figure 10.

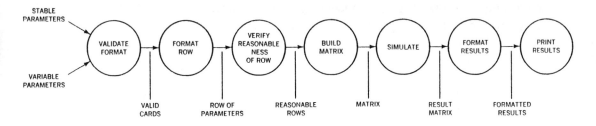

Figure 10. Rough structure of simulation system.

Step Two. Identify the external conceptual streams of data. An *external* stream of data is one that is external to the system. A *conceptual* stream of data is a stream of related data that is independent of any physical I/O device. For instance, we may have several conceptual streams coming from one I/O device or one stream coming from several I/O devices. In our simulation system, the external conceptual streams are the input parameters, and the formatted simulation the result.

Step Three. Identify the *major* external conceptual stream of data (both input and output) in the problem. Then, using the diagram of the problem structure, determine, for this stream, the points of "highest abstraction," as in Figure 11.

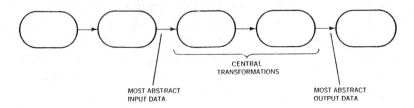

CENTRAL
TRANSFORMATIONS

MOST ABSTRACT
INPUT DATA

MOST ABSTRACT
OUTPUT DATA

Figure 11. Determining points of highest abstraction.

The "point of highest abstraction" for an input stream of data is the point in the problem structure where that data is farthest removed from its physical input form yet can still be viewed as coming in. Hence, in the simulation system, the most abstract form of the input transaction stream might be the built matrix. Similarly, identify the point where the data stream can first be viewed as going out — in the example, possibly the result matrix.

Admittedly, this is a subjective step. However, experience has shown that designers trained in the technique seldom differ by more than one or two blocks in their answers to the above.

Step Four. Design the structure in Figure 12 from the previous information with a source module for each conceptual input stream which exists at the point of most abstract input data; do sink modules similarly. Often only single source and sink branches are necessary. The parameters passed are dependent on the problem, but the general pattern is shown in Figure 12.

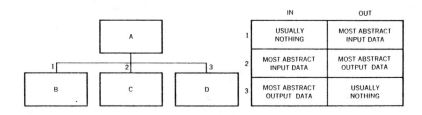

	IN	OUT
1	USUALLY NOTHING	MOST ABSTRACT INPUT DATA
2	MOST ABSTRACT INPUT DATA	MOST ABSTRACT OUTPUT DATA
3	MOST ABSTRACT OUTPUT DATA	USUALLY NOTHING

Figure 12. The top level.

Describe the function of each module with a short, concise, and specific phrase. Describe what transformations occur when that module is called, not how the module is implemented. Evaluate the phrase relative to functional binding.

When module A is called, the program or system executes. Hence, the function of module A is equivalent to the problem being solved. If the problem is "write a FORTRAN compiler," then the function of module A is "compile FORTRAN program."

Module B's function involves obtaining the major stream of data. An example of a "typical module B" is "get next valid source statement in Polish form."

Module C's purpose is to transform the major input stream into the major output stream. Its function should be a nonprocedural description of this transformation. Examples are "convert Polish form statement to machine language statement" or "using key-word list, search abstract file for matching abstracts."

Module D's purpose is disposing of the major output stream. Examples are "produce report" or "display results of simulation."

Step Five. For each source module, identify the last transformation necessary to produce the form being returned by that module. Then identify the form of the input just prior to the last transformation. For sink modules, identify the first process necessary to get closer to the desired output and the resulting output form. This results in the portions of the structure shown in Figure 13.

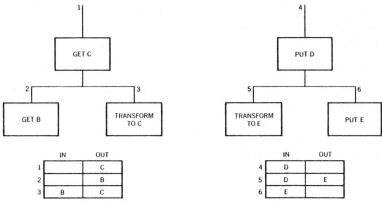

Figure 13. Lower levels.

Repeat Step Five on the new source and sink modules until the original source and final sink modules are reached. The modules may be analyzed in any order, but each module should be done completely before doing any of its subordinates. There are, unfortunately, no detailed guidelines available for dividing the transform modules. Use binding and coupling considerations, size (about one page of source), and usefulness (are there subfunctions that could be useful elsewhere now or in the future) as guidelines on how far to divide.

During this phase, err on the side of dividing too finely. It is always easy to recombine later in the design, but duplicate functions may not be identified if the dividing is too conservative at this point.

Design guidelines

The following concepts are useful for achieving simple designs and for improving the "first-pass" structures.

Match program to problem

One of the most useful techniques for reducing the effect of changes on the program is to make the structure of the design match the structure of the problem, that is, form should follow function. For example, consider a module that dials a telephone and a module that receives data. If receiving immediately follows dialing, one might arrive at design A as shown in Figure 14. Consider, however, whether receiving is part of dialing. Since it is not (usually), have DIAL's caller invoke RECEIVE as in design B.

If, in this example, design A were used, consider the effect of a new requirement to transmit immediately after dialing. The DIAL module receives first and cannot be used, or a switch must be passed, or another DIAL module has to be added.

To the extent that the design structure does match the problem structure, changes to single parts of the problem result in changes to single modules.

Scopes of effect and control

The *scope of control* of a module is that module plus all modules that are ultimately subordinate to that module. In the example of Figure 15, the scope of control of B is B, D, and E. The *scope of effect* of a decision is the set of all modules that contain some code whose execution is based upon the outcome of the decision. The system is simpler when the scope of effect of a decision is in the scope of control of the module containing the decision. The following example illustrates why.

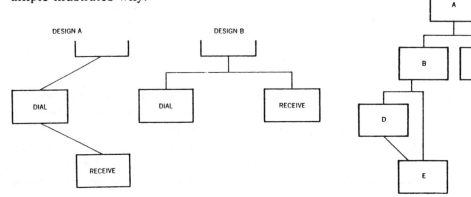

Figure 14. Design form should follow function.   **Figure 15. Scope of control.**

If the execution of some code in A is dependent on the outcome of decision X in module B, then either B will have to return a flag to A or the decision will have to be repeated in A. The former approach results in added coding to implement the flag, and the latter results in some of B's function (decision X) in module A. Duplicates of decision X result in difficulties coordinating changes to both copies whenever decision X must be changed.

The scope of effect can be brought within the scope of control either by moving the decision element "up" in the structure, or by taking those modules that are in the scope of effect but not in the scope of control and moving them so that they fall within the scope of control.

Module size

Size can be used as a signal to look for *potential* problems. Look carefully at modules with less than five or more than 100 executable source statements. Modules with a small number of statements may not perform an entire function, hence, may not have functional binding. Very small modules can be eliminated by placing their statements in the calling modules. Large modules may include more than one function. A second problem with large modules is understandability and readability. There is evidence to the fact that a group of about 30 statements is the upper limit of what can be mastered on the first reading of a module listing [11].

Error and end-of-file

Often, part of a module's function is to notify its caller when it cannot perform its function. This is accomplished with a return error parameter (preferably binary only). A module that handles streams of data must be able to signal end-of-file (EOF), preferably also with a binary parameter. These parameters should not, however, tell the caller what to do about the error or EOF. Nevertheless, the system can be made simpler if modules can be designed without the need for error flags.

Initialization

Similarly, many modules require some initialization to be done. An initialize module will suffer from low binding but sometimes is the simplest solution. It may, however, be possible to eliminate the need for initializing without compromising "black-boxness" (the same inputs *always* produce the same outputs). For example, a read module that detects a return error of file-not-opened from the access method and recovers by opening the file and rereading eliminates the need for initialization without maintaining an internal state.

Selecting modules

Eliminate duplicate functions but not duplicate code. When a function changes, it is a great advantage to only have to change it in one place. But if a module's need for its own copy of a random collection of code changes slightly, it will not be necessary to change several other modules as well.

If a module seems almost, but not quite, useful from a second place in the system, try to identify and isolate the useful subfunction. The remainder of the module might be incorporated in its original caller.

Check modules that have many callers or that call many other modules. While not always a problem, it may indicate missing levels or modules.

Isolate specifications

Isolate all dependencies on a particular data-type, record-layout, index-structure, etc., in one or a minimum of modules. This minimizes the recoding necessary should that particular specification change.

Reduce parameters

Look for ways to reduce the number of parameters passed between modules. Count every item passed as a separate parameter for this objective (independent of how it will be implemented). Do not pass whole records from module to module, but pass only the field or fields necessary for each module to accomplish its function. Otherwise, all modules will have to change if one field expands, rather than only those which directly used that field. Passing only the data being processed by the program system with necessary error and EOF parameters is the ultimate objective. Check binary switches for indications of scope-of-effect/scope-of-control inversions.

Have the designers work together and with the complete structure chart. If branches of the chart are worked on separately, common modules may be missed and incompatibilities result from design decisions made while only considering one branch.

An example

The following example illustrates the use of structured design:

A patient-monitoring program is required for a hospital. Each patient is monitored by an analog device which measures factors such as pulse, temperature, blood pressure, and skin resistance. The program reads these factors on a periodic basis (specified for each patient) and stores these factors in a data base. For each patient, safe ranges for each factor are specified (e.g., patient X's valid temperature range is 98 to 99.5 degrees Fahrenheit). If a factor falls outside of a patient's safe range, or if an analog device fails, the nurse's station is notified.

In a real-life case, the problem statement would contain much more detail. However, this one is of sufficient detail to allow us to design the structure of the program.

The first step is to outline the structure of the problem as shown in Figure 16. In the second step, we identify the external conceptual streams of data. In this case, two streams are present, factors from the analog device and warnings to the nurse. These also represent the major input and output streams.

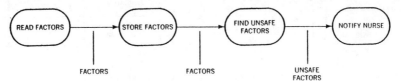

Figure 16. Outline of problem structure.

Figure 17 indicates the point of highest abstraction of the input stream, which is the point at which a patient's factors are in the form to store in the data base. The point of highest abstraction of the output stream is a list of unsafe factors (if any). We can now begin to design the program's structure as in Figure 18.

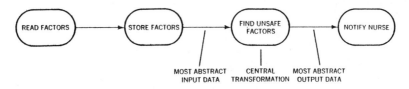

Figure 17. Points of highest abstraction.

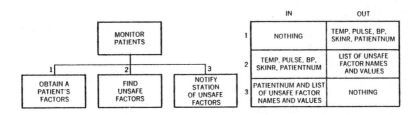

Figure 18. Structure of the top level.

In analyzing the module "OBTAIN A PATIENT'S FACTORS," we can deduce from the problem statement that this function has three parts: (1) Determine which patient to monitor next (based on their specified periodic intervals). (2) Read the analog device. (3) Record the factors in the data base. Hence, we arrive at the structure in Figure 19. (NOTVAL is set if a valid set of factors was not available.)

Further analysis of "READ VALID SET OF FACTORS," "FIND UNSAFE FACTORS," and "NOTIFY STATION OF UNSAFE FACTORS" yields the results shown in the complete structure chart in Figure 20.

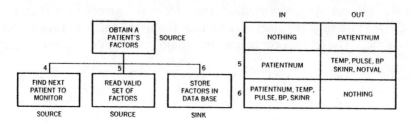

Figure 19. Structure of next level.

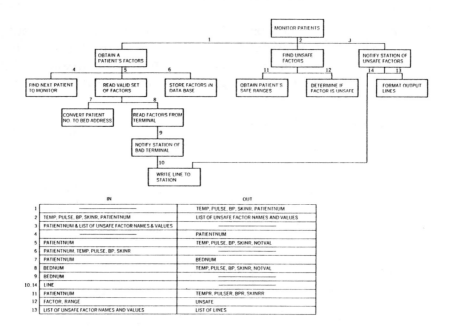

Figure 20. Complete structure chart.

Note that the module "READ FACTORS FROM TERMINAL" contains a decision asking "did we successfully read from the terminal?" If the read was not successful, we have to notify the nurse's station and then find the next patient to process as depicted in Figure 21.

Modules in the scope of effect of this decision are marked with an X. Note that the scope of effect is *not* a subset of the scope of control. To correct this problem, we have to take two steps. First, we will move the decision up to "READ VALID SET OF FACTORS." We do this by merging "READ FACTORS FROM TERMINAL" into its calling module. We now make "FIND NEXT PATIENT TO MONITOR" a subordinate of "READ VALID SET OF FACTORS." Hence, we have the structure in Figure 22. Thus, by slightly altering the structure and the function of a few modules, we have completely eliminated the problem.

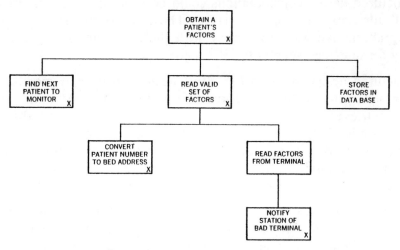

Figure 21. Structure as designed.

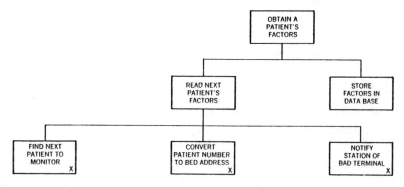

Figure 22. Scope of effect within scope of control.

Concluding remarks

The HIPO Hierarchy chart is being used as an aid during general systems design. The considerations and techniques presented here are useful for evaluating alternatives for those portions of the system that will be programmed on a computer. The charting technique used here depicts more details about the interfaces than the HIPO Hierarchy chart. This facilitates consideration during general program design of each individual connection and its associated passed parameters. The resulting design can be documented with the HIPO charts. (If the designer decides to have more than one function in any module, the structure chart should show them in the same block. However, the HIPO Hierarchy chart would still show all the functions in separate blocks.) The output of the general program design is the input for the detailed module design. The HIPO input-process-output chart is useful for describing and designing each module.

Structured design considerations could be used to review program designs in a walk-through environment [12]. These concepts are also useful for evaluating alternative ways to comply with the requirement of structured programming for one-page segments [7].

Structured design reduces the effort needed to fix and modify programs. If all programs were written in a form where there was one module, for example, which retrieved a record from the master file given the key, then changing operating systems, file access techniques, file blocking, or I/O devices would be greatly simplified. And if *all* programs in the installation retrieved from a given file with the same module, then one properly rewritten module would have *all* the installation's programs working with the new constraints for that file.

However, there are other advantages. Original errors are reduced when the problem at hand is simpler. Each module is self-contained and to some extent may be programmed independently of the others in location, programmer, time, and language. Modules can be tested before all programming is done by supplying simple "stub" modules that merely return preformatted results rather than calculating them. Modules critical to memory or execution overhead can be optimized separately and reintegrated with little or no impact. An entry or return trace-module becomes very feasible, yielding a very useful debugging tool.

Independent of all the advantages previously mentioned, structured design would *still* be valuable to solve the following problem alone. Programming can be considered as an art where each programmer usually starts with a blank canvas — techniques, yes, but still a blank canvas. Previous coding is often not used because previous modules usually contain, for example, *at least* GET and EDIT. If the EDIT is not the one needed, the GET will have to be recoded also.

Programming can be brought closer to a science where current work is built on the results of earlier work. Once a module is written to get a record from the master file given a key, it can be used by all users of the file and need not be rewritten into each succeeding program. Once a module has been written to do a table search, anyone can use it. And, as the module library grows, less and less new code needs to be written to implement increasingly sophisticated systems.

Structured design concepts are not new. The whole assembly-line idea is one of isolating simple functions in a way that still produces a complete, complex result. Circuits are designed by connecting isolatable, functional stages together, not by designing one big, interrelated circuit. Page numbering is being increasingly sectionalized (e.g., 4-101) to minimize the "connections" between written sections, so that expanding one section does not require renumbering other sections. Automobile manufacturers, who have the most to gain from shared system elements, finally abandoned even the coupling of the windshield wipers to the engine vacuum due to effects of the engine load on the performance of the wiping function. Most other industries know well the advantage of isolating functions.

It is becoming increasingly important to the data-processing industry to be able to produce more programming systems and produce them with fewer errors, at a faster rate, and in a way that modifications can be accomplished easily and quickly. Structured design considerations can help achieve this goal.

References

1. This method has not been submitted to any formal IBM test. Potential users should evaluate its usefulness in their own environment prior to implementation.

2. E. Yourdon and L.L. Constantine, *Structured Design: Fundamentals of a Discipline of Computer Program and System Design* (Englewood Cliffs, N.J.: Prentice-Hall, 1979). (1979 edition of YOURDON Press' 1975 text)

3. G.J. Myers, *Composite Design: The Design of Modular Programs*, IBM Corporation, Technical Report No. TR00.2406 (Poughkeepsie, N.Y.: January 29, 1973).

4. _____, "Characteristics of Composite Design," *Datamation,* Vol. 19, No. 9 (September 1973), pp. 100-102.

5. _____, *Reliable Software Through Composite Design* (New York: Petrocelli/Charter, 1975).

6. *HIPO — Hierarchical Input-Process-Output Documentation Technique.* Audio Education Package, Form No. SR20-9413, available through any IBM Branch Office.

7. F.T. Baker, "Chief Programmer Team Management of Production Programming," *IBM Systems Journal,* Vol. 11, No. 1 (1972), pp. 56-73.

8. The use of the HIPO Hierarchy charting format is further illustrated in Figure 6, and its use in this paper was initiated by R. Ballow of the IBM Programming Productivity Techniques Department.

9. L.A. Belady and M.M. Lehman, *Programming System Dynamics or the Metadynamics of Systems in Maintenance and Growth,* IBM Corporation, Report No. RC 3546 (Yorktown Heights, N.Y.: IBM Thomas J. Watson Research Center, 1971).

10. L.L. Constantine, "Control of Sequence and Parallelism in Modular Programs," *AFIPS Proceedings of the 1968 Spring Joint Computer Conference,* Vol. 32 (Montvale, N.J.: AFIPS Press, 1968), p. 409.

11. G.M. Weinberg, *PL/I Programming: A Manual of Style* (New York: McGraw-Hill, 1970).

12. *Improved Programming Technologies: Management Overview,* IBM Corporation (White Plains, N.Y.: Data Processing Division, August 1973).

INTRODUCTION

The following paper by Kernighan and Plauger is one of three chosen from the December 1974 issue of *ACM Computing Surveys.* It's considerably shorter and less theoretical than the companion papers by Knuth [Paper 20] and Wirth [Paper 13]; indeed, it's less theoretical and more down to earth than most of the papers in this book! For that reason, many readers will view it as a breath of fresh air, and will rejoice at the presence of *real* FORTRAN examples and *real* PL/I examples.

The paper is largely excerpted from Kernighan and Plauger's first book, *The Elements of Programming Style,* providing a nice, concise, 21-page summary that you can read in less than an hour. One of the themes of this paper is that structured programming is, in a sense, a secondary issue; the primary concern of programming, according to the authors, is *style.* The elements of programming style consist of such things as *expression* (organizing individual statements so that they read clearly), *structure* (organizing larger blocks of code so that the program "hangs together"), *robustness* (writing code that can "defend itself against bad data from the outside world"), and, finally, *efficiency.*

As I've said, there are examples to illustrate these elements of programming style — examples that are "real," from the kind of programs that one would expect to find in an actual scientific or business-oriented EDP shop. Indeed, the examples *are* real, but in a very special sense: Kernighan and Plauger have taken all of their examples verbatim from other programming textbooks. Although the examples don't include any COBOL or assembler code, the enterprising reader can generalize from the FORTRAN examples so as to apply the lessons to his own work.

There is one other theme in this paper, one that I think is particularly important in these days of elegant programming languages like ALGOL and PASCAL. Rather than trying to restate Kernighan and Plauger's point, let me quote them directly:

". . . many people try to excuse badly written programs by blaming inadequacies of the language that must be used. We have seen repeatedly that even Fortran can be tamed with proper discipline. The presence of bad features is not an invitation to use them, nor is the absence of good features an excuse to avoid simulating them as cleanly as possible. Good languages are nice, but not vital."

FORTRAN and COBOL programmers, take heed!

Programming Style: Examples and Counterexamples

I. Introduction

Five or ten years ago, if you had asked someone what good programming style was, you would likely have received (if you didn't get a blank stare) a lecture on

1) how to save microseconds.

2) how to save words of memory.

3) how to draw neat flowcharts.

4) how many comments to write per line of code.

But our outlook has changed in the last few years. E.W. Dijkstra [1] argues that programming is a job for skilled professionals, not clever puzzle solvers. While attempting to prove the correctness of programs, he found that some coding practices were so difficult to understand that they were best avoided. His now famous letter, "Go To Statement Considered Harmful" [2], began a debate, not yet completed, on how to structure programs properly. (See [3, 4, 5], for instance.)

Harlan D. Mills [6], using chief programmer teams and programming with just a few well understood control structures (which did *not* include the GOTO), was able to report [7] the on-time delivery of a large application package with essentially no bugs. Clearly, if such results could be consistently reproduced, programming would be raised from the status of black art.

The final word is not yet in on how best to write code. G.M. Weinberg [8], approaching the problem as both a psychologist and a programmer, is studying what people do well, and what they do badly, so we can have a more objective basis for deciding what programming tools to use. Programming languages are still evolving as we learn which features encourage good programming [9]. We have learned that the way to make programs more efficient is usually by changing algorithms, not by writing very tight but incomprehensible code [10]. And people who continue to use GOTOs, out of preference or necessity, are at least thinking more carefully about how they use them [11].

We feel, however, that programming style goes beyond even these considerations. While writing *The Elements of Programming Style* [12], we reviewed hundreds of published programs, in textbooks and in the recent literature. It is no secret that imperfect programming practice is common — we found plenty of evidence of that. There are even bug-infested and unreadable "structured" programs. Writing in teams, using proper structures, avoiding GOTOs — all are useful ingredients in the manufacture of good code. But they are not enough.

Today, if you asked someone what good programming style is, you would (or should!) get quite a different lecture, for we now know that neat flowcharts and lots of comments can't salvage bad code, and that all those microseconds and bytes saved don't help when the program doesn't work. Today's lecture on "What is good programming style?" would probably be more like this . . .

Expression:

At the lowest level of coding, individual statements and small groups of statements have to be expressed so they read clearly. Consider the analogy with English — if you can't write a coherent sentence, how will you put together paragraphs, let alone write a book? So if your individual program statements are incoherent and unintelligible, what will your subroutines and operating systems be like?

Structure:

The larger structure of the code should also read clearly — it should hang together the same way a paper or a book in English should. It should be written with only a handful of control-flow primitives, such as *if-then-else, loops, statement groups* (begin-end blocks, subroutines), and it probably shouldn't contain any GOTOs. This is one aspect of what we mean by structured programming. Coding in this set of well-behaved structures makes code readable, and thus more understandable, and thus more likely to be right (and incidentally easier to change and debug).

The data structure of a program should be chosen with the same care as the control flow. Choose a data representation that makes the job easy to program: the program shouldn't have to be convoluted just to get around its data.

Robustness:

A program should *work*. Not just on the easy cases, or on the well-exercised ones, but all the time. It should be written to defend itself against bad data from the outside world. "Garbage in, garbage out" is not a law of nature; it just means that a programmer shirked his responsibility for checking his input. Special cases should work — the program should behave at its boundaries. For instance, does the sorting program correctly sort a list with just one element? Does the table lookup routine work when the table is empty?

Efficiency and instrumentation:

Only now should the lecture on style get around to "efficiency." Not that we don't care how fast a program runs or how much memory it takes, but until we have a working piece of code, we don't always know where it spends its time. And until we know that, talk of changing it "for efficiency" is foolish. Write the whole program clearly. If it is then too slow or too big, change to a better algorithm. (Since you wrote it clearly, change will be easy.) If the algorithm is already the "best," then *measure* the program, and improve the critical parts; leave the rest alone.

Documentation:

If you write code with care in the detailed expression, using the fundamental structures and choosing a good data representation, most of the code will be self-documenting — it can be *read*. Much of the need for detailed flowcharts and comments on every line will go away. And you will have less worry about the inevitable discrepancies between flowchart, comments, and code.

The approach in the "lecture" we just gave seems to lead to better (more reliable, more readable, and usually faster and shorter) code. In this paper we will talk mostly about expression and structure, with occasional digressions to robustness, efficiency, and documentation. Our presentation here is necessarily brief; all of these questions are more fully discussed in [12]. As we did there, to illustrate our points and to show what can go wrong when good style is forgotten, we have chosen a set of "real" programs. Each one is taken verbatim from some programming textbook. (We will not cite any texts by name, for we intend no criticism of textbook authors. We are all human, and it is all too easy to introduce shortcomings into programs.)

The examples are all in Fortran and PL/I; none contain particularly difficult constructions. If you have even a reading knowledge of some high level language you should be able to follow the examples without difficulty. The principles illustrated are applicable in all languages.

II. Expression

Being too clever

Our favorite example, the one we feel best underlines the need for something that can only be called good style, is this three line Fortran program:

```
        DO 1 I=1,N
        DO 1 J=1,N
    1   X(I,J)=(I/J)*(J/I)
```

It is an interesting experiment to ask a group of student Fortran programmers what this excerpt does. After thirty seconds or so, perhaps a third to a half of them will tentatively agree that they know what it does. Even after a minute of study, there are still puzzled looks. When the group is quizzed, one finds that only a few actually got the correct answer.

What does it do? It relies on Fortran's truncating integer division: if I is less than J, I/J is zero; conversely, if J is less than I, J/I is zero. Only when I equals J do we have a non-zero product, which happens to be one. Thus the code puts ones on the diagonal of X and zeros everywhere else.

Clever? Certainly, but it hardly qualifies as a *good* piece of code in any sense. It is neither short nor fast, despite its terse representation in Fortran. Worst of all, it is virtually unreadable, just because it is too clever for its importance. Even if the trick did happen to prove faster than more conventional methods, it should still be avoided, for initializing a matrix must surely be but a small part of the program that uses the matrix. It is far more important to make the code clear, so people can debug, maintain and modify it.

There is a principle of style in English that says, "Say what you mean, as simply and directly as you can." The same principle applies to programming. We mean that if I equals J, X(I,J) should be 1; if I is not equal to J, X(I,J) should be zero. So say it:

```
        DO 20  I = 1, N
            DO 10 J = 1, N
                IF( I .EQ. J ) X(I,J) = 1.0
                IF( I .NE. J ) X(I,J) = 0.0
    10      CONTINUE
    20  CONTINUE
```

If this proves to be too "inefficient," then it may be *refined* into a faster but somewhat less clear version:

```
        DO 20  I = 1, N
            DO 10 J = 1, N
    10          X(I,J) = 0.0
    20      X(I,I) = 1.0
```

It is arguable which of these is better, but both are better than the original. Don't make debugging harder than it already is — don't be too clever.

Being too complicated

Here is another Fortran example, which is an interesting contrast with the previous one:

```
      IF( X .LT. Y ) GO TO 30
      IF ( Y .LT. Z ) GO TO 50
      SMALL = Z
      GO TO 70
   30 IF ( X .LT. Z ) GO TO 60
      SMALL = Z
      GO TO 70
   50 SMALL = Y
      GO TO 70
   60 SMALL = X
   70 . . .
```

Ten and a half lines of code are used, with four statement numbers and six GOTOs — surely something must be happening. Before reading further, test yourself. What does this program do?

The mnemonic SMALL is a giveaway — the sequence sets SMALL to the smallest of X, Y, and Z. Where the first example was too clever, this one is too wordy and simple-minded. Since this code was intended to show how to compute the minimum of three numbers, we should ask why it wasn't written like this:

```
      SMALL = X
      IF( Y .LT. SMALL ) SMALL = Y
      IF( Z .LT. SMALL ) SMALL = Z
```

No labels, no GOTO's, three statements, and clearly correct. And the generalization to computing the minimum of many elements is obvious.

Of course, if our goal is to get the job done, rather than teaching how to compute a minimum, we can write, much more readably than the original, the single statement:

```
      SMALL = AMINO(X, Y, Z)
```

One line replaces ten. How can a piece of code that is an order of magnitude too large be considered reliable? There is that much greater chance for confusion, and hence for the introduction of bugs. There is that much more that must be understood in order to make evolutionary changes.

Clarity versus "efficiency"

It seems obvious that a program should be clear, yet clarity is often sacrificed needlessly in the name of efficiency or expediency.

```
      DO 10 I=1,M
      IF( BP( I )+1.0 )19,11,10
11    IBN1( I ) = BLNK
      IBN2( I ) = BLNK
      GO TO 10
19    BP( I ) = -1.0
      IBN1( I ) = BLNK
      IBN2( I ) = BLNK
10    CONTINUE
```

If BP(I) is less than or equal to -1, this excerpt will set BP(I) to -1 and put blanks in IBN1(I) and IBN2(I). The code uses a hard-to-read Fortran arithmetic IF that branches three ways, two almost-duplicated pieces of code, two labels and an extra GOTO, all to avoid setting BP(I) to -1 if it is already -1.

There is no need to make a special case. Write the code so it can be read:

```
      DO 10 I = 1, M
         IF( BP( I ) .GT. -1.0 ) GOTO 10
            BP( I ) = -1.0
            IBN1( I ) = BLNK
            IBN2( I ) = BLNK
10    CONTINUE
```

Interestingly enough, our version will be more "efficient" on most machines, both in space and in time: although we may reset BP(I) unnecessarily, we do less bookkeeping. What did concern with "efficiency" in the original version produce, besides a bigger, slower, and more obscure program?

Rewriting

These may seem like small things, taken one at a time. But look what happens when the need for clear expression is consistently overlooked, as in this PL/I program which computes a set of approximations to the integral of X**2 between zero and one, by adding up the areas of rectangles of various widths.

```
TRAPZ:  PROCEDURE OPTIONS (MAIN);
     DECLARE MSSG1 CHARACTER (20);
        MSSG1 = 'AREA UNDER THE CURVE';
     DECLARE MSSG2 CHARACTER (23);
        MSSG2 = 'BY THE TRAPAZOIDAL RULE';
     DECLARE MSSG3 CHARACTER (16);
        MSSG3 = 'FOR DELTA X = 1/';
     DECLARE I  FIXED DECIMAL (2);
     DECLARE J  FIXED DECIMAL (2);
     DECLARE L  FIXED DECIMAL (7,6);
     DECLARE M  FIXED DECIMAL (7,6);
     DECLARE N  FIXED DECIMAL (2);
     DECLARE AREA1 FIXED DECIMAL (8,6);
     DECLARE AREA FIXED DECIMAL  (8,6);
     DECLARE LMTS FIXED DECIMAL  (5,4);
        PUT SKIP EDIT  (MSSG1)  (X(9), A(20));
        PUT SKIP EDIT  (MSSG2)  (X(7), A(23));
        PUT SKIP EDIT  (' ') (A(1));
     AREA = 0;
           DO K = 4 TO 10;
            M = 1 / K;
            N = K - 1;
        LMTS = .5 * M;
            I = 1;
            DO J = 1 TO N;
            L = (I / K) ** 2;
     AREA1 = .5 * M * (2 * L);
     AREA = AREA + AREA1;
        IF I = N THEN CALL OUT;
          ELSE I = I + 1;
        END;
       END;
  OUT:  PROCEDURE;
        AREA = AREA + LMTS;
     PUT SKIP EDIT  (MSSG3,K,AREA) (X(2),A(16),F(2),X(6),
           F(9,6));
     AREA = 0;
     RETURN;
    END;
  END;
```

Everything about this program is wordy. The output messages are declared and assigned unnecessarily. There are far too many temporary variables and their associated declarations. The structure sprawls.

Try going through the code, fixing just one thing at a time — put the error messages in the PUT statements where they belong. Eliminate the unnecessary intermediate variables. Combine the remaining declarations. Simplify the initializations. Delete the unnecessary procedure call. You will find that the code shrinks before your very eyes, revealing the simple underlying algorithm.

Here is our revised version:

```
TRAPZ:  PROCEDURE OPTIONS(MAIN);
        DECLARE (J,K)  FIXED DECIMAL (2),
                AREA FIXED DECIMAL (8,6);

        PUT SKIP EDIT    ('AREA UNDER THE CURVE',
                         'BY THE TRAPEZOIDAL RULE')
                         (X(9), A, SKIP, X(7), A);

        PUT SKIP;

        DO K = 4 TO 10;
           AREA = 0.5/K;

           DO J = 1 TO K-1;
              AREA = AREA + ((J/K)**2)/K;
           END;

           PUT SKIP EDIT ('FOR DELTA X=1/', K, AREA)
                         (X(2), A, F(2), X(6), F(9, 6));
        END;
     END TRAPZ;
```

Both versions give the same results, so this was not an exercise in debugging in the traditional sense. But if there were a bug localized to this part of a larger system, which version would you rather try to fix? Which would you give a higher mark to? Which would you rather be in charge of, when changes are necessary?

The original version reads like a hasty first draft which was later patched. Arriving at our "final draft" required no great ingenuity, just a series of almost mechanical steps much as we described. Applying the principles of good style, one at a time, gradually eliminates the features that make the original version so hard to read. The problem is, most programs never get past the "first draft" stage, possibly because the code appears too frightening when viewed all at once.

Programmers sometimes say that they haven't time to worry about niceties like style — they have to get the thing written fast so they can get on to the next one. (What actually happens is they get it written fast so they can get on to the tedious job of debugging it.) But you will soon find that, with practice, you spend less and less time revising, because you do a better and better job the first time.

Much more can be said about how to make code locally more readable (see [12]), but for now we will turn to a topic that has recently become popular — how to specify control flow with good style.

III. Control flow structure

One way to improve the apparently random control flow that several of our examples have demonstrated is to program consciously with just a small set of well-behaved control flow structures. One interpretation of "structured programming," in fact, is this way of coding. Although this is a narrow view, we will keep to just that aspect for the time being.

It has been shown [13] that programs can be written using just:

1. *Alternation,* such as IF-THEN-ELSE, where the ELSE part may be optional.

2. *Looping,* such as WHILE or the Fortran DO loop. Different flavors have the termination test at the beginning or end of the loop.

3. *Grouping,* such as subroutines and compound statements.

While these tools are sufficient, in the same sense that a Turing machine can perform any of a wide class of calculations, it is convenient to add:

4. *CASE switches,* which are essentially multi-way IF statements, and

5. *BREAK and ITERATE statements,* which exit from a loop or skip to the test portion of a loop, respectively.

Most languages have at best a subset of these forms, so the pragmatic programmer cannot hope to avoid the more primitive control statements carried over from earlier days. For example, the simplest way to implement a BREAK in PL/I is to use a GOTO. And in Fortran, of course, GOTOs and statement numbers must be sprinkled liberally throughout the best designed code. But the basic design of a program should be done in terms of the fundamental structures. GOTOs and other primitive language features should be used *only to implement the basic structures outlined above.*

While these are well tried and useful forms, there is a tendency to believe that just by using them (and only them) one can avoid all trouble. This is false — they are not panaceas. Good style, care and intelligence are still needed. We can see this just by studying the use and abuse of the IF-THEN-ELSE, certainly a simple and fundamental structure in any programming language.

Null THEN

The following routine is supposed to sort an array of eight numbers into increasing order of absolute value:

```
DCL A(8);
GET LIST (A);
DO I=1 TO 8;
   IF ABS(A(I))<ABS(A(I+1)) THEN;
      ELSE BEGIN;
         STORE=A(I);
         A(I)=A(I+1);
         A(I+1)=STORE;
         END;
   END;
PUT LIST(A);
```

The heart of this sequence is a "DON'T" statement — if the specified condition is true, do nothing, otherwise do something. Anything so misleading should put us on guard; and indeed we see immediately that the sequence cannot possibly sort correctly because

1.   only one pass is made over the array, and we know simple sorting takes about N passes.

2.   a reference is made outside array bounds when A(I+1) is accessed on the last iteration with I equal to 8.

There are several ways of doing a simple sort correctly. We could make N−1 passes over the array, or we could set a flag every time it is necessary to exchange two elements, so we know that an additional pass over the array is needed. Applying this latter fix to the program above (and eliminating the subscript range error) should give us a working sort.

But there is still a lurking bug. Turning the test around so the IF-THEN is stated more naturally:

```
IF ABS(A(I)) >= ABS(A(I+1)) THEN DO;
   STORE = A(I);
   A(.I) = A(I+1);
   A(I+1) = STORE;
   EXCH = '1' B;
   END;
```

reveals that two elements will be exchanged even if they are equal. If A contains two equal elements, the program goes into an infinite loop exchanging them, because the flag EXCH will be set repeatedly. Using a null THEN may seem a small thing, until it adds a day of debugging time.

Even when code is correct, it can be very hard to read. Here's another sorting program, which sorts into descending order this time, with an almost-null THEN:

```
        DO  M  =  1 TO  N;
        K  =   N−1;
        DO J  =  1 TO  K;
        IF ARAY(J)  −  ARAY(J+1)  >=  0
                    THEN GO TO RETRN;
                        ELSE;
        SAVE  =  ARAY(J);
        ARAY(J)  =  ARAY(J+1);
        ARAY(J+1)  =  SAVE;
    RETRN:    END;
        END;
```

The construction THEN GOTO might be a BREAK statement in disguise, but often it is a tipoff that something is amiss. Here it branches around only three statements and not out of the loop. Why not turn the test around so no GOTO or label is needed? (The null ELSE has no function whatsoever; it only confuses the issue.) And why does the test subtract the two elements and then compare against zero, when a direct comparison would be far easier to understand and free of overflow problems? The program reads like a hasty translation from Fortran into PL/I. Revision is easy:

```
DO M  =  1 TO  N−1;
    DO J  =  1 TO  N−1;
        IF ARAY(J)  <  ARAY(J+1) THEN DO;
            SAVE  =  ARAY(J);
            ARAY(J)  =  ARAY(J+1);
            ARAY(J+1)  =  SAVE;
        END;
    END;
END;
```

The original program worked, but again we were able to improve it with little effort.

In Fortran, there are fewer options when using IFs, for there is no ELSE clause and no way to form compound groups of statements. But in the few cases where the language lets you write clearly, *do so.* Don't write like this:

```
        IF (A(I).GT.GRVAL) GO TO 30
        GO TO 25
    30  GRVAL  =  A(I)
    25  . . .
```

A branch around the branch that branches around what we wanted to do in the first place! Say what you mean, as simply and directly as you can:

```
IF( A( I ) .GT. GRVAL ) GRVAL = A( I )
```

There are now no labels, no GOTOs, and the code can be understood even when read aloud over a telephone. (This is always a good test to apply to your code — if you can't understand it when spoken aloud, how easy will it be to grasp when you read it quietly to yourself?)

ELSE BREAK

The BREAK statement has its uses, but it has to be used judiciously. Consider this sequence for finding the largest of a set of positive numbers:

```
            DCL NEWIN DEC FLOAT (4);
                LARGE DEC FLOAT (4) INIT (.0E1);
                /* .0 × 10**1 = .0 × 10 = 0.0
    NEXT_C:  GET LIST (NEWIN);
             IF NEWIN >=0
                 THEN IF NEWIN > LARGE
                        THEN LARGE = NEWIN;
                        ELSE GO TO NEXT_C;
                 ELSE GO TO FINISH;
             GO TO NEXT_C;
    FINISH:   PUT LIST (LARGE);
```

Ignoring the curious zero in the INIT attribute, and the equally curious explanatory comment, we can see that this program does indeed use just the structures we mentioned above (the GOTOs implement BREAKs and ITERATEs). Therefore it should be readable. But tracing the tortuous flow of control is not a trivial exercise — how does one get to that last GOTO NEXT_C? Why, from the innermost THEN clause, of course.

The ELSE BREAK is just as confusing as the DON'T statement. It tells you where you went if you didn't do the THEN, leaving you momentarily at a loss in finding the successor to the THEN clause. And when ELSE BREAKs are used one after the other, as here, the mind boggles.

Such convolutions are almost never necessary, since an organized statement of the problem leads to a simple series of decisions:

```
            DECLARE (NEWIN, LARGE) DECIMAL FLOAT (4);
            LARGE = 0;
    NEXT_C:    GET LIST (NEWIN);
               IF NEWIN > LARGE THEN LARGE = NEWIN;
               IF NEWIN >= 0 THEN GOTO NEXT_C;
            PUT LIST (LARGE);
```

What we have here is a simple DO-WHILE, done while the number read is not negative, controlling a simple IF-THEN. Of course we have rearranged the order of testing, but the end-of-data marker chosen was a convenient one and does not interfere with the principal work of the routine. True, our version makes one extra test, comparing the marker against LARGE, but that will hardly affect the overall efficiency of the sequence. Readability is certainly improved by avoiding the ELSE GOTOs.

THEN-IF

Now consider:

```
IF QTY > 10 THEN                                        /*A*/
   IF QTY > 200 THEN                                    /*B*/
      IF QTY >= 500 THEN BILL_A = BILL_A + 1.00;        /*C*/
                    ELSE BILL_A = BILL_A + .50;         /*C*/
              ELSE;                                     /*B*/
        ELSE BILL_A = .00;                              /*A*/
```

Those letters down the right hand side are designed to help you figure out what is going on, but as usual, no amount of commenting can rescue bad code. The code requires you to maintain a mental pushdown stack of what tests were made, so that at the appropriate point you can pop them until you determine the corresponding action (if you can still remember). You might time yourself as you determine what this code does when QTY equals 350. How about 150?

Since only one of a set of actions is ever called for here, a frequent occurrence, what we really want is some form of CASE statement. In PL/I, the most general CASE is implemented by a series of ELSE-IFs:

```
IF         cond1 THEN   first case;
ELSE IF    cond2 THEN   second case;
. . .
ELSE IF    condn THEN   nth case;
ELSE                    default;
```

If there is no default action, the last ELSE clause is omitted. We can rewrite the example as:

```
IF         QTY  >=  500 THEN BILL_A = BILL_A + 1.00;
ELSE IF    QTY  >   200 THEN BILL_A = BILL_A + 0.50;
ELSE IF    QTY  <=   10 THEN BILL_A = 0.0;
```

Now all we need do is read down the list of tests until we find one that is met, read across to the corresponding action, and continue after the last ELSE. In Fortran, this can be rendered similarly as

```
IF(QTY .GE. 500.0) BILLA = BILLA + 1.0
IF(QTY .LT. 500.0 .AND. QTY .GT. 200.0) BILLA = BILLA + 0.5
IF(QTY .LE. 10.0) BILLA = 0.0
```

which is best if the relations and actions are simple enough to write one per line and the tests are mutually exclusive. Don't let anyone tell you this is not efficient — it doesn't take all that much time to make the whole set of tests, and you're more likely to get the code right the first time. If it does take too much time, and you have measurements that prove it, then and only then should you re-write it with GOTOs.

The THEN-IF was the culprit in this example, but we could have given the disease another name. Note the null ELSE clause, required to make the unstacking come out right when one of the conditions has no corresponding action. These seemingly useless statements cauterize the stumps of any ill-thought-out THEN-IFs buried in the code. A program containing null ELSE clauses is suspect, if for no other reason than that it was written by someone bitten by THEN-IFs often enough to sprinkle null ELSEs around for insurance.

The THEN-IF does have its uses. It is often the only way to ensure that tests with side effects are performed in the proper order, as in

```
IF I > 0 THEN
    IF A( I ) = B( I ) THEN . . .
```

which ensures that I is in range before its use as an index. Some languages provide special Boolean connectives [14] which guarantee left-to-right evaluation and early exit as soon as the truth value of the expression is determined; but if you are not fortunate enough to be able to program with these useful tools, use THEN-IFs and don't forget to cauterize.

Bushy trees

Most of the IF-THEN-ELSE examples we have shown so far have a characteristic in common, besides the unreadable practices we pointed out. Each approximates, as closely as the programmer could manage, a minimum depth decision tree for the problem at hand. If all outcomes have equal probability, such a tree arrives at the appropriate action with the minimum number of tests on the average, so we are all encouraged to lay out programs accordingly. But a program is a one-dimensional construct, which obscures any two-dimensional connectedness it may have. Perhaps the minimum depth tree is not the best structure for a reliable program.

Let us rewrite the minimum function in PL/I, adhering to the spirit of the original Fortran, but using only IF-THEN-ELSEs:

```
IF X >= Y THEN
    IF Y >= Z THEN SMALL = Z;
    ELSE           SMALL = Y;
ELSE
    IF X >= Z THEN SMALL = Z;
    ELSE           SMALL = X;
```

Even though neatly laid out and properly indented, it is still not easy to grasp. Not all the confusion of the original can be attributed to the welter of GOTOs and statement numbers. What we have here is a "bushy" tree, needlessly complex in any event, but still hard to read simply because it is conceptually short and fat.

The ELSE-IF sequence, on the other hand, is long and skinny as trees go; it seems to more closely reflect how we think. (Note that our revised minimum function was also linear.) It is easier to read down a list of items, considering them one at a time, than to remember the complete path to some interior part of a tree, even if the path has only two or three links. Seldom is it actually necessary to repeat tests in the process of stringing out a tree into a list; often it is just a matter of performing the tests in a judicious order. Yet too often programmers tend to build a thicket of logic where a series of signposts are called for.

Summary of IF-THEN-ELSE

Let us summarize our discussion of IF-THEN-ELSE. The most important principle is to avoid bushy decision trees like:

```
IF  ...
     THEN  IF ...
     ELSE    ...
ELSE IF    ...
     THEN  ...
     ELSE  ...
```

The bushy tree should almost always be reorganized into a CASE statement, which is implemented as a string of ELSE-IFs in PL/I. The resulting long thin tree is much easier to understand:

```
IF       ... THEN  ...
ELSE IF  ... THEN  ...
   ...
ELSE                ...
```

A THEN-IF is an early warning that a decision tree is growing the wrong way. A null ELSE indicates that the programmer knows that trouble lies ahead and is trying to defend against it. And an ELSE BREAK from such a structure may leave the reader at a loss to understand how the following statement is reached.

A null THEN or (more commonly) THEN GOTO usually indicates that a relational test needs to be turned around, and some set of statements made into a block.

The general rule is: after you make a decision, *do something*. Don't just go somewhere or make another decision. If you follow each decision by the action that goes with it, you can see at a glance what each decision implies.

WHILE

Looping is fundamental in programming. Yet explicit loop control in For-tran or PL/I can only be specified by a DO statement, which encourages the be-lief that all loops involve repeated incrementing of an integer variable until it exceeds some predetermined value. Fortran further insists that the loop body be obeyed once before testing to see whether the loop should have been en-tered at all.

Thinking in terms of DO statements, instead of loops, leads to programs like this sine routine:

```
          DOUBLE PRECISION FUNCTION SIN(X,E)
   C      THIS DECLARATION COMPUTES SIN(X) TO ACCURACY E
          DOUBLE PRECISION E,TERM,SUM
          REAL  X
          TERM=X
          DO 20 I=3,100,2
          TERM=TERM*X**2/(I*(I-1))
          IF(TERM.LT.E)GO TO 30
          SUM=SUM+(-1**(1/2))*TERM
    20 CONTINUE
    30 SIN=SUM
          RETURN
          END
```

The program consists entirely of a loop, which computes and sums the terms of a Maclaurin series until the terms get too small or a predetermined number have been included in the sum.

In its most general form, a loop should be laid out as:

```
          initialize
          while (reason for looping)
               body of loop
```

This way, the parts are clearly specified and kept separate. But this approach was evidently not taken here:

1)   The program fails to initialize SUM along with TERM and I.

2)   The program misstates the convergence test, returning im-mediately on negative values of X.

3)   The convergence test is misplaced, so the last TERM computed is not included in SUM. And TERM is computed unnecessarily when the convergence test is met right from the start.

These three bugs can be traced directly to poor structural design. There is also a fourth bug:

4) TERM is computed incorrectly because the "**" operator binds tighter than unary minus (another case of being too clever?).

We first write the code in an anonymous language that includes the WHILE.

```
sin = x
term = x
i = 3
while (i < 100 & abs(term) > e)
    term = −term * x ** 2 /(i * (i − 1))
    sin = sin + term
    i = i + 2
return
```

and then translate into Fortran:

```
      SIN = X
      TERM = X
      DO 20 I = 3, 100, 2
      IF (DABS(TERM) .LT. E) GOTO 30
         TERM = −TERM * X**2 / FLOAT( I * ( I − 1 ))
         SIN = SIN + TERM
 20   CONTINUE
 30   RETURN
```

In this case, the WHILE becomes a DO followed by an IF. The DO neatly summarizes the initialization, incrementing, and testing of I, and keeps the loop control separate from the computation. It is a useful statement. The important thing is to recognize its shortcomings and plan loops in terms of the more general WHILE.

In PL/I, the DO-WHILE and DO I=J TO K constructions make the test at the top of the loop, which is most often what is wanted. Fortran programs, on the other hand, frequently fail to "do nothing gracefully" because DO loops insist on being performed at least once, regardless of their limits, even when action is undesirable. For example, this function finds the smallest element in an array.

```
      FUNCTION SMALL(A,N)
      DIMENSION A(1)
      SMALL = A(1)
      DO 1 K = 2,N
      IF(A(K) − SMALL)2,1,1
 2       SMALL = A(K)
 1    CONTINUE
      RETURN
      END
```

Clearly it's more efficient to use the DO limits of "2,N" − it saves a useless comparison. But what if N is one? Don't kid yourself: N *will* be equal to one some day, and the program will surely fail when it looks at the undefined A(2). Had we first written this routine with a WHILE statement, we would have seen the need for an IF to protect the DO in the translated version. Or, we could have written directly:

```
        SMALL = A(1)
        DO 1 K = 1,N
           IF( A(K) .LT. SMALL ) SMALL = A(K)
     1 CONTINUE
```

This may be less "efficient" in the small, but the cost of finding the bug in the original, and repairing the damage it cost, will certainly outweigh the few microseconds more than our version takes. (You have to weigh for yourself the question of whether to test if N is less than one.)

IV. Data structure

Putting the hard parts of a program into an appropriate data structure is an art, but well worthwhile. (Imagine doing long division in Roman numerals.) This program converts the year and day of the year into the month and day of the month:

```
DATES:    PROC OPTIONS (MAIN);
READ:     GET DATA (IYEAR, IDATE);
          IF IDATE < 1 | IDATE > 366 | IYEAR < 0 THEN RETURN;
          IF IDATE <= 31 THEN GO TO JAN;
          L = 1;
          I = IYEAR/400; IF I = IYEAR/400 THEN GO TO LEAP;
          I = IYEAR/100; IF I = IYEAR/100 THEN GO TO NOLEAP;
          I = IYEAR/4; IF I = IYEAR/4 THEN GO TO LEAP;
NOLEAP:   L = 0;
          IF IDATE > 365 THEN RETURN;
LEAP:     IF IDATE > 181 + L THEN GO TO G181;
          IF IDATE > 90 + L THEN GO TO G90;
          IF IDATE > 59 + L THEN GO TO G59;
          MONTH = 2; IDAY = IDATE − 31; GO TO OUT;
G59:      MONTH = 3; IDAY = IDATE − (59 + L); GO TO OUT;
G90:      IF IDATE > 120 + L THEN GO TO G120;
          MONTH = 4; IDAY = IDATE − (90 + L); GO TO OUT;
G120:     IF IDATE > 151 + L THEN GO TO G151;
          MONTH = 5; IDAY = IDATE − (120 + L); GO TO OUT;
G151:     MONTH = 6; IDAY = IDATE − (151 + L); GO TO OUT;
G181:     IF IDATE > 273 + L THEN GO TO G273;
          IF IDATE > 243 + L THEN GO TO G243;
          IF IDATE > 212 + L THEN GO TO G212;
          MONTH = 7; IDAY = IDATE − (181 + L); GO TO OUT;
G212:     MONTH = 8; IDAY = IDATE − (212 + L); GO TO OUT;
G243:     MONTH = 9; IDAY = IDATE − (243 + L); GO TO OUT;
G273:     IF IDATE > 334 + L THEN GO TO G334;
          IF IDATE > 304 + L THEN GO TO G304;
          MONTH = 10; IDAY = IDATE − (273 + L); GO TO OUT;
G304:     MONTH = 11; IDAY = IDATE − (304 + L); GO TO OUT;
G334:     MONTH = 12; IDAY = IDATE − (334 + L);
OUT:      PUT DATA (MONTH,IDAY,IYEAR) SKIP;
          GO TO READ;
JAN:      MONTH=1; IDAY=IDATE; GO TO OUT;
          END DATES;
```

What we have here is a bushy tree to end all bushy trees. The rococo structure of the calendar is intimately intertwined with the control flow in an attempt to arrive at the proper answer with a minimum number of tests.

Clarity is certainly not worth sacrificing just to save three tests per access (on the average) — the irregularities must be brought under control. Most good programmers are accustomed to using subprocedures to achieve regularity. The procedure body shows what is common to each invocation, and the differences are neatly summarized in the parameter list for each call. Fewer programmers learn to use judiciously designed data layouts to capture the irregularities in a computation. But we can see that structured programming can also apply to the data declarations:

```
DATES:  PROCEDURE OPTIONS (MAIN);
        DECLARE MONSIZE(0:1, 1:12) INITIAL(
           31,28,31,30,31,30,31,31,30,31,30,31,        /* NON-LEAP */
           31,29,31,30,31,30,31,31,30,31,30,31);       /* LEAP */

READ:
        GET LIST (IYEAR, IDATE) COPY;

        IF  MOD(IYEAR,400)=0  |
            (MOD(IYEAR,100)¬=0 & MOD(IYEAR,4)=0)
                THEN LEAP = 1;
                ELSE LEAP = 0;

        IF  IYEAR<1753  | IYEAR>3999  | IDATE<=0  | IDATE>365+LEAP THEN
            PUT SKIP LIST ('BAD YEAR, DATE -', IYEAR, IDATE);

        ELSE DO;
            NDAYS = 0;
            DO MONTH = 1 TO 12
                WHILE ( IDATE > NDAYS + MONSIZE(LEAP, MONTH) ) ;
                NDAYS = NDAYS + MONSIZE(LEAP, MONTH);
            END;
            PUT SKIP LIST(MONTH, IDATE - NDAYS, IYEAR);
        END;

        GOTO READ;
    END DATES;
```

Most people can recognize a table giving the lengths of the different months ("Thirty days hath September . . ."), so this version can be quickly checked for accuracy. The program may take a bit more time counting the number of days every time it is called, but it is more likely to get the right answer than you are, and even if the program is used a lot, I/O conversions are sure to use more time than the actual computation of the date. The double computation of MONSIZE(LEAP,MONTH) falls into the same category — write it clearly so it works; then measure to see if it's worth your while to rewrite parts of it.

Our revised date computation shows an aspect of modularity which is often overlooked. Most people equate modules with procedures, but our program has several distinct modules and only one procedure. A date is input, LEAP is computed, the date is validated, the conversion is made and the result is printed. Each of these pieces could be picked up as a unit and planted as needed in some other environment with a good chance of working unaltered, because there are no unnecessary labels or other cross references between pieces. (The label and GOTO implement a WHILE, done while there is still input.) The control flow structures we have described tend to split programs into *computational units* like these and thus lead to internal modularity.

V. Conclusion

Three topics we have hardly touched, which are usually associated with any discussion of style, are efficiency, documentation, and language design. We think these are straw men, almost always raised improperly in a consideration of only parochial issues.

Opponents of programming reform argue that anything that is readable must automatically be inefficient. This is the same attitude that says that assembly languages are preferable to high level languages. But as we have seen, good programming is not synonymous with GOTO-less programming, and it certainly does not have to be wasteful of time or space. Quite the contrary, we find that nearly all our revised programs take no more time and are about the same size as the originals. And in some cases the revised version is shorter and faster because unnecessary special cases have been eliminated.

We use few comments in our revisions — most of the programs are short enough to speak for themselves. And when a program cannot speak for itself, it is seldom the case that greater reliability or understanding will result by interposing yet another insulating layer of documentation between the code and the reader. Bad programming practice cannot be explained away; it must be rewritten.

Finally, many people try to excuse badly written programs by blaming inadequacies of the language that must be used. We have seen repeatedly that even Fortran can be tamed with proper discipline. The presence of bad features is not an invitation to use them, nor is the absence of good features an excuse to avoid simulating them as cleanly as possible. Good languages are nice, but not vital.

Our survey of programming style has been sketchy, for there are far too many details that must be covered to give a proper treatment here. But there is ample evidence for the existence of some discipline beyond a simple set of restrictions on what types of statements to use. It is called style.

References

1. E.W. Dijkstra, "The Humble Programmer," *Communications of the ACM,* Vol. 15, No. 10 (October 1972), pp. 859-66.

2. _____, "Go To Statement Considered Harmful," *Communications of the ACM,* Vol. 11, No. 3 (March 1968), pp. 147-48.

3. B.M. Leavenworth, "Programming With(out) the GOTO," *Proceedings of the 25th National ACM Conference* (New York: Association for Computing Machinery, August 1972), pp. 782-86.

4. W.A. Wulf, "A Case Against the GOTO," *Proceedings of the 25th National ACM Conference* (New York: Association for Computing Machinery, August 1972), pp. 791-97.

5. O.-J. Dahl, E.W. Dijkstra, and C.A.R. Hoare, *Structured Programming* (New York: Academic Press, 1972).

6. F.T. Baker and H.D. Mills, "Chief Programmer Teams," *Datamation,* Vol. 19, No. 12 (December 1973), pp. 58-61.

7. H.D. Mills, "Top-Down Programming in Large Systems," *Debugging Techniques in Large Systems,* ed. R. Rustin (Englewood Cliffs, N.J.: Prentice-Hall, 1971), pp. 41-55.

8. G.M. Weinberg, *The Psychology of Computer Programming* (New York: Van Nostrand Reinhold, 1971).

9. C.A.R. Hoare, *Hints for Programming Language Design,* Stanford University, Computer Science Report No. STAN-CS-74-403 (Stanford, Calif.: January 1974).

10. D.E. Knuth, "An Empirical Study of FORTRAN Programs," *Software — Practice and Experience,* Vol. 1, No. 2 (April-June 1971), pp. 105-33.

11. _____, "Structured Programming with GOTO Statements," *Computing Surveys,* Vol. 6, No. 4 (December 1974), pp. 261-301; also in *Current Trends in Programming Methodology,* Vol. I, ed. R.T. Yeh (Englewood Cliffs, N.J.: Prentice-Hall, 1977).

12. B.W. Kernighan and P.J. Plauger, *The Elements of Programming Style* (New York: McGraw-Hill, 1974).

13. C. Böhm and G. Jacopini, "Flow Diagrams, Turing Machines and Languages with Only Two Formation Rules," *Communications of the ACM,* Vol. 9, No. 5 (May 1966), pp. 366-71.

14. J. McCarthy, "Recursive Functions of Symbolic Expressions and Their Computation by Machine, Part I," *Communications of the ACM,* Vol. 3, No. 4 (April 1960), pp. 184-95.

INTRODUCTION

For serious students of structured programming, and also for language designers, Knuth's "Structured Programming with go to Statements" is probably *the* paper to read. It is by far the most complete description of structured programming of all the selections in this book. Even though it originally was published in late 1974, Knuth's ideas have not aged a bit.

The title, as Knuth acknowledges, is somewhat of a misnomer: ". . . I should confess that the title of this article was chosen primarily to generate attention." Indeed, he is not arguing that structured programming always should be carried out with goto statements; instead, as he says, "what I am really doing is striving for a reasonably well-balanced viewpoint about the proper role of go to statements." Like a number of other authors whose views are presented in this book, Knuth seems deeply concerned that the average programmer will over-react to the "no goto" philosophy. Reflecting that concern, the first few pages of Knuth's paper give an indication of the fanaticism of its time — a fanaticism that has largely died away.

For history buffs, Knuth has carefully documented the origins of structured programming. He claims that the programming style now referred to as "structured programming" actually was first practiced by D.V. Schorre in 1960, and that was followed by publication of the work of Peter Naur in 1963 and of George Forsythe in 1964 — all of this *before* the better-known works of Dijkstra, and of Böhm and Jacopini.

There are three major themes in Knuth's paper, and a vast number of examples to illustrate each one. One theme — a familiar one, if you've read many of the other papers in this book — is that a program needs to be rewritten several times before it can be considered a truly good program. As Knuth says, ". . . I learned again that I should always keep looking for improvements, even when I have a satisfactory program." Indeed, one gets the impression that Knuth views this as the major virtue of structured programming: The requirement to eliminate gotos forces the programmer to rewrite and thus *think* more about what he was trying to accomplish with his program.

A second theme — one that you *won't* find in any of the other papers — is that efficiency *is* important in some programming applications, and that the programmer needs the freedom to use gotos to optimize critical portions of a program. Actually, Martin Hopkins makes the same point in "A Case for the GOTO" [Paper 9], but he does so much less forcefully than Knuth. Knuth recognizes the danger of overemphasizing optimization; as he says, "premature optimization is the root of all evil." And, he does state that only three percent of the code in a typical program ever needs to be optimized; but for that critical three percent, he demonstrates that structured code often is twenty to thirty percent less efficient than equivalent code with gotos. Unfortunately, the point is repeated so many times, with so many examples, that the average reader is likely to conclude that Knuth is obsessed with efficiency. However, given the number of authors exhorting programmers to ignore efficiency altogether, it is probably very healthy to have someone argue for a careful consideration of program efficiency.

Knuth's third main theme is that structured programming could be made much more practical with the addition of a few language constructs. In addition to constructs like LEAVE and BREAK, Knuth argues for a "situation" construct patterned after a proposal originally made by C.T. Zahn.

In keeping with the heretical title of his paper, Knuth introduces a fourth theme: There are times when the programmer should put gotos *into* his code, rather than take them out. For example, gotos can be used to convert recursion to iteration; or to implement coroutines; or to eliminate Boolean variables by branching into common code. In this context, Knuth suggests the following strategy: First, write the program in a structured manner to convince yourself that it is correct; then, transform it into an efficient program, possibly by introducing some goto statements; and, finally, leave the original structured code behind as documentation, so that subsequent readers can understand how the transformation took place. Whether the average programmer would go through these steps in an orderly, formal way is something worth pondering. My own suspicion is that it won't work, but I'm often branded a skeptic.

To conclude: It's probably best not to read Knuth's paper in one sitting, for you almost surely will become mentally fatigued by the eight major examples, each of which is rewritten three or four (or more!) times in an ALGOL-like pseudocode. Read the paper piece by piece, and *do* read the code — you'll learn a lot from it!

Structured Programming
with go to Statements

> You may go when you will go,
>   And I will stay behind.
> *— Edna St. Vincent Millay* [1]
>
> Most likely you go your way and I'll go mine.
> *— Song title by Bob Dylan* [2]
>
> Do you suffer from painful elimination?
> *— Advertisement, J.B. Williams Co.*

Introduction

A revolution is taking place in the way we write programs and teach programming, because we are beginning to understand the associated mental processes more deeply. It is impossible to read the recent book *Structured Programming* [3, 4] without having it change your life. The reasons for this revolution and its future prospects have been aptly described by E.W. Dijkstra in his 1972 Turing Award Lecture, "The Humble Programmer" [5].

As we experience this revolution, each of us naturally is developing strong feelings one way or the other, as we agree or disagree with the revolutionary leaders. I must admit to being a nonhumble programmer, egotistical enough to believe that my own opinions of the current trends are not a waste of the reader's time. Therefore I want to express in this article several of the things that struck me most forcefully as I have been thinking about structured programming during the last year; several of my blind spots were removed as I was learning these things, and I hope I can convey some of my excitement to the reader. Hardly any of the ideas I will discuss are my own; they are nearly all the work of others, but perhaps I may be presenting them in a new light. I write this article in the first person to emphasize the fact that what I'm saying is just one man's opinion; I don't expect to persuade everyone that my present views are correct.

Before beginning a more technical discussion, I should confess that the title of this article was chosen primarily to generate attention. There are doubtless some readers who are convinced that abolition of **go to** statements is merely a fad, and they may see this title and think, "Aha! Knuth is rehabilitating the **go to** statement, and we can go back to our old ways of programming again." Another class of readers will see the heretical title and think, "When are diehards like Knuth going to get with it?" I hope that both classes of people will read on and discover that what I am really doing is striving for a reasonably well balanced viewpoint about the proper role of **go to** statements. I argue for the elimination of **go to**'s in certain cases, and for their introduction in others.

I believe that by presenting such a view I am not in fact disagreeing sharply with Dijkstra's ideas, since he recently wrote the following: "Please don't fall into the trap of believing that I am terribly dogmatical about [the **go to** statement]. I have the uncomfortable feeling that others are making a religion out of it, as if the conceptual problems of programming could be solved by a single trick, by a simple form of coding discipline!" [6]. In other words, it seems that fanatical advocates of the New Programming are going overboard in their strict enforcement of morality and purity in programs. Sooner or later people are going to find that their beautifully structured programs are running at only half the speed — or worse — of the dirty old programs they used to write, and they will mistakenly blame the structure instead of recognizing what is probably the real culprit — the system overhead caused by typical compiler implementation of Boolean variables and procedure calls. Then we'll have an unfortunate counterrevolution, something like the current rejection of the "New Mathematics" in reaction to its over-zealous reforms.

It may be helpful to consider a further analogy with mathematics. In 1904, Bertrand Russell published his famous paradox about the set of all sets which aren't members of themselves. This antinomy shook the foundations of classical mathematical reasoning, since it apparently brought very simple and ordinary deductive methods into question. The ensuing crisis led to the rise of "intuitionist logic," a school of thought championed especially by the Dutch mathematician, L.E.J. Brouwer; intuitionism abandoned all deductions that were based on questionable nonconstructive ideas. For a while it appeared that intuitionist logic would cause a revolution in mathematics. But the new approach angered David Hilbert, who was perhaps the leading mathematician of the time; Hilbert said, "Forbidding a mathematician to make use of the principle of the excluded middle is like forbidding an astronomer his telescope or a boxer the use of his fists." He characterized the intuitionist approach as seeking "to save mathematics by throwing overboard all that is troublesome. . . . They would chop up and mangle the science. If we would follow such a reform as they suggest, we could run the risk of losing a great part of our most valuable treasures" [7].

Something a little like this is happening in computer science. In the late 1960s we witnessed a "software crisis," which many people thought was paradoxical because programming was supposed to be so easy. As a result of the crisis, people are now beginning to renounce every feature of programming that can be considered guilty by virtue of its association with difficulties. Not only **go to** statements are being questioned; we also hear complaints about floating-point calculations, global variables, semaphores, pointer variables, and even assignment statements. Soon we might be restricted to only a dozen or so programs that are sufficiently simple to be allowable; then we will be almost certain that these programs cannot lead us into any trouble, but of course we won't be able to solve many problems.

In the mathematical case, we know what happened: the intuitionists taught the other mathematicians a great deal about deductive methods, while the other mathematicians cleaned up the classical methods and eventually "won" the battle. And a revolution did, in fact, take place. In the computer science case, I imagine that a similar thing will eventually happen: purists will point the way to clean constructions, and others will find ways to purify their use of floating-point arithmetic, pointer variables, assignments, etc., so that these classical tools can be used with comparative safety.

Of course all analogies break down, including this one, especially since I'm not yet conceited enough to compare myself to David Hilbert. But I think it's an amusing coincidence that the present programming revolution is being led by another Dutchman (although he doesn't have extremist views corresponding to Brouwer's); and I do consider assignment statements and pointer variables to be among computer science's "most valuable treasures."

At the present time I think we are on the verge of discovering at last what programming languages should really be like. I look forward to seeing many responsible experiments with language design during the next few years; and my dream is that by 1984 we will see a consensus developing for a really good programming language (or, more likely, a coherent family of languages). Furthermore, I'm guessing that people will become so disenchanted with the languages they are now using — even COBOL and FORTRAN — that this new language, UTOPIA 84, will have a chance to take over. At present we are far from that goal, yet there are indications that such a language is very slowly taking shape.

Will UTOPIA 84, or perhaps we should call it NEWSPEAK, contain **go to** statements? At the moment, unfortunately, there isn't even a consensus about this apparently trivial issue, and we had better not be hung up on the question too much longer since there are less than ten years left.

I will try in what follows to give a reasonably comprehensive survey of the **go to** controversy, arguing both pro and con, without taking a strong stand one way or the other until the discussion is nearly complete. In order to illustrate different uses of **go to** statements, I will discuss many example programs, some of which tend to negate the conclusions we might draw from the others. There are two reasons why I have chosen to present the material in this apparently vacillating manner. First, since I have the opportunity to choose all the examples, I don't think it's fair to load the dice by selecting only program fragments which favor one side of the argument. Second, and perhaps most important, I tried this approach when I lectured on the subject at UCLA in February 1974, and it worked beautifully: nearly everybody in the audience had the illusion that I was largely supporting his or her views, regardless of what those views were!

Elimination of go to statements

Historical background

At the IFIP Congress in 1971 I had the pleasure of meeting Dr. Eiichi Goto of Japan, who cheerfully complained that he was always being eliminated. Here is the history of the subject, as far as I have been able to trace it.

The first programmer who systematically began to avoid all labels and **go to** statements was perhaps D.V. Schorre, then of UCLA. He has written the following account of his early experiences [8].

> Since the summer of 1960, I have been writing programs in outline form, using conventions of indentation to indicate the flow of control. I have never found it necessary to take exception to these conventions by using *go statements.* I used to keep these outlines as original documentation of a program, instead of using flow charts. . . . Then I would code the program in assembly language from the outline. Everyone liked these outlines better than the flow charts I had drawn before, which were not very neat — my flow charts had been nick-named "balloon-o-grams."

He reported that this method made programs easier to plan, to modify and to check out.

When I met Schorre in 1963, he told me of his radical ideas, and I didn't believe they would work. In fact, I suspected that it was really his rationalization for not finding an easy way to put labels and **go to** statements into his

META-II subset of ALGOL [9], a language which I liked very much except for this omission. In 1964 I challenged him to write a program for the eight-queens problem without using **go to** statements, and he responded with a program using recursive procedures and Boolean variables, very much like the program later published independently by Wirth [10].

I was still not convinced that all **go to** statements could or should be done away with, although I fully subscribed to Peter Naur's observations which had appeared about the same time [11]. Since Naur's comments were the first published remarks about harmful **go to**'s, it is instructive to quote some of them here:

> If you look carefully you will find that surprisingly often a **go to** statement which looks back really is a concealed **for** statement. And you will be pleased to find how the clarity of the algorithm improves when you insert the **for** clause where it belongs. . . . If the purpose [of a programming course] is to teach ALGOL programming, the use of flow diagrams will do more harm than good, in my opinion.

The next year we find George Forsythe also purging **go to** statements from algorithms submitted to *Communications of the ACM* [12]. Incidentally, the second example program at the end of the original ALGOL 60 report [13] contains four **go to** statements, to labels named AA, BB, CC, and DD, so it is clear that the advantages of ALGOL's control structures weren't fully perceived in 1960.

In 1965, Edsger Dijkstra published the following instructive remarks [14]:

> Two programming department managers from different countries and different backgrounds — the one mainly scientific, the other mainly commercial — have communicated to me, independently of each other and on their own initiative, their observation that the quality of their programmers was inversely proportional to the density of goto statements in their programs. . . . I have done various programming experiments . . . in modified versions of ALGOL 60 in which the goto statement was abolished. . . . The latter versions were more difficult to make: we are so familiar with the jump order that it requires some effort to forget it! In all cases tried, however, the program without the goto statement turned out to be shorter and more lucid.

A few months later, at the ACM Programming Languages and Pragmatics Conference, Peter Landin put it this way [15]:

> There is a game sometimes played with ALGOL 60 programs — rewriting them so as to avoid using **go to** statements. It is part of a more embracing game — reducing the extent to which the program conveys its information by explicit sequencing. . . . The game's

significance lies in that it frequently produces a more "transparent" program — easier to understand, debug, modify, and incorporate into a larger program.

Peter Naur reinforced this opinion at the same meeting [16].

The next chapter in the story is what many people regard as the first, because it made the most waves. Dijkstra submitted a short article to *Communications of the ACM* devoted entirely to a discussion of **go to** statements. In order to speed publication, the editor decided to publish Dijkstra's article as a letter, and to supply a new title, "Go to statement considered harmful." This note [17] rapidly became well-known; it expressed Dijkstra's conviction that **go to**'s "should be abolished from all 'higher level' programming languages (i.e., everything except, perhaps, plain machine code). . . . The **go to** statement as it stands is just too primitive; it is too much an invitation to make a mess of one's program." He encouraged looking for alternative constructions which may be necessary to satisfy all needs. Dijkstra also recalled that Heinz Zemanek had expressed doubts about **go to** statements as early as 1959; and that Peter Landin, Christopher Strachey, C.A.R. Hoare and others had been of some influence on his thinking.

By 1967, the entire XPL compiler had been written by McKeeman, Horning, and Wortman, using **go to** only once ([18], pp. 365-458; the **go to** is on page 385). Similarly, Christopher Strachey [19] reported, "It is my aim to write programs with no labels. I am doing quite well. I have got the operating system down to 5 labels and I am planning to write a compiler with no labels at all." In 1972, an entire session of the ACM National Conference was devoted to the subject [20, 21, 22]. The December, 1973, issue of *Datamation* featured five articles about structured programming and elimination of **go to**'s [23, 24, 25, 26, 27]. Thus, it is clear that sentiments against **go to** statements have been building up. In fact, the discussion has apparently caused some people to feel threatened; Dijkstra once told me that he actually received "a torrent of abusive letters" after publication of his article.

The tide of opinion first hit me personally in 1969, when I was teaching an introductory programming course for the first time. I remember feeling frustrated on several occasions at not seeing how to write programs in the new style; I would run to Bob Floyd's office asking for help, and he usually showed me what to do. This was the genesis of our article [28] in which we presented two types of programs which did not submit gracefully to the new prohibition. We found that there was no way to implement certain simple constructions with **while** and conditional statements substituted for **go to**'s, unless extra computation was specified.

During the last few years several languages have appeared in which the designers proudly announced that they have abolished the **go to** statement. Perhaps the most prominent of these is BLISS [29], whose authors originally replaced **go to**'s by eight so-called "escape" statements. And the eight weren't even enough; the authors wrote, "Our mistake was in assuming that there is no need for a label once the **go to** is removed," and they later [30, 22] added a new statement "**leave** ⟨label⟩ **with** ⟨expression⟩" which goes to the place *after* the statement identified by the ⟨label⟩. Other **go to**-less languages for systems programming have similarly introduced other statements which provide "equally powerful" alternative ways to jump.

In other words, it seems that there is widespread agreement that **go to** statements are harmful, yet programmers and language designers still feel the need for some euphemism that "goes to" without saying **go to**.

A searching example

What are the reasons for this? In Knuth and Floyd [28], Floyd and I gave the following example of a typical program for which the ordinary capabilities of **while** and **if** statements are inadequate. Let's suppose that we want to search a table A[1] . . . A[m] of distinct values, in order to find where a given value x appears; if x is not present in the table, we want to insert it as an additional entry. Let's suppose further that there is another array B, where B[i] equals the number of times we have searched for the value A[i]. We might solve such a problem as follows:

Example 1

```
for i := 1 step 1 until m do
  if A[i] = x then go to found fi;
not found: i := m + 1; m := i;
  A[i] := x; B[i] := 0;
found: B[i] := B[i]+1;
```

(In the present article I shall use an ad hoc programming language that is very similar to ALGOL 60, with one exception: the symbol **fi** is required as a closing bracket for all **if** statements, so that **begin** and **end** aren't needed between **then** and **else**. I don't really like the looks of **fi** at the moment; but it is short, performs a useful function, and connotes finality, so I'm confidently hoping that I'll get used to it. Alan Perlis has remarked that **fi** is a perfect example of a cryptic notation that can make programming unnecessarily complicated for beginners; yet I'm more comfortable with **fi** every time I write it. I still balk at spelling *other* basic symbols backwards, and so do most of the people I know; a student's paper containing the code fragment "**esac; comment** bletch **tnemmoc;**" is a typical reaction to this trend!)

There are ways to express Example 1 without **go to** statements, but they require more computation and aren't really more perspicuous. Therefore, this example has been widely quoted in defense of the **go to** statement, and it is appropriate to scrutinize the problem carefully.

Let's suppose that we've been forbidden to use **go to** statements, and that we want to do *precisely* the computation specified in Example 1 (using the obvious expansion of such a **for** statement into assignments and a **while** iteration). If this means not only that we want the same results, but also that we want to do the same operations in the same order, the mission is impossible. But if we are allowed to weaken the conditions just slightly, so that a relation can be tested twice in succession (assuming that it will yield the same result each time, i.e., that it has no side effects), we can solve the problem as follows:

Example 1a

$$i := 1;$$
$$\textbf{while } i \leqslant m \textbf{ and } A[i] \neq x \textbf{ do } i := i + 1$$
$$\textbf{if } i > m \textbf{ then } m := i; A[i] := x; B[i] := 0 \textbf{ fi};$$
$$B[i] := B[i]+1;$$

The **and** operation used here stands for McCarthy's sequential conjunction operator [31]; i.e., "*p* **and** *q*" means "**if** *p* **then** *q* **else false fi**" so that *q* is not evaluated when *p* is false. Example 1a will do exactly the same sequence of computations as Example 1, except for one extra comparison of *i* with *m* (and occasionally one less computation of $m + 1$). If the iteration in this **while** loop is performed a large number of times, the extra comparison has a negligible effect on the running time.

Thus, we can live without the **go to** in Example 1. But Example 1a is slightly less readable, in my opinion, as well as slightly slower; so it isn't clear what we have gained. Furthermore, if we had made Example 1 more complicated, the trick of going to Example 1a would no longer work. For example, suppose we had inserted another statement into the **for** loop, just before the **if** clause; then the relations $i \leqslant m$ and $A[i] = x$ wouldn't have been tested consecutively, and we couldn't in general have combined them with **and**.

John Cocke told me an instructive story relating to Example 1 and to the design of languages. Some PL/I programmers were asked to do the stated search problem without using jumps, and they came up with essentially the following two solutions:

```
a)    DO I = 1 TO M WHILE (A(I) ¬ = X);
      END;
      IF I > M THEN
          DO; M = I; A(I) = X; B(I) = 0; END;
      B(I) = B(I) + 1;

b)    FOUND = 0;
      DO I = 1 TO M WHILE (FOUND = 0);
              IF A(I) = X THEN FOUND = 1;
      END;
      IF FOUND = 0 THEN
              DO; M = I; A(I) = X; B(I) = 0; END;
      B(I) = B(I) + 1;
```

Solution (a) is better, but since it involves a null iteration (with no explicit statements being iterated) most people came up with Solution (b). The instructive point is that Solution (b) doesn't work; there is a serious bug which caused great puzzlement before the reason was found. Can the reader spot the difficulty? (The answer appears on page 315.)

As I've said, Example 1 has often been used to defend the **go to** statement. Unfortunately, however, the example is totally unconvincing in spite of the arguments I've stated so far, because the method in Example 1 is almost *never* a good way to search an array for *x!* The following modification to the data structure makes the algorithm much better:

Example 2

$$A[m + 1] := x; i := 1;$$
while $A[i] \neq x$ **do** $i := i + 1;$
if $i > m$ **then** $m := i; B[i] := 1;$
else $B[i] := B[i]+1$ **fi**;

Example 2 beats Example 1 because it makes the inner loop considerably faster. If we assume that the programs have been handcoded in assembly language, so that the values of i, m, and x are kept in registers, and if we let n be the final value of i at the end of the program, Example 1 will make $6n + 10$ (+3 if not found) references to memory for data and instructions on a typical computer, while the second program will make only $4n + 14$ (+6 if not found). If, on the other hand, we assume that these programs are translated by a typical "90% efficient compiler" with bounds-checking suppressed, the corresponding run-time figures are respectively about $14n + 5$ and $11n + 21$. (The appendix to this article explains the ground rules for these calculations.) Under the first assumption we save about 33% of the run-time, and under the second assumption we save about 21%, so in both cases the elimination of the **go to** has also eliminated some of the running time.

Efficiency

The ratio of running times (about 6 to 4 in the first case when n is large) is rather surprising to people who haven't studied program behavior carefully. Example 2 doesn't look *that* much more efficient, but it is. Experience has shown (see [32, 33]) that most of the running time in non-IO-bound programs is concentrated in about 3% of the source text. We often see a short inner loop whose speed governs the overall program speed to a remarkable degree; speeding up the inner loop by 10% speeds up everything by almost 10%. And if the inner loop has 10 instructions, a moment's thought will usually cut it to 9 or fewer.

My own programming style has of course changed during the last decade, according to the trends of the times (e.g., I'm not quite so tricky anymore, and I use fewer **go to**'s), but the major change in my style has been due to this

268 CLASSICS IN SOFTWARE ENGINEERING

inner loop phenomenon. I now look with an extremely jaundiced eye at every operation in a critical inner loop, seeking to modify my program and data structure (as in the change from Example 1 to Example 2) so that some of the operations can be eliminated. The reasons for this approach are that (a) it doesn't take long, since the inner loop is short; (b) the payoff is real; and (c) I can then afford to be less efficient in the other parts of my programs, which therefore are more readable and more easily written and debugged. Tools are being developed to make this critical-loop identification job easy (see [32, 34]).

Thus, if I hadn't seen how to remove one of the operations from the loop in Example 1 by changing to Example 2, I would probably (at least) have made the **for** loop run from m to 1 instead of from 1 to m, since it's usually easier to test for zero than to compare with m. And if Example 2 were really critical, I would improve on it still more by "doubling it up" so that the machine code would be essentially as follows.

Example 2a

```
A[m + 1] := x; i := 1; go to test;
loop:   i := i + 2;
test:   if A[i] = x then go to found fi;
        if A[i + 1] ≠ x then go to loop fi;
        i := i + 1;
found: if i > m then m := i; B[i] := 1;
        else B[i] := B[i]+1 fi;
```

Here the loop variable i increases by 2 on each iteration, so we need to do that operation only half as often as before; the rest of the code in the loop has essentially been duplicated to make this work. The running time has now been reduced to about $3.5n + 14.5$ or $8.5n + 23.5$ under our respective assumptions — again this is a noticeable saving in the overall running speed, if, say, the average value of n is about 20, and if this search routine is performed a million or so times in the overall program. Such loop-optimizations are not difficult to learn and, as I have said, they are appropriate in just a small part of a program, yet they very often yield substantial savings. (Of course if we want to improve on Example 2a still more, especially for large m, we'll use a more sophisticated search technique; but let's ignore that issue, at the moment, since I want to illustrate loop optimization in general, not searching in particular.)

The improvement in speed from Example 2 to Example 2a is only about 12%, and many people would pronounce that insignificant. The conventional wisdom shared by many of today's software engineers calls for ignoring efficiency in the small; but I believe this is simply an overreaction to the abuses they see being practiced by penny-wise-and-pound-foolish programmers, who can't debug or maintain their "optimized" programs. In established engineering disciplines a 12% improvement, easily obtained, is never considered marginal; and I believe the same viewpoint should prevail in software engineering. Of course I wouldn't bother making such optimizations on a one-shot job, but when it's a question of preparing quality programs, I don't want to restrict myself to tools that deny me such efficiencies.

There is no doubt that the "grail" of efficiency leads to abuse. Programmers waste enormous amounts of time thinking about, or worrying about, the speed of noncritical parts of their programs, and these attempts at efficiency actually have a strong negative impact when debugging and maintenance are considered. We *should* forget about small efficiencies, say about 97% of the time: premature optimization is the root of all evil.

Yet we should not pass up our opportunities in that critical 3%. A good programmer will not be lulled into complacency by such reasoning, he will be wise to look carefully at the critical code; but only *after* that code has been identified. It is often a mistake to make a priori judgments about what parts of a program are really critical, since the universal experience of programmers who have been using measurement tools has been that their intuitive guesses fail. After working with such tools for seven years, I've become convinced that all compilers written from now on should be designed to provide all programmers with feedback indicating what parts of their programs are costing the most; indeed, this feedback should be supplied automatically unless it has been specifically turned off.

After a programmer knows which parts of his routines are really important, a transformation like doubling up of loops will be worthwhile. Note that this transformation introduces **go to** statements — and so do several other loop optimizations; I will return to this point later. Meanwhile I have to admit that the presence of **go to** statements in Example 2a has a negative as well as a positive effect on efficiency; a non-optimizing compiler will tend to produce awkward code, since the contents of registers can't be assumed known when a label is passed. When I computed the running times cited above by looking at a typical compiler's output for this example, I found that the improvement in performance was not quite as much as I had expected.

Error exits

For simplicity I have avoided a very important issue in the previous examples, but it must now be faced. All of the programs we have considered exhibit bad programming practice, since they fail to make the necessary check that m has not gone out of range. In each case before we perform "$m := i$" we should precede that operation by a test such as

if $m = max$ **then go to** memory overflow;

where *max* is an appropriate threshold value. I left this statement out of the examples since it would have been distracting, but we need to look at it now since it is another important class of **go to** statements: an *error exit*. Such checks on the validity of data are very important, especially in software, and it seems to be the one class of **go to**'s that still is considered ugly but necessary by today's leading reformers. (I wonder how Val Schorre has managed to avoid such **go to**'s during all these years.)

Sometimes it is necessary to exit from several levels of control, cutting across code that may even have been written by other programmers; and the most graceful way to do this is a direct approach with a **go to** or its equivalent. Then the intermediate levels of the program can be written under the assumption that nothing will go wrong.

I will return to the subject of error exits later.

Subscript checking

In the particular examples given above we can, of course, avoid testing m vs. *max* if we have dynamic range-checking on all subscripts of A. But this usually aborts the program, giving us little or no control over the error recovery; so we probably want to test m anyway. And ouch, what subscript checking does to the inner loop execution times! In Example 2, I will certainly want to suppress range-checking in the **while** clause since its subscript can't be out of range unless $A[m + 1]$ was already invalid in the previous line. Similarly, in Example 1 there can be no range error in the **for** loop unless a range error occurred earlier. It seems senseless to have expensive range checks in those parts of my programs that I *know* are clean.

In this respect I should mention Hoare's almost persuasive arguments to the contrary [35]. He points out quite correctly that the current practice of compiling subscript range checks into the machine code while a program is being tested, then suppressing the checks during production runs, is like a sailor who wears his life preserver while training on land but leaves it behind when he sails! On the other hand, that sailor isn't so foolish if life vests are extremely expensive, and if he is such an excellent swimmer that the chance of needing one is quite small compared with the other risks he is taking. In the foregoing examples we typically are much more certain that the subscripts will be in range than that other aspects of our overall program will work correctly. John Cocke observes that time-consuming range checks can be avoided by a smart compiler which first compiles the checks into the program and then moves them out of the loop. Wirth [36] and Hoare [37] have pointed out that a well-designed **for** statement can permit even a rather simple-minded compiler to avoid most range checks within loops.

I believe that range-checking should be used far more often than it currently is, but not everywhere. On the other hand I am really assuming infallible hardware when I say this; surely I wouldn't want to remove the parity check mechanism from the hardware, even under a hypothetical assumption that it was slowing down the computation. Additional memory protection is necessary to prevent my program from harming someone else's, and theirs from clobbering mine. My arguments are directed towards compiled-in tests, not towards the hardware mechanisms which are really needed to ensure reliability.

Hash coding

Now let's move on to another example, based on a standard hashing technique but otherwise designed for the same application as the above. Here $h(x)$ is a hash function which takes on values between 1 and m; and $x \neq 0$. In this case m is somewhat larger than the number of items in the table, and "empty" positions are represented by 0.

Example 3

```
i := h(x);
while A[i] ≠ 0 do
  begin if A[i] = x then go to found fi;
    i := i − 1; if i = 0 then i := m fi;
  end;
not found: A[i] := x; B[i] := 0;
found: B[i] := B[i]+1;
```

If we analyze this as we did Example 1, we see that the trick which led to Example 2 doesn't work any more. Yet if we want to eliminate the **go to** we can apply the idea of Example 1a by writing

$$\textbf{while } A[i] \neq 0 \textbf{ and } A[i] \neq x \textbf{ do} \ldots$$

and by testing afterwards which condition caused termination. This version is perhaps a little bit easier to read; unfortunately it makes a redundant test, which we would like to avoid if we were in a critical part of the program.

Why should I worry about the redundant test in this case? After all, the extra test whether $A[i]$ was $\neq 0$ or $\neq x$ is being made outside of the **while** loop, and I said before that we should generally confine our optimizations to inner loops. Here, the reason is that this **while** loop *won't* usually be a loop at all; with a proper choice of h and m, the operation $i := i − 1$ will tend to be executed very infrequently, often less than once per search on the average [38]. Thus, the entire program of Example 3, except perhaps for the line labeled "not found," must be considered as part of the inner loop, if this search process is a dominant part of the overall program (as it often is). The redundant test will therefore be significant in this case.

Despite this concern with efficiency, I should actually have written the first draft of Example 3 without that **go to** statement, probably even using a **while** clause written in an extended language, such as

$$\textbf{while } A[i] \notin \{0, x\} \textbf{ do} \ldots$$

since this formulation abstracts the *real* meaning of what is happening. Someday there may be hardware capable of testing membership in small sets more efficiently than if we program the test sequentially, so that such a program would lead to better code than Example 3. And there is a much more important reason for preferring this form of the **while** clause: it reflects a symmetry between 0 and x that is not present in Example 3. For example, in most software applications it turns out that the condition $A[i] = x$ terminates the loop far more frequently than $A[i] = 0$; with this knowledge, my second draft of the program would be the following.

Example 3a

```
i := h(x);
while A[i] ≠ x do
 begin if A[i] = 0
  then A[i] := x; B[i] := 0;
   go to found;
  fi;
   i := i − 1; if i = 0 then i := m fi;
  end;
 found: B[i] := B[i]+1;
```

This program is easy to derive from the **go to**-less form, but not from Example 3; and it is better than Example 3. So, again we see the advantage of delaying optimizations until we have obtained more knowledge of a program's behavior.

It is instructive to consider Example 3a further, assuming now that the **while** loop is performed many times per search. Although this should not happen in most applications of hashing, there are other programs in which a loop of the above form is present, so it is worth examining what we should do in such circumstances. If the **while** loop becomes an inner loop affecting the overall program speed, the whole picture changes; that redundant test outside the loop becomes utterly negligible, but the test "**if** $i = 0$" suddenly looms large. We generally want to avoid testing conditions that are almost always false, inside a critical loop. Therefore, under these new assumptions I would change the data structure by adding a new element $A[0] = 0$ to the array and eliminating the test for $i = 0$ as follows.

Example 3b

```
i := h(x);
while A[i] ≠ x do
 if A[i] ≠ 0
 then i := i − 1
 else if i = 0
  then i := m;
  else A[i] := x; B[i] := 0;
   go to found;
  fi;
 fi;
 found: B[i] := B[i]+1;
```

The loop now is noticeably faster. Again, I would be unhappy with slow subscript range checks if this loop were critical. Incidentally, Example 3b was derived from Example 3a, and a rather different program would have emerged if the same idea had been applied to Example 3; then a test "**if** $i = 0$" would have been inserted *outside* the loop, at label "not found," and another **go to** would have been introduced by the optimization process.

As in the first examples, the program in Example 3 is flawed in failing to test for memory overflow. I should have done this, for example, by keeping a count, n, of how many items are nonzero. The "not found" routine should then begin with something like "$n := n + 1$; **if** $n = m$ **then go to** memory overflow."

Text scanning

The first time I consciously applied the top-down structured programming methodology to a reasonably complex job was in the late summer of 1972, when I wrote a program to prepare the index to my book *Sorting and Searching* [39]. I was quite pleased with the way that program turned out (there was only one serious bug), but I did use one **go to** statement. In this case the reason was somewhat different, having nothing to do with exiting from loops; I was exiting, in fact, from an **if-then-else** construction.

The following example is a simplified version of the situation I encountered. Suppose we are processing a stream of text, and that we want to read and print the next character from the input; however, if that character is a slash ("/") we want to "tabulate" instead (i.e., to advance in the output to the next tab-stop position on the current line); however, two consecutive slashes means a "carriage return" (i.e., to advance in the output to the beginning of the next line). After printing a period (".") we also want to insert an additional space in the output. The following code clearly does the trick.

Example 4

```
x := read char;
if x = slash
then x := read char;
 if x = slash
 then return the carriage;
  go to char processed;
 else tabulate;
 fi;
fi;
write char (x);
if x = period then write char (space) fi;
char processed:
```

An abstract program with similar characteristics has been studied by Peterson, et al. [40], Fig. 1a. In practice we occasionally run into situations where a sequence of decisions is made via nested **if-then-else**'s, and then two or more of the branches merge into one. We can manage such decision-table tasks without **go to**'s by copying the common code into each place, or by defining it as a **procedure**, but this does not seem conceptually simpler than to make such cases **go to** a common part of the program. Thus in Example 4 I could avoid the **go to** by copying "*write char* (*x*); **if** *x* = *period* **then** *write char* (*space*) **fi**" into the program after "*tabulate;*" and by making corresponding changes. But this would be a pointless waste of energy just to eliminate a perfectly understandable **go to** statement: the resulting program would actually be harder to maintain than the former, since the action of printing a character now appears in two different places. The alternative of declaring procedures avoids the latter problem, but it is not especially attractive either. Still another alternative is:

Example 4a

```
x := read char;
double slash := false;
if x = slash
then x := read char;
  if x = slash
  then double slash := true;
  else tabulate;
  fi;
fi;
if double slash
then return the carriage;
else write char(x);
  if x = period then write char (space) fi;
fi;
```

I claim that this is conceptually no simpler than Example 4; indeed, one can argue that it is actually more difficult, because it makes the *entire* routine aware of the "double slash" exception to the rules, instead of dealing with it in one exceptional place.

A confession

Before we go on to another example, I must admit what many readers already suspect, namely, that I'm subject to substantial bias because I actually have a vested interest in **go to** statements! The style for the series of books I'm writing was set in the early 1960s, and it would be too difficult for me to change it now; I present algorithms in my books using informal English language descriptions, and **go to** or its equivalent is almost the only control structure I have. Well, I rationalize this apparent anachronism by arguing that: (a) an informal English description seems advantageous because many readers tell me they automatically read English, but skip over formal code; (b) when **go to** statements are used judiciously together with comments stating nonobvious loop invariants, they are semantically equivalent to **while** statements, except that indentation is missing to indicate the structure; (c) the algorithms are nearly always short, so that accompanying flowcharts are able to illustrate the structure; (d) I try to present algorithms in a form that is most efficient for implementation, and high-level structures often don't do this; (e) many readers will get pleasure from converting my semiformal algorithms into beautifully structured programs in a formal programming language; and (f) we are still learning much about control structures, and I can't afford to wait for the final consensus.

In spite of these rationalizations, I'm uncomfortable about the situation, because I find others occasionally publishing examples of algorithms in "my" style but without the important parenthesized comments and/or with unrestrained use of **go to** statements. In addition, I also know of places where I have myself used a complicated structure with excessively unrestrained **go to** statements, especially the notorious Algorithm 2.3.3A for multivariate polynomial addition [41]. The original program had at least three bugs; exercise 2.3.3−14, "Give a formal proof (or disproof) of the validity of Algorithm A," was therefore unexpectedly easy. Now in the second edition, I believe that the revised algorithm is correct, but I still don't know any good way to prove it; I've had to raise the difficulty rating of exercise 2.3.3−14, and I hope someday to see the algorithm cleaned up without loss of its efficiency.

My books emphasize efficiency because they deal with algorithms that are used repeatedly as building blocks in a large variety of applications. It is important to keep efficiency in its place, as mentioned above, but when efficiency counts we should also know how to achieve it.

In order to make it possible to derive quantitative assessments of efficiency, my books show how to analyze machine language programs; and these programs are expressed in MIXAL, a symbolic assembly language that explicitly corresponds one-for-one to machine language. This has its uses, but there is a danger of placing too much stress on assembly code. Programs in MIXAL are like programs in machine language, devoid of structure; or, more precisely, it is difficult for our eyes to perceive the program structure. Accompanying comments explain the program and relate it to the global structure illustrated in flowcharts, but it is not so easy to understand what is going on; and it is easy to make mistakes, partly because we rely so much on comments which might possibly be inaccurate descriptions of what the program really does. It is clearly better to write programs in a language that reveals the control structure, even if we are intimately conscious of the hardware at each step; and therefore I will be discussing a structured assembly language called PL/MIX in the fifth volume of *The Art of Computer Programming.* Such a language (analogous to Wirth's PL360 [42]) should really be supported by each manufacturer for each machine in place of the old-fashioned structureless assemblers that still proliferate.

On the other hand I'm not really unhappy that MIXAL programs appear in my books, because I believe that MIXAL is a good example of a "quick and dirty assembler," a genre of software which will always be useful in its proper role. Such an assembler is characterized by language restrictions that make simple one-pass assembly possible, and it has several noteworthy advantages when we are first preparing programs for a new machine: a) it is a great improvement over numeric machine code; b) its rules are easy to state; and c) it can be implemented in an afternoon or so, thus getting an efficient assembler working quickly on what may be very primitive equipment. So far I have implemented six such assemblers, at different times in my life, for machines or interpretive systems or microprocessors that had no existing software of comparable utility; and in each case other constraints made it impractical for me to take the extra time necessary to develop a good, structured assembler. Thus I am sure that the concept of quick-and-dirty-assembler is useful, and I'm glad to let MIXAL illustrate what one is like. However, I also believe strongly that such languages should never be improved to the point where they are too easy or too pleasant to use; one must restrict their use to primitive facilities that are easy to implement efficiently. I would never switch to a two-pass process, or add complex pseudo-operations, macro-facilities, or even fancy error diagnostics to such a language, nor would I maintain or distribute such a language as a standard programming tool for a real machine. All such ameliorations and refinements should appear in a structured assembler. Now that the technology is available, we can condone unstructured languages only as a bootstrap-like means to a limited end, when there are strong economic reasons for not implementing a better system.

Tree searching

But, I'm digressing from my subject of **go to** elimination in higher level languages. A few weeks ago I decided to choose an algorithm at random from my books, to study its use of **go to** statements. The very first example I encountered [38] (Algorithm 6.2.3C) turned out to be another case where existing programming languages have no good substitute for **go to**'s. In simplified form, the loop where the trouble arises can be written as follows.

Example 5

```
compare:
if A[i] < x
then if L[i] ≠ 0
    then i := L[i]; go to compare;
    else L[i] := j; go to insert fi;
else if R[i] ≠ 0
    then i := R[i]; go to compare;
    else R[i] := j; go to insert fi;
fi;
insert: A[j] := x;
L[j] := 0; R[j] := 0; j := j +1;
```

This is part of the well-known "tree search and insertion" scheme, where a binary search tree is being represented by three arrays: $A[i]$ denotes the information stored at node number i, and $L[i]$, $R[i]$ are the respective node numbers for the roots of that node's left and right subtrees; empty subtrees are represented by zero. The program searches down the tree until finding an empty subtree where x can be inserted; and variable j points to an appropriate place to do the insertion. For convenience, I have assumed in this example that x is not already present in the search tree.

Example 5 has four **go to** statements, but the control structure is saved from obscurity because the program is so beautifully symmetric between L and R. I know that these **go to** statements can be eliminated by introducing a Boolean variable which becomes true when $L[i]$ or $R[i]$ is found to be zero. But I don't want to test this variable in the inner loop of my program.

Systematic elimination

A good deal of theoretical work has been addressed to the question of **go to** elimination, and I shall now try to summarize the findings and to discuss their relevance.

S.C. Kleene proved a famous theorem in 1956 [43] which says, in essence, that the set of all paths through any flowchart can be represented as a "regular expression" R built up from the following operations:

s	the single arc s of the flowchart
$R_1; R_2$	concatenation (all paths consisting of a path of R_1 followed by a path of R_2)
$R_1 \cup R_2$	union (all paths of either R_1 or R_2)
R^+	iteration (all paths of the form $p_1; p_2; \dots ;$ p_n for some $n \geq 1$, where each p_i is a path of R)

These regular expressions correspond loosely to programs consisting of statements in a programming language related by the three operations of sequential composition, conditionals (**if-then-else**), and iterations (**while** loops). Thus, we might expect that these three program control structures would be sufficient for all programs. However, closer analysis shows that Kleene's theorem does not relate directly to control structures; the problem is only superficially similar. His result is suggestive but not really applicable in this case.

The analogous result for control structures was first proved by G. Jacopini in 1966, in a paper written jointly with C. Böhm [44]. Jacopini showed, in effect, that any program given, say, in flowchart form can be transformed systematically into another program, which computes the same results and which is built up from statements in the original program using only the three basic operations of composition, conditional, and iteration, plus possible assignment statements and tests on auxiliary variables. Thus, in principle, **go to** statements can always be removed. A detailed exposition of Jacopini's construction has been given by H.D. Mills [45].

Recent interest in structured programming has caused many authors to cite Jacopini's result as a significant breakthrough and as a cornerstone of modern programming technique. Unfortunately, these authors are unaware of the comments made by Cooper [46] and later by Bruno and Steiglitz [47], namely, that from a practical standpoint the theorem is meaningless. Indeed, any program can obviously be put into the "beautifully structured" form

$$
\begin{aligned}
&p := 1; \\
&\textbf{while } p > 0 \textbf{ do} \\
&\quad \textbf{begin if } p = 1 \textbf{ then } \text{perform step 1;} \\
&\qquad p := \text{successor of step 1 } \textbf{fi}; \\
&\quad \textbf{if } p = 2 \textbf{ then } \text{perform step 2;} \\
&\qquad p := \text{successor of step 2 } \textbf{fi}; \\
&\qquad \cdots \\
&\quad \textbf{if } p = n \textbf{ then } \text{perform step } n; \\
&\qquad p := \text{successor of step } n \textbf{ fi}; \\
&\textbf{end}.
\end{aligned}
$$

Here the auxiliary variable p serves as a program counter representing which box of the flowchart we're in, and the program stops when p is set to zero. We have eliminated all **go to**'s, but we've actually lost all the structure.

Jacopini conjectured in his paper that auxiliary variables are necessary in general, and that the **go to**'s in a program of the form

$$
\begin{aligned}
L_1: &\ \textbf{if } B_1 \textbf{ then go to } L_2 \textbf{ fi}; \\
&\ S_1; \\
&\ \textbf{if } B_2 \textbf{ then go to } L_2 \textbf{ fi}; \\
&\ S_2; \\
&\ \textbf{go to } L_1; \\
L_2: &\ S_3;
\end{aligned}
$$

cannot always be removed unless additional computation is done. Floyd and I proved this conjecture with John Hopcroft's help [28]. Sharper results were later obtained by Ashcroft and Manna [48], Bruno and Steiglitz [47], and Peterson, Kasami, and Tokura [40], Kosaraju [49], and Lipton, Eisenstadt, and DeMillo [50]. The theorem of Lipton, Eisenstadt, and DeMillo is especially noteworthy: they have proved that, for all large integers n, there exists an n-statement program using **go to** statements which cannot be converted to any "structured" program of less than $(1.3)^{\sqrt{n}}$ statements unless that program runs at least $\frac{1}{2} \log_2 n$ times slower than the original because of the extra bookkeeping necessary. This holds even if the "structured" program has **go to** statements which jump out of (but not into) loops.

Jacopini's original construction was not merely the trivial flowchart emulation scheme indicated above; he was able to salvage much of the given flowchart structure if it was reasonably well-behaved. A more general technique of **go to** elimination, devised by Ashcroft and Manna [48], made it possible to capture still more of a given program's natural flow; for example, their technique applied to Example 5 yields

Example 5a

```
t := true;
while t do
  begin if A[i] < x
    then if L[i] ≠ 0 then i := L[i];
      else L[i] := j; t := false fi;
    else if R[i] ≠ 0 then i := R[i];
      else R[i] := j; t := false fi;
  end;
  A[j] := x;
```

But, in general, their technique may cause a program to grow exponentially in size; and when error exits or other recalcitrant **go to**'s are present, the resulting programs will indeed look rather like the flowchart emulator sketched above.

If such automatic **go to** elimination procedures are applied to badly structured programs, we can expect the resulting programs to be at least as badly structured. Dijkstra pointed this out already in 1968 [17], saying:

> The exercise to translate an arbitrary flow diagram more or less mechanically into a jumpless one, however, is not to be recommended. Then the resulting flow diagram cannot be expected to be more transparent than the original one.

In other words, we shouldn't merely remove **go to** statements because it's the fashionable thing to do; the presence or absence of **go to** statements is not really the issue. The underlying structure of the program is what counts, and we want only to avoid usages which somehow clutter up the program. Good structure can be expressed in FORTRAN or COBOL, or even in assembly language, although less clearly and with much more trouble. The real goal is to formulate our programs in such a way that they are easily understood.

Program structure refers to the way in which a complex algorithm is built up from successively simpler processes. In most situations this structure can be described very nicely in terms of sequential composition, conditionals, simple iterations, and with **case** statements for multiway branches; undisciplined **go to** statements make program structure harder to perceive, and they are often symptoms of a poor conceptual formulation. But there has been far too much emphasis on **go to** elimination instead of on the really important issues; people have a natural tendency to set up an easily understood quantitative goal like the abolition of jumps, instead of working directly for a qualitative goal like good program structure. In a similar way, many people have set up "zero population growth" as a goal to be achieved, when they really desire living conditions that are much harder to quantify.

Probably the worst mistake any one can make with respect to the subject of **go to** statements is to assume that "structured programming" is achieved by writing programs as we always have and then eliminating the **go to**'s. Most **go to**'s shouldn't be there in the first place! What we really want is to conceive of our program in such a way that we rarely even *think* about **go to** statements, because the real need for them hardly ever arises. The language in which we express our ideas has a strong influence on our thought processes. Therefore, Dijkstra [17] asks for more new language features — structures which encourage clear thinking — in order to avoid the **go to**'s temptations toward complications.

Situation indicators

The best such language feature I know has recently been proposed by C.T. Zahn [51]. Since this is still in the experimental stage, I will take the liberty of modifying his "syntactic sugar" slightly, without changing his basic idea. The essential novelty in his approach is to introduce a new quantity into programming languages, called a *situation indicator*. My current preference is to write his situation-driven construct in the following two general forms.

(a) **loop until** $\langle\text{situation}\rangle_1$ **or** . . . **or** $\langle\text{situation}\rangle_n$:
    $\langle\text{statement list}\rangle_0$;
repeat;
then $\langle\text{situation}\rangle_1 \implies \langle\text{statement list}\rangle_1$;
    .

    .

    $\langle\text{situation}\rangle_n \implies \langle\text{statement list}\rangle_n$;
fi;

(b) **begin until** $\langle\text{situation}\rangle_1$ **or** . . . **or** $\langle\text{situation}\rangle_n$;
    $\langle\text{statement list}\rangle_0$;
end;
then $\langle\text{situation}\rangle_1 \implies \langle\text{statement list}\rangle_1$;
    .

    .

    $\langle\text{situation}\rangle_n \implies \langle\text{statement list}\rangle_n$;
fi;

There is also a new statement, " $\langle\text{situation}\rangle$," which means that the designated situation has occurred: such a statement is allowed only within $\langle\text{statement list}\rangle_0$ of an **until** construct which declares that situation.

In form (a), $\langle\text{statement list}\rangle_0$ is executed repeatedly until control leaves the construct entirely or until one of the named situations occurs; in the latter case, the statement list corresponding to that situation is executed. The behavior in form (b) is similar, except that no iteration is implied; one of the named situations must have occurred before the **end** is reached. The **then** . . . **fi** part may be omitted when there is only one situation name.

The above rules should become clear after looking at what happens when Example 5 above is recoded in terms of this new feature:

Example 5b

```
loop until left leaf hit or
            right leaf hit:
  if A[i] < x
  then if L[i] ≠ 0 then i := L[i];
    else left leaf hit fi;
  else if R[i] ≠ 0 then i := R[i];
    else right leaf hit fi;
  fi;
repeat;
then left leaf hit => L[i] := j;
     right leaf hit => R[i] := j;
fi;
A[j] := x; L[j] := 0; R[j] := 0; j := j + 1;
```

Alternatively, using a single situation name,

Example 5c

```
loop until leaf replaced:
  if A[i] < x
  then if L[i] ≠ 0 then i := L[i]
    else L[i] := j; leaf replaced fi;
  else if R[i] ≠ 0 then i := R[i]
    else R[i] := j; leaf replaced fi;
  fi;
repeat;
A[j] := x; L[j] := 0; R[j] := 0; j := j + 1;
```

For reasons to be discussed later, Example 5b is preferable to 5c.

It is important to emphasize that the first line of the construct merely declares the situation indicator names, and that situation indicators are *not* conditions which are being tested continually; ⟨situation⟩ statements are simply transfers of control which the compiler can treat very efficiently. Thus, in Example 5c the statement "leaf replaced" is essentially a **go to** which jumps out of the loop.

This use of situations is, in fact, semantically equivalent to a restricted form of **go to** statement, which Peter Landin discussed in 1965 [52] before most of us were ready to listen. Landin's device has been reformulated by Clint and Hoare [53] in the following way: Labels are declared at the beginning of each block, just as procedures normally are, and each label also has a ⟨label body⟩ just as a procedure has a ⟨procedure body⟩. Within the block whose heading contains such a declaration of label L, the statement **go to** L according to this scheme means "execute the body of L, then leave the block." It is easy to see that this is exactly the form of control provided by Zahn's situation mechanism, with the ⟨label body⟩s replaced by ⟨statement list⟩s in the **then** ...

fi postlude and with ⟨situation⟩ statements corresponding to Landin's **go to**. Thus, Clint and Hoare would have written Example 5b as follows:

```
while true do
  begin label left leaf hit; L[i] := j;
    label right leaf hit; R[i] := j;
    if A[i] < x
    then if L[i] ≠ 0 then i := L[i];
      else go to left leaf hit fi;
      else if R[i] ≠ 0 then i := R[i];
      else go to right leaf hit fi;
  end;
  A[j] := x; L[j] := 0; R[j] := 0; j := j + 1;
```

I believe the program reads much better in Zahn's form, with the ⟨label body⟩s set in the code between that which logically precedes and follows.

Landin also allowed his "labels" to have parameters like any other procedures; this is a valuable extension to Zahn's proposal, so I shall use situations with value parameters in several of the examples below.

As Zahn [51] has shown, situation-driven statements blend well with the ideas of structured programming by stepwise refinement. Thus, Examples 1 to 3 can all be cast into the following more abstract form, using a situation "found" with an integer parameter:

```
begin until found:
  search table for x and
  insert it if not present;
end;
then found (integer j) => B[j] := B[j]+1;
fi;
```

This much of the program can be written before we have decided how to maintain the table. At the next level of abstraction, we might decide to represent the table as a sequential list, as in Example 1, so that "search table . . ." would expand into

```
for i := 1 step 1 until m do
  if A[i] = x then found (i) fi;
  m := m + 1; A[m] := x; found (m);
```

Note that this **for** loop is more disciplined than the one in our original Example 1, because the iteration variable is not used outside the loop; it now conforms to the rules of ALGOL W and ALGOL 68. Such **for** loops provide convenient documentation and avoid common errors associated with global variables; their advantages have been discussed by Hoare [37].

Similarly, if we want to use the idea of Example 2 we might write the following code as the refinement of "search table . . .":

```
begin integer i;
  A[m + 1] := x; i := 1;
  while A[i] ≠ x do i := i + 1;
  if i > m then m := i; B[m] := 0 fi;
  found(i);
end;
```

And finally, if we decide to use hashing, we obtain the equivalent of Example 3, which might be written as follows.

```
begin integer i;
  i := h(x);
  loop until present or absent;
    if A[i] = x then present fi;
    if A[i] = 0 then absent fi;
    i := i - 1;
    if i = 0 then i := m fi;
  repeat;
  then present => found (i);
       absent => A[i] := x; found(i);
  fi;
end;
```

The **begin until** ⟨situation⟩ construct also provides a natural way to deal with decision-table constructions such as the text-scanning application we have discussed.

Example 4b

```
begin until normal character input
    or double slash:
  char x;
  x := read char;
  if x = slash
  then x := read char;
    if x = slash
    then double slash;
    else tabulate;
      normal character input (x);
    fi;
  else normal character input (x);
  fi;
end;
then normal character input (char x) =>
    write char (x);
    if x = period then write char (space) fi;
  double slash => return the carriage;
fi;
```

This program states the desired actions a bit more clearly than any of our previous attempts were able to do.

Situation indicators handle error exits too. For example, we might write a program as follows:

```
begin until error or normal end:
    . . .
    if m = max then error ('symbol table full') fi;
    . . .
    normal end;
end;
then error (string S) = >
    print ('unrecoverable error', S);
  normal end = >
    print ('computation complete');
fi;
```

Comparison of features

Of course, situation indicators are not the only decent alternatives to **go to** statements that have been proposed. Many authors have suggested language features which provide roughly equivalent facilities, but which are expressed in terms of **exit**, **jumpout**, **break**, or **leave** statements. Kosaraju [49] has proved that such statements are sufficient to express all programs without **go to**'s and without any extra computation, but only if an exit from arbitrarily many levels of control is permitted; furthermore, Kosaraju's construction may require exponential growth in the program size (see the theorem of Lipton, Eisenstadt, and DeMillo cited earlier).

The earliest language features of this kind, besides Landin's proposal, provided essentially only one exit from a loop; this means that the code appearing in the **then** . . . **fi** postlude of our examples would be inserted into the body itself before branching. (See Example 5c.) The separation of such code as in Zahn's proposal is better, mainly because the body of the construct corresponds to code that is written under different "invariant assumptions" which are inoperative after a particular situation has occurred. Thus, each situation corresponds to a particular set of assertions about the state of the program, and the code which follows that situation takes cognizance of these assertions, which are rather different from the assertions in the main body of the construct. (For this reason I prefer Example 5b to Example 5c.)

Language features allowing multiple exits have been proposed by G.V. Bochmann [54], and independently by Shigo, et al. [55]. These are semantically equivalent to Zahn's proposals, with minor variations; but they express such semantics in terms of statements that say "**exit to** ⟨label⟩." I believe Zahn's idea of situation indicators is an improvement on the previous schemes, because the specification of situations instead of labels encourages a better *conception* of the program. The identifier given to a label is often an imperative verb like "insert" or "compare," saying what action is to be done next, while the appropriate identifier for a situation is more likely to be an adjective like "found." The names of situations are very much like the names of Boolean variables, and I believe this accounts for the popularity of Boolean variables as documentation aids, in spite of their inefficiency.

Putting this another way, it is much better from a psychological standpoint to write

loop until found . . . ; found; . . . repeat

than to write

search: while true do
 begin . . . ; leave search; . . . end.

The **leave** or **exit** statement is operationally the same, but intuitively different, since it talks more about the program than about the problem.

The PL/I language allows programmer-defined ON-conditions, which are similar in spirit to situation indicators. A programmer first *executes* a statement "ON CONDITION (identifier) block" which specifies a block of code that is to be executed when the identified situation occurs, and an occurrence of that situation is indicated by writing SIGNAL CONDITION (identifier). However, the analogy is not very close, since control returns to the statement following the SIGNAL statement after execution of the specified block of code, and the block may be dynamically respecified.

Some people have suggested to me that situations should be called "conditions" instead, by analogy with Boolean expressions. However, that terminology would tend to imply a relation which is continually being monitored, instead of a happening. By writing "**loop until** *yprime* is near *y:* . . ." we seem to be saying that the machine should keep track of whether or not *y* and *yprime* are nearly equal; a better choice of words would be a situation name like "**loop until** convergence established: . . ." so that we can write "**if** $abs(yprime - y) <$ $epsilon \times y$ **then** convergence established." A situation arrives when the program has *discovered* that the state of computation has changed.

Simple iterations

So far I haven't mentioned what I believe is really the most common situation in which **go to** statements are needed by an ALGOL or PL/I programmer, namely a simple iterative loop with one entrance and one exit. The iteration statements most often proposed as alternatives to **go to** statements have been "**while** B **do** S" and "**repeat** S **until** B." However, in practice, the iterations I encounter very often have the form

A: S;
 if B then go to Z fi;
 T; go to A;
 Z:

where S and T *both* represent reasonably long sequences of code. If S is empty, we have a **while** loop, and if T is empty we have a **repeat** loop, but in the general case it is a nuisance to avoid the **go to** statements.

A typical example of such an iteration occurs when S is the code to acquire or generate a new piece of data, B is the test for end of data, and T is the processing of that data. Another example is when the code preceding the loop sets initial conditions for some iterative process; then S is a computation of quantities involved in the test for convergence, B is the test for convergence, and T is the adjustment of variables for the next iteration.

Dijkstra [6] aptly named this a loop which is performed "n and a half times." The usual practice for avoiding **go to**'s in such loops is either to duplicate the code for S, writing

$$\text{S; } \textbf{while } \bar{B} \textbf{ do begin } \text{T; S } \textbf{end;}$$

where $\bar{B}$ is the negation of relation B; or to figure out some sort of "inverse" for T so that "T^{-1}; T" is equivalent to a null statement, and writing

$$T^{-1}\text{; } \textbf{repeat } \text{T; S } \textbf{until } \text{B;}$$

or to duplicate the code for B and to make a redundant test, writing

$$\textbf{repeat } \text{S; } \textbf{if } \bar{B} \textbf{ then } \text{T } \textbf{fi}\text{; } \textbf{until } \text{B;}$$

or its equivalent. The reader who studies **go to**-less programs as they appear in the literature will find that all three of these rather unsatisfactory constructions are used frequently.

I discussed this weakness of ALGOL in a letter to Niklaus Wirth in 1967, and he proposed two solutions to the problem, together with many other instructive ideas in an unpublished report on basic concepts of programming languages [36]. His first suggestion was to write

$$\textbf{repeat begin } \text{S; } \textbf{when } \text{B } \textbf{exit}\text{; T; } \textbf{end;}$$

and readers who remember 1967 will also appreciate his second suggestion,

$$\textbf{turn on begin } \text{S; } \textbf{when } \text{B } \textbf{drop out}\text{; T; } \textbf{end.}$$

Neither set of delimiters was felt to be quite right, but a modification of the first proposal (allowing one or more single-level **exit** statements within **repeat begin . . . end**) was later incorporated into an experimental version of the ALGOL W language. Other languages such as BCPL and BLISS incorporated and extended the **exit** idea, as mentioned above. Zahn's construction now allows us to write, for example,

```
loop until all data exhausted:
    S;
    if B then all data exhausted fi;
    T;
repeat;
```

and this is a better syntax for the $n + \frac{1}{2}$ problem than we have had previously.

On the other hand, it would be nicest if our language would provide a single feature which covered all simple iterations without going to a rather "big" construct like the situation-driven scheme. When a programmer uses the simpler feature he is thereby announcing plainly that he has a simple iteration, with exactly one condition which is being tested exactly once each time around the loop. Furthermore, by providing special syntax for this common case we make it easier for a compiler to produce more efficient code, since the compiler can rearrange the machine instructions so that the test appears physically at the end of loop. (Many hours of computer time are now wasted each day executing unconditional jumps to the beginning of loops.)

Ole-Johan Dahl has recently proposed a syntax which I think is the first real solution to the $n + \frac{1}{2}$ problem. He suggests writing the general simple iteration defined above as

$$\textbf{loop: } S; \textbf{ while } \bar{B}: T; \textbf{ repeat};$$

where, as before, S and T denote sequences of one or more statements separated by semicolons. Note that as in two of our original **go to**-free examples, the syntax refers to condition $\bar{B}$ which represents staying *in* the iteration, instead of condition B which represents exiting; and this may be the secret of its success.

Dahl's syntax may not seem appropriate at first, but actually it reads well in every example I have tried, and I hope the reader will reserve judgment until seeing the examples in the rest of this article. One of the nice properties of his syntax is that the word **repeat** occurs naturally at the end of a loop rather than at its beginning, since we read actions of the program sequentially. As we reach the end, we are instructed to repeat the loop, instead of being informed that the *text* of the loop (not its execution) has ended. Furthermore, the above syntax avoids ALGOL's use of the word **do** (and also the more recent unnatural delimiter **od**); the word **do** as used in ALGOL has never sounded quite right to native speakers of English, it has always been rather quaint for us to say "**do** *read* (A[i])" or "**do begin**"! Another feature of Dahl's proposals is that it is easily axiomatized along the lines proposed by Hoare [56]:

$$\frac{\{P\}S\{Q\}}{\{Q \wedge \bar{B}\}T\{P\}}$$
$$\{P\} \textbf{ loop: } S; \textbf{ while } \bar{B}: T; \textbf{ repeat}; \{Q \wedge \neg \bar{B}\}$$

(Here I am using braces around the assertions, as in Wirth's PASCAL language [57], instead of following Hoare's original notation "P {S} Q," since assertions are, by nature, parenthetical remarks.)

The nicest thing about Dahl's proposal is that it works also when S or T is empty, so that we have a uniform syntax for all three cases; the **while** and **repeat** statements found in ALGOL-like languages of the late 1960s are no longer needed. When S or T is empty, it is appropriate to delete the preceding colon.

Thus

> **loop while B̄**:
>   T;
> **repeat**;

takes the place of "**while B̄ do begin** T **end**;" and

> **loop**:
>   S
> **while B̄ repeat**;

takes the place of "**repeat** S **until** B;". At first glance these may seem strange, but probably less strange than the **while** and **repeat** statements did when we first learned them.

If I were designing a programming language today, my current preference would be to use Dahl's mechanism for simple iteration, plus Zahn's more general construct, plus a **for** statement whose syntax would be perhaps

> **loop for** $1 \leq i \leq n$:
>   S;
> **repeat**;

with appropriate extensions. These control structures, together with **if** . . . **then** . . . **else** . . . **fi**, will comfortably handle all the examples discussed so far in this article, without any **go to** statements or loss of efficiency or clarity. Furthermore, none of these language features seem to encourage overly complicated program structure.

Introduction of go to statements

Now that I have discussed how to remove **go to** statements, I will turn around and show why there are occasions when I actually wish to *insert* them into a **go to**-less program. The reason is that I like well-documented programs very much, but I dislike inefficient ones; and there are some cases where I simply seem to need **go to** statements, despite the examples stated above.

Recursion elimination

Such cases come to light primarily when I'm trying to optimize a program (originally well structured), often involving the removal of implicit or explicit recursion. For example, consider the following recursive procedure that prints the contents of a binary tree in symmetric order. The tree is represented by L, A, and R arrays as in Example 5, and the recursive procedure is essentially the *definition* of symmetric order.

Example 6

```
procedure treeprint (t); integer t; value t;
    if t ≠ 0
    then treeprint (L[t]);
        print (A[t]);
        treeprint (R[t]);
    fi;
```

This procedure may be regarded as a model for a great many algorithms which have the same structure, since tree traversal occurs in so many applications; we shall assume for now that printing is our goal, with the understanding that this is only one instance of a general family of algorithms.

It is often useful to remove recursion from an algorithm because of important economies of space or time, even though this tends to cause some loss of the program's basic clarity. (And, of course, we might also have to state our algorithm in a language like FORTRAN or in a machine language that doesn't allow recursion.) Even when we use ALGOL or PL/I, every compiler I know imposes considerable overhead on procedure calls; this is to a certain extent inevitable because of the generality of the parameter mechanisms, especially call by name and the maintenance of proper dynamic environments. When procedure calls occur in an inner loop the overhead can slow a program down by a factor of two or more. But if we hand tailor our own implementation of recursion instead of relying on a general mechanism we can usually find worthwhile simplifications, and in the process we occasionally get a deeper insight into the original algorithm.

There has been a good deal published about recursion elimination, especially in the work of Barron [58], Cooper [46], Manna and Waldinger [59], McCarthy [31], and Strong [60, 61]; but I'm amazed that very little of this is about "down-to-earth" problems. I have always felt that the transformation from recursion to iteration is one of the most fundamental concepts of computer science, and that a student should learn it at about the time he is studying data structures. This topic is the subject of Chapter 8 in my multivolume work; but it's only by accident that recursion wasn't Chapter 3, since it conceptually belongs very early in the table of contents. The material just wouldn't fit comfortably into any of the earlier volumes; yet there are many algorithms in Chapters 1-7 that are recursions in disguise. Therefore it surprises me that the literature on recursion removal is primarily concerned with "baby" examples like computing factorials or reversing lists, instead of with a sturdy toddler like Example 6.

Now let's go to work on the above example. I assume, of course, that the reader knows the standard way of implementing recursion with a stack (Dijkstra [62]), but I want to make simplifications beyond this. Rule number one for simplifying procedure calls is:

If the last action of procedure p before it returns is to call procedure q, simply **go to** the beginning of procedure q instead.

(We must forget for the time being that we don't like **go to** statements.) It is easy to confirm the validity of this rule, if, for simplicity, we assume parameterless procedures. For the operation of calling q is to put a return address on the stack, then to execute q, then to resume p at the return address specified, then to resume the caller of p. The above simplification makes q resume the caller of p. When $q = p$ the argument is perhaps a bit subtle, but it's all right. (I'm not sure who originated this principle; I recall learning it from Gill's paper [63], and then seeing many instances of it in connection with top-down compiler organization. Under certain conditions the BLISS/11 compiler [64] is capable of discovering this simplification. Incidentally, the converse of the above principle is also true (see Knuth and Floyd [28]): **go to** statements can always be eliminated by declaring suitable procedures, each of which calls another as its last action. This shows that procedure calls include **go to** statements as a special case; it cannot be argued that procedures are conceptually simpler than **go to**'s, although some people have made such a claim.)

As a result of applying the above simplification and adapting it in the obvious way to the case of a procedure with one parameter, Example 6 becomes

Example 6a

```
procedure treeprint (t); integer t; value t;
L: if t ≠ 0
   then treeprint (L[t ]);
      print (A[t ]);
      t := R[t ]; go to L;
   fi;
```

But we don't really want that **go to**, so we might prefer to write the code as follows, using Dahl's syntax for iterations as explained above.

Example 6b

```
procedure treeprint (t); integer t; value t;
loop while t ≠ 0:
   treeprint (L[t ]);
   print (A[t ]);
   t := R[t ];
repeat;
```

If our goal is to impress somebody, we might tell them that we thought of Example 6b first, instead of revealing that we got it by straightforward simplification of the obvious program in Example 6.

There is still a recursive call in Example 6b; and this time it's embedded in the procedure, so it looks as though we have to go to the general stack implementation. However, the recursive call now occurs in only one place, so we need not put a return address on the stack; only the local variable t needs to be saved on each call. (This is another simplification which occurs frequently.) The program now takes the following nonrecursive form.

Example 6c

```
procedure treeprint (t); integer t; value t;
   begin integer stack S; S := empty;
L1:   loop while t ≠ 0:
         S <= t; t := L[t ]; go to L1;
L2:   t <= S;
         print (A[t ]);
         t := R[t ];
      repeat;
      if nonempty(S) then go to L2 fi;
   end.
```

Here for simplicity I have extended ALGOL to allow a "stack" data type, where S $<=$ t means "push t onto S" and $t <=$ S means "pop the top of S to t, assuming that S is nonempty."

It is easy to see that Example 6c is equivalent to Example 6b. The statement "**go to** L1" initiates the procedure, and control returns to the following statement (labeled L2) when the procedure is finished. Although Example 6c involves **go to** statements, their purpose is easy to understand, given the knowledge that we have produced Example 6c by a mechanical, completely reliable method for removing recursion. Hopkins [20] has given other examples where **go to** at a low level supports high-level constructions.

But if you look at the above program again, you'll probably be just as shocked as I was when I first realized what has happened. I had always thought that the use of **go to** statements was a bit sinful, say a "venial sin"; but there was one kind of **go to** that I certainly had been taught to regard as a mortal sin, perhaps even unforgivable, namely one which goes into the middle of an iteration! Example 6c does precisely that, and it is perfectly easy to understand Example 6c by comparing it with Example 6b. In this particular case we can remove the **go to**'s without difficulty; but in general, when a recursive call is embedded in several complex levels of control, there is no equally simple way to remove the recursion without resorting to something like Example 6c. As I say, it was a shock when I first ran across such an example. Later, Jim Horning confessed to me that he also was guilty, in the syntax-table-building program for the XPL system [18], because XPL doesn't allow recursion; see also Knuth and Szwarcfiter [65]. Clearly a new doctrine about sinful **go to**'s is needed — some sort of "situation ethics."

The new morality that I propose may perhaps be stated thus: "Certain **go to** statements which arise in connection with well-understood transformations are acceptable, provided that the program documentation explains what the transformation was." The use of four-letter words like **goto** can occasionally be justified even in the best of company.

This situation is very similar to what people have commonly encountered when proving a program correct. To demonstrate the validity of a typical program Q, it is usually simplest and best to prove that some rather simple but less efficient program P is correct and then to prove that P can be transformed into Q by a sequence of valid optimizations. I'm saying that a similar thing should be considered standard practice for all but the simplest software programs: A programmer should create a program P which is readily understood and well-documented, and then he should optimize it into a program Q which is very efficient. Program Q may contain **go to** statements and other low-level features, but the transformation from P to Q should be accomplished by completely reliable and well-documented "mechanical" operations.

At this point many readers will say, "But he should only write P, and an optimizing compiler will produce Q." To this I say, "No, the optimizing compiler would have to be so complicated (much more so than anything we have now) that it will in fact be *un*reliable." I have another alternative to propose, a new class of software which will be far better.

Program manipulation systems

For 15 years or so I have been trying to think of how to write a compiler that really produces top quality code. For example, most of the MIX programs in my books are considerably more efficient than any of today's most visionary compiling schemes would be able to produce. I've tried to study the various techniques that a hand-coder like myself uses, and to fit them into some systematic and automatic system. A few years ago, several students and I looked at a typical sample of FORTRAN programs [33], and we all tried hard to see how a machine could produce code that would compete with our best hand-optimized object programs. We found ourselves always running up against the same problem: the compiler needs to be in a dialog with the programmer; it needs to know properties of the data, and whether certain cases can arise, etc. And we couldn't think of a good language in which to have such a dialog.

For some reason we all (especially me) had a mental block about optimization, namely that we always regarded it as a behind-the-scenes activity, to be done in the machine language, which the programmer isn't supposed to know. This veil was first lifted from my eyes in the fall of 1973, when I ran across a remark by Hoare [66] that, ideally, a language should be designed so that an optimizing compiler can describe its optimizations in the *source* language. Of course! Why hadn't I ever thought of it?

Once we have a suitable language, we will be able to have what seems to be emerging as the programming system of the future: an interactive *program-manipulation system*, analogous to the many symbol-manipulation systems which are presently undergoing extensive development and experimentation. We are gradually learning about program transformations, which are more complicated than formula manipulations but really not very different. A program-manipulation system is obviously what we've been leading up to, and I wonder why I never thought of it before. Of course, the idea isn't original with me; when I told Hoare, he said, "Exactly!" and referred me to a recent work by Darlington and Burstall [67] which describes a system which removes some recursions from a LISP-like language (curiously, without introducing any **go to**'s), and which also does some conversion of data structures (from sets to lists or bit strings) and some restructuring of a program by combining similar loops. I later discovered that program manipulation is just part of a much more ambitious project undertaken by Cheatham and Wegbreit [68]; another publication about source-code optimizations has also recently appeared [69]. Since LISP programs are easily manipulated as LISP data objects, there has also been a rather extensive development of similar ideas in this domain, notably by Warren Teitelman [70, 71]. The time is clearly ripe for program-manipulation systems, and a great deal of further work suggests itself.

The programmer using such a system will write his beautifully-structured, but possibly inefficient, program P; then he will interactively specify transformations that make it efficient. Such a system will be much more powerful and reliable than a completely automatic one. We can also imagine the system manipulating measurement statistics concerning how much of the total running time is spent in each statement, since the programmer will want to know which parts of his program deserve to be optimized, and how much effect an optimization will really have. The original program P should be retained along with the transformation specifications, so that it can be properly understood and maintained as time passes. As I say, this idea certainly isn't my own; it is so exciting I hope that *everyone* soon becomes aware of its possibilities.

A "calculus" of program transformations is gradually emerging, a set of operations which can be applied to programs without rethinking the specific problem each time. I have already mentioned several of these transformations: doubling up of loops (Example 2a), changing final calls to **go to**'s (Example 6a), using a stack for recursions (Example 6c), and combining disjoint loops over the same range [67]. The idea of macro-expansions in general seems to find its most appropriate realization as part of a program-manipulation system.

Another well-known example is the removal of invariant subexpressions from loops. We are all familiar with the fact that a program which includes such subexpressions is more readable than the corresponding program with invariant subexpressions moved out of their loops; yet we consciously remove them when the running time of the program is important.

Still another type of transformation occurs when we go from high-level "abstract" data structures to low-level "concrete" ones (see Hoare's chapter in [72] for numerous examples). In the case of Example 6c, we can replace the stack by an array and a pointer, arriving at

Example 6d

```
procedure treeprint (t); integer t; value t;
  begin integer array S[1:n]; integer k; k := 0;
L1:  loop while t ≠ 0:
       k := k + 1; S[k] := t;
       t := L[t]; go to L1;
L2:  t := S[k]; k := k - 1;
     print (A[t]);
     t := R[t];
   repeat;
   if k ≠ 0 then go to L2 fi;
  end.
```

Here the programmer must specify a safe value for the maximum stack size *n,* in order to make the transformation legitimate. Alternatively, he may wish to implement the stack by a linked list. This choice can usually be made without difficulty, and it illustrates another area in which interaction is preferable to completely automatic transformations.

Recursion vs. iteration

Before leaving the *treeprint* example, I would like to pursue the question of **go to** elimination from Example 6c, since this leads to some interesting issues. It is clear that the first **go to** is just a simple iteration, and a little further study shows that Example 6c is just one simple iteration inside another, namely (in Dahl's syntax)

Example 6e

```
procedure treeprint (t); integer t; value t;
  begin integer stack S; S := empty;
    loop:
      loop while t ≠ 0:
        S <= t;
        t := L[t];
      repeat;
      while nonempty(S):
        t <= S;
        print (A[t]);
        t := R[t];
      repeat;
    end.
```

Furthermore, there is a rather simple way to understand this program, by providing suitable "loop invariants." At the beginning of the first (outer) loop, suppose the stack contents from top to bottom are $t_n, \ldots, t_1$ for some $n \geq 0$; then the procedure's remaining duty is to accomplish the effect of

$$treeprint (t);$$
$$print (A[t_n]);\ treeprint (R[t_n]);$$
$$\ldots;$$
$$print (A[t_1]);\ treeprint (R[t_1]); \qquad (*)$$

In other words, the purpose of the stack is to record postponed obligations to print the A's and right subtrees of certain nodes. Once this concept is grasped, the meaning of the program is clear and we can even see how we might have written it without ever thinking of a recursive formulation or a **go to** statement: The innermost loop ensures $t = 0$, and afterwards the program reduces the stack, maintaining (*) as the condition to be fulfilled, at key points in the outer loop.

A careful programmer might notice a source of inefficiency in this program: when $L[t] = 0$, we put *t* on the stack, then take it off again. If there are *n* nodes in a binary tree, about half of them, on the average, will have $L[t]$

= 0 so we might wish to avoid this extra computation. It isn't easy to do that to Example 6e without major surgery on the structure; but it *is* easy to modify Example 6c (or 6d), by simply bracketing the source of inefficiency, including the **go to**, and the label, and all.

Example 6f

```
procedure treeprint (t); value t; integer t;
  begin integer stack S; S := empty;
L1:  loop while t ≠ 0:
L3:    if L[t] ≠ 0
       then S <= t; t := L[t]; go to L1;
L2:       t <= S;
    fi;
    print (A[t]);
    t := R[t];
  repeat;
  if nonempty(S) then go to L2 fi;
  end.
```

Here we notice that a further simplification is possible: **go to** L1 can become **go to** L3 because *t* is known to be nonzero.

An equivalent **go to**-free program analogous to Example 6e is

Example 6g

```
procedure treeprint (t); value t; integer t;
  begin integer stack S; S := empty;
  loop until finished:
    if t ≠ 0
    then
      loop while L[t] ≠ 0:
        S <= t;
        t := L[t];
      repeat;
    else
      if nonempty(S)
      then t <= S;
      else finished;
      fi;
    fi;
    print (A[t]);
    t := R[t];
  repeat;
  end.
```

I derived this program by thinking of the loop invariant (*) in Example 6e and acting accordingly, *not* by trying to eliminate the **go to**'s from Example 6f. So I know this program is well structured, and I therefore haven't succeeded in finding an example of recursion removal where **go to**'s are strictly necessary. It is interesting, in fact, that our transformations originally intended for efficiency led us to new insights and to programs that still possess decent structure. However, I still feel that Example 6f is easier to understand than 6g, given that the reader is told the recursive program it comes from and the transformations that were used. The recursive program is trivially correct, and the transformations require only routine verification; by contrast, a mental leap is needed to invent (*).

Does recursion elimination help? Clearly there won't be much gain in this example if the *print* routine itself is the bottleneck. But let's replace *print* ($A[t]$) by

$$i := i + 1; B[i] := A[t];$$

i.e., instead of printing the tree, let's assume that we merely want to transfer its contents to some other array B. Then we can expect to see an improvement.

After making this change, I tried the recursive Example 6 vs. the iterative Example 6d on the two main ALGOL compilers available to me. Normalizing the results so that 6d takes 1.0 units of time per node of the tree, with subscript checking suppressed, I found that the corresponding recursive version took about 2.1 units of time per node using our ALGOL W compiler for the 360/67; and the ratio was 1.16 using the SAIL compiler for the PDP-10. (Incidentally, the relative run-times for Example 6f were 0.8 with ALGOL W, and 0.7 with SAIL. When subscript ranges were dynamically checked, ALGOL W took 1.8 units of time per node for the nonrecursive version, and 2.8 with the recursive version; SAIL's figures were 1.28 and 1.34.)

Boolean variable elimination

Another important program transformation, somewhat less commonly known, is the removal of Boolean variables by code duplication. The following example is taken from Dijkstra's treatment [73] of Hoare's "Quicksort" algorithm. The idea is to rearrange array elements $A[m]$ . . . $A[n]$ so that they are partitioned into two parts: The left part $A[m]$ . . . $A[j - 1]$, for some appropriate j, will contain all the elements less than some value, v; the right part $A[j + 1]$ . . . $A[n]$ will contain all the elements greater than v; and the element $A[j]$ lying between these parts will be equal to v. Partitioning is done by scanning from the left until finding an element greater than v, then scanning from the right until finding an element less than v, then scanning from the left again, and so on, moving the offending elements to the opposite side, until the two scans come together; a Boolean variable *up* is used to distinguish the left scan from the right.

Example 7

```
i := m; j := n;
v := A[j]; up := true;
loop:
  if up
  then if A[i] > v
    then A[j] := A[i]; up := false fi;
  else if v > A[j]
    then A[i] := A[j]; up := true fi;
  fi;
  if up then i := i + 1 else j := j − 1 fi;
  while i < j repeat;
A[j] := v;
```

The manipulation and testing of *up* is rather time-consuming here. We can, in general, eliminate a Boolean variable by storing its current value in the program counter, i.e., by duplicating the program, letting one part of the text represent **true** and the other part **false**, with jumps between the two parts in appropriate places. Example 7 therefore becomes

Example 7a

```
      i := m; j := n;
      v := A[j];
      loop: if A[i] > v
            then A[j] := A[i]; go to upf fi;
upt:  i := i + 1;
      while i < j repeat; go to common;
      loop: if v > A[j]
            then A[i] := A[j]; go to upt fi;
upf:  j := j − 1;
      while i < j repeat;
common: A[j] := v;
```

Note that again we have come up with a program which has jumps into the middle of iterations, yet we can understand it since we know that it came from a previously understood program, by way of an understandable transformation.

Of course this program is messier than the first, and we must ask again if the gain in speed is worth this cost. If we are writing a sort procedure that will be used many times, we will be interested in the speed. The average running time of Quicksort was analyzed by Hoare in his 1962 paper on the subject [74], and it turns out that the body of the loop in Example 7 is performed about $2N \ln N$ times while the statement $up := \textbf{false}$ is performed about $1/3N \ln N$ times, if we are sorting N elements. All other parts of the overall sorting program (not shown here) have a running time of order N or less, so when N is reasonably large the speed of the inner loop governs the speed of the entire sorting process. (Incidentally, a recursive version of Quicksort will run just about as fast, since the recursion overhead is not part of the inner loop. But in this case the removal of recursion is of great value for another reason, because it cuts the auxiliary stack space requirement from order N to order $\log N$.)

Using these facts about inner loop times, we can make a quantitative comparison of Examples 7 and 7a. As with Example 1, it seems best to make two comparisons, one with the assembly code that a decent programmer would write for the examples, and the other with the object code produced by a typical compiler that does only local optimizations. The assembly-language programmer will keep i, j, v, and up in registers, while a typical compiler will not keep variables in registers from one statement to another, except if they happen to be there by coincidence. Under these assumptions, the asymptotic running time for an entire Quicksort program based on these routines will be

	Assembled	*Compiled*
Example 7	$20\text{-}2/3N \ln N$	$55\text{-}1/3N \ln N$
Example 7a	$15\text{-}1/3N \ln N$	$40N \ln N$

expressed in memory references to data and instructions. So Example 7a saves more than 25% of the sorting time.

I showed this example to Dijkstra, cautioning him that the **go to** leading into an iteration might be a terrible shock. I was extremely pleased to receive his reply [75]:

> Your technique of storing the value of up in the order counter is, of course, absolutely safe. I did not faint! I am in no sense "afraid" of a program constructed that way, but I cannot consider it beautiful: it is really the same repetition with the same terminating condition, that "changes color" as the computation proceeds.

He went on to say that he looks forward to the day when machines are so fast that we won't be under pressure to optimize our programs; yet

> For the time being I could not agree more with your closing remarks: if the economies matter, apply "disciplined optimalization" to a nice program, the correctness of which has been established beyond reasonable doubt. Your massaging of the program text is then no longer trickery ad hoc, it is perfectly safe and sound.

It is hard for me to express the joy that this letter gave me; it was like having all my sins forgiven, since I need no longer feel guilty about my optimized programs.

Coroutines

Several of the people who read the first draft of this article observed that Example 7a can perhaps be understood more easily as the result of eliminating *coroutine* linkage instead of Boolean variables. Consider the following program:

Example 7b

```
coroutine move i;
  loop:  if A[i] > v
         then A[j] := A[i];
            resume move j;
         fi;
         i := i + 1;
   while i < j repeat;
coroutine move j;
  loop:  if v > A[j]
         then A[i] := A[j];
            resume move i;
         fi;
         j := j - 1;
   while i < j repeat;
   i := m; j := n; v := A[j];
   call move i;
   A[j] := v;
```

When a coroutine is "resumed," let's assume that it begins after its own **resume** statement; and when a coroutine terminates, let's assume that the most recent **call** statement is thereby completed. (Actual coroutine linkage is slightly more involved, see Chapter 3 of Dahl and Dijkstra and Hoare [3], but this description will suffice for our purposes.) Under these conventions, Example 7b is precisely equivalent to Example 7a. At the beginning of *move i* we know that $A[k] \leq v$ for all $k < i$, and that $i < j$, and that $\{A[m], \ldots, A[j-1], A[j+1], \ldots, A[n]\} \cup \{v\}$ is a permutation of the original contents of $\{A[m], \ldots, A[n]\}$; a similar statement holds at the beginning of *move j*. This separation into two coroutines can be said to make Example 7b conceptually simpler than Example 7; but on the other hand, the idea of coroutines admittedly takes some getting used to.

Christopher Strachey once told me about an example which first convinced him that coroutines provided an important control structure. Consider two binary trees represented as in Examples 5 and 6, with their A array information in increasing order as we traverse the trees in symmetric order of their nodes. The problem is to *merge* these two A array sequences into one ordered sequence. This requires traversing both trees more or less asynchronously, in symmetric order, so we'll need two versions of Example 6 running cooperatively. A conceptually simple solution to this problem can be written with coroutines, or by forming an equivalent program which expresses the coroutine linkage in terms of **go to** statements; it appears to be cumbersome (though not impossible) to do the job without using either feature.

Quicksort: A digression

Dijkstra also sent another instructive example in his letter [76]. He decided to create the program of Example 7 from scratch, as if Hoare's algorithm had never been invented, starting instead with modern ideas of semiautomatic program construction based on the following *invariant* relation:

$$v = A[n] \wedge$$
$$\forall k(m \leq k < i => A[k] \leq v) \wedge$$
$$\forall k(j < k \leq n => A[k] \geq v).$$

The resulting program is unusual, yet perhaps cleaner than Example 7:

```
i := m; j := n - 1; v := A[n];
loop while i ≤ j:
  if A[j] ≥ v then j := j - 1;
  else A[i] :=: A[j]; i := i + 1;
  fi;
repeat;
if j ≤ m then A[m] :=: A[n]; j := m fi;
```

Here ":=:" denotes the interchange (i.e., swap) operation. At the conclusion of this program, the A array will be different than before, but we will have the array partitioned as desired for sorting (i.e., $A[m] \ldots A[j]$ are $\leq v$ and $A[j + 1] \ldots A[n]$ are $\geq v$).

Unfortunately, however, this "pure" program is less efficient than Example 7, and Dijkstra noted that he didn't like it very much himself. In fact, Quicksort is really quick in practice because there is a method that is even better than Example 7a: A good Quicksort routine will have a faster inner loop which avoids most of the "$i < j$" tests. Dijkstra recently [75] sent me another approach to the problem which leads to a much better solution. First we can abstract the situation by considering any notions "small" and "large" so that: (a) an element $A[i]$ is never both small and large simultaneously; (b) some elements might be neither small nor large; (c) we wish to rearrange an array so that all small elements precede all large ones; and (d) there is at least one element which is not small, and at least one which is not large. Then we can write the following program in terms of this abstraction.

Example 8

```
i := m; j := n;
loop:
  loop while A[i] is small:
    i := i + 1; repeat;
  loop while A[j] is large:
    j := j - 1; repeat;
  while i < j:
    A[i] :=: A[j];
    i := i + 1; j := j - 1;
repeat;
```

At the beginning of the first (outer) loop we know that $A[k]$ is not large for $m \leq k < i$, and that $A[k]$ is not small for $j < k \leq n$; also that there exists a k such that $i \leq k \leq n$ and $A[k]$ is not small, and a k such that $m \leq k \leq j$ and $A[k]$ is not large. The operations in the loop are easily seen to preserve these "invariant" conditions. Note that the inner loops are now extremely fast, and that they are guaranteed to terminate; therefore the proof of correctness is simple. At the conclusion of the outer loop we know that $A[m] \ldots A[i-1]$ and $A[j]$ are not large, that $A[i]$ and $A[j+1] \ldots A[n]$ are not small, and that $m \leq j \leq i \leq n$.

Applying this to Quicksort, we can set $v := A[n]$ and write

"$A[i] < v$" in place of "$A[i]$ is small"
"$A[j] < v$" in place of "$A[j]$ is large"

in the above program. This gives a very pretty algorithm, which is essentially equivalent to the method published by Hoare [77] in his first major application of the idea of invariants, and discussed in his original paper on Quicksort [74]. Note that since $v = A[n]$, we know that the first execution of "**loop while** $A[j] > v$" will be trivial; we could move this loop to the end of the outer loop just before the final **repeat**. This would be slightly faster, but it would make the program harder to understand, so I would hesitate to do it.

The Quicksort partitioning algorithm actually given in my book [38] is better than Example 7a, but somewhat different from the program we have just derived. My version can be expressed as follows (assuming that $A[m-1]$ is defined and $\leq A[n]$):

```
i := m - 1; j := n; v := A[n];
loop until pointers have met:
  loop: i := i + 1; while A[i] < v repeat;
  if i ≥ j then pointers have met; fi;
  A[j] := A[i];
  loop: j := j - 1; while A[j] > v repeat;
  if i ≥ j then j := i; pointers have met; fi;
  A[i] := A[j];
repeat;
A[j] := v;
```

At the conclusion of this routine, the contents of $A[m] \ldots A[n]$ have been permuted so that $A[m] \ldots A[j-1]$ are $\leq v$ and $A[j+1] \ldots A[n]$ are $\geq v$ and $A[j] = v$ and $m \leq j \leq n$. The assembled version will make about $11N \ln N$ references to memory on the average, so this program saves 28% of the running time of Example 7a.

When I first saw Example 8 I was chagrined to note that it was easier to prove than my program; it was shorter, and (the crushing blow) it also seemed about 3% faster, because it tested "$i < j$" only half as often. My first mathematical analysis of the average behavior of Example 8 indicated that the asymptotic number of comparisons and exchanges would be the same, even though the partitioned subfiles included all N elements instead of $N-1$ as in the classical Quicksort routine. But suddenly it occurred to me that my new analysis was incorrect because one of its fundamental assumptions breaks down: the elements of the two subfiles after partitioning by Example 8 are not in random order! This was a surprise, because randomness *is* preserved by the usual Quicksort routine. When the N keys are distinct, v will be the largest element in the left subfile, and the mechanism of Example 8 shows that v will tend to be near the left of that subfile. When that subfile is later partitioned, it is highly likely that v will move to the extreme right of the resulting right sub-subfile. So that right sub-subfile will be subject to a trivial partitioning by its largest element; we have a subtle loss of efficiency on the third level of recursion. I still haven't been able to analyze Example 8, but empirical tests have borne out my prediction that it is in fact about 15% slower than the book algorithm.

Therefore, there is no reason for anybody to use Example 8 in a sorting routine; although it is slightly cleaner looking than the method in my book, it is noticeably slower, and we have nothing to fear by using a slightly more complicated method once it has been proved correct. Beautiful algorithms are, unfortunately, not always the most useful.

This is not the end of the Quicksort story (although I almost wish it was, since I think the preceding paragraph makes an important point). After I had shown Example 8 to my student, Robert Sedgewick, he found a way to modify it, preserving the randomness of the subfiles, thereby achieving both elegance and efficiency at the same time. Here is his revised program.

Example 8a

```
i := m − 1; j := n; v := A[n];
loop:
  loop: i := i + 1; while A[i] < v repeat;
  loop: j := j − 1; while A[j] > v repeat;
  while i < j:
    A[i] :=: A[j];
  repeat;
  A[i] :=: A[n];
```

(As in the previous example, we assume that $A[m − 1]$ is defined and $\leq A[n]$, since the j pointer might run off the left end.) At the beginning of the outer loop the invariant conditions are now

$$m − 1 \leq i < j \leq n;$$
$$A[k] \leq v \text{ for } m − 1 \leq k \leq i;$$
$$A[k] \geq v \text{ for } j \leq k \leq n;$$
$$A[n] = v.$$

It follows that Example 8a ends with

$$A[m] \ldots A[i − 1] \leq v = A[i] \leq A[i + 1] \ldots A[n]$$

and $m \leq i \leq n$; hence a valid partition has been achieved.

Sedgewick also found a way to improve the inner loop of the algorithm from my book, namely:

```
i := m − 1; j := n; v := A[n];
loop:
  loop: i := i + 1; while A[i] < v repeat;
  A[j] := A[i];
  loop: j := j − 1; while A[j] > v repeat;
  while i < j;
  A[i] := A[j];
  repeat;
  if i ≠ j then j := j + 1;
  A[j] := v;
```

Each of these programs leads to a Quicksort routine that makes about $10-2/3N \ln N$ memory references on the average; the former is preferable (except on machines for which exchanges are clumsy), since it is easier to understand. Thus I learned again that I should always keep looking for improvements, even when I have a satisfactory program.

Axiomatics of jumps

We have now discussed many different transformations on programs; and there are more which could have been mentioned (e.g., the removal of trivial assignments as in Knuth [41], exercise 1.1−3, or Knuth [38], exercise 5.2.1−33). This should be enough to establish that a program-manipulation system will have plenty to do.

Some of these transformations introduce **go to** statements that cannot be handled very nicely by situation indicators, and in general we might expect to find a few programs in which **go to** statements survive. Is it really a formidable job to understand such programs? Fortunately this is not an insurmountable task, as recent work has shown. For many years, the **go to** statement has been troublesome in the definition of correctness proofs and language semantics; for example, Hoare and Wirth have presented an axiomatic definition of PASCAL [78] in which everything but **real** arithmetic and the **go to** is defined formally. Clint and Hoare [53] have shown how to extend this to situation-indicator **go to**'s (i.e., those which don't lead into iterations or conditionals), but they stressed that the general case appears to be fraught with complications. Just recently, however, Hoare has shown that there is, in fact, a rather simple way to give an axiomatic definition of **go to** statements; indeed, he wishes quite frankly that it hadn't been quite so simple. For each label L in a program, the programmer should state a logical assertion $\alpha(L)$ which is to be true whenever we reach L. Then the axioms

$$\{\alpha(L)\}\textbf{go to } L \textbf{ \{false\}}$$

plus the rules of inference

$$\{\alpha(L)\} \text{ S} \{P\} \vdash \{\alpha(L)\} \text{ L: S} \{P\}$$

are allowed in program proofs, and all properties of labels and **go to**'s will follow if the $\alpha(L)$ are selected intelligently. One must, of course, carry out the entire proof using the same assertion $\alpha(L)$ for each appearance of the label L, and some choices of assertions will lead to more powerful results than others.

Informally, $\alpha(L)$ represents the desired state of affairs at label L; this definition says essentially that a program is correct if $\alpha(L)$ holds at L and before all "**go to** L" statements, and that control never "falls through" a **go to** statement to the following text. Stating the assertions $\alpha(L)$ is analogous to formulating loop invariants. Thus, it is not difficult to deal formally with tortuous program structure if it turns out to be necessary; all we need to know is the "meaning" of each label.

Reduction of complication

There is one remaining use of **go to** for which I have never seen a good replacement, and in fact it's a situation where I still think **go to** is the right idea. This situation typically occurs after a program has made a multiway branch to a rather large number of different but related cases. A little computation often suffices to reduce one case to another; and when we've reduced one problem to a simpler one, the most natural thing is for our program to **go to** the routine which solves the simpler problem.

For example, consider writing an interpretive routine (e.g., a microprogrammed emulator), or a simulator of another computer. After decoding the address and fetching the operand from memory, we do a multiway branch based on the operation code. Let's say the operations include no-op, add, subtract, jump on overflow, and unconditional jump. Then the subtract routine might be

$$\text{subtract: } operand := - \ operand; \textbf{ go to } \text{add};$$

the add routine might be

```
add:    accum := accum + operand;
        tyme := tyme + 1;
        go to no op;
```

and jump on overflow might be

```
jov:    if overflow
        then overflow := false; go to jump;
        else go to no op;
        fi;
```

I still believe that this is the correct way to write such a program.

Such situations aren't restricted to interpreters and simulators, although the foregoing is a particularly dramatic example. Multiway branching is an important programming technique which is all too often replaced by an inefficient sequence of **if** tests. Peter Naur recently wrote me that he considers the use of tables to control program flow as a basic idea of computer science that has been nearly forgotten; but he expects it will be ripe for rediscovery any day now. It is the key to efficiency in all the best compilers I have studied.

Some hints of this situation, where one problem reduces to another, have occurred in previous examples of this article. Thus, after searching for x and discovering that it is absent, the "not found" routine can insert x into the table, thereby reducing the problem to the "found" case. Consider also our decision-table Example 4, and suppose that each period was to be followed by a carriage return instead of by an extra space. Then it would be natural to reduce the post-processing of periods to the return-carriage part of the program. In each case, a **go to** would be easy to understand.

If we need to find a way to do this without saying **go to**, we could extend Zahn's situation indicator scheme so that some situations are allowed to appear in the **then** . . . **fi** part after we have begun to process other situations. This accommodates the above-mentioned examples very nicely; but of course it can be dangerous when misused, since it gives us back all the power of **go to**. A restriction which allows ⟨statement list⟩ to refer to ⟨situation⟩$_j$ only for $j > i$ would be less dangerous.

With such a language feature, we can't "fall through" a label (i.e., a situation indicator) when the end of the preceding code is reached; we must explicitly name each situation when we go to its routine. Prohibiting "fall through" means forcing a programmer to write "**go to** common" just before the label "common:" in Example 7a; surprisingly, such a change actually makes that program more readable, since it makes the symmetry plain. Also, the program fragment

```
subtract: operand := − operand; go to add;
add:      accum := accum + operand;
```

seems to be more readable than if "**go to** add" were deleted. It is interesting to ponder why this is so.

Conclusions

This has been a long discussion, and very detailed, but a few points stand out. First, there are several kinds of programming situations in which **go to** statements are harmless, even desirable, if we are programming in ALGOL or PL/I. But secondly, new types of syntax are being developed that provide good substitutes for these harmless **go to**'s, without encouraging a programmer to create "logical spaghetti."

One thing we haven't spelled out clearly, however, is what makes some **go to**'s bad and others acceptable. The reason is that we've really been directing our attention to the wrong issue, to the objective question of **go to** elimination instead of the important subjective question of program structure. In the words of John Brown [79], "The act of focusing our mightiest intellectual resources on the elusive goal of **go to**-less programs has helped us get our minds off all those really tough and possibly unresolvable problems and issues with which today's professional programmer would otherwise have to grapple." By writing this long article I don't want to add fuel to the controversy about **go to** elimination, since that topic has already assumed entirely too much significance; my goal is to lay that controversy to rest, and to help direct the discussion towards more fruitful channels.

Structured programming

The real issue is structured programming, but unfortunately this has become a catch phrase whose meaning is rarely understood in the same way by different people. Everybody knows it is a Good Thing, but as McCracken [26] has said, "Few people would venture a definition. In fact, it is not clear that there exists a simple definition as yet." Only one thing is really clear: Structured programming is *not* the process of writing programs and then eliminating their **go to** statements. We should be able to define structured programming without referring to **go to** statements at all; then the fact that **go to** statements rarely need to be introduced as we write programs should follow as a corollary.

Indeed, Dijkstra's original article [80] which gave structured programming its name never mentioned **go to** statements at all! He directed attention to the critical question, "For what program structures can we give correctness proofs without undue labor, even if the programs get large?" By correctness proofs he explained that he does not mean formal derivations from axioms, he means any sort of proof (formal or informal) that is "sufficiently convincing"; and a proof really means an understanding. By program structure he means data structure as well as control structure.

We understand complex things by systematically breaking them into successively simpler parts and understanding how these parts fit together locally. Thus, we have different levels of understanding, and each of these levels corresponds to an *abstraction* of the detail at the level it is composed from. For example, at one level of abstraction, we deal with an integer without considering whether it is represented in binary notation or two's complement, etc., while at deeper levels this representation may be important. At more abstract levels the precise value of the integer is not important except as it relates to other data.

David J. Wheeler mentioned this principle as early as 1952, at the first ACM National Conference [81]:

> When a programme has been made from a set of sub-routines the breakdown of the code is more complete than it would otherwise be. This allows the coder to concentrate on one section of a programme at a time without the overall detailed programme continually intruding.

Abstraction is easily understood in terms of BNF notation. A metalinguistic category like ⟨assignment statement⟩ is an abstraction which is composed of two abstractions (a ⟨left part list⟩ and an ⟨arithmetic expression⟩), each of which is composed of abstractions such as ⟨identifier⟩ or ⟨term⟩, etc. We understand the program syntax as a whole by knowing the structural details that relate these abstract parts. The most difficult things to understand about a program's syntax are the identifiers, since their meaning is passed across several levels of structure. If all identifiers of an ALGOL program were changed to random meaningless strings of symbols, we would have great difficulty seeing what the type of a variable is and what the program means, but we would still easily recognize the more local features, such as assignment statements, expressions, subscripts, etc. (This inability for our eyes to associate a type or mode with an identifier has led to what I believe are fundamental errors of human engineering in the design of ALGOL 68, but that's another story. My own notation for stacks in Example 6c suffers from the same problem; it works in these examples chiefly because t is lower case and S is upper case.) Larger nested structures are harder for the eye to see unless they are indented, but indentation makes the structure plain.

It would probably be still better if we changed our source language concept so that the program wouldn't appear as one long string. John McCarthy says, "I find it difficult to believe that whenever I see a tree I am really seeing a string of symbols." Instead, we should give meaningful names to the larger constructs in our program that correspond to meaningful levels of abstraction, and we should define those levels of abstraction in one place, and merely use their names (instead of including the detailed code) when they are used to build larger concepts. Procedure names do this, but the language could easily be designed so that no action of calling a subroutine is implied.

From these remarks it is clear that sequential composition, iteration, and conditional statements present syntactic structures that the eye can readily assimilate; but a **go to** statement does not. The visual structure of **go to** statements is like that of flowcharts, except reduced to *one* dimension in our source languages. In two dimensions it is possible to perceive **go to** structure in small examples, but we rapidly lose our ability to understand larger and larger flowcharts; some intermediate levels of abstraction are necessary. As an undergraduate, in 1959, I published an octopus flowchart which I sincerely hope is the most horribly complicated that will ever appear in print; anyone who believes that flowcharts are the best way to understand a program is urged to look at this example [82]. (See also [25] for a nice illustration of how **go to**'s make a PL/I program obscure, and see R. Lawrence Clark's hilarious spoof about linear representation of flowcharts by means of a "**come from** statement" [24].)

I have felt for a long time that a talent for programming consists largely of the ability to switch readily from microscopic to macroscopic views of thing, i.e., to change levels of abstraction fluently. I mentioned this [4] to Dijkstra, and he replied [6] with an excellent analysis of the situation:

I feel somewhat guilty when I have suggested that the distinction or introduction of "different levels of abstraction" allow you to think about only one level at a time, ignoring completely the other levels. This is not true. You are trying to organize your thoughts; that is, you are seeking to arrange matters in such a way that you can concentrate on some portion, say with 90% of your conscious thinking, while the rest is temporarily moved away somewhat towards the background of your mind. But that is something quite different from "ignoring completely": you allow yourself temporarily to ignore details, but some overall appreciation of what is supposed to be or to come there continues to play a vital role. You remain alert for little red lamps that suddenly start flickering in the corners of your eye.

I asked Hoare for a short definition of structured programming, and he replied that it is "the systematic use of abstraction to control a mass of detail, and also a means of documentation which aids program design." I hope that my remarks above have made the abstract concept of abstraction clear; the second part of Hoare's definition (which was also stressed by Dijkstra in his original paper [80]) states that a good way to express the abstract properties of an unwritten piece of program often helps us to write that program, and to "know" that it is correct as we write it.

Syntactic structure is just one part of the picture, and BNF would be worthless if the syntactic constructs did not correspond to semantic abstractions. Similarly, a good program will be composed in such a way that each semantic level of abstraction has a reasonably simple relation to its constituent parts. We noticed in our discussion of Jacopini's theorem that every program can trivially be expressed in terms of a simple iteration which simulates a computer; but that iteration has to carry the entire behavior of the program through the loop, so it is worthless as a level of abstraction.

An iteration statement should have a purpose that is reasonably easy to state; typically, this purpose is to make a certain Boolean relation true while maintaining a certain invariant condition satisfied by the variables. The Boolean condition is stated in the program, while the invariant should be stated in a comment, unless it is easily supplied by the reader. For example, the invariant in Example 1 is that $A[k] \neq x$ for $1 \leq k < i$, and in Example 2 it is the same, plus the additional relation $A[m + 1] = x$. Both of these are so obvious that I didn't bother to mention them; but in Examples 6e and 8, I stated the more complicated invariants that arose. In each of those cases the program almost wrote itself once the proper invariant was given. Note that an "invariant assertion" actually does vary slightly as we execute statements of the loop, but it comes back to its original form when we repeat the loop.

Thus, an iteration makes a good abstraction if we can assign a meaningful invariant describing the local states of affairs as it executes, and if we can describe its purpose (e.g., to change one state to another). Similarly, an **if** . . . **then** . . . **else** . . . **fi** statement will be a good abstraction if we can state an overall purpose for the statement as a whole.

We also need well-structured *data;* i.e., as we write the program we should have an abstract idea of what each variable means. This idea is also usually describable as an invariant relation, e.g., "m is the number of items in the table" or "x is the search argument" or "$L[t]$ is the number of the root node of node t's left subtree, or 0 if this subtree is empty" or "the contents of stack S are postponed obligations to do such and such."

Now let's consider the slightly more complex case of a situation-driven construct. This should also correspond to a meaningful abstraction, and our examples show what is involved: For each situation we give an (invariant) assertion which describes the relations which must hold when that situation occurs, and for the **loop until** we also give an invariant for the loop. A situation statement typically corresponds to an abrupt change in conditions so that a different assertion from the loop invariant is necessary.

An error exit can be considered well-structured for precisely this reason — it corresponds to a situation that is impossible according to the local invariant assertions; it is easiest to formulate assertions that assume nothing will go wrong, rather than to make the invariants cover all contingencies. When we jump out to an error exit we go to another level of abstraction having different assumptions.

As another simple example, consider binary search in an ordered array using the invariant relation $A[i] < x < A[j]$:

```
loop while i + 1 < j;
k := (i + j) ÷ 2;
  if A[k] < x then i := k;
  else if A[k] > x then j := k;
    else cannot preserve the invariant fi;
  fi;
repeat;
```

Upon normal exit from this loop, the conditions $i + 1 \geq j$ and $A[i] < x < A[j]$ imply that $A[i] < x < A[i + 1]$, i.e., that x is not present. If the program comes to "cannot preserve the invariant" (because $x = A[k]$), it wants to **go to** another set of assumptions. The situation-driven construct provides a level at which it is appropriate to specify the other assumptions.

Another good illustration occurs in Example 6g; the purpose of the main **if** statement is to find the first node whose A value should be printed. If there is no such t, the event "finished" has clearly occurred; it is better to regard the

if statement as having the stated abstract purpose without considering that t might not exist.

With go to statements

We can also consider **go to** statements from the same point of view; when do they correspond to a good abstraction? We've already mentioned that **go to**'s do not have a syntactic structure that the eye can grasp automatically; but in this respect they are no worse off than variables and other identifiers. When these are given a meaningful name corresponding to the abstraction (N.B. *not* a numeric label!), we need not apologize for the lack of syntactic structure. And the appropriate abstraction itself is an invariant essentially like the assertions specified for a situation.

In other words, we can indeed consider **go to** statements as part of systematic abstraction; all we need is a clearcut notion of exactly what it means to **go to** each label. This should come as no great surprise. After all, a lot of computer programs have been written using **go to** statements during the last 25 years, and these programs haven't all been failures! Some programmers have clearly been able to master structure and exploit it; not as consistently, perhaps, as in modern-day structured programming, but not inflexibly either. By now, many people who have never had any special difficulty writing correct programs have naturally been somewhat upset after being branded as sinners, especially when they know perfectly well what they're doing; so they have understandably been less than enthusiastic about "structured programming" as it has been advertised to them.

My feeling is that it's certainly possible to write well-structured programs with **go to** statements. For example, Dijkstra's 1968 program about concurrent process control [83] used three **go to** statements, all of which were perfectly easy to understand; and I think at most two of these would have disappeared from his code if ALGOL 60 had had a **while** statement. But **go to** is hardly ever the best alternative now, since better language features are appearing. If the invariant for a label is closely related to another invariant, we can usually save complexity by combining those two into one abstraction, using something other than **go to** for the combination.

There is also another problem, namely, at what level of abstraction should we introduce a label? This however is like the analogous problem for variables, and the general answer is still unclear in both cases. Aspects of data structure are often postponed, but sometimes variables are defined and passed as "parameters" to other levels of abstraction. There seems to be no clearcut idea as yet about a set of syntax conventions, relating to the definition of variables, which would be most appropriate to structured programming methodology; but for each particular problem there seems to be an appropriate level.

Efficiency

In our previous discussion we concluded that premature emphasis on efficiency is a big mistake which may well be the source of most programming complexity and grief. We should ordinarily keep efficiency considerations in the background when we formulate our programs. We need to be subconsciously aware of the data processing tools available to us, but we should strive most of all for a program that is easy to understand and almost sure to work. (Most programs are probably only run once; and I suppose in such cases we needn't be too fussy about even the structure, much less the efficiency, as long as we are happy with the answers.)

When efficiencies do matter, however, the good news is that usually only a very small fraction of the code is significantly involved. And when it is desirable to sacrifice clarity for efficiency, we have seen that it *is* possible to produce reliable programs that can be maintained over a period of time, if we start with a well-structured program and then use well-understood transformations that can be applied mechanically. We shouldn't attempt to understand the resulting program as it appears in its final form; it should be thought of as the result of the original program modified by specified transformations. We can envision program-manipulation systems which will facilitate making and documenting these transformations.

In this regard I would like to quote some observations made recently by Pierre-Arnoul de Marneffe [84]:

> In civil engineering design, it is presently a mandatory concept known as the "Shanley Design Criterion" to collect several functions into one part . . . If you make a cross-section of, for instance, the German V-2, you find external skin, structural rods, tank wall, etc. If you cut across the Saturn-B moon rocket, you find only an external skin which is at the same time a structural component and the tank wall. Rocketry engineers have used the "Shanley Principle" thoroughly when they use the fuel pressure inside the tank to improve the rigidity of the external skin! . . . People can argue that structured programs, even if they work correctly, will look like laboratory prototypes where you can discern all the individual components, but which are not daily usable. Building "integrated" products is an engineering principle as valuable as structuring the design process.

He goes on to describe plans for a prototype system that will automatically assemble integrated programs from well-structured ones that have been written top-down by stepwise refinement.

Today's hardware designers certainly know the advantages of integrated circuitry, but of course they must first understand the separate circuits before the integration is done. The V-2 rocket would never have been airborne if its designers had originally tried to combine all its functions. Engineering has two phases, structuring and integration; we ought not to forget either one, but it is best to hold off the integration phase until a well-structured prototype is working and understood. As stated by Weinberg [85], the former regimen of analysis/coding/debugging should be replaced by analysis/coding/debugging/improving.

The future

It seems clear that languages somewhat different from those in existence today would enhance the preparation of structured programs. We will perhaps eventually be writing only small modules which are identified by name as they are used to build larger ones, so that devices like indentation, rather than delimiters, might become feasible for expressing local structure in the source language. (See the discussion following Landin's paper [15].) Although our examples don't indicate this, it turns out that a given level of abstraction often involves several related routines and data definitions; for example, when we decide to represent a table in a certain way, we simultaneously want to specify the routines for storing and fetching information from that table. The next generation of languages will probably take into account such related routines.

Program-manipulation systems appear to be a promising future tool which will help programmers to improve their programs, and to enjoy doing it. Standard operating procedure nowadays is usually to hand code critical portions of a routine in assembly language. Let us hope such assemblers will die out, and we will see several levels of language instead: at the highest levels we will be able to write abstract programs, while at the lowest levels we will be able to control storage and register allocation, and to suppress subscript range checking, etc. With an integrated system it will be possible to do debugging and analysis of the transformed program using a higher level language for communication. All levels will, of course, exhibit program structure syntactically so that our eyes can grasp it.

I guess the big question, although it really shouldn't be so big, is whether or not the ultimate language will have **go to** statements in its higher levels, or whether **go to** will be confined to lower levels. I personally wouldn't mind having **go to** in the highest level, just in case I really need it; but I probably would never use it, if the general iteration and situation constructs suggested in this article were present. As soon as people learn to apply principles of abstraction consciously, they won't see the need for **go to**, and the issue will just fade away. On the other hand, W.W. Peterson told me about his experience teaching PL/I to beginning programmers: he taught them to use **go to** only in unusual special cases where **if** and **while** aren't right, but he found [86] that

"A disturbingly large percentage of the students ran into situations that require **go to**'s, and sure enough, it was often because **while** didn't work well to their plan, but almost invariably because their plan was poorly thought out." Because of arguments like this, I'd say we should, indeed, abolish **go to** from the high-level language, at least as an experiment in training people to formulate their abstractions more carefully. This does have a beneficial effect on style, although I would not make such a prohibition if the new language features described above were not available. The question is whether we should ban it, or educate against it; should we attempt to legislate program morality? In this case I vote for legislation, with appropriate legal substitutes in place of the former overwhelming temptations.

A great deal of research must be done if we're going to have the desired language by 1984. Control structure is merely one simple issue, compared to questions of abstract data structure. It will be a major problem to keep the total number of language features within tight limits. And we must especially look at problems of input/output and data formatting, in order to provide a viable alternative to COBOL.

Acknowledgments

I've benefited from a truly extraordinary amount of help while preparing this article. The individuals named provided me with a total of 144 pages of single-spaced comments, plus six hours of conversation and four computer listings:

Frances E. Allen	Ralph L. London
Forest Baskett	Zohar Manna
G.V. Bochmann	W.M. McKeeman
Per Brinch Hansen	Harlan D. Mills
R.M. Burstall	Peter Naur
Vinton Cerf	Kjell Overholt
T.E. Cheatham, Jr.	James Peterson
John Cocke	W. Wesley Peterson
Ole-Johan Dahl	Mark Rain
Peter J. Denning	John Reynolds
Edsger Dijkstra	Barry K. Rosen
James Eve	E. Satterthwaite, Jr.
K. Friedenbach	D.V. Schorre
Donald I. Good	Jacob T. Schwartz
Ralph E. Gorin	Richard L. Sites
Leo Guibas	Richard Sweet
C.A.R. Hoare	Robert D. Tennent
Martin Hopkins	Niklaus Wirth
James J. Horning	M. Woodger
B.M. Leavenworth	William A. Wulf
Henry F. Ledgard	Charles (Carroll) T. Zahn

These people unselfishly devoted hundreds of man-hours to helping me revise the first draft; and I'm sorry that I wasn't able to reconcile all of their interesting points of view. In many places I have shamelessly used their suggestions without an explicit acknowledgment; this article is virtually a joint paper with 30 to 40 co-authors! However, any mistakes it contains are my own.

Appendix

In order to make some quantitative estimates of efficiency, I have counted memory references for data and instructions, assuming a multiregister computer without cache memory. Thus, each instruction costs one unit, plus another if it refers to memory; small constants and base addresses are assumed to be either part of the instruction or present in a register. Here are the code sequences developed for the first two examples, assuming that a typical assembly-language programmer or a very good optimizing compiler is at work.

Label	Instruction	Cost	Times
Example 1	$r1 \leftarrow 1$	1	1
	$r2 \leftarrow m$	2	1
	$r3 \leftarrow x$	2	1
	to test	1	1
loop:	$A[r1]:r3$	2	$n - a$
	to found **if** $=$	1	$n - a$
	$r1 \leftarrow r1 + 1$	1	$n - 1$
test:	$r1:r2$	1	n
	to loop **if** $\leq$	1	n
notfound:	$m \leftarrow r1$	2	a
	$A[r1] \leftarrow r3$	2	a
	$B[r1] \leftarrow 0$	2	a
found:	$r4 \leftarrow B[r1]$	2	1
	$r4 \leftarrow r4 + 1$	1	1
	$B[r1] \leftarrow r4$	2	1
Example 2	$r2 \leftarrow m$	2	1
	$r3 \leftarrow x$	2	1
	$A[r2 + 1] \leftarrow r3$	2	1
	$r1 \leftarrow 0$	1	1
loop:	$r1 \leftarrow r1 + 1$	1	n
	$A[r1]:r3$	2	n
	to loop **if** $\neq$	1	n
	$r1:r2$	1	1
	to found **if** $\leq$	1	1
notfound:	$m \leftarrow r1$ etc., as in Example 1.		

A traditional "90% efficient compiler" would render the first example as follows:

Label	Instruction	Cost	Times
Example 1	$r1 \leftarrow 1$	1	1
	to test	1	1
incr:	$r1 \leftarrow i$	2	$n-1$
	$r1 \leftarrow r1 + 1$	1	$n-1$
test:	$r1:m$	2	n
	to notfound **if** $>$	1	n
	$i \leftarrow r1$	2	$n-a$
	$r2 \leftarrow A[r1]$	2	$n-a$
	$r2:x$	2	$n-a$
	to found **if** $=$	1	$n-a$
	to incr	1	$n-1$
notfound:	$r1 \leftarrow m$	2	a
	$r1 \leftarrow r1 + 1$	1	a
	$i \leftarrow r1$	2	a
	$m \leftarrow r1$	2	a
	$r1 \leftarrow x$	2	a
	$r2 \leftarrow i$	2	a
	$A[r2] \leftarrow r1$	2	a
	$B[r2] \leftarrow 0$	2	a
found:	$r1 \leftarrow i$	2	1
	$r2 \leftarrow B[r1]$	2	1
	$r2 \leftarrow r2 + 1$	1	1
	$B[r1] \leftarrow r2$	2	1

Answer to PL/I problem, page 267

The variable I is increased before FOUND is tested. One way to fix the program is to insert "I = I − FOUND;" before the last statement. (Unfortunately.)

References

1. Edna St. Vincent Millay, "Elaine," *Bartlett's Familiar Quotations.*

2. B. Dylan, "Blonde on Blonde," produced by Bob Johnston (New York: Columbia Records, March 1966).

3. O.-J. Dahl, E.W. Dijkstra, and C.A.R. Hoare, *Structured Programming* (New York: Academic Press, 1972).

4. D.E. Knuth, *A Review of Structured Programming,* Stanford University, Computer Science Department Report No. CS371 (Stanford, Calif.: June 1973).

5. E.W. Dijkstra, "The Humble Programmer," *Communications of the ACM,* Vol. 15, No. 10 (October 1972), pp. 859-66.

6. _____, Personal communication (January 3, 1973).

7. C. Reid, *Hilbert* (New York: Springer-Verlag, 1970).

8. D.V. Schorre, *Improved Organization for Procedural Languages,* Systems Development Corporation, Technical Memorandum TM 3086/002/00 (Santa Monica, Calif.: September 8, 1966).

9. _____, "META-II — A Syntax-Directed Compiler Writing Language," *Proceedings of the ACM National Conference* (Philadelphia, Pa.: 1964).

10. N. Wirth, "Program Development by Stepwise Refinement," *Communications of the ACM,* Vol. 14, No. 4 (April 1971), pp. 221-27.

11. P. Naur, "GOTO Statements and Good Algol Style," *BIT,* Vol. 3, No. 3 (1963), pp. 204-208.

12. D.E. Knuth, "George Forsythe and the Development of Computer Science," *Communications of the ACM,* Vol. 15, No. 8 (August 1972), pp. 721-26.

13. P. Naur, ed., "Report on the Algorithmic Language ALGOL 60," *Communications of the ACM,* Vol. 3, No. 5 (May 1960), pp. 299-314.

14. E.W. Dijkstra, "Programming Considered as a Human Activity," *Proceedings of the 1965 IFIP Congress* (Amsterdam, The Netherlands: North-Holland Publishing Co., 1965), pp. 213-17.

15. P.J. Landin, "The Next 700 Programming Languages," *Communications of the ACM,* Vol. 9, No. 3 (March 1966), pp. 157-66.

16. P. Naur, "Program Translation Viewed as a General Data Processing Problem," *Communications of the ACM,* Vol. 9, No. 3 (March 1966), pp. 176-79.

17. E.W. Dijkstra, "Go To Statement Considered Harmful," *Communications of the ACM,* Vol. 11, No. 3 (March 1968), pp. 147-48.

18. W.M. McKeeman, J.J. Horning, and D.B. Wortman, *A Compiler Generator* (Englewood Cliffs, N.J.: Prentice-Hall, 1970).

19. C. Strachey, "Varieties of Programming Language," *High Level Languages,* ed. C. Boon, Infotech State of the Art Report, Vol. 7 (1972).

20. M.E. Hopkins, "A Case for the GOTO," *Proceedings of the 25th National ACM Conference* (New York: Association for Computing Machinery, 1972), pp. 787-90.

21. B.M. Leavenworth, "Programming With(out) the GOTO," *Proceedings of the 25th National ACM Conference* (New York: Association for Computing Machinery, 1972), pp. 782-86.

22. W.A. Wulf, "A Case Against the GOTO," *Proceedings of the 25th National ACM Conference* (New York: Association for Computing Machinery, 1972), pp.791-97.

23. F.T. Baker and H.D. Mills, "Chief Programmer Teams," *Datamation,* Vol. 19, No. 12 (December 1973), pp. 58-61.

24. R.L. Clark, "A Linguistic Contribution to GOTO-less Programming," *Datamation,* Vol. 19, No. 12 (December 1973), pp. 62-63.

25. J.R. Donaldson, "Structured Programming," *Datamation,* Vol. 19, No. 12 (December 1973), pp. 52-54.

26. D.D. McCracken, "Revolution in Programming: An Overview," *Datamation,* Vol. 19, No. 12 (December 1973), pp. 50-52.

27. E.F. Miller, Jr. and G.E. Lindamood, "Structured Programming: Top-Down Approach," *Datamation,* Vol. 19, No. 12 (December 1973), pp. 55-57.

28. D.E. Knuth and R.W. Floyd, "Notes on Avoiding 'go to' Statements," *Information Processing Letters,* Vol. 1, No. 1 (February 1971), pp. 23-31; also Stanford University, Computer Science Technical Report Vol. CS148 (Stanford, Calif.: January 1970).

29. W.A. Wulf, D.B. Russell and A.N. Habermann, "BLISS: A Language for Systems Programming," *Communications of the ACM,* Vol. 14, No. 12 (December 1971), pp. 780-90.

30. W.A. Wulf, "Programming Without the GOTO," *Proceedings of the 1971 IFIP Congress,* Vol. 1 (Amsterdam, The Netherlands: North-Holland Publishing Co., 1972), pp. 408-13.

31. J. McCarthy, "Recursive Functions of Symbolic Expressions and Their Computation by Machine, Part 1," *Communications of the ACM,* Vol. 3, No. 4 (April 1960), pp. 184-95.

32. D. Ingalls, "The Execution-Time Profile as a Programming Tool," *Compiler Optimization, 2d Courant Computer Science Symposium,* ed. R. Rustin (Englewood Cliffs, N.J.: Prentice-Hall, 1972), pp. 107-28.

33. D.E. Knuth, "An Empirical Study of FORTRAN Programs," *Software — Practice and Experience,* Vol. 1, No. 2 (April-June 1971), pp. 105-33.

34. E.H. Satterthwaite, "Debugging Tools for High Level Languages," *Software — Practice and Experience,* Vol. 2, No. 3 (July-September 1972), pp. 197-217.

35. C.A.R. Hoare, "Prospects for a Better Programming Language," *High-level Languages,* ed. C. Boon, Infotech State of the Art Report, Vol. 7 (1972), pp. 327-43.

36. N. Wirth, *On Certain Basic Concepts of Programming Languages,* Stanford University, Computer Science Report Vol. CS65 (Stanford, Calif.: May 1967).

37. C.A.R. Hoare, "A Note on the For Statement," *BIT,* Vol. 12 (1972), pp. 334-41.

38. D.E. Knuth, *The Art of Computer Programming,* 2nd ed., Vol. 1, *Fundamental Algorithms* (Reading, Mass.: Addison-Wesley, 1973.)

39. _____, *The Art of Computer Programming,* 2nd ed., Vol. 3, *Sorting and Searching* (Reading, Mass.: Addison-Wesley, 1973).

40. W.W. Peterson, T. Kasami, and N. Tokura, "On the Capabilities of While, Repeat and Exit Statements," *Communications of the ACM,* Vol. 16, No. 8 (August 1973), pp. 503-12.

41. D.E. Knuth, *The Art of Computer Programming,* 1st ed., Vol. 1 (Reading, Mass.: Addison-Wesley, 1968).

42. N. Wirth, "PL360, a Programming Language for the 360 Computers," *Journal of the ACM,* Vol. 15, No. 1 (January 1968), pp. 37-74.

43. S.C. Kleene, "Representation of Events in Nerve Nets," *Automata Studies,* eds. C.E. Shannon and J. McCarthy (Princeton, N.J.: Princeton University Press, 1956), pp. 3-40.

44. C. Böhm and G. Jacopini, "Flow Diagrams, Turing Machines and Languages with Only Two Formation Rules," *Communications of the ACM,* Vol. 9, No. 5 (May 1966), pp. 366-71.

45. H.D. Mills, *Mathematical Foundations for Structured Programming,* IBM Federal Systems Division, Report No. FSC 72-6012 (Gaithersburg, Md.: February 1972).

46. D.C. Cooper, "Böhm and Jacopini's Reduction of Flowcharts," *Communications of the ACM,* Vol. 10, No. 8 (August 1967), pp. 463-73.

47. J. Bruno and K. Steiglitz, "The Expression of Algorithms by Charts," *Journal of the ACM,* Vol. 19, No. 3 (July 1972), pp. 517-25.

48. E. Ashcroft and Z. Manna, "The Translation of 'go to' Programs to 'while' Programs," *Proceedings of the 1971 IFIP Congress,* Vol. 1 (Amsterdam, The Netherlands: North-Holland Publishing Co., 1972), pp. 250-55; also Stanford University, AIM-138, STAN CS-71-88 (Stanford, Calif., January 1971).

49. S.R. Kosaraju, "Analysis of Structured Programs," *Proceedings of the Fifth Annual ACM Symposium on Theory of Computing* (May 1973), pp. 240-52; also in *Journal of Computer and System Sciences,* Vol. 9, No. 3 (December 1974).

50. R.J. Lipton, S.C. Eisenstadt, and R.A. DeMillo, "The Complexity of Control Structures and Data Structures," *Proceedings of the ACM Symposium on the Theory of Computing,* Vol. 7 (1975), pp. 186-93.

51. C.T. Zahn, "A Control Statement for Natural Top-Down Structured Programming," Presented at the Symposium on Programming Languages (Paris, France: 1974).

52. P.J. Landin, "A Correspondence Between ALGOL 60 and Church's Lambda-Notation: Part I," *Communications of the ACM,* Vol. 8, No. 2 (February 1965), pp. 89-101.

53. M. Clint and C.A.R. Hoare, "Program Proving: Jumps and Functions," *Acta Informatica,* Vol. 1, No. 3 (1972), pp. 214-24.

54. G.V. Bochmann, "Multiple Exits from a Loop Without the GOTO," *Communications of the ACM,* Vol. 16, No. 7 (July 1973), pp. 443-44.

55. O. Shigo, et al., "Spot: An Experimental System for Structured Programming," (in Japanese), *Conference Record* (Japan: Information Processing Society of Japan, 1973).

56. C.A.R. Hoare, "An Axiomatic Approach to Computer Programming," *Communications of the ACM,* Vol. 12, No. 10 (October 1969), pp. 576-80, 583.

57. N. Wirth, "The Programming Language Pascal," *Acta Informatica,* Vol. 1, No. 1 (1971), pp. 35-63.

58. D.W. Barron, *Recursive Techniques in Programming* (New York: American Elsevier, 1968).

59. Z. Manna and R.J. Waldinger, "Towards Automatic Program Synthesis," *Communications of the ACM,* Vol. 14, No. 3 (March 1971), pp. 151-65.

60. H.R. Strong, Jr., "Translating Recursion Equations into Flowcharts," *Journal of the Computer and System Sciences,* Vol. 5, No. 3 (June 1971), pp. 254-85.

61. S.A. Walker and H.R. Strong, "Characterizations of Flowchartable Recursions," *Journal of Computer and System Sciences,* Vol. 7, No. 4 (August 1973), pp. 404-47.

62. E.W. Dijkstra, "Recursive Programming," *Numerische Mathematik,* Vol. 2, No. 5 (1960), pp. 312-18.

63. S. Gill, "Automatic Computing: Its Problems and Prizes," *Computer Journal,* Vol. 8, No. 3 (October 1965), 177-89.

64. W.A. Wulf, et al., *The Design of an Optimizing Compiler,* Carnegie-Mellon University, Computer Science Department Report (Pittsburgh, Pa.: December 1973).

65. D.E. Knuth and J.L. Szwarcfiter, "A Structured Program to Generate All Topological Sorting Arrangements," *Information Processing Letters,* Vol. 2, No. 6 (April 1974), pp. 153-57.

66. C.A.R. Hoare, *Hints for Programming Language Design,* Stanford University, Computer Science Report STAN-CS-74-403 (Stanford, Calif.: January 1974).

67. J. Darlington and R.M. Burstall, *A System Which Automatically Improves Programs,* Stanford University, IJCAI Vol. 73 (Stanford, Calif.: 1973), pp. 479-85.

68. T.E. Cheatham, Jr. and B. Wegbreit, "A Laboratory for the Study of Automatic Programming," *AFIPS Proceedings of the 1972 Spring Joint Computer Conference,* Vol. 40 (Montvale, N.J.: AFIPS Press, 1972), pp. 11-21.

69. P.B. Schneck and E. Angel, "A FORTRAN to FORTRAN Optimizing Compiler," *Computer Journal,* Vol. 16, No. 4 (1973), pp. 322-30.

70. W. Teitelman, "Toward a Programming Laboratory," *Software Engineering, Concepts and Techniques,* eds. J.N. Buxton, P. Naur, and B. Randall (New York: Petrocelli/Charter, 1976).

71. _____, et al., *INTERLISP Reference Manual,* Xerox Palo Alto Research Center (Palo Alto, Calif.: Bolt Beranek and Newman, Inc., 1974).

72. O.-J. Dahl, E.W. Dijkstra, and C.A.R. Hoare, *Structured Programming* (New York: Academic Press, 1972).

73. E.W. Dijkstra, *A Short Introduction to the Art of Programming,* Technische Hogeschool Eindhoven, Report No. EWD-316 (Eindhoven, The Netherlands: August 1971).

74. C.A.R. Hoare, "Quicksort," *Computer Journal,* Vol. 5, No. 1 (1962), pp. 10-15.

75. E.W. Dijkstra, Personal communication (January 30, 1974).

76. _____, Personal communication (November 19, 1973).

77. C.A.R. Hoare, "Proof of a Program: FIND," *Communications of the ACM,* Vol. 14, No. 1 (January 1971), pp. 39-45.

78. _____ and N. Wirth, "An Axiomatic Definition of the Programming Language Pascal," *Acta Informatica,* Vol. 2 (1973), pp. 335-55.

79. P.J. Brown, "Programming and Documenting Software Projects," *ACM Computing Surveys,* Vol. 6, No. 4 (December 1974).

80. E.W. Dijkstra, "Structured Programming," *Software Engineering, Concepts and Techniques, Proceedings of the NATO Conferences,* eds. J.N. Buxton, P. Naur, and B. Randell (New York: Petrocelli/Charter, 1976), pp. 222-26.

81. D.J. Wheeler, unpublished proceedings, First ACM National Conference (1952).

82. D.E. Knuth, "RUNCIBLE — Algebraic Translation on a Limited Computer," *Communications of the ACM,* Vol. 2, No. 11 (November 1959), pp. 18-21.

83. E.W. Dijkstra, "Solution of a Problem in Concurrent Programming Control," *Communications of the ACM,* Vol. 9, No. 9 (September 1968), p. 569.

84. P.A. de Marneffe, *Holon Programming: A Survey,* Université de Liège, Service Informatique (Liège, Belgium: 1973), p. 135.

85. G.M. Weinberg, "The Psychology of Improved Computer Programming Performance," *Datamation,* Vol. 17, No. 11 (November 1972), pp. 82-85.

86. W.W. Peterson, Personal communication (April 2, 1974).

INTRODUCTION

If someone said to me, "I have time to read only one of the papers in your collection," I would recommend this paper by Barry Boehm — not because it is brilliant (although I think some of Boehm's insights border on brilliance) or because it revolutionized the field (the way some of Dijkstra's papers did), but simply because it is probably the best overall summary of the software field that I have yet seen published. If nothing else, Boehm's bibliography is stupendous, even outdoing the bibliography that Knuth provides in his "Structured Programming with go to Statements"!

"Software Engineering" serves both as the title of Boehm's paper, and as a phrase used throughout his discussion. Like structured programming, it is a term that has been around for a few years, and now gradually is becoming accepted as the successor to the various phrases that incorporate the word "structured." As Boehm says in his introduction,

> "*Software engineering* is the means by which we attempt to produce all of this software in a way that is both cost-effective and reliable enough to deserve our trust. . . . [It is] the practical application of scientific knowledge in the design and construction of computer programs and the associated documentation required to develop, operate, and maintain them."

Thus, the term clearly subsumes structured programming, structured design, and structured analysis, and it also includes some areas that largely have been ignored by other authors represented in this book.

In essence, Boehm's paper is a survey of a wide range of topics, dealing with specific aspects of software development: requirements definition, software design, programming, testing and reliability, maintenance, and software management. Each section contains a short summary of current practice in the area, a survey of the frontier technology, and a summary of future trends. Boehm's treatment of frontier technology provides a barometer: For more information, the reader is directed to more than a hundred books and papers listed in the bibliography.

As you read the survey, it will become evident that much of the EDP developmental work is being done either in the universities (where its real-world application always is suspect), or in the large aerospace/defense companies (where EDP problems are usually large, and where errors in systems analysis, design, or coding cannot be tolerated). Because such government/military projects may lead the industry by five to ten years in terms of technological development, we should see such frontier concepts as automated design systems appear in business applications in the mid-1980s.

One of the most important aspects of Boehm's paper, in my opinion, is its emphasis on software testing and software maintenance. In the section on testing, there is a survey of software reliability models; software error data; half a dozen automated testing aids, such as test monitoring and output checking; test sufficiency; symbolic execution; and proofs of program correctness.

In the maintenance area, Boehm provides statistics that should scare any responsible EDP manager to death: It is evident that by the mid-1980s, most organizations will spend more than sixty percent of their EDP budget on maintenance. Boehm devotes most of his attention to a discussion of how to do "good" maintenance on "good" programs; he largely ignores the issue of how to grapple with the maintenance of "bad" programs. Much of the EDP industry desperately needs help in this area, but there seems to be very little help to offer.

Boehm concludes his paper with a review of software management, which he argues is in an even worse state than our programming and design technology. Once again, there are developments underway in this field, but they seem to be mostly restricted to large defense projects.* Boehm closes with a note of concern:

> "What is rather surprising, and a bit disappointing, is the reluctance of the computer science field to address itself to the more difficult and diffuse problems . . . as compared to the more tractable . . . subjects of automata theory, parsing, computability, etc."

Unfortunately, that concern, expressed in December 1976, still is valid today, and probably will be so for a number of years to come.

---

*Boehm mentions IBM's Chief Programmer Team as one possible solution to the management vacuum; unfortunately, most organizations already have decided that the concept won't work for them. For more on CPT, see Baker's "Chief Programmer Team Management of Production Programming" in [Paper 7], or Baker and Mills's "Chief Programmer Teams" [Paper 17].

Software Engineering

I. Introduction

The annual cost of software in the U.S. is approximately 20 billion dollars. Its rate of growth is considerably greater than that of the economy in general. Compared to the cost of computer hardware, the cost of software is continuing to escalate along the lines predicted in Fig. 1 [1].* A recent SHARE study [2] indicates further that software demand over the years 1975-1985 will grow considerably faster (about 21-23 percent per year) than the growth rate in software supply at current estimated growth rates of the software labor force and its productivity per individual, which produce a combined growth rate of about 11.5-17 percent per year over the years 1975-1985.

In addition, as we continue to automate many of the processes which control our life-style — our medical equipment, air traffic control, defense system, personal records, bank accounts — we continue to trust more and more in the reliable functioning of this proliferating mass of software. *Software engineering* is the means by which we attempt to produce all of this software in a way that is both cost-effective and reliable enough to deserve our trust. Clearly, it is a discipline which is important to establish well and to perform well.

---

*Another trend has been added to Fig.1: the growth of software maintenance, which will be discussed later.

This paper will begin with a definition of "software engineering." It will then survey the current state of the art of the discipline, and conclude with an assessment of likely future trends.

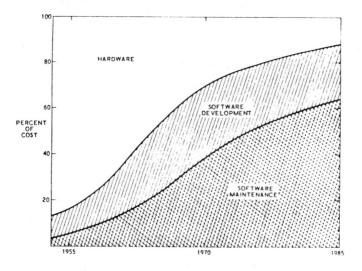

Figure 1. Hardware-software cost trends.

II. Definitions

Let us begin by defining "software engineering." We will define software to include not only computer programs, but also the associated documentation required to develop, operate, and maintain the programs. By defining software in this broader sense, we wish to emphasize the necessity of considering the generation of timely documentation as an integral portion of the software development process. We can then combine this with a definition of "engineering" to produce the following definition.

> *Software Engineering:* The practical application of scientific knowledge in the design and construction of computer programs and the associated documentation required to develop, operate, and maintain them.

Three main points should be made about this definition. The first concerns the necessity of considering a broad enough interpretation of the word "design" to cover the extremely important activity of software requirements engineering. The second point is that the definition should cover the entire software life cycle, thus including those activities of redesign and modification often termed "software maintenance." (Fig. 2 indicates the overall set of activities thus encompassed in the definition.) The final point is that our store of knowledge about software which can really be called "scientific knowledge" is a rather small base upon which to build an engineering discipline. But, of course, that is what makes software engineering such a fascinating challenge at this time.

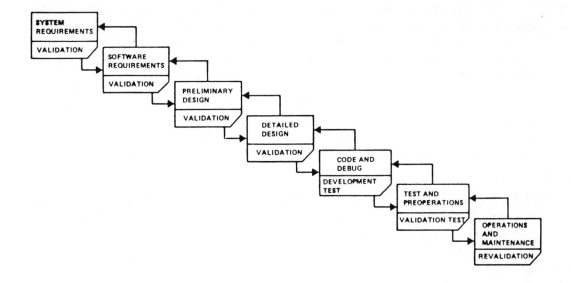

Figure 2. Software life cycle.

The remainder of this paper will discuss the state of the art of software engineering along the lines of the software life cycle depicted in Fig. 2. Section III contains a discussion of software requirements engineering, with some mention of the problem of determining overall system requirements. Section IV discusses both preliminary design and detailed design technology trends. Section V contains only a brief discussion of programming, as this topic is also covered in a companion article in this issue [3]. Section VI covers both software testing and the overall life cycle concern with software reliability. Section VII discusses the highly important but largely neglected area of software maintenance. Section VIII surveys software management concepts and techniques, and discusses the status and trends of integrated technology-management approaches to software development. Finally, Section IX concludes with an assessment of the current state of the art of software engineering with respect to the definition above.

Each section (sometimes after an introduction) contains a short summary of current practice in the area, followed by a survey of current frontier technology, and concluding with a short summary of likely trends in the area. The survey is oriented primarily toward discussing the domain of applicability of techniques (where and when they work) rather than how they work in detail. An extensive set of references is provided for readers wishing to pursue the latter.

III. Software requirements engineering

A. Critical nature of software requirements engineering

Software requirements engineering is the discipline for developing a complete, consistent, unambiguous specification — which can serve as a basis for common agreement among all parties concerned — describing *what* the software product will do (but *not how* it will do it; this is to be done in the design specification).

The extreme importance of such a specification is only now becoming generally recognized. Its importance derives from two main characteristics: 1) it is easy to delay or avoid doing thoroughly; and 2) deficiencies in it are very difficult and expensive to correct later.

Fig. 3 shows a summary of current experience at IBM [4], GTE [5], and TRW on the relative cost of correcting software errors as a function of the phase in which they are corrected. Clearly, it pays off to invest effort in finding requirements errors early and correcting them in, say, 1 man-hour rather than waiting to find the error during operations and having to spend 100 man-hours correcting it.

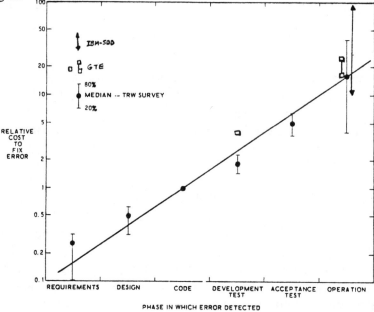

Figure 3. Software validation: the price of procrastination.

Besides the cost-to-fix problems, there are other critical problems stemming from a lack of a good requirements specification. These include [6]: 1) top-down designing is impossible, for lack of a well-specified "top"; 2) testing is impossible, because there is nothing to test against; 3) the user is frozen out, because there is no clear statement of what is being produced for him; and 4) management is not in control, as there is no clear statement of what the project team is producing.

B. Current practice

Currently, software requirements specifications (when they exist at all) are generally expressed in free-form English. They abound with ambiguous terms ("suitable," "sufficient," "real-time," "flexible") or precise-sounding terms with unspecified definitions ("optimum," "99.9 percent reliable") which are potential seeds of dissension or lawsuits once the software is produced. They have numerous errors; one recent study [7] indicated that the first independent review of a fairly good software requirements specification will find from one to four nontrivial errors per page.

The techniques used for determining software requirements are generally an ad hoc manual blend of systems analysis principles [8] and common sense. (These are the good ones; the poor ones are based on ad hoc manual blends of politics, preconceptions, and pure salesmanship.) Some formalized manual techniques have been used successfully for determining business system requirements, such as accurately defined systems (ADS), and time automated grid (TAG). The book edited by Couger and Knapp [9] has an excellent summary of such techniques.

C. Current frontier technology: Specification languages and systems

1) *ISDOS:* The pioneer system for machine-analyzable software requirements is the ISDOS system developed by Teichroew and his group at the University of Michigan [10]. It was primarily developed for business system applications, but much of the system and its concepts are applicable to other areas. It is the only system to have passed a market and operations test; several commercial, aerospace, and government organizations have paid for it and are successfully using it. The U.S. Air Force is currently using and sponsoring extensions to ISDOS under the Computer Aided Requirements Analysis (CARA) program.

ISDOS basically consists of a problem statement language (PSL) and a problem statement analyzer (PSA). PSL allows the analyst to specify his system in terms of formalized entities (INPUTS, OUTPUTS, REAL WORLD ENTITIES), classes (SETS, GROUPS), relationships (USES, UPDATES, GENERATES), and other information on timing, data volume, synonyms, attributes, etc. PSA operates on the PSL statements to produce a number of useful summaries, such as: formatted problem statements; directories and keyword indices; hierarchical structure reports; graphical summaries of flows and relationships; and statistical summaries. Some of these capabilities are actually more suited to supporting system design activities; this is often the mode in which ISDOS is used.

Many of the current limitations of ISDOS stem from its primary orientation toward business systems. It is currently difficult to express real-time performance requirements and man-machine interaction requirements, for example. Other capabilities are currently missing, such as support for configuration control, traceability to design and code, detailed consistency checking, and automatic simulation generation. Other limitations reflect deliberate, sensible design choices: the output graphics are crude, but they are produced in standard 8½ × 11 in size on any standard line printer. Much of the current work on ISDOS/CARA is oriented toward remedying such limitations, and extending the system to further support software design.

2) *SREP:* The most extensive and powerful system for software requirements specification in evidence today is that being developed under the Software Requirements Engineering Program (SREP) by TRW for the U.S. Army Ballistic Missile Defense Advanced Technology Center (BMDATC) [11, 12, 13]. Portions of this effort are derivative of ISDOS; it uses the ISDOS data management system, and is primarily organized into a language, the requirements statement language (RSL), and an analyzer, the requirements evaluation and validation system (REVS).

SREP contains a number of extensions and innovations which are needed for requirements engineering in real-time software development projects. In order to represent real-time performance requirements, the individual functional requirements can be joined into stimulus-response networks called R-Nets. In order to focus early attention on software testing and reliability, there are capabilities for designating "validation points" within the R-Nets. For early requirements validation, there are capabilities for automatic generation of functional simulators from the requirements statements. And, for adaptation to changing requirements, there are capabilities for configuration control, traceability to design, and extensive report generation and consistency checking.

Current SREP limitations again mostly reflect deliberate design decisions centered around the autonomous, highly real-time process-control problem of ballistic missile defense. Capabilities to represent large file processing and man-machine interactions are missing. Portability is a problem: although some parts run on several machines, other parts of the system run only on a TI-ASC computer with a very powerful but expensive multicolor interactive graphics terminal. However, the system has been designed with the use of compiler generators and extensibility features which should allow these limitations to be remedied.

3) *Automatic programming and other approaches:* Under the sponsorship of the Defense Advanced Research Projects Agency (DARPA), several researchers are attempting to develop "automatic programming" systems to replace the functions of those currently performed by programmers. If successful, could they drive software costs down to zero? Clearly not, because there would still

be the need to determine what software the system should produce, i.e., the software requirements. Thus, the methods, or at least the forms, of capturing software requirements are of central concern in automatic programming research.

Two main directions are being taken in this research. One, exemplified by the work of Balzer at USC-ISI [14], is to work within a general problem context, relying on only general rules of information processing (items must be defined or received before they are used, an "if" should have both a "then" and an "else," etc.) to resolve ambiguities, deficiencies, or inconsistencies in the problem statement. This approach encounters formidable problems in natural language processing and may require further restrictions to make it tractable.

The other direction, exemplified by the work of Martin at MIT [15], is to work within a particular problem area, such as inventory control, where there is enough of a general model of software requirements and acceptable terminology to make the problems of resolving ambiguities, deficiencies, and inconsistencies reasonably tractable.

This second approach has, of course, been used in the past in various forms of "programming-by-questionnaire" and application generators [1, 2]. Perhaps the most widely used are the parameterized application generators developed for use on the IBM System/3. IBM has some more ambitious efforts on requirements specification underway, notably one called the Application Software Engineering Tool [16] and one called the Information Automat [17], but further information is needed to assess their current status and directions.

Another avenue involves the formalization and specification of required properties in a software specification (reliability, maintainability, portability, etc.). Some success has been experienced here for small-to-medium systems, using a "Requirements-Properties Matrix" to help analysts infer additional requirements implied by such considerations [18].

D. Trends

In the area of requirements statement languages, we will see further efforts either to extend the ISDOS-PSL and SREP-RSL capabilities to handle further areas of application, such as man-machine interactions, or to develop language variants specific to such areas. It is still an open question as to how general such a language can be and still retain its utility. Other open questions are those of the nature, "which representation scheme is best for describing requirements in a certain area?" BMDATC is sponsoring some work here in representing general data-processing system requirements for the BMD problem, involving Petri nets, state transition diagrams, and predicate calculus [11], but its outcome is still uncertain.

A good deal more can and will be done to extend the capability of requirements statement analyzers. Some extensions are fairly straightforward consistency checking; others, involving the use of relational operators to deduce derived requirements and the detection (and perhaps generation) of missing requirements are more difficult, tending toward the automatic programming work.

Other advances will involve the use of formal requirements statements to improve subsequent parts of the software life cycle. Examples include requirements-design-code consistency checking (one initial effort is underway), the automatic generation of test cases from requirements statements, and, of course, the advances in automatic programming involving the generation of code from requirements.

Progress will not necessarily be evolutionary, though. There is always a good chance of a breakthrough: some key concept which will simplify and formalize large regions of the problem space. Even then, though, there will always remain difficult regions which will require human insight and sensitivity to come up with an acceptable set of software requirements.

Another trend involves the impact of having formal, machine-analyzable requirements (and design) specifications on our overall inventory of software code. Besides improving software reliability, this will make our software much more portable; users will not be tied so much to a particular machine configuration. It is interesting to speculate on what impact this will have on hardware vendors in the future.

IV. Software design

A. The requirements/design dilemma

Ideally, one would like to have a complete, consistent, validated, unambiguous, machine-independent specification of software requirements before proceeding to software design. However, the requirements are not really validated until it is determined that the resulting system can be built for a reasonable *cost* — and to do so requires developing one or more software *designs* (and any associated hardware designs needed).

This dilemma is complicated by the huge number of degrees of freedom available to software/hardware system designers. In the 1950's, as indicated by Table 1, the designer had only a few alternatives to choose from in selecting a central processing unit (CPU), a set of peripherals, a programming language, and an ensemble of support software. In the 1970's, with rapidly evolving mini- and microcomputers, firmware, modems, smart terminals, data management systems, etc., the designer has an enormous number of alternative design components to sort out (possibilities) and to seriously choose from (likely choices). By the 1980's, the number of possible design combinations will be formidable.

Table 1
Design Degrees of Freedom for New Data Processing Systems
(Rough Estimates)

Element	Choices (1950's)	Possibilities (1970's)	Likely Choices (1970's)
CPU	5	200	100
Op-Codes	fixed	variable	variable
Peripherals (per function)	1	200	100
Programming language	1	50	5–10
Operating system	0–1	10	5
Data management system	0	100	30

The following are some of the implications for the designer. 1) It is easier for him to do an outstanding design job. 2) It is easier for him to do a terrible design job. 3) He needs more powerful analysis tools to help him sort out the alternatives. 4) He has more opportunities for designing-to-cost. 5) He has more opportunities to design and develop tunable systems. 6) He needs a more flexible requirements-tracking and hardware procurement mechanism to support the above flexibility (particularly in government systems). 7) Any rational standardization (e.g., in programming languages) will be a big help to him, in that it reduces the number of alternatives he must consider.

B. Current practice

Software design is still almost completely a manual process. There is relatively little effort devoted to design validation and risk analysis before committing to a particular software design. Most software errors are made during the design phase. As seen in Fig. 4, which summarizes several software error analyses by IBM [4, 19] and TRW [20, 21], the ratio of design to coding errors generally exceeds 60:40. (For the TRW data, an error was called a design error if and only if the resulting fix required a change in the detailed design specification.)

Most software design is still done bottom-up, by developing software components before addressing interface and integration issues. There is, however, increasing successful use of top-down design. There is little organized knowledge of what a software designer does, how he does it, or of what makes a good software designer, although some initial work along these lines has been done by Freeman [22].

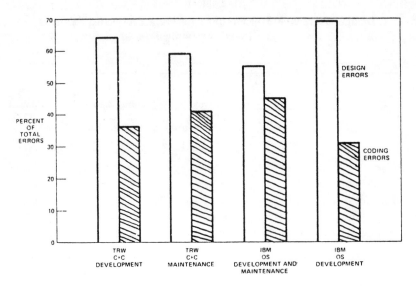

Figure 4. Most errors in large software systems are in early stages.

C. Current frontier technology

Relatively little is available to help the designer make the overall hardware-software tradeoff analyses and decisions to appropriately narrow the large number of design degrees of freedom available to him. At the micro level, some formalisms such as LOGOS [23] have been helpful, but at the macro level, not much is available beyond general system engineering techniques. Some help is provided via improved techniques for simulating information systems, such as the Extendable Computer System Simulator (ECSS) [24, 25], which make it possible to develop a fairly thorough functional simulation of the system for design analysis in a considerably shorter time than it takes to develop the complete design itself.

1) *Top-down design:* Most of the helpful new techniques for software design fall into the category of "top-down" approaches, where the "top" is already assumed to be a firm, fixed requirements specification and hardware architecture. Often, it is also assumed that the data structure has also been established. (These assumptions must in many cases be considered potential pitfalls in using such top-down techniques.)

What the top-down approach does well, though, is to provide a procedure for organizing and developing the control structure of a program in a way which focuses early attention on the critical issues of integration and interface definition. It begins with a top-level expression of a hierarchical control structure (often a top level "executive" routine controlling an "input," a "process," and an "output" routine) and proceeds to iteratively refine each successive lower-level component until the entire system is specified. The successive refinements, which may be considered as "levels of abstraction" or "virtual machines" [26], provide a number of advantages in improved understanding, communication, and verification of complex designs [27, 28]. In general, though, experience shows that some degree of early attention to bottom-level design issues is necessary on most projects [29].

The technology of top-down design has centered on two main issues. One involves establishing guidelines for *how to perform* successive refinements and to group functions into modules; the other involves techniques of *representing* the design of the control structure and its interaction with data.

2) *Modularization:* The techniques of structured design [30] (or composite design [31]) and the modularization guidelines of Parnas [32] provide the most detailed thinking and help in the area of module definition and refinement. Structured design establishes a number of successively stronger types of binding of functions into modules (coincidental, logical, classical, procedural, communicational, informational, and functional) and provides the guideline that a function should be grouped with those functions to which its binding is the strongest. Some designers are able to use this approach quite successfully; others find it useful for reviewing designs but not for formulating them; and others simply find it too ambiguous or complex to be of help. Further experience will be needed to determine how much of this is simply a learning curve effect. In general, Parnas' modularization criteria and guidelines are more straightforward and widely used than the levels-of-binding guidelines, although they may also be becoming more complicated as they address such issues as distribution of responsibility for erroneous inputs [33]. Along these lines, Draper Labs' Higher Order Software (HOS) methodology [34] has attempted to resolve such issues via a set of six axioms covering relations between modules and data, including responsibility for erroneous inputs. For example, Axiom 5 states, "Each module controls the rejection of invalid elements of its own, and only its own, input set."*

3) *Design representation:* Flow charts remain the main method currently used for design representation. They have a number of deficiencies, particularly in representing hierarchical control structures and data interactions. Also, their free-form nature makes it too easy to construct complicated, unstructured designs which are hard to understand and maintain. A number of representation schemes have been developed to avoid these deficiencies.

---

*Problems can arise, however, when one furnishes such a *design choice* with the power of an *axiom.* Suppose, for example, the input set contains a huge table or a master file. Is the module stuck with the job of checking it, by itself, every time?

The hierarchical input-process-output (HIPO) technique [35] represents software in a hierarchy of modules, each of which is represented by its inputs, its outputs, and a summary of the processing which connects the inputs and outputs. Advantages of the HIPO technique are its ease of use, ease of learning, easy-to-understand graphics, and disciplined structure. Some general disadvantages are the ambiguity of the control relationships (are successive lower level modules in sequence, in a loop, or in an if/else relationship?), the lack of summary information about data, the unwieldiness of the graphics on large systems, and the manual nature of the technique. Some attempts have been made to automate the representation and generation of HIPO's such as Univac's PROVAC System [36].

The structure charts used in structured design [30, 31] remedy some of these disadvantages, although they lose the advantage of representing the processes connecting the inputs with the outputs. In doing so, though, they provide a more compact summary of a module's inputs and outputs which is less unwieldy on large problems. They also provide some extra symbology to remove at least some of the sequence/loop/branch ambiguity of the control relationships.

Several other similar conventions have been developed [37, 38, 39], each with different strong points, but one main difficulty of any such manual system is the difficulty of keeping the design consistent and up-to-date, especially on large problems. Thus, a number of systems have been developed which store design information in machine-readable form. This simplifies updating (and reduces update errors) and facilitates generation of selective design summaries and simple consistency checking. Experience has shown that even a simple set of automated consistency checks can catch dozens of potential problems in a large design specification [21]. Systems of this nature that have been reported include the Newcastle TOPD system [40], TRW's DACC and DEVISE systems [21], Boeing's DECA system [41], and Univac's PROVAC [36]; several more are under development.

Another machine-processable design representation is provided by Caine, Farber, and Gordon's Program Design Language (PDL) System [42]. This system accepts constructs which have the form of hierarchical structured programs, but instead of the actual code, the designer can write some English text describing what the segment of code will do. (This representation was originally called "structured pidgin" by Mills [43].) The PDL system again makes updating much easier; it also provides a number of useful formatted summaries of the design information, although it still lacks some wished-for features to support terminology control and version control. The program-like representation makes it easy for programmers to read and write PDL, albeit less easy for nonprogrammers. Initial results in using the PDL system on projects have been quite favorable.

D. *Trends*

Once a good deal of design information is in machine-readable form, there is a fair amount of pressure from users to do more with it: to generate core and time budgets, software cost estimates, first-cut data base descriptions, etc. We should continue to see such added capabilities, and generally a further evolution toward computer-aided-design systems for software. Besides improvements in determining and representing control structures, we should see progress in the more difficult area of data structuring. Some initial attempts have been made by Hoare [44] and others to provide a data analog of the basic control structures in structured programming, but with less practical impact to date. Additionally, there will be more integration and traceability between the requirements specification, the design specification, and the code — again with significant implications regarding the improved portability of a user's software.

The proliferation of minicomputers and microcomputers will continue to complicate the designer's job. It is difficult enough to derive or use principles for partitioning software jobs on single machines; additional degrees of freedom and concurrency problems just make things so much harder. Here again, though, we should expect at least some initial guidelines for decomposing information processing jobs into separate concurrent processes.

It is still not clear, however, how much one can formalize the software design process. Surveys of software designers have indicated a wide variation in their design styles and approaches, and in their receptiveness to using formal design procedures. The key to good software design still lies in getting the best out of good people, and in structuring the job so that the less-good people can still make a positive contribution.

V. **Programming**

This section will be brief, because much of the material will be covered in the companion article by Wegner on "Computer Languages" [3].

A. *Current practice*

Many organizations are moving toward using structured code [28, 43] (hierarchical, block-oriented code with a limited number of control structures — generally SEQUENCE, IFTHENELSE, CASE, DOWHILE, and DOUNTIL — and rules for formatting and limiting module size). A great deal of terribly unstructured code is still being written, though, often in assembly language and particularly for the rapidly proliferating minicomputers and microcomputers.

B. Current frontier technology

Languages are becoming available which support structured code and additional valuable features such as data typing and type checking (e.g., Pascal [45]). Extensions such as concurrent Pascal [46] have been developed to support the programming of concurrent processes. Extensions to data typing involving more explicit binding of procedures and their data have been embodied in recent languages such as ALPHARD [47] and CLU [48]. Metacompiler and compiler writing system technology continues to improve, although much more slowly in the code generation area than in the syntax analysis area.

Automated aids include support systems for top-down structured programming such as the Program Support Library [49], Process Construction [50], TOPD [40], and COLUMBUS [51]. Another novel aid is the Code Auditor program [50] for automated standards compliance checking — which guarantees that the standards are more than just words. Good programming practices are now becoming codified into style handbooks, i.e., Kernighan and Plauger [52] and Ledgard [53].

C. Trends

It is difficult to clean up old programming languages or to introduce new ones into widespread practice. Perhaps the strongest hope in this direction is the current Department of Defense (DoD) effort to define requirements for its future higher order programming languages [54], which may eventually lead to the development and widespread use of a cleaner programming language. Another trend will be an increasing capability for automatically generating code from design specifications.

VI. Software testing and reliability

A. Current practice

Surprisingly often, software testing and reliability activities are still not considered until the code has been run the first time and found not to work. In general, the high cost of testing (still 40-50 percent of the development effort) is due to the high cost of reworking the code at this stage (see Fig. 3), and to the wasted effort resulting from the lack of an advance test plan to efficiently guide testing activities.

In addition, most testing is still a tedious manual process which is error-prone in itself. There are few effective criteria used for answering the question, "How much testing is enough?" except the usual "when the budget (or schedule) runs out." However, more and more organizations are now using disciplined test planning and some objective criteria such as "exercise every instruction" or "exercise every branch," often with the aid of automated test monitoring tools and test case planning aids. But other technologies, such as mathematical proof techniques, have barely begun to penetrate the world of production software.

B.   Current frontier technology

1) *Software reliability models and phenomenology:* Initially, attempts to predict software reliability (the probability of future satisfactory operation of the software) were made by applying models derived from hardware reliability analysis and fitting them to observed software error rates [55]. These models worked at times, but often were unable to explain actual experienced error phenomena. This was primarily because of fundamental differences between software phenomenology and the hardware-oriented assumptions on which the models were based. For example, software components do not degrade due to wear or fatigue; no imperfection or variations are introduced in making additional copies of a piece of software (except possibly for a class of easy-to-check copying errors); repair of a software fault generally results in a different software configuration than previously, unlike most hardware replacement repairs.

Models are now being developed which provide explanations of the previous error histories in terms of appropriate software phenomenology. They are based on a view of a software program as a mapping from a space of inputs into a space of outputs [56], of program operation as the processing of a sequence of points in the input space, distributed according to an operational profile [57], and of testing as a sampling of points from the input space [56] (see Fig. 5). This approach encounters severe problems of scale on large programs, but can be used conceptually as a means of appropriately conditioning time-driven reliability models [58]. Still, we are a long way off from having truly reliable reliability-estimation methods for software.

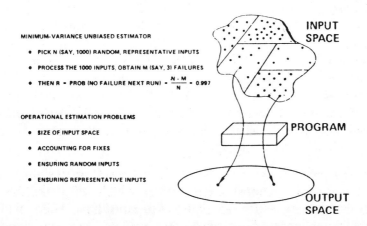

MINIMUM-VARIANCE UNBIASED ESTIMATOR

- PICK N (SAY, 1000) RANDOM, REPRESENTATIVE INPUTS
- PROCESS THE 1000 INPUTS, OBTAIN M (SAY, 3) FAILURES
- THEN R = PROB (NO FAILURE NEXT RUN) = $\frac{N-M}{N}$ = 0.997

OPERATIONAL ESTIMATION PROBLEMS

- SIZE OF INPUT SPACE
- ACCOUNTING FOR FIXES
- ENSURING RANDOM INPUTS
- ENSURING REPRESENTATIVE INPUTS

INPUT SPACE

PROGRAM

OUTPUT SPACE

Figure 5. Input space sampling provides a basis for software reliability measurement.

2) *Software error data:* Additional insights into reliability estimation have come from analyzing the increasing data base of software errors. For example, the fact that the distributions of serious software errors are dissimilar from the distributions of minor errors [59] means that we need to define "errors" very carefully when using reliability prediction models. Further, another study [60] found that the rates of fixing serious errors and of fixing minor errors vary with management direction. ("Close out all problems quickly" generally gets minor simple errors fixed very quickly, as compared to "Get the serious problems fixed first.")

Other insights afforded by software data collection include better assessments of the relative efficacy of various software reliability techniques [4, 19, 60], identification of the requirements and design phases as key leverage points for cost savings by eliminating errors earlier (Figs. 2 and 3), and guidelines for organizing test efforts (for example, one recent analysis indicated that over half the errors were experienced when the software was handling data singularities and extreme points [60]). So far, however, the proliferation of definitions of various terms (error, design phase, logic error, validation test), still make it extremely difficult to compare error data from different sources. Some efforts to establish a unified software reliability data base and associated standards, terminology and data collection procedures are now under way at USAF Rome Air Development Center, and within the IEEE Technical Committee on Software Engineering.

3) *Automated aids:* Let us sketch the main steps of testing between the point the code has been written and the point it is pronounced acceptable for use, and describe for each step the main types of automated aids which have been found helpful. More detailed discussion of these aids can be found in the surveys by Reifer [61] and Ramamoorthy and Ho [62] which in turn have references to individual contributions to the field.

a) *Static code analysis:* Automated aids here include the usual compiler diagnostics, plus extensions involving more detailed data-type checking. Code auditors check for standards compliance, and can also perform various type-checking functions. Control flow and reachability analysis is done by structural analysis programs (flow charters have been used for some of the elementary checks here, "structurizers" can also be helpful). Other useful static analysis tools perform set-use analysis of data elements, singularity analysis, units consistency analysis, data base consistency checking, and data-versus-code consistency checking.

b) *Test case preparation:* Extensions to structural analysis programs provide assistance in choosing data values which will make the program execute along a desired path. Attempts have been made to automate the generation of such data values; they can generally succeed for simple cases, but run into difficulty in handling loops or branching on complex calculated values (e.g., the results of numerical integration). Further, these programs only help generate the *inputs;* the tester must still calculate the expected outputs himself.

Another set of tools will automatically insert instrumentation to verify that a desired path has indeed been exercised in the test. A limited capability exists for automatically determining the minimum number of test cases required to exercise all the code. But, as yet, there is no tool which helps to determine the most appropriate sequence in which to run a series of tests.

c) *Test monitoring and output checking:* Capabilities have been developed and used for various kinds of dynamic data-type checking and assertion checking, and for timing and performance analysis. Test output post-processing aids include output comparators and exception report capabilities, and test-oriented data reduction and report generation packages.

d) *Fault isolation, debugging:* Besides the traditional tools — the core dump, the trace, the snapshot, and the breakpoint — several capabilities have been developed for interactive replay or backtracking of the program's execution. This is still a difficult area, and only a relatively few advanced concepts have proved generally useful.

e) *Retesting (once a presumed fix has been made):* Test data management systems (for the code, the input data, and the comparison output data) have been shown to be most valuable here, along with comparators to check for the differences in code, inputs, and outputs between the original and the modified program and test case. A promising experimental tool performs a comparative structure analysis of the original and modified code, and indicates which test cases need to be rerun.

f) *Integration of routines into systems:* In general, automated aids for this process are just larger scale versions of the test data management systems above. Some additional capabilities exist for interface consistency checking, e.g., on the length and form of parameter lists or data base references. Top-down development aids are also helpful in this regard.

g) *Stopping:* Some partial criteria for thoroughness of testing can and have been automatically monitored. Tools exist which keep a cumulative tally of the number or percent of the instructions or branches which have been exercised during the test program, and indicate to the tester what branch conditions must be satisfied in order to completely exercise all the code or branches. Of course, these are far from complete criteria for determining when to stop testing; the completeness question is the subject of the next section.

4) *Test sufficiency and program proving:* If a program's input space and output space are finite (where the input space includes not only all possible incoming inputs, but also all possible values in the program's data base), then one can construct a set of "black box" tests (one for each point in the input space) which can show conclusively that the program is correct (that its behavior matches its specification).

In general, though, a program's input space is infinite; for example, it must generally provide for rejecting unacceptable inputs. In this case, a finite set of black-box tests is not a sufficient demonstration of the program's correctness (since, for any input x, one must assure that the program does not wrongly treat it as a special case). Thus, the demonstration of correctness in this case involves some formal argument (e.g., a proof using induction) that the dynamic performance of the program indeed produces the static transformation of the input space indicated by the formal specification for the program. For finite portions of the input space, a successful exhaustive test of all cases can be considered as a satisfactory formal argument. Some good initial work in sorting out the conditions under which testing is equivalent to proof of a program's correctness has been done by Goodenough and Gerhart [63] and in a review of their work by Wegner [64].

5) *Symbolic execution:* An attractive intermediate step between program testing and proving is "symbolic execution," a manual or automated procedure which operates on symbolic inputs (e.g., variable names) to produce symbolic outputs. Separate cases are generated for different execution paths. If there are a finite number of such paths, symbolic execution can be used to demonstrate correctness, using a finite symbolic input space and output space. In general, though, one cannot guarantee a finite number of paths. Even so, symbolic execution can be quite valuable as an aid to either program testing or proving. Two fairly powerful automated systems for symbolic execution exist, the EFFIGY system [65] and the SELECT system [66].

6) *Program proving (program verification):* Program proving (increasingly referred to as program verification) involves expressing the program specifications as a logical proposition, expressing individual program execution statements as logical propositions, expressing program branching as an expansion into separate cases, and performing logical transformations on the propositions in a way which ends by demonstrating the equivalence of the program and its specification. Potentially infinite loops can be handled by inductive reasoning.

In general, nontrivial programs are very complicated and time-consuming to prove. In 1973, it was estimated that about one man-month of expert effort was required to prove 100 lines of code [67]. The largest program to be proved correct to date contained about 2000 statements [68]. Again, automation can help out on some of the complications. Some automated verification systems exist, notably those of Good *et al.* [69] and von Henke and Luckham [70]. In general, such systems do not work on programs in the more common languages such as Fortran or Cobol. They work in languages such as Pascal [45], which has (unlike Fortran or Cobol) an axiomatic definition [71] allowing clean expression of program statements as logical propositions. An excellent survey of program verification technology has been given by London [72].

Besides size and language limitations, there are other factors which limit the utility of program proving techniques. Computations on "real" variables involving truncation and roundoff errors are virtually impossible to analyze with adequate accuracy for most nontrivial programs. Programs with nonformalizable inputs (e.g., from a sensor where one has just a rough idea of its bias, signal-to-noise ratio, etc.) are impossible to handle. And, of course, programs can be proved to be consistent with a specification which is itself incorrect with respect to the system's proper functioning. Finally, there is no guarantee that the proof is correct or complete; in fact, many published "proofs" have subsequently been demonstrated to have holes in them [63].

It has been said and often repeated that "testing can be used to demonstrate the presence of errors but never their absence" [73]. Unfortunately, if we must define "errors" to include those incurred by the two limitations above (errors in specifications and errors in proofs), it must be admitted that "program proving can be used to demonstrate the presence of errors but never their absence."

7) *Fault-tolerance:* Programs do not have to be error-free to be reliable. If one could just detect erroneous computations as they occur and compensate for them, one could achieve reliable operation. This is the rationale behind schemes for fault-tolerant software. Unfortunately, both detection and compensation are formidable problems. Some progress has been made in the case of software detection and compensation for hardware errors; see, for example, the articles by Wulf [74] and Goldberg [75]. For software errors, Randell has formulated a concept of separately-programmed, alternate "recovery blocks" [76]. It appears attractive for parts of the error compensation activity, but it is still too early to tell how well it will handle the error detection problem, or what the price will be in program slowdown.

C. Trends

As we continue to collect and analyze more and more data on how, when, where, and why people make software errors, we will get added insights on how to avoid making such errors, how to organize our validation strategy and tactics (not only in testing but throughout the software life cycle), how to develop or evaluate new automated aids, and how to develop useful methods for predicting software reliability. Some automated aids, particularly for static code checking, and for some dynamic-type or assertion checking, will be integrated into future programming languages and compilers. We should see some added useful criteria and associated aids for test completeness, particularly along the lines of exercising "all data elements" in some appropriate way. Symbolic execution capabilities will probably make their way into automated aids for test case generation, monitoring, and perhaps retesting.

Continuing work into the theory of software testing should provide some refined concepts of test validity, reliability, and completeness, plus a better theoretical base for supporting hybrid test/proof methods of verifying programs. Program proving techniques and aids will become more powerful in the size and range of programs they handle, and hopefully easier to use and harder to misuse. But many of their basic limitations will remain, particularly those involving real variables and nonformalizable inputs.

Unfortunately, most of these helpful capabilities will be available only to people working in higher order languages. Much of the progress in test technology will be unavailable to the increasing number of people who find themselves spending more and more time testing assembly language software written for minicomputers and microcomputers with poor test support capabilities. Powerful cross-compiler capabilities on large host machines and microprogrammed diagnostic emulation capabilities [77] should provide these people some relief after a while, but a great deal of software testing will regress back to earlier generation "dark ages."

VII. Software maintenance

A. Scope of software maintenance

Software maintenance is an extremely important but highly neglected activity. Its importance is clear from Fig. 1: about 40 percent of the overall hardware-software dollar is going into software maintenance today, and this number is likely to grow to about 60 percent by 1985. It will continue to grow for a long time, as we continue to add to our inventory of code via development at a faster rate than we make code obsolete.

The figures above are only very approximate, because our only data so far are based on highly approximate definitions. It is hard to come up with an unexceptional definition of software maintenance. Here, we define it as "the process of modifying existing operational software while leaving its primary functions intact." It is useful to divide software maintenance into two categories: software *update,* which results in a changed functional specification for the software, and software *repair,* which leaves the functional specification intact. A good discussion of software repair is given in the paper by Swanson [78], who divides it into the subcategories of corrective maintenance (of processing, performance, or implementation failures), adaptive maintenance (to changes in the processing or data environment), and perfective maintenance (for enhancing performance or maintainability).

For either update or repair, three main functions are involved in software maintenance [79].

Understanding the existing software: This implies the need for good documentation, good traceability between requirements and code, and well-structured and well-formatted code.

Modifying the existing software: This implies the need for software, hardware, and data structures which are easy to expand and which minimize side effects of changes, plus easy-to-update documentation.

Revalidating the modified software: This implies the need for software structures which facilitate selective retest, and aids for making retest more thorough and efficient.

Following a short discussion of current practice in software maintenance, these three functions will be used below as a framework for discussing current frontier technology in software maintenance.

B. Current practice

As indicated in Fig. 6, probably about 70 percent of the overall cost of software is spent in software maintenance. A recent paper by Elshoff [80] indicates that the figure for General Motors is about 75 percent, and that GM is fairly typical of large business software activities. Daly [5] indicates that about 60 percent of GTE's 10-year life cycle costs for real-time software are devoted to maintenance. On two Air Force command and control software systems, the maintenance portions of the 10-year life cycle costs were about 67 and 72 percent. Often, maintenance is not done very efficiently. On one aircraft computer, software development costs were roughly $75/instruction, while maintenance costs ran as high as $4000/instruction [81].

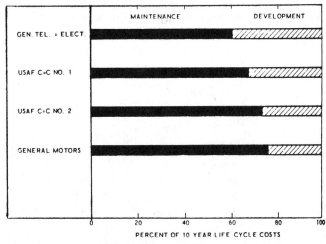

Figure 6. Software life-cycle cost breakdown.

Despite its size, software maintenance is a highly neglected activity. In general, less-qualified personnel are assigned to maintenance tasks. There are few good general principles and few studies of the process, most of them inconclusive.

Further, data processing practices are usually optimized around other criteria than maintenance efficiency. Optimizing around development cost and schedule criteria generally leads to compromises in documentation, testing, and structuring. Optimizing around hardware efficiency criteria generally leads to use of assembly language and skimping on hardware, both of which correlate strongly with increased software maintenance costs [1].

C. Current frontier technology

1) *Understanding the existing software:* Aids here have largely been discussed in previous sections: structured programming, automatic formatting, and code auditors for standards compliance checking to enhance code readability; machine-readable requirements and design languages with traceability support to and from the code. Several systems exist for automatically updating documentation by excerpting information from the revised code and comment cards.

2) *Modifying the existing software:* Some of Parnas' modularization guidelines [32] and the data abstractions of the CLU [48] and ALPHARD [47] languages make it easier to minimize the side effects of changes. There may be a maintenance price, however. In the past, some systems with highly coupled programs and associated data structures have had difficulties with data base updating. This may not be a problem with today's data dictionary capabilities, but the interactions have not yet been investigated. Other aids to modification are structured code, configuration management techniques, programming support libraries, and process construction systems.

3) *Revalidating the modified software:* Aids here were discussed earlier under testing; they include primarily test data management systems, comparator programs, and program structure analyzers with some limited capability for selective retest analysis.

4) *General aids:* On-line interactive systems help to remove one of the main bottlenecks involved in software maintenance: the long turnaround times for retesting. In addition, many of these systems are providing helpful capabilities for text editing and software module management. They will be discussed in more detail under "Management and Integrated Approaches" below. In general, a good deal more work has been done on the maintainability aspects of data bases and data structures than for program structures; a good survey of data base technology is given in a recent special issue of *ACM Computing Surveys* [82].

D. Trends

The increased concern with life cycle costs, particularly within the U.S. DoD [83], will focus a good deal more attention on software maintenance. More data collection and analysis on the growth dynamics of software systems, such as the Belady-Lehman studies of OS/360 [84], will begin to point out the high-leverage areas for improvement. Explicit mechanisms for confronting maintainability issues early in the development cycle, such as the requirements-properties matrix [18] and the design inspection [4] will be refined and used more extensively. In fact, we may evolve a more general concept of software quality assurance (currently focussed largely on reliability concerns), involving such activities as independent reviews of software requirements and design specifications by experts in software maintainability. Such activities will be enhanced considerably with the advent of more powerful capabilities for analyzing machine-readable requirements and design specifications. Finally, advances in automatic programming [14, 15] should reduce or eliminate some maintenance activity, at least in some problem domains.

VIII. Software management and integrated approaches

A. Current practice

There are more opportunities for improving software productivity and quality in the area of management than anywhere else. The difference between software project successes and failures has most often been traced to good or poor practices in software management. The biggest software management problems have generally been the following.

Poor Planning: Generally, this leads to large amounts of wasted effort and idle time because of tasks being unnecessarily performed, overdone, poorly synchronized, or poorly interfaced.

Poor Control: Even a good plan is useless when it is not kept up-to-date and used to manage the project.

Poor Resource Estimation: Without a firm idea of how much time and effort a task should take, the manager is in a poor position to exercise control.

Unsuitable Management Personnel: As a very general statement, software personnel tend to respond to problem situations as designers rather than as managers.

Poor Accountability Structure: Projects are generally organized and run with very diffuse delineation of responsibilities, thus exacerbating all the above problems.

Inappropriate Success Criteria: Minimizing development costs and schedules will generally yield a hard-to-maintain product. Emphasizing "percent coded" tends to get people coding early and to neglect such key activities as requirements and design validation, test planning, and draft user documentation.

Procrastination on Key Activities: This is especially prevalent when reinforced by inappropriate success criteria as above.

B. Current frontier technology

1) *Management guidelines:* There is no lack of useful material to guide software management. In general, it takes a book-length treatment to adequately cover the issues. A number of books on the subject are now available [85-95], but for various reasons they have not strongly influenced software management practice. Some of the books (e.g., Brooks [85] and the collections by Horowitz [86], Weinwurm [87], and Buxton, Naur, and Randell [88]) are collections of very good advice, ideas, and experiences, but are fragmentary and lacking in a consistent, integrated life cycle approach. Some of the books (e.g., Metzger [89], Shaw and Atkins [90], Hice *et al.* [91], Ridge and Johnson [92], and Gildersleeve [93]) are good on checklists and procedures but (except to some extent the latter two) are light on the human aspects of management, such as staffing, motivation, and conflict resolution. Weinberg [94] provides the most help on the human aspects, along with Brooks [85] and Aron [95], but in turn, these three books are light on checklists and procedures. (A second volume by Aron is intended to cover software group and project considerations.) None of the books have an adequate treatment of some items, largely because they are so poorly understood: chief among these items are software cost and resource estimation, and software maintenance.

In the area of software cost estimation, the paper by Wolverton [96] remains the most useful source of help. It is strongly based on the number of object instructions (modified by complexity, type of application, and novelty) as the determinant of software cost. This is a known weak spot, but not one for which an acceptable improvement has surfaced. One possible line of improvement might be along the "software physics" lines being investigated by Halstead [97] and others; some interesting initial results have been obtained here, but their utility for practical cost estimation remains to be demonstrated. A good review of the software cost estimation area is contained in [98].

2) *Management-technology decoupling:* Another difficulty of the above books is the degree to which they are decoupled from software technology. Except for the Horowitz and Aron books, they say relatively little about the use of such advanced-technology aids as formal, machine-readable requirements, top-down design approaches, structured programming, and automated aids to software testing.

Unfortunately, the management-technology decoupling works the other way, also. In the design area, for example, most treatments of top-down software design are presented as logical exercises independent of user or economic considerations. Most automated aids to software design provide little support for such management needs as configuration management, traceability to code or requirements, and resource estimation and control. Clearly, there needs to be a closer coupling between technology and management than this. Some current efforts to provide integrated management-technology approaches are presented next.

3) *Integrated approaches:* Several major integrated systems for software development are currently in operation or under development. In general, their objectives are similar: to achieve a significant boost in software development efficiency and quality through the synergism of a unified approach. Examples are the utility of having a complementary development approach (top-down, hierarchical) and set of programming standards (hierarchical, structured code); the ability to perform a software update and at the same time perform a set of timely, consistent project status updates (new version number of module, closure of software problem report, updated status logs); or simply the improvement in software system integration achieved when all participants are using the same development concept, ground rules, and support software.

The most familiar of the integrated approaches is the IBM "top-down structured programming with chief programmer teams" concept. A good short description of the concept is given by Baker [49]; an extensive treatment is available in a 15-volume series of reports done by IBM for the U.S. Army and Air Force [99]. The top-down structured approach was discussed earlier. The Chief Programmer Team centers around an individual (the Chief) who is responsible for designing, coding, and integrating the top-level control structure as well as the key components of the team's product; for managing and motivating the team personnel and personally reading and reviewing all their code; and also for performing traditional management and customer interface functions. The Chief is assisted by a Backup programmer who is prepared at anytime to take the Chief's place, a Librarian who handles job submission, configuration control, and project status accounting, and additional programmers and specialists as needed.

In general, the overall ensemble of techniques has been quite successful, but the Chief Programmer concept has had mixed results [99]. It is difficult to find individuals with enough energy and talent to perform all the above functions. If you find one, the project will do quite well; otherwise, you have concentrated most of the project risk in a single individual, without a good way of finding out whether or not he is in trouble. The Librarian and Programming Support Library concept have generally been quite useful, although to date the concept has been oriented toward a batch-processing development environment.

Another "structured" integrated approach has been developed and used at SofTech [38]. It is oriented largely around a hierarchical-decomposition design approach, guided by formalized sets of principles (modularity, abstraction, localization, hiding, uniformity, completeness, confirmability), processes (purpose, concept, mechanism, notation, usage), and goals (modularity, efficiency, reliability, understandability). Thus, it accommodates some economic considerations, although it says little about any other management considerations. It appears to work well for SofTech, but in general has not been widely assimilated elsewhere.

A more management-intensive integrated approach is the TRW software development methodology exemplified in the paper by Williams [50] and the TRW Software Development and Configuration Management Manual [100], which has been used as the basis for several recent government in-house software manuals. This approach features a coordinated set of high-level and detailed management objectives, associated automated aids — standards compliance checkers, test thoroughness checkers, process construction aids, reporting systems for cost, schedule, core and time budgets, problem identification and closure, etc. — and unified documentation and management devices such as the Unit Development Folder. Portions of the approach are still largely manual, although additional automation is underway, e.g., via the Requirements Statement Language [13].

The SDC Software Factory [101] is a highly ambitious attempt to automate and integrate software development technology. It consists of an interface control component, the Factory Access and Control Executive (FACE), which provides users access to various tools and data bases: a project planning and monitoring system, a software development data base and module management system, a top-down development support system, a set of test tools, etc. As the system is still undergoing development and preliminary evaluation, it is too early to tell what degree of success it will have.

Another factory-type approach is the System Design Laboratory (SDL) under development at the Naval Electronics Laboratory Center [102]. It currently consists primarily of a framework within which a wide range of aids to software development can be incorporated. The initial installment contains text editors, compilers, assemblers, and microprogrammed emulators. Later additions are envisioned to include design, development, and test aids, and such management aids as progress reporting, cost reporting and user profile analysis.

SDL itself is only a part of a more ambitious integrated approach, ARPA's National Software Works (NSW) [102]. The initial objective here has been to develop a "Works Manager" which will allow a software developer at a terminal to access a wide variety of software development tools on various computers available over the ARPANET. Thus, a developer might log into the NSW, obtain his source code from one computer, text-edit it on another, and perhaps continue to hand the program to additional computers for test instrumentation, compiling, executing, and postprocessing of output data. Currently, an initial version of the Works Manager is operational, along with a few tools, but it is too early to assess the likely outcome and payoffs of the project.

C. Trends

In the area of management techniques, we are probably entering a consolidation period, particularly as the U.S. DoD proceeds to implement the upgrades in its standards and procedures called for in the recent DoD Directive 5000.29 [104]. The resulting government-industry efforts should produce a set of software management guidelines which are more consistent and up-to-date with today's technology than the ones currently in use. It is likely that they will also be more comprehensible and less encumbered with DoD jargon; this will make them more useful to the software field in general.

Efforts to develop integrated, semiautomated systems for software development will continue at a healthy clip. They will run into a number of challenges which will probably take a few years to work out. Some are technical, such as the lack of a good technological base for data structuring aids, and the formidable problem of integrating complex software support tools. Some are economic and managerial, such as the problems of pricing services, providing tool warranties, and controlling the evolution of the system. Others are environmental, such as the proliferation of minicomputers and microcomputers, which will strain the capability of any support system to keep up-to-date.

Even if the various integrated systems do not achieve all their goals, there will be a number of major benefits from the effort. One is of course that a larger number of support tools will become available to a larger number of people (another major channel of tools will still continue to expand, though: the independent software products marketplace). More importantly, those systems which achieve a degree of conceptual integration (not just a free-form tool box) will eliminate a great deal of the semantic confusion which currently slows down our group efforts throughout the software life cycle. Where we have learned how to talk to each other about our software problems, we tend to do pretty well.

IX. Conclusions

Let us now assess the current state of the art of tools and techniques which are being used to solve software development problems, in terms of our original definition of software engineering: the practical application of *scientific knowledge* in the design and construction of software. Table II presents a summary assessment of the extent to which current software engineering techniques are based on solid scientific principles (versus empirical heuristics). The summary assessment covers four dimensions: the extent to which existing scientific principles apply across the entire software life cycle, across the entire range of software applications, across the range of engineering-economic analyses required for software development, and across the range of personnel available to perform software development.

Table II
Applicability of Existing Scientific Principles

Dimension	Software Engineering	Hardware Engineering
Scope Across Life Cycle	Some principles for component construction and detailed design, virtually none for system design and integration, e.g., algorithms, automata theory.	Many principles applicable across life cycle, e.g., communication theory, control theory.
Scope Across Application	Some principles for "systems" software, virtually none for applications software, e.g., discrete mathematical structures.	Many principles applicable across entire application system, e.g., control theory application.
Engineering Economics	Very few principles which apply to system economics, e.g., algorithms.	Many principles apply well to system economics, e.g., strength of materials, optimization, and control theory.
Required Training	Very few principles formulated for consumption by technicians, e.g., structured code, basic math packages.	Many principles formulated for consumption by technicians, e.g., handbooks for structural design, stress testing, maintainability.

For perspective, a similar summary assessment is presented in Table II for hardware engineering. It is clear from Table II that software engineering is in a very primitive state as compared to hardware engineering, with respect to its range of scientific foundations. Those scientific principles available to support software engineering address problems in an area we shall call *Area 1: detailed design and coding* of *systems software* by *experts* in a relatively *economics-independent* context. Unfortunately, the most pressing software development problems are in an area we shall call *Area 2: requirements analysis design, test, and maintenance* of *applications software* by *technicians** in an *economics-driven*

---

*For example, a recent survey of 14 installations in one large organization produced the following profile of its "average coder": 2 years college-level education, 2 years software experience, familiarity with 2 programming languages and 2 applications, and generally introverted, sloppy, inflexible, "in over his head," and undermanaged. Given the continuing increase in demand for software personnel, one should not assume that this typical profile will improve much. This has strong implications for effective software engineering technology which, like effective software, must be well-matched to the people who must use it.

context. And in Area 2, our scientific foundations are so slight that one can seriously question whether our current techniques deserve to be called "software engineering."

Hardware engineering clearly has available a better scientific foundation for addressing its counterpart of these Area 2 problems. This should not be too surprising, since "hardware science" has been pursued for a much longer time, is easier to experiment with, and does not have to explain the performance of human beings.

What is rather surprising, and a bit disappointing, is the reluctance of the computer science field to address itself to the more difficult and diffuse problems in Area 2, as compared with the more tractable Area 1 subjects of automata theory, parsing, computability, etc. Like most explorations into the relatively unknown, the risks of addressing Area 2 research problems in the requirements analysis, design, test and maintenance of applications software are relatively higher. But the prizes, in terms of payoff to practical software development and maintenance, are likely to be far more rewarding. In fact, as software engineering begins to solve its more difficult Area 2 problems, it will begin to lead the way toward solutions to the more difficult large-systems problems which continue to beset hardware engineering.

References

1. B.W. Boehm, "Software and Its Impact: A Quantitative Assessment," *Datamation,* Vol. 19, No. 5 (May 1973), pp. 48-59.

2. T.A. Dolotta, et al., *Data Processing in 1980-85* (New York: Wiley-Interscience, 1976).

3. P. Wegner, "Computer Languages," *IEEE Transactions on Computers,* Vol. C-25, No. 12 (December 1976), pp. 1207-25.

4. M.E. Fagan, *Design and Code Inspections and Process Control in the Development of Programs,* IBM Corporation, Report No. IBM-SDD TR-21.572 (December 1974).

5. E.B. Daly, "Management of Software Development," *IEEE Transactions on Software Engineering,* Vol. SE-3, No. 3 (May 1977), pp. 230-42.

6. W.W. Royce, "Software Requirements Analysis, Sizing, and Costing," *Practical Strategies for the Development of Large Scale Software,* ed. E. Horowitz (Reading, Mass.: Addison-Wesley, 1975).

7. T.E. Bell and T.A. Thayer, "Software Requirements: Are They a Problem?" *Proceedings of the IEEE/ACM Second International Conference on Software Engineering* (October 1976), pp. 61-68.

8. E.S. Quade, ed., *Analysis for Military Decisions* (Chicago: Rand-McNally, 1964).

9. J.D. Couger and R.W. Knapp, eds., *System Analysis Techniques* (New York: Wiley & Sons, 1974).

10. D. Teichroew and H. Sayani, "Automation of System Building," *Datamation,* Vol. 17, No. 16 (August 15, 1971), pp. 25-30.

11. C.G. Davis and C.R. Vick, "The Software Development System," *IEEE Transactions on Software Engineering,* Vol. SE-3, No. 1 (January 1977), pp. 69-84.

12. M. Alford, "A Requirements Engineering Methodology for Real-Time Processing Requirements," *IEEE Transactions on Software Engineering,* Vol. SE-3, No. 1 (January 1977), pp. 60-69.

13. T.E. Bell, D.C. Bixler, and M.E. Dyer, "An Extendable Approach to Computer-Aided Software Requirements Engineering," *IEEE Transactions on Software Engineering,* Vol. SE-3, No. 1 (January 1977), pp. 49-60.

14. R.M. Balzer, *Imprecise Program Specification,* University of Southern California, Report No. ISI/RR-75-36 (Los Angeles: December 1975).

15. W.A. Martin and M. Bosyj, "Requirements Derivation in Automatic Programming," *Proceedings of the MRI Symposium on Computer Software Engineering* (April 1976).

16. N.P. Dooner and J.R. Lourie, *The Application Software Engineering Tool,* IBM Corporation, Research Report No. RC 5434 (Yorktown Heights, N.Y.: IBM Research Center, May 29, 1975).

17. M.L. Wilson, *The Information Automat Approach to Design and Implementation of Computer-Based Systems,* IBM Corporation (Gaithersburg, Md.: IBM Federal Systems Division, June 27, 1975).

18. B.W. Boehm, "Some Steps Toward Formal and Automated Aids to Software Requirements Analysis and Design," *Proceedings of the IFIP Congress* (Amsterdam, The Netherlands: North-Holland Publishing Co., 1974), pp. 192-97.

19. A.B. Endres, "An Analysis of Errors and Their Causes in System Programs," *IEEE Transactions on Software Engineering,* Vol. SE-1, No. 2 (June 1975), pp. 140-49.

20. T.A. Thayer, "Understanding Software Through Analysis of Empirical Data," *AFIPS Proceedings of the 1975 National Computer Conference,* Vol. 44 (Montvale, N.J.: AFIPS Press, 1975), pp. 335-41.

21. B.W. Boehm, R.L. McClean, and D.B. Urfrig, "Some Experience with Automated Aids to the Design of Large-Scale Reliable Software," *IEEE Transactions on Software Engineering,* Vol. SE-1, No. 1 (March 1975), pp. 125-33.

22. P. Freeman, *Software Design Representation: Analysis and Improvements,* University of California, Technical Report No. 81 (Irvine, Calif.: May 1976).

23. E.L. Glaser, et al., "The LOGOS Project," *Proceedings of the IEEE Computer Conference* (1972), pp. 175-92.

24. N.R. Nielsen, *ECSS: Extendable Computer System Simulator,* Rand Corporation, Report No. RM-6132-PR/NASA (January 1970).

25. D.W. Kosy, *The ECSS II Language for Simulating Computer Systems,* Rand Corporation, Report No. R-1895-GSA (December 1975).

26. E.W. Dijkstra, "Complexity Controlled by Hierarchical Ordering of Function and Variability," *Software Engineering, Concepts and Techniques,* P. Naur, B. Randell, and J.N. Buxton, eds. (New York: Petrocelli/Charter, 1976).

27. H.D. Mills, *Mathematical Foundations for Structured Programming,* IBM Corporation, Report No. FSC 72-6012 (Gaithersburg, Md.: IBM Federal Systems Division, February 1972).

28. C.L. McGowan and J.R. Kelly, *Top-Down Structured Programming Techniques* (New York: Petrocelli/Charter, 1975).

29. B.W. Boehm, et al., "Structured Programming: A Quantitative Assessment," *Computer,* Vol. 8, No. 6 (June 1975), pp. 38-54.

30. W.P. Stevens, G.J. Myers, and L.L. Constantine, "Structured Design," *IBM Systems Journal,* Vol. 13, No. 2 (1974), pp. 115-39.

31. G.J. Myers, *Reliable Software Through Composite Design* (New York: Petrocelli/Charter, 1975).

32. D.L. Parnas, "On the Criteria to be Used in Decomposing Systems Into Modules," *Communications of the ACM,* Vol. 15, No. 12 (December 1972), pp. 1053-58.

33. _____, "The Influence of Software Structure on Reliability," *Proceedings of the 1975 International Conference on Reliable Software* (April 1975), pp. 358-62.

34. M. Hamilton and S. Zeldin, "Higher Order Software — A Methodology for Defining Software," *IEEE Transactions on Software Engineering,* Vol. SE-2, No. 1 (March 1976), pp. 9-32.

35. *HIPO — A Design Aid and Documentation Technique,* IBM Corporation, Manual No. GC20-1851-0 (White Plains, N.Y.: IBM Data Processing Division, October 1974).

36. J. Mortison, "Tools and Techniques for Software Development Process Visibility and Control," *Proceedings of the ACM Computer Science Conference* (February 1976).

37. I. Nassi and B. Shneiderman, "Flowchart Techniques for Structured Programming," *SIGPLAN Notices,* Vol. 8, No. 8 (August 1973), pp. 12-26.

38. D.T. Ross, J.B. Goodenough, and C.A. Irvine, "Software Engineering: Process, Principles, and Goals," *Computer,* Vol. 8, No. 5 (May 1975), pp. 17-27.

39. M.A. Jackson, *Principles of Program Design* (New York: Academic Press, 1975).

40. P. Henderson and R.A. Snowden, "A Tool For Structured Program Development," *Proceedings of the 1974 IFIP Congress,* (Amsterdam, The Netherlands: North-Holland Publishing Co.), pp. 204-07.

41. L.C. Carpenter and L.L. Tripp, "Software Design Validation Tool," *Proceedings of the 1975 International Conference on Reliable Software* (April 1975), pp. 395-400.

42. S.H. Caine and E.K. Gordon, "PDL: A Tool for Software Design," *AFIPS Proceedings of the 1975 National Computer Conference,* Vol. 44 (Montvale, N.J.: AFIPS Press, 1975), pp. 271-76.

43. H.D. Mills, *Structured Programming in Large Systems,* IBM Corporation (Gaithersburg, Md.: IBM Federal Systems Division, November 1970).

44. C.A.R. Hoare, "Notes on Data Structuring," *Structured Programming,* O.-J. Dahl, E.W. Dijkstra, and C.A.R. Hoare (New York: Academic Press, 1972).

45. N. Wirth, "An Assessment of the Programming Language Pascal," *IEEE Transactions on Software Engineering,* Vol. SE-1, No. 2 (June 1975), pp. 192-98.

46. P. Brinch-Hansen, "The Programming Language Concurrent Pascal," *IEEE Transactions on Software Engineering,* Vol. SE-1, No. 2 (June 1975), pp. 199-208.

47. W.A. Wulf, *ALPHARD: Toward a Language to Support Structured Programs,* Carnegie-Mellon University, Internal Report (Pittsburgh, Pa.: April 30, 1974).

48. B.H. Liskov and S. Zilles, "Programming with Abstract Data Types," *SIGPLAN Notices,* Vol. 9, No. 4 (April 1974), pp. 50-59.

49. F.T. Baker, "Structured Programming in a Production Programming Environment," *IEEE Transactions on Software Engineering,* Vol. SE-1, No. 2 (June 1975), pp. 241-52.

50. R.D. Williams, "Managing the Development of Reliable Software," *Proceedings of the 1975 International Conference on Reliable Software* (April 1975), pp. 3-8.

51. J. Witt, "The COLUMBUS Approach," *IEEE Transactions on Software Engineering,* Vol. SE-1, No. 4 (December 1975), pp. 358-63.

52. B.W. Kernighan and P.J. Plauger, *The Elements of Programming Style* (New York: McGraw-Hill, 1974).

53. H.F. Ledgard, *Programming Proverbs* (Rochelle Park, N.J.: Hayden, 1975).

54. W.A. Whitaker, et al., *Department of Defense Requirements for High Order Computer Programming Languages: 'Tinman,'* Defense Advanced Research Projects Agency (April 1976).

55. *Proceedings of the 1973 IEEE Symposium on Computer Software Reliability* (April-May 1973).

56. E.C. Nelson, *A Statistical Basis for Software Reliability Assessment,* TRW Systems Group, Report No. TRW-SS-73-03 (Redondo Beach, Calif.: March 1973).

58. J.D. Musa, "Theory of Software Reliability and Its Application," *IEEE Transactions on Software Engineering,* Vol. SE-1, No. 3 (September 1975), pp. 312-27.

59. R.J. Rubey, J.A. Dana, and P.W. Biche, "Quantitative Aspects of Software Validation," *IEEE Transactions on Software Engineering,* Vol. SE-1, No. 2 (June 1975), pp. 150-55.

60. T.A. Thayer, M. Lipow, and E.C. Nelson, *Software Reliability Study,* TRW Systems Group, Report to RADC, Contract No. F30602-74-C-0036 (Redondo Beach, Calif.: March 1976).

61. D.J. Reifer, "Automated Aids for Reliable Software," *Proceedings of the 1975 International Conference on Reliable Software* (April 1975), pp. 131-42.

62. C.V. Ramamoorthy and S.B.F. Ho, "Testing Large Software With Automated Software Evaluation Systems," *IEEE Transactions on Software Engineering,* Vol. SE-1, No. 1 (March 1975), pp. 46-58.

63. J.B. Goodenough and S.L. Gerhart, "Toward a Theory of Test Data Selection," *IEEE Transactions on Software Engineering,* Vol. SE-1, No. 2 (June 1975), pp. 156-73.

64. P. Wegner, "Report on the 1975 International Conference on Reliable Software," in *Findings and Recommendations of the Joint Logistics Commanders' Software Reliability Work Group,* Vol. II (November 1975), pp. 45-88.

65. J.C. King, "A New Approach to Program Testing," *Proceedings of the 1975 International Conference on Reliable Software* (April 1975), pp. 228-33.

66. R.S. Boyer, B. Elspas, and K.N. Levitt, "Select — A Formal System for Testing and Debugging Programs," *Proceedings of the 1975 International Conference on Reliable Software* (April 1975), pp. 234-45.

67. J. Goldberg, ed., *Proceedings of the Symposium on High Cost of Software,* Stanford Research Institute (Stanford, Calif.: September 1973), p. 63.

68. L.C. Ragland, "A Verified Program Verifier," Ph.D. Dissertation, University of Texas, 1973.

69. D.I. Good, R.L. London, and W.W. Bledsoe, "An Interactive Program Verification System," *IEEE Transactions on Software Engineering,* Vol. SE-1, No. 1 (March 1975), pp. 59-67.

70. F.W. von Henke and D.C. Luckham, "A Methodology for Verifying Programs," *Proceedings of the 1975 International Conference on Reliable Software* (April 1975), pp. 156-64.

71. C.A.R. Hoare and N. Wirth, "An Axiomatic Definition of the Programming Language PASCAL," *Acta Informatica,* Vol. 2 (1973), pp. 335-55.

72. R.L. London, "A View of Program Verification," *Proceedings of the 1975 International Conference on Reliable Software* (April 1975), pp. 534-45.

73. E.W. Dijkstra, "Notes on Structured Programming," *Structured Programming,* O.-J. Dahl, E.W. Dijkstra and C.A.R. Hoare (New York: Academic Press, 1972).

74. W.A. Wulf, "Reliable Hardware-Software Architectures," *IEEE Transactions on Software Engineering,* Vol. SE-1, No. 2 (June 1975), pp. 233-40.

75. J. Goldberg, "New Problems in Fault-Tolerant Computing," *Proceedings of the 1975 International Symposium on Fault-Tolerant Computing* (Paris, France: June 1975), pp. 29-36.

76. B. Randell, "System Structure for Software Fault-Tolerance," *IEEE Transactions on Software Engineering,* Vol. SE-1, No. 2 (June 1975), pp. 220-32.

77. R.K. McClean and B. Press, "Improved Techniques for Reliable Software Using Microprogrammed Diagnostic Emulation," *Proceedings of the IFAC Congress,* Vol. IV (August 1975).

78. E.B. Swanson, "The Dimensions of Maintenance," *Proceedings of the IEEE/ACM Second International Conference on Software Engineering* (October 1976).

79. B.W. Boehm, J.R. Brown, and M. Lipow, "Quantitative Evaluation of Software Quality," *Proceedings of the IEEE/ACM Second International Conference on Software Engineering* (October 1976), pp. 592-605.

80. J.L. Elshoff, "An Analysis of Some Commercial PL/I Programs," *IEEE Transactions on Software Engineering,* Vol. SE-2, No. 2 (June 1976), pp. 113-20.

81. W.L. Trainor, "Software: From Satan to Saviour," *Proceedings of the NAECON* (May 1973).

82. E.H. Sibley, ed., *ACM Computing Surveys,* Vol. 8, No. 1 (March 1976). Special issue on data base management systems.

83. *Defense Management Journal,* Vol. II (October 1975). Special issue on software management.

84. L.A. Belady and M.M. Lehman, *The Evolution Dynamics of Large Programs,* IBM Corporation (Yorktown Heights, N.Y.: IBM Research Center, September 1975).

85. F.P. Brooks, *The Mythical Man-Month* (Reading, Mass.: Addison-Wesley, 1975).

86. E. Horowitz, ed., *Practical Strategies for Developing Large-Scale Software* (Reading, Mass.: Addison-Wesley, 1975).

87. G.F. Weinwurm, ed., *On the Management of Computer Programming* (New York: Auerbach, 1970).

88. P. Naur, B. Randell, and J.N. Buxton, eds., *Software Engineering, Concepts and Techniques, Proceedings of the NATO Conferences* (New York: Petrocelli/Charter, 1976).

89. P.J. Metzger, *Managing a Programming Project* (Englewood Cliffs, N.J.: Prentice-Hall, 1973).

90. J.C. Shaw and W. Atkins, *Managing Computer System Projects* (New York: McGraw-Hill, 1970).

91. G.F. Hice, W.S. Turner, and L.F. Cashwell, *System Development Methodology* (New York: American Elsevier, 1974).

92. W.J. Ridge and L.E. Johnson, *Effective Management of Computer Software* (Homewood, Ill.: Dow Jones-Irwin, 1973).

93. T.R. Gildersleeve, *Data Processing Project Management* (New York: Van Nostrand Reinhold, 1974).

94. G.M. Weinberg, *The Psychology of Computer Programming* (New York: Van Nostrand Reinhold, 1971).

95. J.D. Aron, *The Program Development Process: The Individual Programmer* (Reading, Mass.: Addison-Wesley, 1974).

96. R.W. Wolverton, "The Cost of Developing Large-Scale Software," *IEEE Transactions on Computers,* Vol. C-23, No. 6 (June 1974).

97. M.H. Halstead, "Toward a Theoretical Basis for Estimating Programming Effort," *Proceedings of the ACM Conference* (October 1975), pp. 222-24.

98. *Summary Notes, Government/Industry Software Sizing and Costing Workshop,* USAF Electronic Systems Division (October 1974).

99. B.S. Barry and J.J. Naughton, *Chief Programmer Team Operations Description,* U.S. Air Force, Report No. RADC-TR-74-300, Vol. X (of 15-volume series), pp. 1-2-1-3.

100. *Software Development and Configuration Management Manual,* TRW Systems Group, Report No. TRW-SS-73-07 (Redondo Beach, Calif.: December 1973).

101. H. Bratman and T. Court, "The Software Factory," *Computer,* Vol. 8, No. 5 (May 1975), pp. 28-37.

102. *Systems Design Laboratory: Preliminary Design Report,* Naval Electronics Laboratory Center, Preliminary Working Paper TN-3145 (March 1976).

103. W.E. Carlson and S.D. Crocker, "The Impact of Networks on the Software Marketplace," *Proceedings of EASCON* (October 1974).

104. *Management of Computer Resources in Major Defense Systems,* U.S. Department of Defense, Directive 6000.29 (April 1976).

INTRODUCTION

The next article, by Ross and Schoman, is one of three papers chosen for inclusion in this book that deal with the subject of structured analysis. With its companion papers — by Teichroew and Hershey [Paper 23] and by DeMarco [Paper 24] — the paper gives a good idea of the direction that the software field probably will be following for the next several years.

The paper addresses the problems of traditional systems analysis, and anybody who has spent any time as a systems analyst in a large EDP organization immediately will understand the problems and weaknesses of "requirements definition" that Ross and Schoman relate — clearly *not* the sort of problems upon which academicians like Dijkstra, Wirth, Knuth, and most other authors in this book have focused! To stress the importance of proper requirements definition, Ross and Schoman state that "even the best structured programming code will not help if the programmer has been told to solve the wrong problem, or, worse yet, has been given a correct description, but has not understood it."

In their paper, the authors summarize the problems associated with conventional systems analysis, and describe the steps that a "good" analysis approach should include. They advise that the analyst separate his *logical,* or *functional,* description of the system from the *physical* form that it eventually will take; this is difficult for many analysts to do, since they assume, a priori, that the physical implementation of the system will consist of a computer.

Ross and Schoman also emphasize the need to achieve a consensus among typically disparate parties: the user liaison personnel who interface with the developers, the "professional" systems analyst, and management. Since all of these people have different interests and different viewpoints, it becomes all the more important that they have a common frame of reference — a common way of *modeling* the system-to-be. For this need, Ross and Schoman propose their solution: a proprietary package, known as SADT, that was developed by the consulting firm of SofTech for which the authors work.

The SADT approach utilizes a top-down, partitioned, graphic model of a system. The model is presented in a logical, or abstract, fashion that allows for eventual implementation as a manual system, a computer system, or a mixture of both. This emphasis on graphic models of a system is distinctly different from that of the Teichroew and Hershey paper. It is distinctly similar to the approach suggested by DeMarco in "Structured Analysis and System Specification," the final paper in this collection. The primary difference between DeMarco and Ross/Schoman is that DeMarco and his colleagues at YOURDON inc. prefer circles, or "bubbles," whereas the SofTech group prefers rectangles.

Ross and Schoman point out that their graphic modeling approach can be tied in with an "automated documentation" approach of the sort described by Teichroew and Hershey. Indeed, this approach gradually is beginning to be adopted by large EDP organizations; but for installations that can't afford the overhead of a computerized, automated systems analysis package, Ross and Schoman neglect one important aspect of systems modeling. That is the "data dictionary," in which *all* of the data elements pertinent to the new system are defined *in the same logical top-down fashion as the rest of the model.* There also is a need to formalize mini-specifications, or "mini-specs" as DeMarco calls them; that is, the "business policy" associated with each bottom-level functional process of the system must be described in a manner far more rigorous than currently is being done.

A weakness of the Ross/Schoman paper is its lack of detail about problem solutions: More than half the paper is devoted to a description of the problems of conventional analysis, but the SADT package is described in rather sketchy detail. There are additional documents on SADT available from SofTech, but the reader still will be left with the fervent desire that Messrs. Ross and Schoman and their colleagues at SofTech eventually will sit down and put their ideas into a full-scale book.

Structured Analysis for Requirements Definition

I. The problem

The obvious assertion that "a problem unstated is a problem unsolved" seems to have escaped many builders of large computer application systems. All too often, design and implementation begin before the real needs and system functions are fully known. The results are skyrocketing costs, missed schedules, waste and duplication, disgruntled users, and an endless series of patches and repairs euphemistically called "system maintenance." Compared to other phases of system development, these symptoms reflect, by a large margin, the lack of an adequate approach to requirements definition.

Given the wide range of computer hardware now available and the emergence of software engineering as a discipline, most problems in system development are becoming less traceable to either the machinery or the programming [1]. Methods for handling the hardware and software components of systems are highly sophisticated, but address only part of the job. For example, even the best structured programming code will not help if the programmer has been told to solve the wrong problem, or, worse yet, has been given a correct description, but has not understood it. The results of requirements definition must be both complete and understandable.

In efforts to deal with these needs, the expressions "system architecture," "system design," "system analysis," and "system engineering" seem to be accepted terminology. But in truth, there is no widely practiced methodology for systems work that has the clarity and discipline of the more classical techniques used in construction and manufacturing enterprises. In manufacturing, for example, a succession of blueprints, drawings, and specifications captures all of the relevant requirements for a product. This complete problem definition and implementation plan allows the product to be made almost routinely, by "business as usual," with no surprises. In a good manufacturing operation, major troubles are avoided because even the first production run does not create an item for the first time. The item was created and the steps of forming and assembly were done mentally, in the minds of designers and engineers, long before the set of blueprints and specifications ever arrived at the production shop. That simulation is made possible only because the notations and discipline of the blueprinting methodology are so complete and so consistent with the desired item that its abstract representation contains all the information needed for its imaginary preconstruction.

Software system designers attempt to do the same of course, but being faced with greater complexity and less exacting methods, their successes form the surprises, rather than their failures!

Experience has taught us that system problems are complex and ill-defined. The complexity of large systems is an inherent fact of life with which one must cope. Faulty definition, however, is an artifact of inadequate methods. It can be eliminated by the introduction of well-thought-out techniques and means of expression. That is the subject of this paper. Systems can be manufactured, like other things, if the right approach is used. That approach must start at the beginning.

Requirements definition

Requirements definition includes, but is not limited to, the problem analysis that yields a functional specification. It is much more than that. Requirements definition must encompass everything necessary to lay the groundwork for subsequent stages in system development (Fig. 1). Within the total process, which consists largely of steps in a solution to a problem, only once is the problem itself stated and the solution justified — in requirements definition.

Requirements definition is a careful assessment of the needs that a system is to fulfill. It must say *why* a system is needed, based on current or foreseen conditions, which may be internal operations or an external market. It must say *what* system features will serve and satisfy this context. And it must say *how* the system is to be constructed. Thus, requirements definition must deal with three subjects.

1) *Context analysis:* The reasons *why* the system is to be created and why certain technical, operational, and economic feasibilities are the criteria which form *boundary conditions* for the system.

2) *Functional specification:* A description of *what* the system is to be, in terms of the functions it must accomplish. Since this is part of the problem statement, it must only present *boundary conditions* for considerations later to be taken up in system design.

3) *Design constraints:* A summary of conditions specifying *how* the required system is to be constructed and implemented. This does not necessarily specify which things will be in the system. Rather it identifies *boundary conditions* by which those things may later be selected or created.

Each of these subjects must be fully documented during requirements definition. But note that these are subjects, not documents. The contents of resulting documents will vary according to the needs of the development organization. In any case, they must be reference documents which justify all aspects of the required system, not design or detailed specification documents.

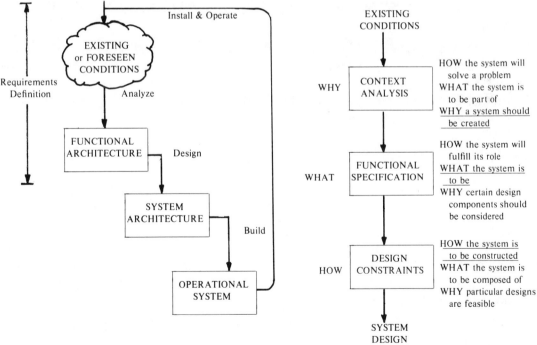

Figure 1. Simplified view
of development cycle.

Figure 2. Each subject has
a fundamental purpose.

Each of the subjects has a specific and limited role in justifying the required system. Collectively, they capture on paper, at the appropriate time, all relevant knowledge about the system problem in a complete, concise, comprehensive form. Taken together, these subjects define the whole need. Separately, they say *what* the system is to be part of, *what* the system is to be, and of *what* the system is to be composed (Fig. 2). The process known as "analysis" must apply to all three.

Descriptions of these subjects just frame the problem; they do not solve it. Details are postponed, and no binding implementation decisions are yet made. Even detailed budget and schedule commitments are put off, except those for the next phase, system design, because they depend on the results of that design. Requirements definition only (but completely) provides *boundary conditions* for the subsequent design and implementation stages. A problem well-stated is well on its way to a sound solution.

The problem revisited

The question still remains: why is requirements definition not a standard part of every system project, especially since not doing it well has such disastrously high costs [2]? Why is project start-up something one muddles through and why does it seem that requirements are never completely stated? What goes wrong?

The answer seems to be that just about everything goes wrong. Stated requirements are often excessive, incomplete, and inconsistent. Communication and documentation are roadblocks, too. Because they speak with different vocabularies, users and developers find it difficult to completely understand each other. Analysts are often drawn from the development organization, and are unable to document user requirements without simultaneously stating a design approach.

Good requirements are complete, consistent, testable, traceable, feasible, and flexible. By just stating necessary boundary conditions, they leave room for tradeoffs during system design. Thus, a good set of requirements documents can, in effect, serve as a user-developer contract. To attain these attributes, simply proposing a table of contents for requirements documentation is not enough. To do the job, one must emphasize the *means* of defining requirements, rather than prescribe the contents of documentation (which would, in any case, be impossible to do in a generic way).

Even in organizations which do stipulate some document or another, the process of defining requirements remains laborious and inconclusive. Lacking a complete definition of the job to be done, the effect of a contract is lacking, and the designers will make the missing assumptions and decisions because they must, in order to get the job done. Even when the value of requirements definition is recognized, it takes more than determination to have an effective approach. To define requirements, one must understand: 1) the nature of that which is to be described; 2) the form of the description; and 3) the process of analysis.

Many remedies to these problems have been proposed. Each project management, analysis, or specification scheme, whether "structured" or not, has its own adherents. Most do indeed offer some improvements, for any positive steps are better than none. But a significant impact has not been achieved, because each partial solution omits enough of the essential ingredients to be vulnerable.

The key to successful requirements definition lies in remembering that people define requirements. Thus, any useful discussion of requirements definition must combine: 1) a generic understanding of systems which is scientifically sound; 2) a notation and structure of documenting specific system knowledge in a rigorous, easy-to-read form; 3) a process for doing analysis which includes definition of people roles and interpersonal procedures; and 4) a way to technically manage the work, which enables allocation of requirements and postponement of design.

Academic approaches won't do. A pragmatic methodology must itself be: 1) technically feasible, i.e., consistent with the systems to be developed; 2) operationally feasible, i.e., people will use it to do the job well; and 3) economically feasible, i.e., noticeably improve the system development cycle.

This paper sketches such an approach, which has been successful in bringing order and direction to a wide range of system contexts. In even the most trying of circumstances, something can be done to address the need for requirements definition.

II. The process of requirements definition

The nature of systems

One fundamental weakness in current approaches to requirements definition is an inability to see clearly what the problem is, much less measure it, envision workable solutions, or apply any sort of assessment.

It is common practice to think of system architecture in terms of devices, languages, transmission links, and record formats. Overview charts of computer systems typically contain references to programs, files, terminals, and processors. At the appropriate time in system development, this is quite proper. But as an initial basis for system thinking, it is premature and it blocks from view precisely the key idea that is essential to successful requirements definition — the algorithmic nature of all systems. This important concept can best be envisioned by giving it a new name, the *functional architecture*, as distinct from the system architecture.

Systems consist of things that perform activities that interact with other things, each such interaction constituting a happening. A functional architecture is a rigorous layout of the activities performed by a system (temporarily disregarding who or what does them) and the things with which those activities interact. Given this, a design process will create a system architecture which implements, in good order, the functions of the functional architecture. Requirements definition is founded on showing what the functional architecture is (Fig. 3), also showing why it is what it is, and constraining how the system architecture is to realize it in more concrete form.

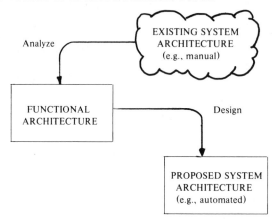

Figure 3. Functional architecture is extracted by analysis.

The concepts of functional architecture are universally applicable, to manual as well as automated systems, and are perfectly suited to the multiple needs of context analysis, functional specification, and design constraints found in requirements definition. Suppose, for example, that an operation, currently being performed manually is to be automated. The manual operation has a system architecture, composed of people, organizations, forms, procedures, and incentives, even though no computer is involved. It also has a functional architecture outlining the purposes for which the system exists. An automated system will implement the functional architecture with a different system architecture. In requirements definition, we must be able to extract the functional architecture (functional specification), and link it both to the boundary conditions for the manual operation (context analysis) and to the boundary conditions for the automated system (design constraints).

Functional architecture is founded on a generic universe of *things* and *happenings:*

objects	operations
data	activities
nouns	verbs
information	processing
substances	events
passive	active

Things and happenings are so intimately related that they can only exist together. A functional architecture always has a very strong structure making explicit these relationships. Functional architecture is, perhaps surprisingly, both abstract and precise.

Precision in functional architecture is best achieved by emphasizing only one primary structural relationship over and over — that of parts and wholes. Parts are related by interfaces to constitute wholes which, in turn, are parts of still larger wholes. It is always valid to express a functional architecture from the generic view that systems are made of components (parts and interfaces) and yet are themselves components.

So like all other architectures, the structure of functional architecture is both modular and hierarchic (even draftsmen and watchmakers use "top-down" methods). Like other architectures, it can be seen from different viewpoints (even the construction trades use distinct structural, electrical, heating, and plumbing blueprints). And like other architectures, it may not necessarily be charted as a physical system would be (even a circuit diagram does not show the actual layout of components, but every important electrical characteristic is represented).

This universal way to view any system is the key to successful requirements definition. From our experience, people do not tend to do this naturally, and not in an organized fashion. In fact, we find that the most basic problem in requirements definition is the fact that most people do not even realize that such universality exists! When it is explained, the usual reaction is, "that is just common sense." But, as has been remarked for ages, common sense is an uncommon commodity. The need is to structure such concepts within a discipline which can be learned.

The form of documentation

To adequately define requirements, one must certainly realize that functional architecture exists, can be measured, and can be evaluated. But to describe it, one needs a communication medium corresponding to the blueprints and specifications that allow manufacturing to function smoothly. In fact, the form of documentation is the key to achieving communication. "Form" includes paging, paragraphing, use of graphics, document organization, and so forth. Because the distinction between form and content is so poorly understood, many adequate system descriptions are unreadable, simply because they are so hard to follow. When Marshall McLuhan said, "The medium is the message," he was apparently ignored by most system analysts.

Analysis of functional architecture (and design of system architecture) cannot be expressed both concisely and unambiguously in natural language. But by imbedding natural language in a blueprint-like graphic framework, all necessary relationships can be shown compactly and rigorously. Well-chosen graphic components permit representation of all aspects of the architecture in an artificial language which is natural for the specific function of communicating that architecture.

The universal nature of systems being both wholes and parts can be expressed by a graphic structure which is both modular and hierarchic (Fig. 4). Because parts are constrained to be wholes, interfaces must be shown explicitly. Interface notation must allow one to distinguish input from output from control (the concept of "control" will not be defended here). Most important, the notation itself must distinguish the things with which activities interact from the things which perform the activities. And because the graphics are a framework for the descriptive abilities of natural language, one must be able to name everything.

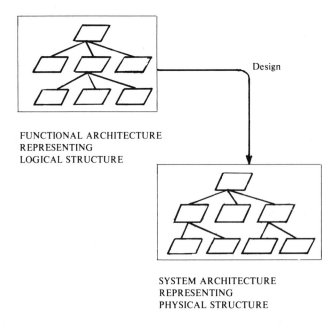

FUNCTIONAL ARCHITECTURE
REPRESENTING
LOGICAL STRUCTURE

SYSTEM ARCHITECTURE
REPRESENTING
PHYSICAL STRUCTURE

Figure 4. Physical structure is seldom identical to logical structure.

To achieve communication, the form of the diagram in which graphic symbols appear is also important. They must be bounded — to a single page or pair of facing pages — so that a reader can see at once everything which can be said about something. Each topic must be carefully delineated so a reader can grasp the whole message. A reader must be able to mentally walk through the architectural structure which is portrayed, just as blueprints enable a manufacturer to "see" the parts working together. And finally, everything must be indexed so that the whole set of diagrams will form a complete model of the architecture.

This appears to be a tall order, but when done elegantly, it yields documentation that is clear, complete, concise, consistent, and convincing. In addition, the hierarchic structure of the documentation can be exploited both to do and to manage the process of analysis. By reviewing the emergent documentation incrementally, for example, while requirements are being delineated, all interested parties can have a voice in directing the process. This is one of the features that results in the standardized, business-as-usual, "no surprises" approach found in manufacturing.

The analysis team

When thinking about why requirements are neither well-structured nor well-documented, one must not forget that any proposed methodology must be people-oriented. Technical matters matter very much, but it is the wishes, ideas, needs, concerns, and skills of people that determine the outcome. Technical aspects can only be addressed through the interaction of all people who have an interest in the system. One of the current difficulties in requirements definition, remember, is that system developers are often charged with documenting requirements. Their design background leads them (however well-intentioned they may be) to think of system architecture rather than functional architecture, and to define requirements in terms of solutions.

Consider a typical set of people who must actively participate in requirements definition. The *customer* is an organization with a need for a system. That customer authorizes a *commissioner* to acquire a system which will be operated by users. The commissioner, although perhaps technically oriented, probably knows less about system technology than the *developers* who will construct the system. These four parties may or may not be within one organization. For each administrative structure, there is a *management* group. Requirements definition must be understood by all these parties, answer the questions they have about the system, and serve as the basis for a development contract.

Each of these parties is a partisan whose conflicting, and often vague, desires must be amalgamated through requirements definition. There is a need at the center for trained, professional *analysts* who act as a catalyst to get the assorted information on paper and to structure from it adequate requirements documentation. The mental facility to comprehend abstraction, the ability to communicate it with personal tact, along with the ability to accept and deliver valid criticism, are all hallmarks of a professional analyst.

Analysts, many of whom may be only part-time, are not expected to supply expertise in all aspects of the problem area. As professionals, they are expected to seek out requirements from experts among the other parties concerned. To succeed, the task of analysis must be properly managed and coordinated, and the requirements definition effort must embody multiple viewpoints. These viewpoints may be overlapping and, occasionally, contradictory.

Managing the analysis

Because many interests are involved, requirements definition must serve multiple purposes. Each subject — context analysis, functional specification, and design constraints — must be examined from at least three points of view: technical, operational, and economic. Technical assessment or feasibility concerns the architecture of a system. Operational assessment concerns the performance of that system in a working environment. Economic feasibility concerns the costs and impacts of system implementation and use. The point is simply that a wide variety of topics must be considered in requirements definition (Fig. 5). Without a plan for assembling the pieces into coherent requirements, it is easy for the analysis team to lose their sense of direction and overstep their responsibility.

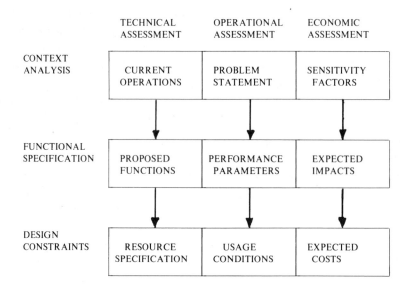

Figure 5. **Multiple viewpoints of requirements definition.**

Requirements definition, like all system development stages, should be an orderly progression. Each task is a logical successor to what has come before and is completed before proceeding to what comes after. Throughout, one must be able to answer the same three questions. 1) What are we doing? 2) Why are we doing it? 3) How do we proceed from here? Adequate management comes from asking these questions, iteratively, at every point in the development process. And if management is not to be a chameleon-like art, the same body of procedural knowledge should be applicable every time, although the subject at hand will differ.

It is precisely the lack of guidance about the process of analysis that makes requirements definition such a "hot item" today. People need to think about truly analyzing problems ("divide and conquer"), secure in the knowledge that postponed decisions will dovetail because the process they use enforces consistency. Analysis is an art of considering everything relevant at a given point, and nothing more. Adequate requirements will be complete, without over-specification, and will postpone certain decisions to later stages in the system development process without artifice. This is especially important in the development of those complex systems where requirements are imposed by higher level considerations (Fig. 6). Decisions must be *allocated* (i.e., postponed) because too many things interrelate in too many complicated ways for people to understand, all at once, what is and is not being said.

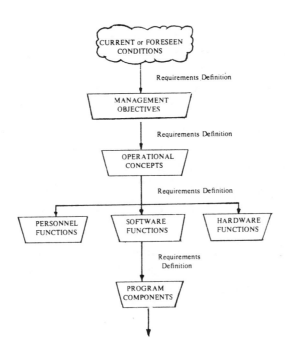

Figure 6. Analysis is repetitive in a complex environment.

Controlling a system development project is nearly impossible without reviews, walk-throughs, and configuration management. Such techniques become workable when the need for synthesis is recognized. Quite simply, system architectures and allocated requirements must be justifiable in light of previously stated requirements. One may choose, by plan or by default, not to enforce such traceability. However, validation and verification of subsequent project stages must not be precluded by ill-structured and unfathomable requirements.

Obviously, decisions on paper are the only ones that count. Knowing that an alternative was considered and rejected, and why, may often be as important as the final requirement. Full documentation becomes doubly necessary when the many parties involved are geographically separated and when staff turnover or expansion may occur before the project is completed.

The features just discussed at length — functional architecture, documentation, analysis teamwork, and the orderly process of analyzing and synthesizing multiple viewpoints — all must be integrated when prescribing a methodology for requirements definition.

III. Structured analysis

Outline of the approach

For several years, the senior author and his colleagues at SofTech have been developing, applying, and improving a general, but practical approach to handling complex system problems. The method is called Structured Analysis and Design Technique (SADT®) [3]. It has been used successfully on a wide range of problems by both SofTech and clients. This paper has presented some of the reasons why SADT works so well, when properly applied.

SADT evolved naturally from earlier work on the foundations of software engineering. It consists of both techniques for performing system analysis and design, and a process for applying these techniques in requirements definition and system development. Both features significantly increase the productivity and effectiveness of teams of people involved in a system project. Specifically, SADT provides methods for: 1) thinking in a structured way about large and complex problems; 2) working as a team with effective division and coordination of effort and roles; 3) communicating interview, analysis, and design results in clear, precise notation; 4) documenting current results and decisions in a way which provides a complete audit of history; 5) controlling accuracy, completeness and quality through frequent review and approval procedure; and 6) planning, managing, and assessing progress of the team effort. Two aspects of SADT deserve special mention: the graphic techniques and the definition of personnel roles.

Graphic techniques

The SADT graphic language provides a limited set of primitive constructs from which analysts and designers can compose orderly structures of any required size. The notation is quite simple — just boxes and arrows. *Boxes* represent parts of a whole in a precise manner. *Arrows* represent interfaces between parts. *Diagrams* represent wholes and are composed of boxes, arrows, natural language names, and certain other notations. The same graphics are applicable to both activities and data.

An SADT model is an organized sequence of diagrams, each with concise supporting text. A high-level overview diagram represents the whole subject. Each lower level diagram shows a limited amount of detail about a well-constrained topic. Further, each lower level diagram connects exactly into higher level portions of the model, thus preserving the logical relationship of each component to the total system (Fig. 7).

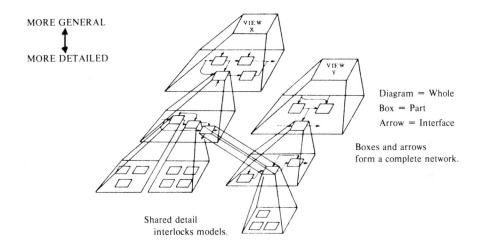

Figure 7. SADT provides practical, rigorous decomposition.

An SADT model is a graphic representation of the hierarchic structure of a system, decomposed with a firm purpose in mind. A model is structured so that it gradually exposes more and more detail. But its depth is bounded by the restriction of its vantage point and its content is bounded by its viewpoint. The priorities dictated by its purpose determine the layering of the top-down decomposition. Multiple models accommodate both multiple viewpoints and the various stages of system realization.

The arrow structure on an SADT diagram represents a constraint relationship among the boxes. It does not represent flow of control or sequence, as for example, on a flowchart for a computer program. Constraint arrows show necessary conditions imposed on a box.

Most arrows represent interfaces between boxes, whether in the same or different models. Some arrows represent noninterface interlocking between models. Together, these concepts achieve both overlapping of multiple viewpoints and the desirable attributes of good analysis and design projects (e.g., modularity, flexibility, and so forth [4]). The interface structure, particularly, passes through several levels of diagrams, creating a web that integrates all parts of the decomposition and shows the whole system's environmental interfaces with the topmost box.

Process overview

Clearly, requirements definition requires cooperative teamwork from many people. This in turn demands a clear definition of the kinds of interactions which should occur between the personnel involved. SADT anticipates this need by establishing titles and functions of appropriate roles (Fig. 8). In a requirements definition effort, for example, the "authors" would be analysts, trained and experienced in SADT.

Name	Function
Authors	Personnel who study requirements and constraints, analyze system functions and represent them by models based on SADT diagrams.
Commenters	Usually authors, who must review and comment in writing on the work of other authors.
Readers	Personnel who read SADT diagrams for information but are not expected to make written comments.
Experts	Persons from whom authors obtain specialized information about requirements and constraints by means of interviews.
Technical Committee	A group of senior technical personnel assigned to review the analysis at every major level of decomposition. They either resolve technical issues or recommend a decision to the project management.
Project Librarian	A person assigned the responsibility of maintaining a centralized file of all project documents, making copies, distributing reader kits, keeping records, etc.
Project Manager	The member of the project who has the final technical responsibility for carrying out the system analysis and design.
Monitor (or Chief Analyst)	A person fluent in SADT who assists and advises project personnel in the use and application of SADT.
Instructor	A person fluent in SADT, who trains Authors and Commenters using SADT for the first time.

Figure 8. Personnel roles for SADT.

The SADT process, in which these roles interact, meets the needs of requirements definition for continuous and effective communication, for understandable and current documentation, and for regular and critical review. The process exploits the structure of an SADT model so that decisions can be seen in context and can be challenged while alternatives are still viable.

Throughout a project, draft versions of diagrams in evolving models are distributed to project members for review. Commenters make their suggestions in writing directly on copies of the diagrams. Written records of decisions and alternatives are retained as they unfold. As changes and corrections are made, all versions are entered in the project files. A project librarian provides filing, distribution, and record-keeping support, and, not so incidentally, also ensures configuration control.

This process documents all decisions and the reasons why decisions were made. When commenters and authors reach an understanding, the work is reviewed by a committee of senior technical and management personnel. During the process, incorrect or unacceptable results are usually spotted early, and oversights or errors are detected before they can cause major disruptions. Since everything is on record, future enhancement and system maintenance can reference previous analysis and design decisions.

When documentation is produced as the model evolves, the status of the project becomes highly visible. Management can study the requirements (or the design) in a "top-down" manner, beginning with an overview and continuing to any relevant level of detail. Although presentations to upper management usually follow standard summary and walk-through methods, even senior executives sometimes become direct readers, for the blueprint language of SADT is easily learned.

Implementing the approach

How the ideas discussed in this paper are employed will vary according to organization needs and the kinds of systems under consideration. The methodology which has been described is not just a theory, however, and has been applied to a wide range of complex problems from real-time communications to process control to commercial EDP to organization planning. It is, in fact, a total systems methodology, and not merely a software technique. ITT Europe, for example, has used SADT since early 1974 for analysis and design of both hardware/software systems (telephonic and telegraphic switches) and nonsoftware people-oriented problems (project management and customer engineering). Other users exhibit similar diversity, from manufacturing (AFCAM [5]) to military training (TRAIDEX [6]). Users report that it is a communications vehicle which focuses attention on well-defined topics, that it increases management control through visibility and standardization, that it creates a systematic work breakdown structure for project teams, and that it minimizes errors through disciplined flexibility.

There is no set pattern among different organizations for the contents of requirements documentation. In each case, the needs of the users, the commissioner, and the development organization must be accommodated. Government agencies tend to have fixed standards, while other organizations encourage flexibility. In a numerical control application, almost 40 models were generated in requirements definition (SINTEF, University of Trondheim, Norway). At least one supplier of large-scale computer-based systems mandates consideration of system, hardware, software, commercial, and administrative constraints. Among all distinct viewpoints, the only common ground lies in the vantage points of context analysis, functional specification, and design constraints. Experience has shown that use of well-structured models together with a well-defined process of analysis, when properly carried out, does provide a strong foundation for actual system design [7].

Because local needs are diverse, implementation of the approach discussed in this paper cannot be accomplished solely by the publication of policy or standards. It is very much a "learn by doing" experience in which project personnel acquire ways of understanding the generic nature of systems. One must recognize that a common sense approach to system manufacturing is not now widely appreciated. A change in the ways that people think about systems and about the systems work that they themselves perform cannot be taught or disseminated in a short period of time.

Further developments

In manufacturing enterprises, blueprinting and specification methods evolved long before design support tools. In contrast to that analogy, a number of current efforts have produced systems for automating requirements information, independent of the definition and verification methodology provided by SADT. To date, SADT applications have been successfully carried out manually, but in large projects, where many analysts are involved and frequent changes do occur, the question is not whether or how to automate but simply what to automate.

Existing computer tools which wholly or partly apply to requirements [8] are characterized by a specification (or a design) database which, once input, may be manipulated. All such attempts, however, begin with user requirements recorded in a machine-readable form. Two impediments immediately become evident. The first is that requirements stated in prose texts cannot be translated in a straightforward manner to interface with an automated problem language. The second is that no computer tool will ever perform the process of requirements definition. Defining and verifying requirements is a task done by users and analysts [9].

Given the right kind of information, however, computer tools can provide capabilities to insure consistency, traceability, and allocation of requirements. A good example of this match to SADT is PSL/PSA, a system resulting from several years' effort in the ISDOS Project at the University of Michigan [10, 11]. The PSL database can represent almost every relationship which appears on SADT diagrams, and the input process from diagrams to database can be done by a project librarian. Not only does SADT enhance human communication (between user and analyst and between analyst and designer), but the diagrams become machine-readable in a very straightforward manner.

The PSA data analyzer and report generator is useful for summarizing database contents and can provide a means of controlling revisions. If the database has been derived by SADT, enhancements to existing PSA capabilities are possible to further exploit the structure of SADT models. For example, SADT diagrams are not flow diagrams, but the interface constraints are directed. These precedence relations, systematically pursued in SADT to specify quantities (volumes and rates) and sequences, permit any desired degree of simulation of a model (whether performed mentally or otherwise).

Computer aids are created as support tools. SADT provides a total context, within which certain automated procedures can play a complementary role. The result will be a complete, systematized approach which both suits the needs of the people involved and enables automation to be used in and extended beyond requirements definition. Such comprehensive methods will enable arbitrary systems work to attain the fulfillment that blueprint techniques deliver in traditional manufacturing.

IV. Conclusion

Requirements definition is an important source of costly oversights in present-day system innovation, but something can be done about it. None of the thoughts presented here are mere speculation. All have produced real achievements. The methods described have been successfully applied to a wide range of planning, analysis and design problems involving men, machines, software, hardware, databases, communications, procedures, and finances. The significance of the methods seems to be that a well-structured approach to documenting what someone thinks about a problem or a system can materially aid both that person's thinking and his ability to convey his understanding to others. Properly channeled, the mind of man is indeed formidable. But only by considering all aspects of the task ahead can teamwork be more productive and management be more effective. Communication with nontechnical readers, an understanding of the nature and structure of systems [12], and indeed a thorough knowledge of the process of analysis itself are the essential ingredients of successful requirements definition.

Appendix

Asking the right questions

The basic difficulty in requirements definition is not one of seeing the woods instead of the trees. The real need is for a methodology which, in any given circumstance, will enable an analyst to distinguish one from the other. It is always more important to ask the right questions than it is to assert possibly wrong answers. It is said that when a famous rabbi was asked, "Rabbi, why does a rabbi always answer a question with a question?" he replied, "Is there a better way?" This is the famous dialectic method used by Socrates to lead his students to understanding. Answering questions with questions leaves options open, and has the nature of breaking big questions into a top-down structure of smaller questions, easier and easier to address. The answers, when they are ultimately supplied, are each less critical and more tractable, and their relations with other small answers are well-structured.

This is the focus of requirement definition. The appropriate questions — *why, what, how* — applied systematically, will distinguish that which must be considered from that which must be postponed. A sequence of such questions, on a global, system-wide scale, will break the complexity of various aspects of the system into simpler, related questions which can be analyzed, developed, and documented. The context analysis, functional specification, and design constraints — subjects which are part of requirements definition — are merely parts of an overlapping chain of responses to the appropriate why, what, how questions (Fig. 9). In different circumstances, the subjects may differ, but the chaining of questions will remain the same. *Why* some feature is needed molds *what* it has to be, which in turn molds *how* it is to be achieved.

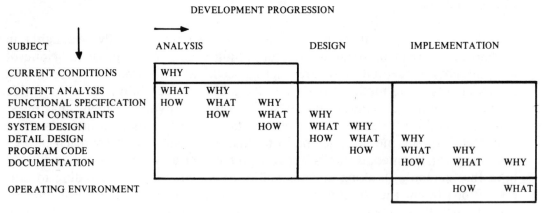

Figure 9. **System development is a chain of overlapping questions, documented at each step.**

These questions form an overlapping repetition of a common pattern. Each time, the various aspects of the system are partitioned, and the understanding which is developed must be documented in a form consistent with the pattern. It is not sufficient merely to break big problems into little problems by shattering them. "Decompose" is the inverse of "compose"; at every step, the parts being considered must reassemble to make the whole context within which one is working.

The English word "cleave" captures the concept exactly. It is one of those rare words that has antithetical meanings. It means both to separate and to cling to! Thus, in the orderly process of top-down decomposition which describes the desired system, multiple views must intersect in order to supply the whole context for the next stage of system development (Fig. 10).

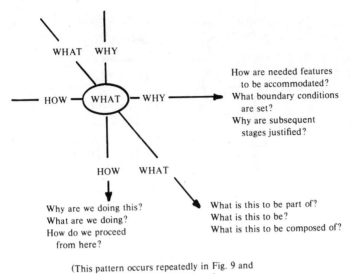

(This pattern occurs repeatedly in Fig. 9 and
constitutes its primary structure.)

Figure 10. Right questions occur within a context and form a context as well.

And finding the right answers

Probably the most important aspect of this paper is its emphasis on a common approach to all phases of system development, starting with requirements definition. Knowing how postponed decisions will be handled in later phases (by the same methods) allows their essence to be established by boundary conditions, while details are left open (Fig. 11). The knowledge that all requirements must ultimately be implemented somehow (again by the same methods) allows their completeness and consistency to be verified. Finally, an orderly sequence of questions enforces gradual exposition of detail. All information is presented in well-structured documentation which allows first-hand participation by users and commissioners in requirements definition.

The way to achieve such coherence is to seek the right kind of answers to every set of why, what, how questions. By this is meant to establish the viewpoint, vantage point, and purpose of the immediate task before writing any document or conducting any analysis.

The initial *purpose* of the system development effort is established by context analysis. Proper cleaving of subjects and descriptions then takes two different forms, the exact natures of which are governed by the overall project purpose. One cleaving creates partial but overlapping delineations according to *viewpoint* — viewpoint makes clear what aspects are considered relevant to achieving some component of the overall purpose. The other cleaving creates rigorous functional architectures according to *vantage point* — vantage point is a level of abstraction that relates the viewpoints and component purposes which together describe a given whole subject (Fig. 12).

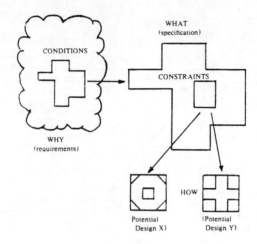

Figure 11. Postponed decisions occur within a prior framework.

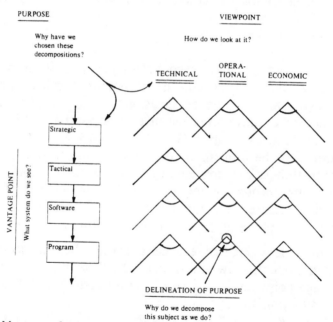

Figure 12. Subjects are decomposed according to viewpoint, vantage point, and purpose.

Depending on the system, any number of viewpoints may be important in requirements definition and may continue to be relevant as the vantage point shifts to designing, building, and finally using the system. Any single viewpoint always highlights some aspects of a subject, while other aspects will be lost from view. For example, the same system may be considered from separate viewpoints which emphasize physical characteristics, functional characteristics, operation, management, performance, maintenance, construction cost, and so forth.

Picking a vantage point always abstracts a functional architecture, while muting implementation-defined aspects of the system architecture. The placement of a vantage point within a viewpoint establishes an all-important *bounded context* — a subset of purpose which then governs the decomposition and exposition of a particular subject regarding the system.

Can give the right results

Requirements definition, beginning with context analysis, can occur whenever there is a need to define, redefine, or further delineate purpose. Context analysis treats the most important, highest level questions first, setting the conditions for further questioning each part in turn. Each subsequent question is asked within the bounded context of a prior response. Strict discipline ensures that each aspect of any question is covered by exactly one further question. Getting started is difficult, but having done so successfully, one is introduced to a "top-down" hierarchy of leading questions, properly sequenced, completely decomposed, and successively answered.

Whether explicitly stated or not, vantage points, viewpoints, and purposes guide the activities of *any* analysis team which approaches a requirements definition task. With the global understanding offered by the above discussion, analysts should realize that a place can be found for every item of information gathered. Structuring this mass of information still must be done, on paper, in a way that ensures completeness and correctness, without overspecification and confusion. That is the role of SADT.

Acknowledgment

The authors would like to thank J.W. Brackett and J.B. Goodenough of SofTech, Inc., Waltham, MA, who made several helpful suggestions incorporated into the presentation of these ideas. Many people at SofTech have, of course, contributed to the development and use of SADT.

References

1. B.W. Boehm, "Software and Its Impact: A Quantitative Assessment," *Datamation,* Vol. 19, No. 5 (May 1973), pp. 48-59.

2. P. Hirsch, "GAO Hits Wimmix Hard: FY'72 Funding Prospects Fading Fast," *Datamation,* Vol. 17, No. 7 (March 1, 1971), p. 41.

3. *An Introduction to SADT^{TM},* SofTech, Inc., Report No. 9022-78 (Waltham, Mass.: February 1976).

4. D.T. Ross, J.B. Goodenough, and C.A. Irvine, "Software Engineering: Process, Principles, and Goals," *Computer,* Vol. 8, No. 5 (May 1975), pp. 17-27.

5. Air Force Materials Laboratory, *Air Force Computer-Aided Manufacturing (AFCAM) Master Plan,* Vol. II, App. A, and Vol. III, AFSC, Wright Patterson Air Force Base, Report No. AFML-TR-74-104 (Ohio: July 1974). Available from DDC as AD 922-041L and 922-171L.

6. *TRAIDEX Needs and Implementation Study,* SofTech, Inc., Final Report (Waltham, Mass.: May 1976). Available as No. ED-129244 from ERIC Printing House on Information Resources (Stanford, Calif.).

7. B.W. Boehm, "Software Design and Structure," *Practical Strategies for Developing Large Software Systems,* ed. E. Horowitz (Reading, Mass.: Addison-Wesley, 1975), pp. 115-22.

8. R.V. Head, "Automated System Analysis," *Datamation,* Vol. 17, No. 16 (Aug. 15, 1971), pp. 22-24.

9. J.T. Rigo, "How to Prepare Functional Specifications," *Datamation,* Vol. 20, No. 5 (May 1974), pp. 78-80.

10. D. Teichroew and H. Sayani, "Automation of System Building," *Datamation,* Vol. 17, No. 16 (Aug. 15, 1971), pp. 25-30.

11. D. Teichroew and E.A. Hershey, "PSL/PSA: A Computer-Aided Technique for Structured Documentation and Analysis of Information Processing Systems," *IEEE Transactions on Software Engineering,* Vol. SE-3, No. 1 (January 1977), pp. 41-48.

12. F.M. Haney, "What It Takes to Make MAC, MIS, and ABM Fly," *Datamation,* Vol. 20, No. 6 (June 1974), pp. 168-69.

INTRODUCTION

I vividly remember a *Datamation* article, written by Daniel Teichroew in 1967, predicting that within ten years programmers would be obsolete. All we had to do, he said, was make it possible for users to state *precisely* what they wanted a computer system to do for them; at that point, it should be possible to mechanically generate the code. Having been in the computer field for only a few years, I was profoundly worried. Maybe it was time to abandon data processing and become a farmer?

Those early ideas of Professor Teichroew perhaps were ahead of their time — after all, there still were a sizable number of programmers in existence in 1977! — but some of his predictions are beginning to take concrete form today. The following paper, written by Teichroew and Hershey and originally published in the January 1977 *IEEE Transactions on Software Engineering,* is the best single source of information on a system for automated analysis, known as "ISDOS" or "PSL/PSA."

The Teichroew/Hershey paper deals specifically with structured analysis, and, as such, is radically different from the earlier papers on programming and design. Throughout the 1960s, it was fashionable to blame all of our EDP problems on *programming;* structured programming and the related disciplines were deemed the ideal solution. Then, by the mid-1970s, emphasis shifted toward *design,* as people began to realize that brilliant code would not save a mediocre design. But now our emphasis has shifted even further: Without an adequate statement of the user's requirements, the best design and the best code in the world won't do the job. Indeed, without benefit of proper requirements definition, structured design and structured programming may simply help us arrive at a systems disaster faster.

So, what can be done to improve the requirements definition process? There are, of course, the methods proposed by Ross and Schoman in the previous paper, as well as those set forth by DeMarco in the paper that appears after this one. In this paper, Teichroew and Hershey concentrate on the *documentation* associated with requirements definition, and on the difficulty of producing and managing manually generated documentation.

The problems that Teichroew and Hershey address certainly are familiar ones, although many systems analysts probably have come to the sad conclusion that things always were meant to be like this. They observe, for example, that much of the documentation associated with an EDP system is not formally recorded until the *end* of the project, by which time, as DeMarco points out, the final document is "of historical significance only" [Paper 24]. The documentation generated is notoriously ambiguous, verbose, and redundant, and, worst of all, it is *manually* produced, *manually* examined for possible errors and inconsistencies, and *manually* updated and revised as user requirements change.

So, the answer to all of this, in Teichroew and Hershey's opinion, is a computer program that allows the systems analyst to input the user requirements in a language that can be regarded as a subset of English; those requirements then can be changed, using facilities similar to those on any modern text-editing system, throughout the analysis phase of the project — *and throughout the entire system life cycle!* Perhaps most important, the requirements definition can be subjected to automated analysis to determine such things as contradictory definitions of data elements, missing definitions, and data elements that are generated but never used.

The concept for PSL was documented by Teichroew more than ten years ago, but it is in this 1977 paper that we begin to get some idea of the impact on the real world. Automated analysis slowly is becoming an option, with a number of large, prestigious organizations using PSL/PSA.

One would expect continued growth; ironically, though, a reported problem is *machine inefficiency!* PSL/PSA apparently consumes significant amounts of CPU time and other computer resources, although Teichroew and Hershey maintain that such tangible, visible costs probably are smaller than the intangible, hidden costs of time wasted during "manual" analysis. It appears that PSL/PSA is most successfully used in organizations that already have vast computer installations and several hundred (or thousand) EDP people. A significant drawback to widespread adoption of PSL/PSA is the fact that it is written in FORTRAN! Admittedly this has helped make it portable — but FORTRAN?

PSL/PSA: A Computer-Aided Technique
for Structured Documentation and Analysis
of Information Processing Systems

I. Introduction

Organizations now depend on computer-based information processing systems for many of the tasks involving data (recording, storing, retrieving, processing, etc.). Such systems are man-made, the process consists of a number of activities: perceiving a need for a system, determining what it should do for the organization, designing it, constructing and assembling the components, and finally testing the system prior to installing it. The process requires a great deal of effort, usually over a considerable period of time.

Throughout the life of a system it exists in several different "forms." Initially, the system exists as a concept or a proposal at a very high level of abstraction. At the point where it becomes operational it exists as a collection of rules and executable object programs in a particular computing environment. This environment consists of hardware and hard software such as the operating system, plus other components such as procedures which are carried out manually. In between the system exists in various intermediary forms.

The process by which the initial concept evolves into an operational system consists of a number of activities each of which makes the concept more concrete. Each activity takes the results of some of the previous activities and produces new results so that the progression eventually results in an operational system. Most of the activities are data processing activities, in that they use data and information to produce other data and information. Each activity can be regarded as receiving specifications or requirements from preceding activities and producing data which are regarded as specifications or requirements by one or more succeeding activities.

Since many individuals may be involved in the system development process over considerable periods of time and these or other individuals have to maintain the system once it is operating, it is necessary to record descriptions of the system as it evolves. This is usually referred to as "documentation."

In practice, the emphasis in documentation is on describing the system in the final form so that it can be maintained. Ideally, however, each activity should be documented so that the results it produces become the specification for succeeding activities. This does not happen in practice because the communications from one activity to succeeding activities is accomplished either by having the same person carrying out the activities, by oral communication among individuals in a project, or by notes which are discarded after their initial use.

This results in projects which proceed without any real possibility for management review and control. The systems are not ready when promised, do not perform the function the users expected, and cost more than budgeted.

Most organizations, therefore, mandate that the system development process be divided into phases and that certain documentation be produced by the end of each phase so that progress can be monitored and corrections made when necessary. These attempts, however, leave much to be desired and most organizations are attempting to improve the methods by which they manage their system development [20, 6].

This paper is concerned with one approach to improving systems development. The approach is based on three premises. The first is that more effort and attention should be devoted to the front end of the process where a proposed system is being described from the user's point of view [2, 14, 3]. The second premise is that the computer should be used in the development process since systems development involves large amounts of information processing. The third premise is that a computer-aided approach to systems development must start with "documentation."

This paper describes a computer-aided technique for documentation which consists of the following:

1)   The results of each of the activities in the system development process are recorded in computer processible form as they are produced.

2) A computerized data base is used to maintain all the basic data about the system.

3) The computer is used to produce hard copy documentation when required.

The part of the technique which is now operational is known as PSL/PSA. Section II is devoted to a brief description of system development as a framework in which to compare manual and computer-aided documentation methods. The Problem Statement Language (PSL) is described in Section III. The reports which can be produced by the Problem Statement Analyzer (PSA) are described in Section IV. The status of the system, results of experience to date, and planned developments are outlined in Section V.

II. Logical systems design

The computer-aided documentation system described in Sections III and IV of this paper is designed to play an integral role during the initial stages in the system development process. A generalized model of the whole system development process is given in Section II-A. The final result of the initial stage is a document which here will be called the System Definition Report. The desired contents of this document are discussed in Section II-B. The activities required to produce this document manually are described in Section II-C and the changes possible through the use of computer-aided methods are outlined in Section II-D.

A. A model of the system development process

The basic steps in the life cycle of information systems (initiation, analysis, design, construction, test, installation, operation, and termination) appeared in the earliest applications of computers to organizational problems (see for example, [17, 1, 4, 7]). The need for more formal and comprehensive procedures for carrying out the life cycle was recognized; early examples are the IBM SOP publications [5], the Philips ARDI method [8], and the SDC method [23]. In the last few years, a large number of books and papers on this subject have been published [11, 19].

Examination of these and many other publications indicate that there is no general agreement on what phases the development process should be divided into, what documentation should be produced at each phase, what it should contain, or what form it should be presented in. Each organization develops its own methods and standards.

In this section a generalized system development process will be described as it might be conducted in an organization which has a Systems Department responsible for developing, operating, and maintaining computer based information processing systems. The System Department belongs to some higher unit in the organization and itself has some subunits, each with certain functions (see for example, [24]). The System Department has a system development standard procedure which includes a project management system and documentation standards.

A request for a new system is initiated by some unit in the organization or the system may be proposed by the System Department. An initial document is prepared which contains information about why a new system is needed and outlines its major functions. This document is reviewed and, if approved, a senior analyst is assigned to prepare a more detailed document. The analyst collects data by interviewing users and studying the present system. He then produces a report describing his proposed system and showing how it will satisfy the requirements. The report will also contain the implementation plan, benefit/cost analysis, and his recommendations. The report is reviewed by the various organizational units involved. If it passes this review it is then included with other requests for the resources of the System Department and given a priority. Up to this point the investment in the proposed system is relatively small.

At some point a project team is formed, a project leader and team members are assigned, and given authority to proceed with the development of the system. A steering group may also be formed. The project is assigned a schedule in accordance with the project management system and given a budget. The schedule will include one or more target dates. The final target date will be the date the system (or its first part if it is being done in parts) is to be operational. There may also be additional target dates such as beginning of system test, beginning of programming, etc.

B. *Logical system design documentation*

In this paper, it is assumed that the system development procedure requires that the proposed system be reviewed before a major investment is made in system construction. There will therefore be another target date at which the "logical" design of the proposed system is reviewed. On the basis of this review the decision may be to proceed with the physical design and construction, to revise the proposed system, or to terminate the project.

The review is usually based on a document prepared by the project team. Sometimes it may consist of more than one separate document; for example, in the systems development methodology used by the U.S. Department of Defense [21] for non-weapons systems, development of the life cycle is divided into phases. Two documents are produced at the end of the Definition subphase of the Development phase: a Functional Description, and a Data Requirements Document.

Examination of these and many documentation requirements show that a Systems Definition Report contains five major types of information:

1) a description of the organization and where the proposed system will fit; showing how the proposed system will improve the functioning of the organization or otherwise meet the needs which lead to the project;

2) a description of the operation of the proposed system in sufficient detail to allow the users to verify that it will in fact accomplish its objectives, and to serve as the specification for the design and construction of the proposed system if the project continuation is authorized;

3) a description of its proposed system implementation in sufficient detail to estimate the time and cost required;

4) the implementation plan in sufficient detail to estimate the cost of the proposed system and the time it will be available;

5) a benefit/cost analysis and recommendations.

In addition, the report usually also contains other miscellaneous information such as glossaries, etc.

C. Current logical system design process

During the initial stages of the project the efforts of the team are directed towards producing the Systems Definition Report. Since the major item this report contains is the description of the proposed system from the user or logical point of view, the activities required to produce the report are called the logical system design process. The project team will start with the information already available and then perform a set of activities. These may be grouped into five major categories.

1) *Data collection.* Information about the information flow in the present system, user desires for new information, potential new system organization, etc., is collected and recorded.

2) *Analysis.* The data that have been collected are summarized and analyzed. Errors, omissions, and ambiguities are identified and corrected. Redundancies are identified. The results are prepared for review by appropriate groups.

3) *Logical design.* Functions to be performed by the system are selected. Alternatives for a new system or modification of the present system are developed and examined. The "new" system is described.

4) *Evaluation.* The benefits and costs of the proposed system are determined to a suitable level of accuracy. The operational and functional feasibility of the system are examined and evaluated.

5) *Improvements.* Usually as a result of the evaluation a number of deficiencies in the proposed system will be discovered. Alternatives for improvement are identified and evaluated until further possible improvements are not judged to be worth additional effort. If major changes are made, the evaluation step may be repeated; further data collection and analysis may also be necessary.

In practice the type of activities outlined above may not be clearly distinguished and may be carried out in parallel or iteratively with increasing level of detail. Throughout the process, however it is carried out, results are recorded and documented.

It is widely accepted that documentation is a weak link in system development in general and in logical system design in particular. The representation in the documentation that is produced with present manual methods is limited to:

1) text in a natural language;

2) lists, tables, arrays, cross references;

3) graphical representation, figures, flowcharts.

Analysis of two reports showed the following number of pages for each type of information.

Form	Report A	Report B
text	90	117
lists and tables	207	165
charts and figures	28	54
total	335	336

The systems being documented are very complex and these methods of representation are not capable of adequately describing all the necessary aspects of a system for all those who must, or should, use the documentation. Consequently, documentation is

1) ambiguous: natural languages are not precise enough to describe systems and different readers may interpret a sentence in different ways;

2) inconsistent: since systems are large the documentation is large and it is very difficult to ensure that the documentation is consistent;

3)   incomplete: there is usually not a sufficient amount of time to devote to documentation and with a large complex system it is difficult to determine what information is missing.

The deficiencies of manual documentation are compounded by the fact that systems are continually changing and it is very difficult to keep the documentation up-to-date.

Recently there have been attempts to improve manual documentation by developing more formal methodologies [16, 12, 13, 22, 15, 25]. These methods, even though they are designed to be used manually, have a formal language or representation scheme that is designed to alleviate the difficulties listed above. To make the documentation more useful for human beings, many of these methods use a graphical language.

D. Computer-aided logical system design process

In computer-aided logical system design the objective, as in the manual process, is to produce the System Definition Report and the process followed is essentially similar to that described above. The computer-aided design system has the following capabilities:

1)   capability to describe information systems, whether manual or computerized, whether existing or proposed, regardless of application area;

2)   ability to record such description in a computerized data base;

3)   ability to incrementally add to, modify, or delete from the description in the data base;

4)   ability to produce "hard copy" documentation for use by the analyst or the other users.

The capability to describe systems in computer processable form results from the use of the system description language called PSL. The ability to record such description in a data base, incrementally modify it, and on demand perform analysis and produce reports comes from the software package called the Problem Statement Analyzer (PSA). The Analyzer is controlled by a Command Language which is described in detail in [9] (Fig. 1).

The Problem Statement Language is outlined in Section III and described in detail in [10]. The use of PSL/PSA in computer-aided logical system design is described in detail in [18].

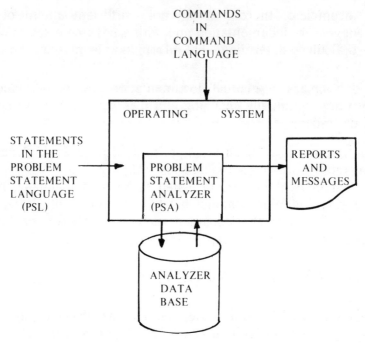

Figure 1. The problem statement analyzer.

The use of PSL/PSA does not depend on any particular structure of the system development process or any standards on the format and content of hard copy documentation. It is therefore fully compatible with current procedures in most organizations that are developing and maintaining systems. Using this system, the data collected or developed during all five of the activities are recorded in machine-readable form and entered into the computer as it is collected. A data base is built during the process. These data can be analyzed by computer programs and intermediate documentation prepared on request. The Systems Definition Report then includes a large amount of material produced automatically from the data base.

The activities in logical system design are modified when PSL/PSA is used as follows:

1) Data collection: since most of the data must be obtained through personal contact, interviews will still be required. The data collected are recorded in machine-readable form. The intermediate outputs of PSA also provide convenient checklists for deciding what additional information is needed and for recording it for input.

2) Analysis: a number of different kinds of analysis can be performed on demand by PSA, and therefore need no longer be done manually.

3) Design: design is essentially a creative process and cannot be automated. However, PSA can make more data available to the designer and allow him to manipulate it more extensively. The results of his decisions are also entered into the data base.

4) Evaluation: PSA provides some rudimentary facilities for computing volume or work measures from the data in the problem statement.

5) Improvements: identification of areas for possible improvements is also a creative task; however, PSA output, particularly from the evaluation phase, may be useful to the analyst.

The System Definition Report will contain the same material as that described since the documentation must serve the same purpose. Furthermore, the same general format and representation is desirable.

1) Narrative information is necessary for human readability. This is stored as part of the data but is not analyzed by the computer program. However, the fact that it is displayed next to, or in conjunction with, the final description improves the ability of the analyst to detect discrepancies and inconsistencies.

2) Lists, tables, arrays, matrices. These representations are prepared from the data base. They are up-to-date and can be more easily rearranged in any desired order.

3) Diagrams and charts. The information from the data base can be represented in various graphical forms to display the relationships between objects.

III. PSL, a problem statement language

PSL is a language for describing systems. Since it is intended to be used to describe "proposed" systems it was called a Problem Statement Language because the description of a proposed system can be considered a "problem" to be solved by the system designers and implementors.

PSL is intended to be used in situations in which analysts now describe systems. The descriptions of systems produced using PSL are used for the same purpose as that produced manually. PSL may be used both in batch and interactive environments, and therefore only "basic" information about the system need to be stated in PSL. All "derived" information can be produced in hard copy form as required.

The model on which PSL is based is described in Section III-A. A general description of the system and semantics of PSL is then given in Section III-B to illustrate the broad scope of system aspects that can be described using PSL. The detailed syntax of PSL in given in [10].

A. Model of information systems

The Problem Statement Language is based first on a model of a general system, and secondly on the specialization of the model to a particular class of systems, namely information systems.

The model of a general system is relatively simple. It merely states that a system consists of things which are called OBJECTS. These objects may have PROPERTIES and each of these PROPERTIES may have PROPERTY VALUES. The objects may be connected or interrelated in various ways. These connections are called RELATIONSHIPS.

The general model is specialized for an information system by allowing the use of only a limited number of predefined objects, properties, and relationships.

B. An overview of the problem statement language syntax and semantics

The objective of PSL is to be able to express in syntactically analyzable form as much of the information which commonly appears in System Definition Reports as possible.

System Descriptions may be divided into eight major aspects:

1) System Input/Output Flow,
2) System Structure,
3) Data Structure,
4) Data Derivation,
5) System Size and Volume,
6) System Dynamics,
7) System Properties,
8) Project Management.

PSL contains a number of types of objects and relationships which permit these different aspects to be described.

The *System Input/Output Flow* aspect of the system deals with the interaction between the target system and its environment.

System Structure is concerned with the hierarchies among objects in a system. Structures may also be introduced to facilitate a particular design approach such as "top down." All information may initially be grouped together and called by one name at the highest level, and then successively subdivided. System structures can represent high-level hierarchies which may not actually exist in the system, as well as those that do.

The *Data Structure* aspect of system description includes all the relationships which exist among data used and/or manipulated by the system as seen by the "users" of the system.

The *Data Derivation* aspect of the system description specifies which data objects are involved in particular PROCESSES in the system. It is concerned with what information is used, updated, and/or derived, how this is done, and by which processes.

Data Derivation relationships are internal in the system, while System Input/Output Flow relationships describe the system boundaries. As with other PSL facilities System Input/Output Flow need not be used. A system can be considered as having no boundary.

The *System Size and Volume* aspect is concerned with the size of the system and those factors which influence the volume of processing which will be required.

The *System Dynamics* aspect of system description presents the manner in which the target system "behaves" over time.

All objects (of a particular type) used to describe the target system have characteristics which distinguish them from other objects of the same type. Therefore, the PROPERTIES of particular objects in the system must be described. The PROPERTIES themselves are objects and given unique names.

The *Project Management* aspect requires that, in addition to the description of the target system being designed, documentation of the project designing (or documenting) the target system be given. This involves identification of people involved and their responsibilities, schedules, etc.

IV. Reports

As information about a particular system is obtained, it is expressed in PSL and entered into a data base using the Problem Statement Analyzer. At any time standard outputs or reports may be produced on request. The various reports can be classified on the basis of the purposes which they serve.

1) *Data Base Modification Reports:* These constitute a record of changes that have been made, together with diagnostics and warnings. They constitute a record of changes for error correction and recovery.

2) *Reference Reports:* These present the information in the data base in various formats. For example, the Name List Report presents all the objects in the data base with their type and date of last change. The Formatted Problem Statement Report shows all properties and relationships for a particular object

(Fig. 2). The Dictionary Report gives only data dictionary type
information.

```
Parameters:  DB=-EXBDB  NAME=hourly-employee-processing  NOINDEX  NOPUNCHED-NAMES  PRINT  EMPTY
    NOPUNCH  SMARG=5  NMARG=20  AMARG=10  BMARG=25  RNMARG=70  CMARG=1  HMARG=60  NODESIGNATE
    SEVERAL-PER-LINE  DEFINE  COMMENT  NONEW-PAGE  NONEW-LINE  NOALL-STATEMENTS
    COMPLEMENTARY-STATEMENTS  LINE-NUMBERS  PRINTEOF  DLC-COMMENT

 1 PROCESS                                                hourly-employee-processing;
 2    /*    DATE OF LAST CHANGE - JUN 26, 1976, 13:56:44 */
 3    DESCRIPTION;
 4          this process performs those actions needed to interpret
 5          time cards to produce a pay statement for each hourly
 6          employee.;
 7    KEYWORDS:      independent;
 8    ATTRIBUTES ARE:
 9          complexity-level
10               high;
11    GENERATES:     pay-statement, error-listing,
12                   hourly-employee-report;
13    RECEIVES:      time-card;
14    SUBPARTS ARE:  hourly-paycheck-validation, hourly-emp-update,
15                   h-report-entry-generation,
16                   hourly-paycheck-production;
17    PART OF:       payroll-processing;
18    DERIVES:       pay-statement
19      USING:       time-card, hourly-employee-record;
20    DERIVES:       hourly-employee-report
21      USING:       time-card, hourly-employee-record;
22    DERIVES:       error-listing
23      USING:       time-card, hourly-employee-record;
24    PROCEDURE;
25          1. compute gross pay from time card data.
26          2. compute tax from gross pay.
27          3. subtract tax from gross pay to obtain net pay.
28          4. update hourly employee record accordingly.
29          5. update department record accordingly.
30          6. generate paycheck.
31          note: if status code specifies that the employee did not work
32             this week, no processing will be done for this employee.;
33    HAPPENS:
34          number-of-payments TIMES-PER pay-period;
35    TRIGGERED BY:  hourly-emp-processing-event;
36    TERMINATION-CAUSES:
37                   new-employee-processing-event;
38    SECURITY IS:   company-only;
39
40 EOF EOF EOF EOF EOF
```

Figure 2. Example of a FORMATTED PROBLEM STATEMENT for one PROCESS.

3)   *Summary Reports:* These present collections of information in
     summary from, or gathered from several different relation-
     ships. For example, the Data Base Summary Report provides
     project management information by showing the totals of vari-
     ous types of objects and how much has been said about them.
     The Structure Report shows complete or partial hierarchies.
     The Extended Picture Report shows the data flows in a graphi-
     cal form.

4)   *Analysis Reports:* These provide various types of analysis of the
     information in the data base. For example, the Contents
     Comparison Report analyzes similarity of Inputs and Outputs.
     The Data Process Interaction Report (Fig. 3) can be used to
     detect gaps in the information flow, or unused data objects.
     The Process Chain Report shows the dynamic behavior of the
     system (Fig. 4).

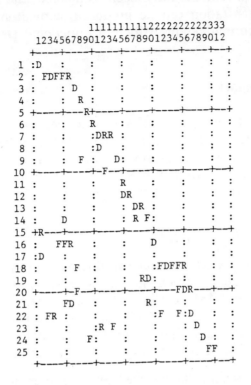

```
             1111111111222222222333
      12345678901234567890123456789012
      +---+---+---+---+---+---+---+---+
   1  :D   :   :   :   :   :   :  :
   2  : FDFFR   :   :   :   :   :  :
   3  :   : D   :   :   :   :   :  :
   4  :   : R   :   :   :   :   :  :
   5  +---+---R+---+---+---+---+---+
   6  :   :   R   :   :   :   :  :
   7  :   :  :DRR  :   :   :   :  :
   8  :   :  :D   :   :   :   :  :
   9  :   : F   D:   :   :   :  :
  10  +---+---+-F-+---+---+---+---+
  11  :   :   :   R   :   :   :  :
  12  :   :   :   DR  :   :   :  :
  13  :   :   :   : DR :   :   :  :
  14  :   D   :   : R F:   :   :  :
  15  +R--+---+---+---+---+---+---+
  16  :  FFR  :   :   D   :   :  :
  17  :D  :   :   :   :   :   :  :
  18  :   : F :   :   :FDFFR   :  :
  19  :   :   :   : RD:   :   :  :
  20  +---+---F-+---+---+---+--FDR---+---+
  21  :   FD  :   :   R:   :   :  :
  22  : FR :   :   :   :F  F:D  :  :
  23  :   :   :R F :   :   : D  :  :
  24  :   : F:   :   :   : D :  :
  25  :   :   :   :   :   : FF  :
      +---+---+---+---+---+---+---+---+
```

Figure 3. Example of part of a Data Process Interaction Report.

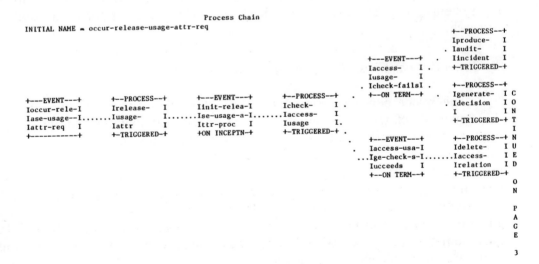

Figure 4. Example of a Process Chain Report.

After the requirements have been completed, the final documentation required by the organization can be produced semiautomatically to a presented format, e.g., the format required for the Functional Description and Data Requirements in [21].

V. Concluding remarks

The current status of PSL/PSA is described briefly in Section V-A. The benefits that should accrue to users of PSL/PSA are discussed in Section V-B. The information on benefits actually obtained by users is given in Section V-C. Planned extensions are outlined in Section V-D. Some conclusions reached as a result of the developments to date are given in Section V-E.

A. Current status

The PSL/PSA system described in this paper is operational on most larger computing environments which support interactive use, including IBM 370 series (OS/VS/TSO/CMS), Univac 1100 series (EXEC-8), CDC 6000/7000 series (SCOPE, TSS), Honeywell 600/6000 series (MULTICS, GCOS), AMDAHL 470/VS (MTS), and PDP-10 (TOPS 10). Portability is achieved at a relatively high level; almost all of the system is written in ANSI Fortran.

PSL/PSA is currently being used by a number of organizations including AT&T Long Lines, Chase Manhattan Bank, Mobil Oil, British Railways, Petroleos Mexicanos, TRW Inc., the U.S. Air Force and others for documenting systems. It is also being used by academic institutions for education and research.

B. Benefit/cost analysis of computer-aided documentation

The major benefits claimed for computer-aided documentation are that the "quality" of the documentation is improved and that the cost of design, implementation, and maintenance will be reduced. The "quality" of the documentation, measured in terms of preciseness, consistency, and completeness is increased because the analysts must be more precise, the software performs checking, and the output reports can be reviewed for remaining ambiguities, inconsistencies, and omissions. While completeness can never be fully guaranteed, one important feature of the computer-aided method is that all the documentation that "exists" is the data base, and therefore the gaps and omissions are more obvious. Consequently, the organization knows what data it has, and does not have to depend on individuals who may not be available when a specific item of data about a system is needed. Any analysis performed and reports produced are up-to-date as of the time it is performed. The coordination among analysts is greatly simplified since each can work in his own area and still have the system specifications be consistent.

Development will take less time and cost less because errors, which usually are not discovered until programming or testing, have been minimized. It is recognized that one reason for the high cost of systems development is the fact that errors, inconsistencies, and omissions in specifications are frequently not detected until later stages of development: in design, programming, systems tests, or even operation. The use of PSL/PSA during the specification stage reduces the number of errors which will have to be corrected later. Maintenance costs are considerably reduced because the effect of a proposed change can easily be isolated, thereby reducing the probability that one correction will cause other errors.

The cost of using a computer-aided method during logical system design must be compared with the cost of performing the operations manually. In practice the cost of the various analyst functions of interviewing, recording, analyzing, etc., are not recorded separately. However, it can be argued that direct cost of documenting specifications for a proposed system using PSL/PSA should be approximately equal to the cost of producing the documentation manually. The cost of typing manual documentation is roughly equal to the cost of entering PSL statements into the computer. The computer cost of using PSA should not be more than the cost of analyst time in carrying out the analyses manually. (Computer costs, however, are much more visible than analysts costs.) Even though the total cost of logical system design is not reduced by using computer-aided methods, the elapsed time should be reduced because the computer can perform clerical tasks in a shorter time than analysts require.

C. Benefits/costs evaluation in practice

Ideally the adoption of a new methodology such as that represented by PSL/PSA should be based on quantitative evaluation of the benefits and costs. In practice this is seldom possible; PSL/PSA is no exception.

Very little quantitative information about the experience in using PSL/PSA, especially concerning manpower requirements and system development costs, is available. One reason for this lack of data is that the project has been concerned with developing the methodology and has not felt it necessary or worthwhile to invest resources in carrying out controlled experiments which would attempt to quantify the benefits. Furthermore, commercial and government organizations which have investigated PSL/PSA have, in some cases, started to use it without a formal evaluation; in other cases, they have started with an evaluation project. However, once the evaluation project is completed and the decision is made to use the PSL/PSA, there is little time or motivation to document the reasons in detail.

Organizations carrying out evaluations normally do not have the comparable data for present methods available and so far none have felt it necessary to run controlled experiments with both methods being used in parallel. Even when evaluations are made, the results have not been made available to the project, because the organizations regard the data as proprietary.

The evidence that the PSL/PSA is worthwhile is that almost without exception the organizations which have seriously considered using it have decided to adopt it either with or without an evaluation. Furthermore, practically all organizations which started to use PSL/PSA are continuing their use (the exceptions have been caused by factors other than PSL/PSA itself) and in organizations which have adopted it, usage has increased.

D. Planned developments

PSL as a system description language was intended to be "complete" in that the logical view of a proposed information system could be described, i.e., all the information necessary for functional requirements and specifications could be stated. On the other hand, the language should not be so complicated that it would be difficult for analysts to use. Also, deliberately omitted from the language was any ability to provide procedural "code" so that analysts would be encouraged to concentrate on the requirements rather than on low-level flow charts. It is clear, however, that PSL must be extended to include more precise statements about logical and procedural information.

Probably the most important improvement in PSA is to make it easier to use. This includes providing more effective and simple data entry and modification commands and providing more help to the users. A second major consideration is performance. As the data base grows in size and the number of users increases, performance becomes more important. Performance is very heavily influenced by factors in the computing environment which are outside the control of PSA development. Nevertheless, there are improvements that can be made.

PSL/PSA is clearly only one step in using computer-aided methods in developing, operating, and maintaining information processing systems. The results achieved to date support the premise that the same general approach can successfully be applied to the rest of the system life cycle and that the data base concept can be used to document the results of the other activities in the system life cycle. The resulting data bases can be the basis for development of methodology, generalized systems, education, and research.

E. Conclusions

The conclusions reached from the development of PSL/PSA to date and from the effort in having it used operationally may be grouped into five major categories.

1) The determination and documentation of requirements and functional specifications can be improved by making use of the computer for recording and analyzing the collected data and statements about the proposed system.

2) Computer-aided documentation is itself a system of which the software is only a part. If the system is to be used, adequate attention must be given to the whole methodology, including: user documentation, logistics and mechanics of use, training, methodological support, and management encouragement.

3) The basic structure of PSL and PSA is correct. A system description language should be of the relational type in which a description consists of identifying and naming objects and relationships among them. The software system should be database oriented, i.e., the data entry and modification procedures should be separated from the output report and analysis facilities.

4) The approach followed in the ISDOS project has succeeded in bringing PSL/PSA into operational use. The same approach can be applied to the rest of the system life cycle. A particularly important part of this approach is to concentrate first on the documentation and then on the methodology.

5) The decision to use a computer-aided documentation method is only partly influenced by the capabilities of the system. Much more important are factors relating to the organization itself and system development procedures. Therefore, even though computer-aided documentation is operational in some organizations, that does not mean that all organizations are ready to immediately adopt it as part of their system life cycle methodology.

References

1. T. Aiken, "Initiating an Electronics Program," in *Proceedings of the 7th Annual Meeting of the Systems and Procedures Association* (1954).

2. B.W. Boehm, "Software and Its Impact: A Quantitative Assessment," *Datamation,* Vol. 19, No. 5 (May 1973), pp. 48-59.

3. _____, "Some Steps Toward Formal and Automated Aids to Software Requirements Analysis and Design," *Information Processing* (1974), pp. 192-97.

4. R.G. Canning, *Electronic Data Processing for Business and Industry* (New York: Wiley, 1956).

5. T.B. Glans, et al., *Management Systems* (New York: Holt, Rinehart, & Winston, 1968). Based on IBM's study Organization Plan, 1961.

6. J. Goldberg, ed., *Proceedings of the Symposium on High Cost of Software* (Stanford, Calif.: Stanford Research Institute, September 1973).

7. R.H. Gregory and R.L. Van Horn, *Automatic Data Processing Systems* (Belmont, Calif.: Wadsworth Publishing Co., 1960).

8. W. Hartman, H. Matthes, and A. Proeme, *Management Information Systems Handbook* (New York: McGraw-Hill, 1968).

9. E.A. Hershey and M. Bastarache, "PSA — Command Descriptions," University of Michigan, ISDOS Working Paper No. 91 (Ann Arbor, Mich.: 1975).

10. E.A. Hershey, et al., "Problem Statement Language — Language Reference Manual," University of Michigan, ISDOS Working Paper No. 68 (Ann Arbor, Mich.: 1975).

11. G.F. Hice, W.S. Turner, and L.F. Cashwell, *System Development Methodology* (Amsterdam, The Netherlands: North-Holland Publishing Co., 1974).

12. *HIPO — A Design Aid and Documentation Technique,* IBM Corporation, Manual No. GC-20-1851 (White Plains, N.Y.: IBM Data Processing Division, October 1974).

13. M.N. Jones, "Using HIPO to Develop Functional Specifications," *Datamation,* Vol. 22, No. 3 (March 1976), pp. 112-25.

14. G.H. Larsen, "Software: Man in the Middle," *Datamation,* Vol. 19, No. 11 (November 1973), pp. 61-66.

15. G.J. Myers, *Reliable Software Through Composite Design* (New York: Petrocelli/Charter, 1975).

16. D.T. Ross and K.E. Schoman, Jr., "Structured Analysis for Requirements Definition," *IEEE Transactions on Software Engineering*, Vol. SE-3, No. 1 (January 1977), pp. 41-48.

17. H.W. Schrimpf and C.W. Compton, "The First Business Feasibility Study in the Computer Field," *Computers and Automation*, Vol. 18, No. 1 (January 1969), pp. 48-53.

18. D. Teichroew and M. Bastarache, "PSL User's Manual," University of Michigan, ISDOS Working Paper No. 98 (Ann Arbor, Mich.: 1975).

19. *Software Development and Configuration Management Manual,* TRW Systems Group, Manual No. TRW-55-73-07 (Redondo Beach, Calif.: December 1973).

20. U.S. Air Force, *Support of Air Force Automatic Data Processing Requirements Through the 1980's,* Electronics Systems Division, L.G. Hanscom Field, Report SADPR-85 (June 1974).

21. U.S. Department of Defense, *Automated Data Systems Documentation Standards Manual,* Manual 4120.17M (December 1972).

22. J.D. Warnier and B. Flanagan, *Entrainement de la Construction des Programs D'Informatique,* Vols. I and II (Paris: Editions d'Organization, 1972).

23. N.E. Willworth, ed., *System Programming Management,* System Development Corporation, TM 1578/000/00 (Santa Monica, Calif.: March 13, 1964).

24. F.G. Withington, *The Organization of the Data Processing Function* (New York: Wiley Business Data Processing Library, 1972).

25. E. Yourdon and L.L. Constantine, *Structured Design: Fundamentals of a Discipline of Computer Program and Systems Design* (Englewood Cliffs, N.J.: Prentice-Hall, 1979). (1979 edition of YOURDON's 1975 text.)

INTRODUCTION

DeMarco's "Structured Analysis and System Specification" is the final paper chosen for inclusion in this book of classic articles on the structured revolution. It is last of three on the subject of analysis, and, together with Ross/Schoman [Paper 22] and Teichroew/Hershey [Paper 23], provides a good idea of the direction that structured analysis will be taking in the next few years.

Any competent systems analyst undoubtedly could produce a five-page essay on "What's Wrong with Conventional Analysis." DeMarco, being an ex-analyst, does so with pithy remarks, describing conventional analysis as follows:

> "Instead of a meaningful interaction between analyst and user, there is often a period of fencing followed by the two parties' studiously ignoring each other. . . The cost-benefit study is performed backwards by deriving the development budget as a function of expected savings. (Expected savings were calculated by prorating cost reduction targets handed down from On High.)"

In addition to providing refreshing prose, DeMarco's approach differs somewhat — in terms of emphasis — from that of Teichroew/Hershey and of Ross/Schoman. Unlike his colleagues, DeMarco stresses the importance of the *maintainability* of the specification. Take, for instance, the case of one system consisting of six *million* lines of COBOL and written over a period of ten years by employees no longer with the organization. Today, *nobody knows what the system does!* Not only have the program listings and source code been lost — a relatively minor disaster that we all have seen too often — but the specifications are completely out of date. Moreover, the system has grown so large that neither the users nor the data processing people have the faintest idea of *what* the system is supposed to be doing, let alone *how* the mysterious job is being accomplished! The example is far from hypothetical, for this is the fate that all large systems eventually will suffer, unless steps are taken to keep the *specifications* both current and understandable across generations of users.

The approach that DeMarco suggests — an approach generally known today as structured analysis — is similar in form to that proposed by Ross and Schoman, and emphasizes a top-down, partitioned, graphic model of the system-to-be. However, in contrast to Ross and Schoman, DeMarco also stresses the important role of a *data dictionary* and the role of scaled-down specifications, or mini-specs, to be written in a rigorous subset of the English language known as *Structured English*.

DeMarco also explains carefully how the analyst proceeds from a physical description of the user's current system, through a logical description of that same system, and eventually into a logical description of the new system that the user wants. Interestingly, DeMarco uses top-down, partitioned dataflow diagrams to illustrate this part of the so-called Project Life Cycle — thus confirming that such a graphic model can be used to portray virtually any system.

As in other short papers on the subject, the details necessary for carrying out DeMarco's approach are missing or are dealt with in a superficial manner. Fortunately, the details *can* be found: Listed at the end of the paper are references to three full-length books and one videotape training course, all dealing with the kind of analysis approach recommended by DeMarco.

Structured Analysis
and System Specification

When Ed Yourdon first coined the term Structured Analysis [1], the idea was largely speculative. He had no actual results of completed projects to report upon. His paper was based on the simple observation that some of the principles of top-down partitioning used by designers could be made applicable to the Analysis Phase. He reported some success in helping users to work out system details using the graphics characteristic of structured techniques.

Since that time, there has been a revolution in the methodology of analysis. More than 2000 companies have sent employees to Structured Analysis training seminars at YOURDON alone. There are numerous working texts and papers on the subject [2, 3, 4, 5]. In response to the YOURDON 1977 Productivity Survey [6, 7], more than one quarter of the respondents answered that they were making some use of Structured Analysis. The 1978 survey [8] shows a clear increase in that trend.

In this paper, I shall make a capsule presentation of the subject of Structured Analysis and its effect on the business of writing specifications of to-be-developed systems. I begin with a set of definitions:

1. What is analysis?

The analysis transformation.

Analysis is the process of transforming a stream of information about current operations and new requirements into some sort of rigorous description of a system to be built. That description is often called a Functional Specification or System Specification.

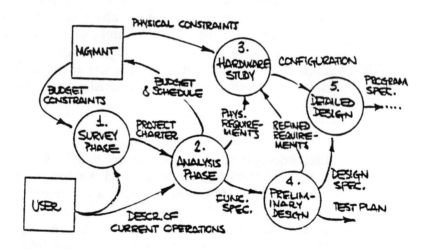

The Analysis Phase in context of the project life cycle.

In the context of the project life cycle for system development, analysis takes place near the beginning. It is preceded only by a Survey or Feasibility Study, during which a project charter (statement of changes to be considered, constraints governing development, etc.) is generated. The Analysis Phase is principally concerned with generating a specification of the system to be built.

But there are numerous required by-products of the phase, including budget, schedule and physical requirements information. The specification task is compounded of the following kinds of activities:

- user interaction,

- study of the current environment,

- negotiation,

- external design of the new system,

- I/O format design,

- cost-benefit study,

- specification writing, and

- estimating.

Well, that's how it works when it works. In practice, some of these activities are somewhat shortchanged. After all, everyone is eager to get on to the real work of the project (writing code). Instead of a meaningful interaction between analyst and user, there is often a period of fencing followed by the two parties' studiously ignoring each other. The study of current operations is frequently bypassed. ("We're going to change all that, anyway.") Many organizations have given up entirely on writing specifications. The cost-benefit study is performed backwards by deriving the development budget as a function of expected savings. (Expected savings were calculated by prorating cost reduction targets handed down from On High.) And the difficult estimating process can be conveniently replaced by simple regurgitation of management's proposed figures. So the Analysis Phase often turns out to be a set of largely disconnected and sometimes fictitious processes with little or no input from the user:

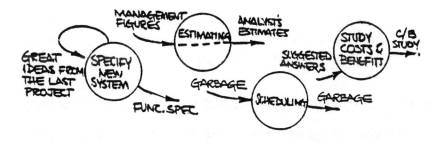

Analysis Phase activities.

2. What is Structured Analysis?

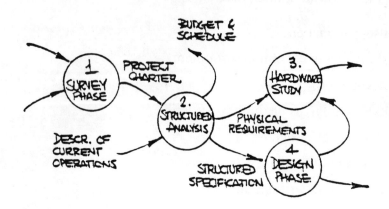

Figure 0: Structured Analysis in context of the project life cycle.

Structured Analysis is a modern discipline for conduct of the Analysis Phase. In the context of the project life cycle, its major apparent difference is its new principal product, called a Structured Specification. This new kind of specification has these characteristics:

- It is *graphic,* made up mostly of diagrams.

- It is *partitioned,* not a single specification, but a network of connected "mini-specifications."

- It is *top-down,* presented in a hierarchical fashion with a smooth progression from the most abstract upper level to the most detailed bottom level.

- It is *maintainable,* a specification that can be updated to reflect change in the requirement.

- It is *a paper model of the system-to-be;* the user can work with the model to perfect his vision of business operations as they will be with the new system in place.

I'll have more to say about the Structured Specification in a later section.

In the preceding figure, I have represented Structured Analysis as a single process (transformation of the project charter and description of current operations into outputs of budget, schedule, physical requirements and the Structured Specification). Let's now look at the details of that process:

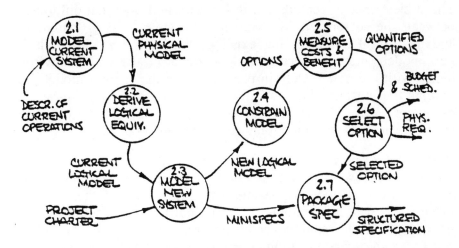

Figure 2: Details of Bubble 2, Structured Analysis.

Note that Figure 2 portrays exactly the same transformation as *Bubble 2* of the previous figure (same inputs, same outputs). But it shows that transformation in considerably more detail. It declares the component processes that make up the whole, as well as the information flows among them.

I won't insult your intelligence by giving you the thousand words that the picture in Figure 2 is worth. Rather than discuss it directly, I'll let it speak for itself. All that is required to complement the figure is a definition of the component processes and information flows that it declares:

Process 2.1. Model the current system: There is almost always a current system (system = integrated set of manual and perhaps automated processes, used to accomplish some business aim). It is the environment that the new system will be dropped into. Structured Analysis would have us build a paper model of the current system, and use it to perfect our understanding of the present environment. I term this model "physical" in that it makes use of the user's terms, procedures, locations, personnel names and particular ways of carrying out business policy. The justification for the physical nature of this first model is that its purpose is to be a verifiable representation of current operations, so it must be easily understood by user staff.

Process 2.2. Derive logical equivalent: The logical equivalent of the physical model is one that is divorced from the "hows" of the current operation. It concentrates instead on the "whats." In place of a description of a way to carry out policy, it strives to be a description of the policy itself.

Process 2.3. Model the new system: This is where the major work of the Analysis Phase, the "invention" of the new system, takes place. The project charter records the differences and potential differences between the current environment and the new. Using this charter and the logical model of the existing system, the analyst builds a new model, one that documents operations of the future environment (with the new system in place), just as the current model documents the present. The new model presents the system-to-be as a partitioned set of elemental processes. The details of these processes are now specified, one mini-spec per process.

Process 2.4. Constrain the model: The new logical model is too logical for our purposes, since it does not even establish how much of the declared work is done inside and how much outside the machine. (That is physical information, and thus not part of a logical model.) At this point, the analyst establishes the man-machine boundary, and hence the scope of automation. He/she typically does this more than once in order to create meaningful alternatives for the selection process. The physical considerations are added to the model as annotations.

Process 2.5. Measure costs and benefits: A cost-benefit study is now performed on each of the options. Each of the tentatively physicalized models, together with its associated cost-benefit parameters, is passed on in the guise of a "Quantified Option."

Process 2.6. Select option: The Quantified Options are now analyzed and one is selected as the best. The quanta associated with the option are formalized as budget, schedule, and physical requirements and are passed back to management.

Process 2.7. Package the specification: Now all the elements of the Structured Specification are assembled and packaged together. The result consists of the selected new physical model, the integrated set of mini-specs and perhaps some overhead (table of contents, short abstract, etc.).

3. What is a model?

The models that I have been referring to throughout are paper representations of systems. A system is a set of manual and automated procedures used to effect some business goal. In the convention of Structured Analysis, a model is made up of *Data Flow Diagrams* and a *Data Dictionary*. My definitions of these two terms follow:

A *Data Flow Diagram* is a network representation of a system. It presents the system in terms of its component processes, and declares all the interfaces among the components. All of the figures used so far in this paper have been Data Flow Diagrams.

A *Data Dictionary* is a set of definitions of interfaces declared on Data Flow Diagrams. It defines each of these interfaces (dataflows) in terms of its components. If I had supplied an entire model of the project life cycle (instead of just an incomplete Data Flow Diagram portion), you would turn to the Data Dictionary of that model to answer any questions that might have arisen in your study of Figure 0 and Figure 2 above. For instance, if you had puzzled over what the Data Flow Diagram referred to as a Quantified Option, you would look it up in the Data Dictionary. There you would find that Quantified Option was made up of the physicalized Data Flow Diagram, Data Dictionary, purchase cost of equipment, schedule and budget for development, monthly operating cost, risk factors, etc.

Data Flow Diagrams are often constructed in leveled sets. This allows a top-down partitioning: The system is divided into subsystems with a top-level Data Flow Diagram; the subsystems are divided into sub-subsystems with second-level Data Flow Diagrams, and so on. The Data Flow Diagrams describing the project life cycle were presented as part of a leveled set. Figure 0 was the parent (top of the hierarchy), and Figure 2, a child. If the model were complete, there would be other child figures as well, siblings of Figure 2. Figure 2 might have some children of its own (Figure 2.1, describing the process of modeling the current system in more detail; Figure 2.2, describing the derivation of logical equivalents, etc.).

The system model plays a number of different roles in Structured Analysis:

- *It is a communication tool.* Since user and analyst have a long-standing history of failure to communicate, it is essential that their discussions be conducted over some workable negotiating instrument, something to point to as they labor to reach a common understanding. Their discussion concerns systems, both past and present, so a useful system model is the most important aid to communication.

- *It is a framework for specification.* The model declares the component pieces of the system, and the pieces of those pieces, all the way down to the bottom. All that remains is to specify the bottom-level processes (those that are not further subdivided). This is accomplished by writing one mini-spec for each bottom-level process.

- *It is a starting point for design.* To the extent that the model is the most eloquent statement of requirement, it has a strong shaping influence on work of the Design Phase. To the extent that the resultant design reflects the shape of the model, it will be conceptually easy to understand for maintainers and user staff. The natural relationship between the Analysis Phase model and the design of the system (its internal structure) is akin to the idea that "form ever follows function."

So far, all I've done is define terms, terms relevant to the analysis process and to Structured Analysis in particular. With these terms defined, we can turn our attention to two special questions: What has been wrong with our approach to computer systems analysis in the past? and, How will Structured Analysis help?

4. What is wrong with classical analysis?

Without going into a long tirade against classical methods, the major problem of analysis has been this: Analysts and users have not managed to communicate well enough — the systems delivered too often have not been the systems the users wanted. Since analysis establishes development goals, failures of analysis set projects moving in wrong directions. The long-standing responses of management to all development difficulties (declaration of the 70-hour work week, etc.) do not help. They only goad a project into moving more quickly, still in the wrong direction. The more manpower and dedication added, the further the project will move away from its true goals. Progress made is just more work to be undone later. There is a word that aptly describes such a project, one that is set off in the wrong direction by early error and cannot be rescued by doubling and redoubling effort. The word is "doomed." Most of the Great Disasters of EDP were projects doomed by events and decisions of the Analysis Phase. All the energies and talents expended thereafter were for naught.

The major failures of classical analysis have been failures of the specification process. I cite these:

The monolithic approach. Classical Functional Specifications read like Victorian novels: heavy, dull and endless. No piece has any meaning by itself. The document can only be read serially, from front to back. No one ever reads the whole thing. (So no one reads the end.)

The poured-in-concrete effect. Functional Specifications are impossible to update. (I actually had one analyst tell me that the change we were considering could be more easily made to the system itself, when it was finally delivered, than to the specification.) Since they can't be updated, they are always out of date.

The lack of feedback. Since pieces of Functional Specifications are unintelligible by themselves, we have nothing to show the user until the end of analysis. Our author-reader cycle may be as much as a year. There is no possibility of iteration (that is, frequently repeated attempts to refine and perfect the product). For most of the Analysis Phase, there is no product to iterate. The famous user-analyst dialogue is no dialogue at all, but a series of monologues.

The Classical Functional Specification is an unmaintainable monolith, the result of "communication" without benefit of feedback. No wonder it is *neither functional nor specific.*

5. How does Structured Analysis help?

I would not be writing this if I did not believe strongly in the value of Structured Analysis; I have been known to wax loquacious on its many virtues. But in a few words, these are the main ways in which Structured Analysis helps to resolve Analysis Phase problems:

- It attacks the problem of largeness by *partitioning.*

- It attacks the many problems of communication between user and analyst by *iterative communication* and an *inversion of viewpoint.*

- It attacks the problem of specification maintenance by *limited redundancy.*

Since all of these ideas are rather new in their application to analysis, I provide some commentary on each:

The concept of *partitioning* or "functional decomposition" may be familiar to designers as the first step in creating a structured design. Its potential value in analysis was evident from the beginning — clearly, large systems cannot be analyzed without some form of concurrent partitioning. But the direct application of Design Phase functional decomposition tools (structure charts and HIPO) caused more problems than it solved. After some early successful experiments [9], negative user attitudes toward the use of hierarchies became apparent, and the approach was largely abandoned. Structured Analysis teaches use of leveled Data Flow Diagrams for partitioning, in place of the hierarchy. The advantages are several:

- The appearance of a Data Flow Diagram is not at all frightening. It seems to be simply a picture of the subject matter being discussed. You never have to explain an arbitrary convention to the user — you don't explain anything at all. You simply use the diagrams. I did precisely that with you in this paper; I used Data Flow Diagrams as a descriptive tool, long before I had even defined the term.

- Network models, like the ones we build with Data Flow Diagrams, are already familiar to some users. Users may have different names for the various tools used — Petri Networks or Paper Flow Charts or Document Flow Diagrams — but the concepts are similar.

- The act of partitioning with a Data Flow Diagram calls attention to the interfaces that result from the partitioning. I believe this is important, because the complexity of interfaces is a valuable indicator of the quality of the partitioning effort: the simpler the interfaces, the better the partitioning.

I use the term *iterative communication* to describe the rapid two-way interchange of information that is characteristic of the most productive work sessions. The user-analyst dialogue has got to be a dialogue. The period over which communication is turned around (called the author-reviewer cycle) needs to be reduced from months to minutes. I quite literally mean that fifteen minutes into the first meeting between user and analyst, there should be some feedback. If the task at hand requires the user to describe his current operation, then fifteen minutes into that session is not too early for the analyst to try telling the user what he has learned. "OK, let me see if I've got it right. I've drawn up this little picture of what you've just explained to me, and I'll explain it back to you. Stop me when I go wrong."

Of course, the early understanding is always imperfect. But a careful and precise declaration of an imperfect understanding is the best tool for refinement and correction. The most important early product on the way to developing a good product is an imperfect version. The human mind is an iterative processor. It never does anything precisely right the first time. What it does consummately well is to make a slight improvement to a flawed product. This it can do again and again. The idea of developing a flawed early version and then refining and refining to make it right is a very old one. It is called *engineering*. What I am proposing is an engineering approach to analysis and to the user-analyst interface.

The product that is iterated is the emerging system model. When the user first sees it, it is no more than a rough drawing made right in front of him during the discussion. At the end, it is an integral part of the Structured Specification. By the time he sees the final specification, each and every page of it should have been across his desk a half dozen times or more.

I mentioned that Structured Analysis calls for an *inversion of viewpoint*. This point may seem obscure because it is not at all obvious what the viewpoint of classical analysis has been. From my reading of hundreds of Classical Functional Specifications over the past fifteen years, I have come to the conclusion that their viewpoint is most often that of the computer. The classical specification describes what the computer does, in the order that it does it, using terms that are relevant to computers and computer people. It frequently limits itself to a discussion of processing inside the machine and data transferred in and out. Almost never does it specify anything that happens outside the man-machine boundary.

The machine's viewpoint is natural and useful for those whose concerns lie inside (the development staff), and totally foreign to those whose concerns lie outside (the user and his staff). Structured Analysis adopts a different viewpoint, that of the data. A Data Flow Diagram follows the data paths wherever they lead, through manual as well as automated procedure. A correctly drawn system model describes the outside as well as the inside of the automated portion. In fact, it describes the automated portion *in the context of the complete system.* The viewpoint of the data has two important advantages over that of any of the processors:

- The data goes everywhere, so its view is all-inclusive.

- The viewpoint of the data is common to those concerned with the inside as well as those concerned with the outside of the man-machine boundary.

The use of *limited redundancy* to create a highly maintainable product is not new. Any programmer worth his salt knows that a parameter that is likely to be changed ought to be defined in one place and one place only. What is new in Structured Analysis is the idea that the specification ought to be maintainable at all. After all, aren't we going to "freeze" it? If we have learned anything over the past twenty years, it is that the concept of freezing specifications is one of the great pipe dreams of our profession. Change cannot be forestalled, only ignored. Ignoring change assures the building of a product that is out of date and unacceptable to the user. We may endeavor to hold off selected changes to avoid disruption of the development effort, but we can no longer tolerate being *obliged* to ignore change just because our specification is impossible to update. It is equally intolerable to accept the change, without updating the specification. The specification is our mechanism for keeping the project on target, tracking a moving goal. Failure to keep the specification up to date is like firing away at a moving target with your eyes closed. A key concept of Structured Analysis is development of a specification with little or no redundancy. This is a serious departure from the classical method that calls for specification of everything at least eleven times in eleven places. Reducing redundancy, as a by-product, makes the resultant specification considerably more concise.

6. What is a Structured Specification?

Structured Analysis is a discipline for conduct of the Analysis Phase. It includes procedures, techniques, documentation aids, logic and policy description tools, estimating heuristics, milestones, checkpoints and by-products. Some of these are important, and the rest merely convenient. What is most important is this simple idea: Structured Analysis involves building a new kind of specification, a Structured Specification, made up of Data Flow Diagrams, Data Dictionary and mini-specs.

The roles of the constituent parts of the Structured Specification are presented below:

The *Data Flow Diagrams* serve to partition the system. The system that is treated by the Data Flow Diagram may include manual as well as automated parts, but the same partitioning tool is used throughout. The purpose of the Data Flow Diagram is not to specify, but to declare. It declares component processes that make up the whole, and it declares interfaces among the components. Where the target system is large, several successive partitionings may be required. This is accomplished by lower-level Data Flow Diagrams of finer and finer detail. All the levels are combined into a leveled DFD set.

The *Data Dictionary* defines the interfaces that were declared on the Data Flow Diagrams. It does this with a notational convention that allows representation of dataflows and stores in terms of their components. (The components of a dataflow or store may be lower-level dataflows, or they may be data elements.) Before the Structured Specification can be called complete, there must be one definition in the Data Dictionary for each dataflow or data store declared on any of the Data Flow Diagrams.

The *mini-specs* define the elemental processes declared on the Data Flow Diagrams. A process is considered elemental (or "primitive") when it is not further decomposed into a lower-level Data Flow Diagram. Before the Structured Specification can be called complete, there must be one mini-spec for each primitive process declared on any of the Data Flow Diagrams.

The YOURDON Structured Analysis convention includes a set of rules and methods for writing mini-specs using Structured English, decision tables and trees and certain non-linguistic techniques for specification. For the purposes of this paper, such considerations are at the detail level — once you have partitioned to the point at which each of the mini-specs can be written in a page or less, it doesn't matter too terribly much how you write them.

7. What does it all mean?

Structured Analysis is here to stay. I estimate that its serious user community now includes more than 800 companies worldwide. Users as far away as Australia and Norway have published results of the application of Structured Analysis techniques to real-world projects [10, 11]. There are courses, texts and even a video-tape series [12] on the subject. There are automated support tools for use in Structured Analysis [13]. There are rival notations and symbologies [3, 14, 15]. Working sessions have been cropping up at GUIDE, NCC, AMA and the DPMA. There are user groups, templates and T-shirts.

The fundamentals of Structured Analysis are not new. Most of the ideas have been used piecemeal for years. What is new is the emerging discipline. The advantages of this discipline are substantial. They include a much more methodical approach to specification, a more usable and maintainable product and fewer surprises when the new system is installed. These are especially attractive when compared to the advantages of the classical discipline for analysis. There were no advantages. There was no discipline.

References

1. E. Yourdon, "The Emergence of Structured Analysis," *Computer Decisions,* Vol. 8, No. 4 (April 1976), pp. 58-59.

2. T. DeMarco, *Structured Analysis and System Specification* (New York: YOURDON Press, 1978).

3. C. Gane and T. Sarson, *Structured Systems Analysis* (New York: Improved System Technologies, Inc., 1977).

4. T. DeMarco, "Breaking the Language Barrier," *Computerworld,* Vol. XII, Nos. 32, 33 and 34 (August 7, 14 and 21, 1978) [published in parts].

5. *IEEE Transactions on Software Engineering,* Vol. SE-3, No. 1 (January 1977). Special issue on structured analysis.

6. *The YOURDON Report,* Vol. 2, No. 3 (March 1977).

7. T. DeMarco, "Report on the 1977 Productivity Survey" (New York: YOURDON inc., September 1977).

8. *The YOURDON Report,* Vol. 3, No. 3 (June-July 1978).

9. M. Jones, "Using HIPO to Develop Functional Specifications," *Datamation,* Vol. 22, No. 3 (March 1976), pp. 112-25.

10. J. Simpson, "Analysis and Design — A Case Study in a Structured Approach," *Australasian Computerworld,* Vol. 1, No. 2 (July 21, 1978), pp. 2-11, 13.

11. J. Pedersen and J. Buckle, "Kongsberg's Road to an Industrial Software Methodology," *IEEE Transactions on Software Engineering,* Vol. SE-4, No. 4 (July 1978).

12. *Structured Analysis,* Videotape series (Chicago: DELTAK inc., 1978).

13. D. Teichroew and E. Hershey III, "PSL/PSA: A Computer-Aided Technique for Structured Documentation and Analysis of Information Processing Systems," *IEEE Transactions on Software Engineering,* Vol. SE-3, No. 1 (January 1977), pp. 41-48.

14. *Introduction to SADT,* SofTech Inc., Document No. 9022-78 (Waltham, Mass.: February 1976).

15. V. Weinberg, *Structured Analysis* (New York: YOURDON Press, 1978).